HU-105 COLLEGIATE LEARNING AND COGNITIVE DEVELOPMENT

BRIARCLIFFE COLLEGE

2nd Edition

Dave Ellis | Gwenn Wilson

CENGAGE
Learning·

Australia • Brazil • Japan • Korea • Mexico • Singapore • Spain • United Kingdom • United States

CENGAGE Learning®

HU-105 Collegiate Learning and Cognitive Development: Briarcliffe College, 2nd Edition

Senior Manager, Student Engagement:
Linda deStefano
Janey Moeller

Manager, Student Engagement:
Julie Dierig

Marketing Manager:
Rachael Kloos

Manager, Production Editorial:
Kim Fry

Manager, Intellectual Property Project Manager:
Brian Methe

Senior Manager, Production and Manufacturing:
Donna M. Brown

Manager, Production:
Terri Daley

Compositor:
Integra Software Services

For product information and technology assistance, contact us at
Cengage Learning Customer & Sales Support, 1-800-354-9706

For permission to use material from this text or product,
submit all requests online at **cengage.com/permissions**
Further permissions questions can be emailed to
permissionrequest@cengage.com

This book contains select works from existing Cengage Learning resources and was produced by Cengage Learning Custom Solutions for collegiate use. As such, those adopting and/or contributing to this work are responsible for editorial content accuracy, continuity and completeness.

Compilation © 2014 Cengage Learning

ISBN-13: 978-1-305-01006-2
ISBN-10: 1-305-01006-X

WCN: 01-100-101

Cengage Learning
5191 Natorp Boulevard
Mason, Ohio 45040
USA

Cengage Learning is a leading provider of customized learning solutions with office locations around the globe, including Singapore, the United Kingdom, Australia, Mexico, Brazil, and Japan. Locate your local office at:
international.cengage.com/region.

Cengage Learning products are represented in Canada by Nelson Education, Ltd.
For your lifelong learning solutions, visit **www.cengage.com/custom.**
Visit our corporate website at **www.cengage.com.**

Table of Contents

2 DETERMINING THE INFORMATION YOU NEED 37

3   HOW DO YOU FIND AND ACCESS INFORMATION? 77

4 · EVALUATING INFORMATION **107**

5 ORGANIZING INFORMATION 149

6 **LEGAL AND ETHICAL ISSUES RELATED
TO INFORMATION** **187**

12 TESTS 365

Preface

● HOW WILL THIS TEXT HELP ME?

Your enrollment in college says that you have made a decision to grow and develop as a person and a professional. Your college experience and your future professional activities will require you to locate, evaluate, organize, and communicate information in carrying out your responsibilities and achieving your professional goals. *100% Information Literacy Success* will provide you with tools to accomplish your objectives.

100% Information Literacy Success discusses skills that are fundamental to becoming an information-literate student and professional, which in turn will contribute to your academic and career success. The text is divided into the following topics: *Introduction to Information Literacy in the Digital Age, Determining the Information You Need, How Do You Find and Access Information?, Evaluating Information, Organizing Information,* and concluding with *Legal and Ethical Issues Related to Information.* Use the following summaries of these sections to get an overview of the book and to determine how each topic supports you in the development of information literacy skills.

▶ *Defining information:* You will be introduced to the concept of information literacy and why it is important to academic and career success. The abundance and rapid flow of data in the Information Era requires understanding, finding, using, evaluating, and communicating information effectively and efficiently in all fields of study.

▶ *Understanding information resources:* You will become familiar with common and more obscure information resources available to you in libraries and on the Internet and how to use them.

▶ *Finding information sources:* Here you will learn how to locate and access information from a variety of sources so that you can effectively solve problems and answer questions for school and workplace situations.

▶ *Evaluating information:* Because anyone can publish anything on the Internet, you will have to know how to evaluate and determine the credibility of Internet information. You will learn how to evaluate whether an Internet information source is credible and appropriate for your needs. In addition, you will learn how to assess an author's expertise, as well as the currency and relevancy of print and other resources.

▶ *Organizing information:* As a professional, you will have to be able to logically organize the information you find so you can use it for your information needs and communicate it to others. Effectively organized information will enable you to accomplish your communication goals.

▶ *Communicating information:* Finally, you will explore the many ways that students and professionals communicate information to others. You will become familiar with channels of communication and guidelines for communicating effectively in a variety of professional settings. The emphasis is on using information ethically and legally, and acknowledging others correctly for their intellectual property.

The Third Edition of *100% Information Literacy Success* has been revised to actively help you develop skills beyond the classroom, focusing on those strategies necessary for 21st-century learners and workers.

● HOW TO USE THIS BOOK

100% Information Literacy Success is designed to actively involve you in developing information literacy skills. The text includes the following features that will guide you through the material and provide opportunities for you to practice what you've learned.

▶ *Learning Objectives:* Learning Objectives, like those provided on course syllabi, are provided to outline what you should be learning from the chapter and guide you to the main concepts of the chapter. Use the objectives to identify important points and to understand what you are supposed to learn, to measure what you have mastered, and to identify what you still need to work on. You are encouraged to expand your knowledge beyond the learning objectives according to your goals and interests.

▶ *Be in the Know:* A new feature to the third edition of *100% Information Literacy Success*, Be in the Know provides vignettes on real-world situations as they relate to the chapter content. The intent of this feature is to help students focus on the subject at hand, and how they can learn from the provided examples in these content areas.

▶ *Case in Point:* In the middle of each chapter, a case study demonstrates the application of chapter concepts to the real world. Use the questions following each case study to stimulate your critical thinking and analytical skills. Discuss the questions with classmates. You are encouraged to think of your own application of ideas and to raise additional questions.

▶ *Self-Assessment Questions:* The Self-Assessment Questions ask you to evaluate your personal development. They are intended to increase your self-awareness and ability to understand your decisions and actions.

▶ *Critical Thinking Questions:* The Critical Thinking Questions challenge you to examine ideas and thoughtfully apply concepts presented in the text. These questions encourage the development of thinking skills that are crucial for efficient performance in school and in the workplace.

▶ *Apply It!:* At the end of each chapter are activities that will help you apply the concepts discussed in practical situations. Your instructor may assign these activities as part of the course requirements. Or, if they are not formally assigned, you will want to complete them for your own development.

▶ *Success Steps:* Scattered throughout the text are Success Steps that offer a pathway to achieve various goals. They essentially summarize the detailed processes that are discussed fully in the body of the text. To achieve a specific information literacy goal, use the Table of Contents to locate the information quickly.

▶ *Check Your Understanding:* Check Your Understanding, found on the companion web site, provides an opportunity for you to assess the effectiveness of your learning and to set goals to expand your knowledge in a given area.

▶ *Suggested Items for Learning Portfolio:* A portfolio is a collection of the work that you have done. A *learning portfolio* is used to track your progress through school and a *professional portfolio* showcases your professional accomplishments. A *developmental portfolio* typically contains documents that illustrate your development over time. A professional portfolio contains finished projects and work that represents your best efforts and achievements and will be the emphasis of the portfolio you create as part of *100% Information Literacy Success.* Throughout *100% Information Literacy Success,* there are suggestions to include completed activities in your portfolio. Arranging your portfolio in a way that illustrates your professional development and showcases your best work will be useful for reviewing your progress and demonstrating your abilities.

As you read and complete the activities in *100% Information Literacy Success*, keep your long-term goals in mind and think about how you can apply these concepts to your everyday activities. Application is the key—and the more you practice, the more proficient you will become in using and communicating information.

Visit the companion web site for this textbook by visiting www.cengagebrain.com, where you will find practice quizzes, flashcards, and additional resources to help support your success in college.

TEACHING WITH 100% INFORMATION LITERACY SUCCESS

WHAT IS NEW IN THE THIRD EDITION OF *100% INFORMATION LITERACY SUCCESS?*

Instructors who have previously used *100% Information Literacy Success* in their classrooms will find the following changes throughout the textbook:

▶ A new feature, Be in the Know, has been added to the beginning of each chapter.

▶ Cases in Point have been moved to the middle of each chapter and have been changed to encourage student participation and discussion.

The following list includes changes by chapter to assist instructors in transitioning to the Third Edition of *100% Information Literacy Success*:

Chapter 1 changes:

▶ The section Information Literacy in the 21st Century: An Overview has been renamed Information Literacy in the Digital Age: An Overview, and describes the topics of information work and information workers.

▶ The section Why Is Information Literacy Important? has been moved up within the chapter and contains information about the advantages of being information-literate.

▶ The topic of visual literacy has been added to the section Components of Information Literacy in the Digital Age.

Chapter 2 changes:

▶ A new section, Solving Information Problems: Defining the Need and the Audience, has been added.

▶ Information about identifying one's writing style and defining the audience has been added to The Research Process section.

Chapter 3 changes:

▶ A new section, Solving Information Problems: Find the Information, was added.

▶ A new section, The Evolution of Libraries, was added.

▶ A new section, Working with Your Librarian, was added.

▶ The sections Library Classification Systems and Using Library Classification Systems have been removed.

▶ A new section, Types of Electronic Resources, was added and includes topics such as e-journals, streaming video, blogs, graphics and images, wikis, and social media.

▶ The section Collecting Information has been updated to includes online highlighting and keeping and organizing information on the computer. The topics of note taking and photocopying were removed.

Chapter 4 changes:

▶ The section The Importance of Critical Analysis has been renamed Solving Information Problems: Evaluate the Information.

▶ A new section, Evaluating Web Sources, has been added.

Chapter 5 changes:

▶ The section Information Organization: An Overview was renamed Solving Information Problems: Organize the Information.

▶ The section Organizing Web Pages was removed and was replaced by the section Other Presentation Software.

Chapter 6 changes:

▶ A new section, Solving Information Problems: Communicate the Information, has been added.

▶ The Plagiarism section has been updated to include strategies for avoiding plagiarism and the potential consequences of plagiarism.

▶ The section on Citing Information Sources has been updated to include how to cite information for videos (including online videos), motion pictures, pictures and images, and graphics.

▶ The section Communicating Information has been removed.

▶ A new section, The Importance of Information Literacy in the Workplace, has been added.

Ancillary Materials

100% Information Literacy Success has a companion web site for students. Visit www.cengagebrain.com to access the web site. Available materials include practice quizzes, flashcards, and additional resources to help your students be successful in college; exercises for students to complete, a glossary of terms, Scenic Route links to web sites, and recommended readings.

An Instructor's Companion Site includes an Instructor's Manual, PowerPoint Slides, and a Test Bank. The instructor's resources can be accessed at login.cengage.com. A WebTutor Toolbox is available for this textbook to be used with WebCT or Blackboard.

If you're looking for more ways to assess your students, Cengage Learning has additional resources to consider:

▶ College Success Factors Index 2.0

▶ Noel-Levitz College Student Inventory

▶ The *Myers-Briggs Type Indicator® (MBTI®) Instrument**

You can also package this textbook with the College Success Planner to assist students in making the best use of their time both on and off campus.

An additional service available with this textbook is support from TeamUP Faculty Program Consultants. For more than a decade, our consultants have helped faculty reach and engage first-year students by offering peer-to-peer consulting on curriculum and assessment, faculty training, and workshops. Consultants are available to help you establish or improve our student success program and provide training on the implementation of our textbooks and technology. To connect with your TeamUP Faculty Program Consultant, call 1-800-528-8323 or visit www.cengage.com/teamup.

For more in-depth information on any of these items, talk with your sales rep, or visit www.cengagebrain.com.

*MBTI and Myers-Briggs Type Indicator are registered trademarks of Consulting Psychologists Press, Inc.

1

Introduction to Information Literacy in the Digital Age

LEARNING OBJECTIVES

By the end of this chapter, students will achieve the following objectives:

▶ Describe information work and information workers.

▶ Define *information literacy*.

▶ List the specific skills required for an individual to be an information-literate student or professional in the digital age.

▶ Explain the importance of knowing how to locate, access, retrieve, evaluate, use, and communicate information effectively in school and in the workplace.

▶ Explain the challenges facing an individual who does not possess information skills in school and in the workplace.

1

BE IN THE KNOW

Information Literacy and Professionalism

While you are in school, one of the smartest things you can do is groom yourself for becoming a professional in the workplace. Professionalism is defined as showing behaviors that meet the standards and expectations of the workplace. Demonstrating professionalism in both the classroom and at your place of employment is paramount to your success.

One of the ways you can demonstrate professionalism is to become information-literate. As you will read throughout this text, being an information-literate person encompasses a wide array of competencies that, when combined, make you a well-rounded student or worker who can effectively find, evaluate, and communicate credible, meaningful information that is used to solve information problems.

As you will read in Chapter 6, when interviewing and recruiting recent graduates, employers seek out those who not only exhibit excellent computer skills such as being able to conduct online research, but they also place great value on graduates who go beyond the first two or three entries from a search engine to get answers that solve information problems. This means finding and evaluating information from myriad sources, and in the workplace, this often means seeking out coworkers, supervisors, or other trusted sources. As you complete your coursework, think about those people beyond your instructors who can help you with your information needs, such as librarians and professionals in your field of study. The ability to critically assess the information you find and correlate it back to the subject at hand is a skill that will help you both in your studies and in the workplace.

It is not too early to start down the path to professionalism now. Exhibiting professionalism using your information literacy skills while you are in school and on the job should become a manner of daily life. Strive to demonstrate those skills and professionalism in everything that you do as a student and in your work position. Your diligence will pay off as you move forward in your career.

INFORMATION LITERACY IN THE DIGITAL AGE: AN OVERVIEW

In this digital age of enormous amounts of quickly changing information, students and professionals alike must be able to find information and put it to use effectively. Students must be able to access information beyond textbooks and classroom instructors to prepare for the workplace. Professionals must keep current and continuously expand their body of knowledge to be successful and to advance in their careers. Staying successfully updated requires individuals to become information workers who are *information-literate*.

INFORMATION WORK AND INFORMATION WORKERS

If you use a computer, the Internet, and e-mail while you are in school, regardless of your field of study, you are doing *information work* and can be considered an *information worker*. Your "job" while attending classes is to seek out, analyze, and disseminate information on a particular topic or area in the form of papers, projects, and presentations. The information work that you complete while you are in school contributes to your own learning goals.

The same is said to be true for those who enter the workforce in most instances. Rasmus (2012, p. 1) defines an information worker as "a person who uses information to assist in making decisions or taking actions, or a person who creates information that informs the decisions or actions of others." These days, finding, evaluating, organizing, and communicating information in a meaningful way to the organization are fundamental components of most jobs, no matter what the job title or position on the organizational chart. Corporations harness useful information to achieve organizational goals, such as increasing their bottom line and maintaining a competitive edge, among other things.

Infoengineering.net (n.d.) identifies eight must-have skills in order to be a successful information worker. Some of these may be considered "soft information technology (IT) skills" and include:

- The ability to search online for the information you need.
- The ability to determine if the retrieved information is accurate and reliable.

▶ The ability to communicate the found information to others through the best communication channel(s).

▶ The ability to use computers and operating systems.

▶ The ability to use word processing, spreadsheets, and presentation software to collect and disseminate information.

▶ The ability to put information into the proper file format (such as .jpg for photos) and how to back up files.

▶ The ability to perform computer security, including technical security (protecting against viruses and using security software such as firewalls), and information security (access to personal information, sending confidential information, etc.).

▶ The ability to focus your attention on finding the information you need in the most efficient manner possible.

All of these "must-haves," as well as many other skills, comprise what is known as *information literacy*. The remainder of this text focuses on the components of information literacy and the importance of mastering these abilities in order to become a proficient and professional information worker in the digital age.

WHAT IS INFORMATION LITERACY?

Webber (2010, p. 1) has defined information literacy for the 21st century as "the adoption of appropriate information behavior to identify, through whatever channel or medium, information well fitted to information needs, leading to wise and ethical use of information in society." Today, information comes to us from a myriad of sources: the Internet, podcasts, and traditional media, to name just a few. Webber's definition points to the importance of selecting appropriate information from a suitable source and using the information in a credible manner within legal and ethical boundaries. Excellent students will pursue the development of these skills and practice them in each course they take. They will apply the concepts specifically to their field of study and career goals. Information-literate individuals also are able to critically assess information and to use it effectively to solve personal and workplace problems.

1

WHY IS INFORMATION LITERACY IMPORTANT?

Homes, schools, libraries, and workplaces are becoming increasingly outfitted with advanced technology, including powerful computers, higher-speed Internet connections, sophisticated software applications, convenient searching tools, and numerous media devices such as digital cameras, scanners, and wireless devices. We know that the technology is available, but do we know how to harness this technology to solve our problems and answer our questions? What do we do when we are faced with so much information? How will we know that what we find is credible? How will we communicate this information to everyone who needs to know? How do we even know what questions to ask to begin to solve our information problems?

Without advanced knowledge and skills, students and professionals alike are at a significant disadvantage in their work environments. Problems facing individuals who lack information skills include:

- asking the wrong questions (and consequently getting the wrong answers!)
- using limited or inappropriate sources of information
- using inaccurate or misleading information
- accessing outdated information
- finding incomplete information
- using biased or one-sided resources
- being inefficient in research and wasting time
- being disorganized
- communicating the information ineffectively.

We cannot just be excellent learners. We must be lifelong learners to keep pace with advancing technology and new information. A college graduate's first job represents only the first step. Career advancement requires continuous development of knowledge and skills, as well as the ability and willingness to adapt quickly to the constantly changing tools of the industry. Career advancement in today's information world requires well-developed information skills. Lifelong

SELF-ASSESSMENT QUESTIONS

- Think carefully about your career field or a field in which you might be interested. What technologies do you predict for this field in the next 10 years? How do you see a job in this field changing because of these technologies? Write down as many different ideas as you can.
- How might you prepare yourself for continued success and career advancement in a specific field? What about the workplace in general?

1

learning requires lifelong students to take the initiative to continue to learn and also to figure out what they need to learn.

ADVANTAGES OF BEING INFORMATION-LITERATE

When learners become information-literate, they increase their advantages in school and in the workplace. The following list represents just a few of these potential advantages:

- ❯ Learners sharpen their critical and creative thinking skills.
- ❯ Learners develop higher-order thinking skills essential for excellence in school and the workplace.
- ❯ Students develop a deeper and more applicable understanding of the content they are learning and become better prepared for their jobs.
- ❯ Individuals are able to communicate in knowledgeable, logical, and defensible ways regarding their work.
- ❯ Learners' ability to effectively participate in problem solving and decision making is enhanced.
- ❯ Professionals are able to keep up with advancements in their field of study, making them more competent and valuable as employees.

DEFINING DIGITAL LITERACY

As we move further into the 21st century and into an ever-expanding digital age, we find that how information literacy is defined takes on additional significance. According to Jones and Flannigan (n.d. p.5),

> *Digital literacy* represents a person's ability to perform tasks effectively in a digital environment. The term *digital* means information represented in numeric form and primarily for use by a computer. The term *literacy* includes the ability to read and interpret media (text, sound, images, etc.), to reproduce data and images through digital manipulation, and to evaluate and apply new knowledge gained from digital environments.

The American Library Association (2013, p. 2) defines digital literacy as "the ability to use information and communication technologies to find, understand, evaluate, create, and communicate digital information, an ability that requires both cognitive and technical skills."

The Association defines a *digitally literate person* as one who:

▶ "possesses the variety of skills—cognitive and technical—required to find, understand, evaluate, create, and communicate digital information in a wide variety of formats;

▶ is able to use diverse technologies appropriately and effectively to search for and retrieve information, interpret search results, and judge the quality of the information retrieved;

▶ understands the relationships among technology, lifelong learning, personal privacy, and appropriate stewardship of information;

▶ uses these skills and the appropriate technologies to communicate and collaborate with peers, colleagues, family, and on occasion the general public;

▶ uses these skills to participate actively in civic society and contribute to a vibrant, informed, and engaged community" (American Library Association 2013, p. 2).

Today, the information-literate learner must combine the knowledge of how to find, evaluate, and communicate information within the context of a digitized environment.

COMPONENTS OF INFORMATION LITERACY IN THE DIGITAL AGE

To execute information-related tasks effectively, students and professionals must develop an efficient information-gathering process and enhance specific information-related skills. The American Library Association (ALA, 2000) has published information literacy standards for students in higher education. Although technology and information sources have expanded significantly since publications of these standards, the standards are not medium-specific, which makes their concepts applicable today. According to the ALA Standards, an information-literate individual should be able to complete the following information-related tasks:

▶ **DEFINE:** *Define the need, problem, or question.*

For example, a small training company wants to start offering its training workshops to customers in another state.

1

To do so legally, efficiently, and wisely, the company first must answer several questions about the new area: (1) Does the new state have any laws or regulations for this type of business? (2) Does the new area have competition that would make the decision to expand unwise? (3) Does the new area have enough potential customers—those who would be interested in the type of training the company offers—to make the training cost-effective? These are examples of the many questions that should be asked.

▶ **FIND:** *Locate, access, and retrieve the information from a variety of print, electronic, and human information sources.*

In the example, the company must find the information to answer the questions about expansion into the new state. The training manager responsible for the expansion must understand the specific resources that are available and that will provide her with the correct and current information. She then must be able to locate the resources and access the information. Understanding current search techniques and tools will be necessary for the training manager to access the most current information.

Once she has accessed the information, she must be able to retrieve it so she can organize it and present it to the company president later. The needed information might include state and local regulations, market reports, and demographic information. Sources might include state and local governments, market surveys, directories, and other data services. From numerous resources, the training manager must select the information that best serves the purpose.

▶ **EVALUATE:** *Assess the credibility, currency, reliability, validity, and appropriateness of the information retrieved.*

Before the training manager actually uses the information, she must ensure that it is credible, current, reliable, and valid. For example, an information resource that provides market data from 2005 is not useful. Likewise, information published by a competing company may be biased. Credible resources must be used as a basis for making sound business decisions. The information-literate individual is able to assess the source of information for relevance appropriate to the needs of the current situation as well as evaluate sources for accuracy and conflicts of interest with present needs.

▶ **ORGANIZE:** *Compile the information so it can be used to meet the information need, solve the problem, or answer the question.*

Once the training manager has gathered all of the needed information, she must organize it so it can be used to answer her specific questions. For example, she might want to show trends in population, the influx of new companies that require her training, and specific data showing that her training has little competition. Organizing the information according to each question will allow her to prepare her presentation more effectively.

▶ **COMMUNICATE:** *Communicate the information legally and ethically using a variety of channels directed at a range of audiences.*

Finally, the training manager must communicate the information to the president and other decision makers in the company. She has been asked to make a formal presentation to a board of directors and will use charts, graphs, PowerPoint presentations, and other visual representations of the data. She also has been asked to write a formal proposal and will have to provide accurate information about her information sources. The training manager's ability to present the information clearly, using professional language, will be vital to her success. She must cite her sources accurately and present her references in a way that gives appropriate credit to her information sources.

Information literacy assumes several professional skills that are important to every successful student and professional. These skills, sometimes referred to as transferable skills or generic skills, are abilities that are vital to career success, regardless of industry or job title. Critical thinking, creative thinking, problem solving, higher-order thinking, effective communication, and organization are transferable skills that provide a foundation for information literacy.

CRITICAL THINKING

By definition, critical thinking employs skills that contribute to information literacy. Critical thinking and information literacy both require distinguishing between assumption and fact, suspending

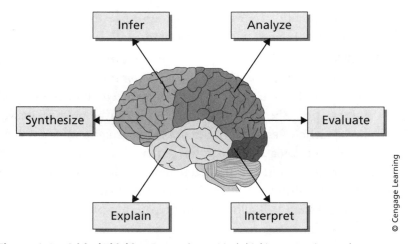

Figure 1-1 Critical Thinking Strategies. Critical thinking strategies can be categorized into six major areas.

personal opinion and bias in favor of objectivity, and considering issues from multiple perspectives and in adequate depth. The wealth of information available today from a wide variety of sources requires sharp analytical skills to determine both appropriateness and credibility. To achieve these objectives, one must think actively and systematically about information using a variety of strategies. Figure 1-1 illustrates only a few of the important critical thinking strategies. Critical thinking is more than just thinking, which sometimes can be biased, uninformed, distorted, superficial, or incomplete. Critical thinking is necessary for effective use of information.

The following processes involve critical thinking:

▶ **INFER:** *To draw conclusions from evidence or facts.*

In the training company expansion case, the training manager responsible for the expansion inferred, from the lack of any significant training companies in the business directories she viewed, that her training company would have a good chance of being successful in the new state.

▶ **ANALYZE:** *To break down complex concepts into parts and then study how the parts are related to each other in making up the whole.*

In the training company case, the training manager had to analyze the various data she found. For example, from all of the companies doing business in the new area, she had to identify those that might utilize her training. Her analysis involved multiple factors, including assessing the needs of companies and their ability to fund the training. She had to consider the perspectives of the decision makers in the companies, as well as the perspective of her own organization. She also had to find out how many other companies provide the same type of training. These are examples of the data analysis needed to make a good decision.

▶ **EVALUATE:** *To examine critically, given a specific set of criteria.*

After broadly analyzing the training situation, the training manager had to critically examine the specific data, such as population statistics, marketing data, financial information, and the human resource requirements for the new training. In addition, to ensure effectiveness, she had to evaluate her performance on each of the steps.

▶ **INTERPRET:** *To comprehend the meaning or significance of something.*

In the case, the training manager had to interpret the significance of the influx of new businesses into the state and relate this influx to the existing training options in the area. She also had to interpret the significance of the online training options and how these options were meeting the actual needs of the businesses. She had to consider the meaning of her analysis in light of these additional factors.

▶ **EXPLAIN:** *To make clear the thought process, facts, or concepts.*

The training manager had to clearly explain and illustrate her recommendation to expand the company's training to the new state. She had to show how she arrived at the decision by presenting accurate, thorough, and effectively organized data.

▶ **SYNTHESIZE:** *To combine separate thoughts to form a concept.*

Finally, to make a sound recommendation, the training manager had to take all of the information, including the recommendations of her subordinates, the state agency representatives she talked with, and potential customers, and combine this information with the empirical data (facts and figures) that she obtained in her research, to draw a logical and workable conclusion.

CREATIVE THINKING

Creative thinking is the process of actively exploring possibilities, generating alternatives, keeping an open mind toward change, and

1

combining ideas to create something new or to view old concepts in new ways. The common phrase "think outside the box" refers to thinking creatively. Effective creative thinking is innovative, yet takes into consideration facts and realistic constraints. Creative thinkers use their imagination, are highly expressive, and are not restricted by existing ideas or barriers. They seek and embrace support from others to gain different perspectives.

For example, a construction foreman faced with increasing safety at the jobsite might hand out safety pamphlets and ask each laborer to read the information. A more creative solution, though, might be to create performance competition among three different teams by giving a safety quiz that identifies safety issues on the jobsite, and by rewarding the team that accrues the most points over the life of the project. Or the foreman might seek input from others to find out what safety programs have been effective in the past.

Effective information users combine critical thinking and creative thinking in their approach to an information need or a problem-solving situation.

PROBLEM SOLVING

Problem solving entails a systematic process to find a solution to a question or an issue. Being information-literate requires knowing how to analyze and apply information to solve problems successfully. Steps in the problem-solving process consist of: (1) defining the problem, (2) looking for possible causes of the problem, (3) developing possible solutions to the problem, (4) evaluating each possible solution to determine the best one, (5) implementing the best solution, and (6) evaluating the results. Figure 1-2 illustrates a simplified version of this process.

▶ **DEFINE THE PROBLEM.** *A problem must be well understood before it can be solved. To define a problem, the training manager uses information to answer the questions: Who? What? Where? When? How? Why? How much?*

As an example, consider an office network situation in which the process of backing up the information on the office network is inefficient and is taking too long. Most important, the system is ineffective, partially because of the office manager's

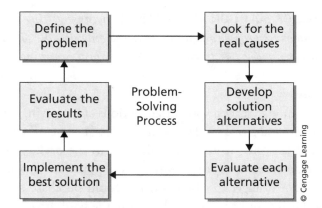

Figure 1-2   The Problem-Solving Process. Effective problem solving involves six major steps.

lack of knowledge regarding data backup and appropriate backup equipment and options. In this situation, the problem first must be defined by thoroughly reviewing the facts and assessing the processes used by the office manager who is responsible for the biweekly backups. Many of the files are crucial and contain information that, if lost, would cost the company money and time.

In the current backup system, the office manager saves the latest files to a flash drive and takes the flash drive home to store the backups offsite for safekeeping. The problem is that this process is too time-consuming, the flash drive is not as reliable as other data-storage options over time, and the offsite storage is not secure.

▶ **LOOK FOR THE REAL CAUSES.** *Office managers have to ensure that they know the exact cause(s) of the problem and understand these causes thoroughly. With only a superficial study of the situation, the real causes of a problem may be hidden, so careful analysis and consideration of multiple perspectives may be necessary.*

In the data-storage case, a closer look at this situation reveals that the office manager lacks knowledge about data backup and storage, and that using a flash drive is the only method he knows. At least part of the real cause of the problem is lack of skill on the part of the person responsible for the network and data.

1

▶ **DEVELOP SOLUTION ALTERNATIVES.** *Because getting input from appropriate people contributes to developing possible solutions, the office manager has to engage others in brainstorming as part of the creative thinking process to generate as many alternatives as possible.*

Among several potential options for solving the data backup and storage dilemma are these: (1) The office manager could continue to use the flash drive as the backup and data-storage method; (2) the company could purchase a tape backup for data storage; (3) the company could purchase an external hard drive for backup and then store the hard drive offsite; and (4) the company could use an online data backup and storage system offered by a third party. An issue related to both the problem and the solution is the need to provide the office manager with training on data backup and storage.

▶ **EVALUATE EACH ALTERNATIVE.** *The office manager has to consider each alternative to determine which solution or combination of solutions works best. Getting an outside opinion from a neutral party contributes another perspective and additional data to the evaluation.*

In the data backup and storage case, each alternative should be evaluated, using a set of predetermined criteria. Because the criteria and the questions asked vary with each situation, knowing the kind of information needed is necessary to define the relevant questions. In this case, the following questions are important: (1) How much does each system cost? (2) How reliable is each system, and how long does each system last? (3) How difficult is each system to implement and maintain? (4) How long does the actual backup process take? (5) How secure is each system? (6) What is the process for data recovery?

▶ **IMPLEMENT THE BEST SOLUTION.** *After selecting the best solution, the office manager has to implement it carefully.*

In the data backup and storage case, the company has chosen the solution of contracting with a third party for offsite data backup and storage. Research revealed a relatively low cost, a high level of security and reliability, ease of implementation, and quick recovery of data, if needed. The company signed on with a reliable data backup and storage company and implemented the process within a few days. Also, the office manager received free training from that company on how to use the new system. He also learned how to increase the security and organization of the company's data and file system.

▶ **EVALUATE THE RESULTS.** *Finally, the office manager has to assess whether the solution worked. Is the problem solved? If not, further evaluation is needed to determine what worked, what did not, and what changes are appropriate. The office manager has to assess whether the information was adequate, whether it was used effectively, and whether the way the information was communicated influenced the outcome in any way. After any changes have been implemented, the cycle is repeated.*

In the data backup and storage case, the company compared the results to the old system, assessed the overall security, and reviewed the existing data-management system. It was determined that, although the service did incur a monthly expense, the extra cost was offset by increased security and the office manager's increased efficiency. The company also decided to revisit the problem in one month to ensure that the data was being backed up as planned, and was stored appropriately.

HIGHER-ORDER THINKING

Higher-order thinking contributes to both critical and creative thinking processes. Bloom (1956) conceptualizes thinking as a pyramid having six levels, beginning with the lowest level (Knowledge) and increasing to the highest level (Evaluation). Each level describes a different way to think about information. The lowest level is superficial, considering straightforward facts. An example of this level is being able to name the states and their capitals. The highest level reflects deep, complex thinking, in which information is judged critically to reach a decision. The training company manager's process is an example of using the higher levels of Bloom's taxonomy.

The diagram in Figure 1-3 illustrates Bloom's taxonomy with its six levels of thinking about information. Information-literate individuals will use all levels of thinking at various times, depending on the information needed and the goal they are trying to achieve. Academic and professional activities tend to require the higher levels of thinking more often.

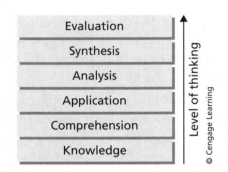

Figure 1-3   Bloom's Taxonomy. The six levels in Bloom's higher-order thinking taxonomy begin with broad, basic thinking (knowledge) and end with more advanced, complex thinking (evaluation).

The following action verbs represent strategies for thinking effectively at each level of Bloom's taxonomy:

▶ *Knowledge: Define, identify, describe, recognize, label, list, match, name, reproduce, outline, recall.* In the training manager case introduced earlier in this chapter, knowledge is exemplified by the information regarding businesses, state laws and regulations, and other factual information relevant to her goal.

▶ *Comprehension: Explain, generalize, extend, comprehend, give examples, summarize, translate, paraphrase, rewrite, predict.* An example of the *comprehension* level from this case is the manager's pulling her factual data into a general statement to condense and summarize the information.

▶ *Application: Apply, compute, change, construct, develop, manipulate, solve, show, illustrate, produce, relate, use, operate, discover, modify.* In the example, the manager might construct scenarios, applying the data related to doing business in the new state to her own company.

▶ *Analysis: Analyze, break down, infer, separate, diagram, differentiate, contrast, compare.* Following the application of the data to her own situation, the manager will assess her findings and compare and contrast doing business in the new state with that in her current location.

▶ *Synthesis: Categorize, generate, design, devise, compile, rearrange, reorganize, revise, reconstruct, combine, write, tell.* After completing her analysis, the manager will compile her conclusions and generate suggestions for following through on the project.

▶ *Evaluation: Conclude, defend, critique, discriminate, judge, interpret, justify, support.* To conclude the process, the training manager will critique her conclusions to ensure that they are logical and that her conclusions are sound.

Note that the level of thinking complexity increases when moving from basic knowledge to evaluation.

EFFECTIVE COMMUNICATION

Successful students and professionals must be able to communicate information effectively to many different types of audiences and in a variety of situations. To be able to communicate effectively, the sender of a message should understand the basic communication process shown in Figure 1-4.

The context in which a communication occurs influences the way information and messages are used, expressed, and received. For example, a student's communication style in a group of friends is likely to differ from the student's communication style with a group of professors. The concept of discourse communities refers to different groups and the unique rules and standards (formal and informal) of each group for communicating. Effective communication takes place when the standards of a specific discourse community are considered and information is communicated according to those standards.

The standards include aspects of communication such as level of formality, language, and style guidelines. For example, communication with your professors (one discourse community) will be more effective when you observe standards of professionalism and appropriate formality. Conversely, your friends (another discourse

Figure 1-4   The Communication Process. The communication process involves a sender who encodes a message and then selects and utilizes an appropriate channel so a receiver can receive and decode the message.

1

community) would find you stuffy and overly formal if you were to use the same communication style with them. Messages are sent and received effectively when the conventions of a discourse community are observed (Trupe, 2001; DePaul University, n.d.).

Communicating to Discourse Communities

The following brief scenario illustrates discourse communities and the basic communication process: Dr. Stewart has just received the results from a series of blood tests for his patient, John, who is suffering from extreme fatigue. Dr. Stewart has to tell John that he has hypoglycemia, a severely lowered blood glucose (blood sugar) level. First, Dr. Stewart must consider the discourse community. She is communicating with a member of the patient community (versus the medical community), so she must encode the message into a form that the receiver (John) can understand. Because John is not at all familiar with technical medical terms, Dr. Stewart must use simple, layperson terms so John can clearly understand the details of his condition.

Next, Dr. Stewart must select and properly use a medium or channel to send this message. With confidential medical information, Dr. Stewart considers the most effective way to be able to answer John's questions, in keeping with the Health Information Portability and Accountability Act (HIPAA), which provides legal and ethical guidelines on the dissemination of a patient's health information. Based on these considerations, Dr. Stewart decides to meet with John in person to answer his questions and maintain confidentiality. Dr. Stewart also decides to use as a visual aid an anatomical illustration of the digestive system and blood pathway to help John understand the importance of eating regular meals. Finally, John must actually receive this information and decode it accurately so he will understand his medical condition.

Dr. Stewart has selected illustrations and explanations that are understandable to a member of the patient community. Consider how this might be different if Dr. Stewart were providing this information to a member of the medical community.

If any part of the communication process is missing or misunderstood, the message will not be communicated as intended. Accordingly, an effective communicator must develop specific skills related to each step in the communication process and be able to select the most effective approach based on the situation.

? CRITICAL THINKING QUESTIONS

- If a workplace professional were said to be computer-literate, how would you describe his or her skills specifically?
- Assuming that you are not the librarian but are said to be a great researcher and literate in using the library, what kind of skills do you think you would have?
- To be media-literate, what specific workplace or school situations might you need? What specific skills would you have?
- Think about the careers that intrigue you and where you might see yourself working. How might you have to be visually literate? How would this help you communicate or achieve some other workplace or school goal?
- What skills do you think are essential for someone who is visually-literate? Do these skills differ in different career areas?

To encode and send a message successfully, the communicator must develop the abilities to:

▶ write well,

▶ organize information logically and coherently,

▶ speak in public,

▶ interact effectively with others,

▶ use visual elements in communicating an idea,

▶ use a variety of technologies (telephone, computer, e-mail, other Internet communication tools, scanners and cameras, audio and video recorders, etc.) to send the message.

A careful study of this process reveals that the sender is responsible for ensuring that the message is received as intended. The receiver also plays a role in the communication process by asking clarifying questions and actively participating in the discourse.

ORGANIZATION

A person who is organized has a systematic way to group information, take notes on research so the main points can be identified, categorize material so the information is easily found, and log steps and resources for later reference. An information-literate individual must understand how to use a variety of organizational strategies to gather information and communicate it effectively. Specific skills include understanding and logically using electronic and print file management systems, practicing time-management techniques, breaking down complex tasks into manageable objectives, and appropriately using a variety of graphic organizers such as Venn diagrams, flowcharts, tables, Gantt charts, organizational charts, concept maps, and so forth. Each of these tools will be described later in the text.

Information literacy is an umbrella term that encompasses several types of literacy. An information-literate individual recognizes that all types of literacy are important and strives to become proficient in the skill sets required for each. These skill sets often overlap and support each other, and all rely on the transferable skills described earlier. The following types of literacy and their associated skills are important components of information literacy.

COMPUTER LITERACY

Computer literacy involves a basic understanding of how a computer works and how it can be applied to complete a task. A computer-literate individual understands the various terms associated with computer hardware, as well as common computer software applications. Figure 1-5 illustrates the various competency areas that make up computer literacy.

LIBRARY LITERACY

Library literacy encompasses an understanding of the different kinds of information resources housed in a library—books, encyclopedias, reference materials, directories, catalogs, indexes, databases, periodicals, visual resources, audio resources, graphic resources, and so forth. Library literacy also includes knowing how to locate the resources in the library physically or electronically, understanding how to find and access information within each resource, being knowledgeable about correct referencing processes, and being able to get help from a librarian when necessary. Today, libraries use both print and sophisticated electronic resources and search tools. An important aspect of library literacy is to know which technology is

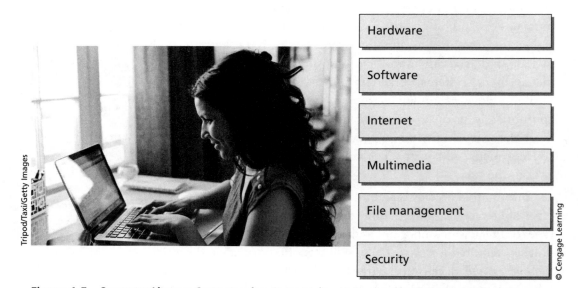

Hardware

Software

Internet

Multimedia

File management

Security

Tripod/Taxi/Getty Images

© Cengage Learning

Figure 1-5   Computer Literacy Competencies. Computer literacy involves knowledge and skills in six major areas related to computers.

Books and periodicals

Databases and directories

Catalogs and indexes

Media resources

Reference materials

© Cengage Learning

Bananastock Ltd./Jupiter Images

Figure 1-6   Knowledge Areas of Library Literacy. Library literacy involves knowledge and skills in five major areas.

most appropriate for the task. Figure 1-6 illustrates only a few of the many knowledge areas required for library literacy.

MEDIA LITERACY

One definition of media literacy is provided by the Center for Media Literacy (n.d.):

> In many cases, print form (print media) is appropriate and sufficient. At other times, audio, visual, graphic, Internet-based, interactive, electronic, and other forms of media are better suited for the communication. The information-literate individual must understand the many options available and know how to translate the information into the best choice. Media-literate individuals also understand the advantages, disadvantages, challenges, and purposes of each type of media.

VISUAL LITERACY

A component of media literacy is visual literacy (and thus a component of information literacy), which is the ability to use visual media effectively to learn and communicate (International Visual Learning Association, 2012). We live in an increasingly visual culture, and the

❝ *Media Literacy is a 21st century approach to education.*

It provides a framework to access, analyze, evaluate, create, and participate using messages in a variety of forms—from print to video to the Internet. Media literacy builds an understanding of the role of the media in society as well as essential skills of inquiry and self-expression necessary for citizens of a democracy.❞

SELF-ASSESSMENT QUESTION

Review the following quote: "In this knowledge-oriented workplace, information literacy is the key to power." What does this mean to you in your own career path? Write down some specific examples of how this might be true for you.

1

SELF-ASSESSMENT QUESTIONS

- Reflect on your area of study and the job-related tasks in your current or future career. What sources and information will you have to be able to locate, access, retrieve, and use information? List as many different areas and types of information as you can. Expand this list as you think of additional types of information and sources.
- How do you think you might be asked to communicate new information in your workplace? List as many different ways or formats as you can. Be specific.
- Imagine yourself in the role of manager or owner of a company, organization, or facility similar to the kind in which you want to work during your career. Relative to information literacy, what information skills would you want your new employees to have? Why? As the owner/manager, how would you be at a disadvantage if your employees were information-illiterate? (Think about this question as you compare your facility to a competing facility with highly skilled employees in information areas.)

information-literate person recognizes that understanding how to view, interpret, and produce visual media is paramount.

The American Library Association (ALA, 2011) defines visual literacy as

> a set of abilities that enables an individual to effectively find, interpret, evaluate, use, and create images and visual media. Visual literacy skills equip a learner to understand and analyze the contextual, cultural, ethical, aesthetic, intellectual, and technical components involved in the production and use of visual materials. A visually literate individual is both a critical consumer of visual media and a competent contributor to a body of shared knowledge and culture.

Though information-literate individuals do not have to be graphic designers or accomplished artists, in many cases visual elements are the best choice for conveying a message. Information-literate individuals must understand how to find, create, format, alter, and embed visual elements into the message, using basic computer software and other tools.

TECHNOLOGY LITERACY

Finally, the information-literate individual must be able to use a variety of technologies to find and access information, as well as to effectively organize, use, and communicate information. These skills make up technology literacy. Included in technology skills are the ability to use basic computer software programs (e.g., word-processing, spreadsheets, presentation tools, databases), the Internet, social media, and supporting tools such as search engines, file-management systems, social networking sites, weblogs (blogs), Really Simple Syndication (RSS) feeds, and so forth. And, because technology changes quickly, information-literate individuals must update their technology skills continuously to stay current and be able to use their existing skills in new ways.

Information literacy is not just for the technical student or the business and technology professional. Information skills are required in every career, and continued growth of this trend can be expected. For example, the health professions (which at one time were considered "nontechnical") are using technology for managing patient records, charting patient progress, and operating equipment. By 2014, all medical records must be in electronic format. All professionals rely on some type of information to complete their job tasks successfully. To be successful in a career, the college graduate no longer can rely solely on the information learned in school. Information is changing constantly.

Today's professionals must acquire new knowledge and skills continuously. For example, an allied health professional will have to keep up with new procedures, medication, diseases, and treatments. A construction professional must keep up with new materials, codes, and techniques. A business professional must be able to gather data on markets, the competition, and new avenues for products and services. Technology has resulted in information being easily updated. The successful professional knows how to use technology to access information that is constantly being added to the body of knowledge in every field. Individuals who lack information literacy skills may rely on outdated information and data, and as a result, be hindered significantly in job success and advancement.

CASE IN POINT: SEEK AND YE SHALL FIND

Read the scenario below. Then, in groups or as a class, discuss the questions at the end.

Derrick Washington just graduated from college with an associate's degree in nursing and was hired at a long-term nursing facility as a caregiver. This facility has the philosophy that true patient care stems from a genuine concern for each individual patient and in-depth knowledge about the individual diseases and disorders challenging each patient. In light of this philosophy, the administration asks all staff members, regardless of position, to attend weekly inservice training sessions to learn more about the care of patients. The staff members take turns presenting information about selected diseases, disorders, and other healthcare issues, including healthcare ethics, legal issues, economic issues, related community issues, aging issues, communication topics, and diversity topics.

Continued

1

Continued

Each staff member is assigned a topic and is asked to fully research the subject, select the most relevant information for the staff as a whole, develop a one- to two-page information sheet with a "Resources for Additional Learning" section, and create a "Tips for Patient Education" page for distribution to each staff member. In addition, staff members are required to deliver a 20-minute presentation on their topic to the entire group of care providers. All staff members are expected to participate, provide current and accurate information, and use excellent professional communication skills.

The facility administration considers these inservice training sessions as essential to the facility's continued excellence and as a contributing factor in salary increases and promotions. Accordingly, all staff members are assessed quarterly on the effectiveness of the inservices they have given during the quarter. All staff members are expected to achieve 80 percent or better on these assessments.

Through self-reflection and honest evaluation, Derrick has found that he does not have the information skills required to excel in this workplace expectation. He realizes that he does not know how to determine what kind of information he will need for the inservices, how to find current information efficiently, or how to assess the credibility of information. In addition, he does not feel confident in his ability to organize the information effectively into a brief written summary or to make a professional presentation, even though he took related courses for these skills in school. He is significantly stressed about this employment requirement.

- How well do you think you could determine the kind and extent of information you might be asked to find to be able to accomplish a professional task?
- How efficient would you be at finding the information in a library or on the Internet?
- How would you know that the information you find is credible?
- How skilled are you at pulling significant points from a large body of information and organizing them into a one- to two-page summary for review by professionals in your field?
- How effectively could you make a presentation that would both engage and teach your colleagues?

STEPS IN EFFECTIVE RESEARCH

Successfully using information to meet a need can be defined in the series of steps illustrated in Figure 1-7. The remainder of this text discusses factors contributing to each step in detail and explores the related information skills.

STEP 1: DEFINE THE NEED AND THE AUDIENCE

Before even beginning to seek the proper information, individuals must establish and articulate the need for that information. This requires consulting with appropriate individuals to communicate and define the need. A need can be a problem that must be solved, a question that must be answered, or a task that must be performed. For example, an instructor may assign to students the task of writing an essay on a controversial issue. In this case, information is needed to describe each side of the issue in depth. The student also must be able to communicate the information in the required format. In the workplace, a departmental team may be asked to solve a production problem. In this case, the information need is to find information about potential technology solutions. and then to evaluate which solution is the best option in light of the company's financial and time constraints. Finally, the team must communicate this solution to decision makers.

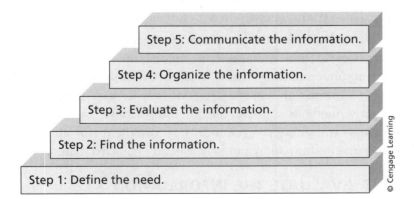

Figure 1-7   Steps in Effective Research. There are five steps to effective research.

1

? CRITICAL THINKING QUESTIONS

- An obsolete employee is one who no longer has the skills required to do the job. What specifically might an obsolete employee in your career field look like in 10 years?
- How do ambitious employees prevent themselves from becoming obsolete? Be specific, and relate your ideas specifically to your field of study.

● ● ● **questions to ask to find useful information**

- What kind of information do I need? (facts, figures, statistics, opinions, sides of an issue, historical/background, profile, interview, primary, secondary, etc.)
- How much information do I need? (limited scope, in-depth coverage, summary or overview, etc.)
- What parameters should I follow? (time period, geographical location, age or gender, point of view, etc.)
- Who will be receiving this information? (practitioners, professionals, laypeople, scientists, team members, colleagues, clients, patients, etc.)

STEP 2: FIND THE INFORMATION

Step 2 involves creating a research strategy customized to the task at hand. A research strategy is a kind of map that is used to avoid wasting time and wandering aimlessly through the massive amounts of information available in libraries, on the Internet, and elsewhere. A research strategy includes deciding what resources to use, whether the resources are available and cost-effective, if using specific resources provides significant benefit, how the resources can be accessed, and the timeline required to accomplish the research. To develop this map, the information gatherer must understand how information is produced, organized, and communicated, in both formal and informal situations.

With a plan in hand, the information gatherer then must call upon a variety of information skills to conduct the research. This step assumes an understanding of how to locate information using search tools and information-retrieval systems, how to apply appropriate investigative methods to obtain the best information, how to find the information within a given resource, how to take useful notes, and how to extract information and save it in an organized manner.

STEP 3: EVALUATE THE INFORMATION

Evaluating the research results requires the information gatherer to apply a set of criteria to determine if the information is reliable, valid, accurate, current, and free from bias. In this part of the evaluation, the

> **● ● ● questions to ask to find useful information**
>
> - What information sources should I use? (encyclopedias, professional journals, people, directories, databases, popular magazines, maps, videos, etc.)
> - Where do I find these resources? (library, Internet, individuals, companies, government resources, librarian, etc.)
> - How do I search for the information within each resource? (index, electronic search engine, etc.)
> - How should I retrieve the information once I find it? (download, photocopy, interlibrary loan, print, etc.)
> - How should I manage the information that I retrieve? (electronic files, print file folders, etc.)

credibility of the actual information sources is assessed. Information also must be evaluated to determine if it meets the research need. This type of evaluation requires filtering, from all of the collected data, information that is important to the original question or problem.

In the next chapters we will define more extensively what is involved in answering each of these questions.

STEP 4: ORGANIZE THE INFORMATION

An information-literate individual uses systematic strategies to organize information so it can be communicated in the most effective way. Organization starts with managing the information retrieved in the

> **● ● ● questions to ask to evaluate information effectively**
>
> - Is the information current?
> - Is the information credible?
> - Is the information accurate?
> - Is the information relevant to the need?
> - Is the information useful?
> - Is the information free from bias?

> **● ● ● questions to ask to organize information effectively**
>
> - How do I organize the information so I can find main ideas, key issues, different viewpoints, etc.?
> - How can I think about the information in new ways?
> - How should I manage a large amount of information?
> - How do I organize the information so it is presented logically and appropriately? (chronologically, priority of elements, problem/solution, deductive order, inductive order, etc.)

research process. For many research projects, a large amount of information is available, some of which may not be useful or directly related to the need. Sometimes it is difficult to know if all of the information is important until the information gathering is complete. Keeping information organized as it is collected simplifies the evaluation process. Information also must be organized to achieve the communication goal. Information can be organized and presented according to several criteria, which will be discussed in-depth in Chapter 5.

STEP 5: COMMUNICATE THE INFORMATION

The information-literate individual must communicate the information to others effectively so it can be used to solve the problem, answer the question, or meet the original need. Effective communication considers many factors and can be transmitted through a variety of channels: written documents, verbal presentations, visual presentations, and a variety of electronic formats. The communication also must be legal and ethical according to copyright laws, intellectual property standards, and the accurate citation of information sources.

Finally, the entire research process and results should be evaluated to determine if the information has met the need sufficiently, solved the problem, or answered the original questions. If not, the process should be evaluated and changes made if appropriate.

Each of the next five chapters in this text will address one of the steps in the research process and explain the specific skills that an information-literate professional needs.

● ● ● questions to ask to communicate information effectively

- Who is my audience? Am I communicating on a casual topic or for business? Is the setting formal or relaxed? The type of audience and the setting will determine how to deliver the information.

- What channel should be used to communicate the research results? (written, verbal, visual, electronic, etc.)

- For the selected channel, what specific format best meets the communication need? (proposal, narrative, research report, slide presentation, image, diagram, etc.)

- How do I properly reference the resources I use and give appropriate credit to the original authors of the information?

success steps for effective research

- Define the need and the audience.
- Find the information.
- Evaluate the information.
- Organize the information.
- Communicate the information.

SELF-ASSESSMENT QUESTIONS

- Which steps in the research process do you think you currently do well?
- In which steps do you think you need to develop more knowledge and skill?
- What do you think are the most difficult steps for you to complete? Why?
- What do you think are the easiest steps for you to complete? Why?

CHAPTER SUMMARY

Chapter 1 introduced you to the concept of information literacy. You now are familiar with what you need to do to be an information-literate individual and why being information-literate is important to your success. Conversely, you are aware of the challenges that can face an individual who is not.

POINTS TO KEEP IN MIND

▶ Information literacy is the ability to locate, access, retrieve, evaluate, use, and communicate information effectively.

▶ The information-literate individual has the knowledge to locate, access, retrieve, evaluate, use, and effectively communicate information.

▶ Information literacy is essential to success in school and in the workplace.

apply it

- Define *information literacy.*
- Name the specific skills required for an individual to be an information-literate student or professional.
- Explain the importance of knowing how to locate, access, retrieve, evaluate, use, and effectively communicate information in school and in the workplace.
- Outline the challenges facing an individual who does not possess information skills in school and in the workplace.

 Activity #1: Self-Analysis: Research Process

GOAL: To reflect critically on your current process for finding and using information and to generate a list of areas for improvement.

Think carefully and write down your answers for agreement to each of the following questions:

1. When you are given a research task, what typically is your first step? Then what do you do? Sketch your personal and realistic research process from beginning to end.

2. What resources do you typically use to find information? List each resource you have used in recent years (e.g., Internet, encyclopedia, dictionary, journal, newspaper, directory).

3. What resources do you commonly use in a library?

4. What online resources do you commonly use for research?

5. What search tools are you proficient at using (printed and/or electronic)?

6. How specifically do you copy down and organize the information you find?

7. How do you organize your electronic files on your computer?

8. On a scale from 1 to 5 where 1 = need significant improvement and 5 = expert, rate yourself in each of the following areas. Be honest.

Rating Table

Area	Rating 1–5
Critical thinking	
Creative thinking	
Problem solving	
Higher-order thinking	
Effective communication	
Organization	
Computer literacy	
Library literacy	
Media literacy	
Visual literacy	
Technology literacy	
Effective research	

Activity #2: Predicting the Future of Information

GOAL: To emphasize the importance of information literacy for the future.

STEP 1: As a group, brainstorm answers to the following questions. Use your imagination. Think critically and creatively. Remember that in brainstorming, the goal is to generate as many ideas as possible but not to judge or evaluate these ideas.

• What will libraries look like in 10 years? In 20 years?

• How will people communicate with each other in 10 years? In 20 years?

• What will computers look like in 10 years? What will they be able to do that they cannot do now? In 20 years?

continued

1

continued

STEP 2: Organize your list into descriptive categories, and be prepared to compare your list with those of other groups in your class.

 Activity #3: Web Research

GOAL: To develop a full understanding of the importance of information literacy in career success.

STEP 1: Go to the American Library Association's web site: www.ala.org

STEP 2: Once there, use the site's search tool to find the Information Literacy resources. Read the information provided.

STEP 3: Go to Google and complete a search for "information literacy." Explore at least two additional web sites related to information literacy. What are others doing in the area of information literacy, and how do they describe the various skill sets?

STEP 4: List at least 20 different specific skills that you know you need to personally develop related to finding, accessing, retrieving, evaluating, using, and communicating information. Be prepared to share your list with your classmates.

STEP 5: Place the List of 20 Information Skills You Know You Need to Develop in your Learning Portfolio.

CHECK YOUR UNDERSTANDING

Visit www.cengagebrain.com to see how well you have mastered the material in Chapter 1.

SUGGESTED ITEMS FOR LEARNING PORTFOLIO

Refer to the "Developing Portfolios" section at the beginning of this textbook for more information on learning portfolios.

▶ List of 20 Information Skills You Know You Need to Develop.

REFERENCES

American Library Association (ALA). (2000). *Information literacy competency standards for higher education.* Retrieved June 10, 2013, from http://www.ala.org/ala/mgrps/divs/acrl/standards/standards.pdf

American Library Association. (2011). *ACRL visual literacy competency standards for higher education.* Retrieved June 10, 2013, from http://www.ala.org/acrl/standards/visualliteracy

American Library Association Digital Literacy Task Force. (2013). *Digital literacy, libraries, and public policy.* Retrieved June 5, 2013, from http://www.districtdispatch.org/wp-content/uploads/2013/01/2012 _OITP_digilitreport_1_22_13.pdf

Bloom B. S. (1956). *Taxonomy of educational objectives, Handbook I: The cognitive domain.* New York: David McKay.

Center for Media Literacy. (n.d.). *What is media literacy? A definition… and more.* Retrieved June 10, 2013, from http://www.medialit.org /reading-room/what-media-literacy-definitionand-more

DePaul University. (n.d.). *What is a discourse community?* Retrieved June 10, 2013, from http://shrike.depaul.edu/~jwhite7/discoursecommunitydef .htm

Infoengineering.net. (n.d.). *The 8 must-have skills for information workers.* Retrieved June 7, 2013, from http://www.infogineering.net/information -worker-skills.htm

International Visual Learning Association. (2012). *What is "visual literacy?"* Retrieved June 10, 2013, from http://www.ivla.org/drupal2/content /what-visual-literacy

Jones, B. and Flannigan, S. (n.d.). *Connecting the digital dots: literacy of the 21st century.* Retrieved June 6, 2013, from http://www.nmc.org/pdf /Connecting%20the%20Digital%20Dots.pdf

Rasmus, D. (2012). *What is an information worker?* Retrieved June 7, 2013, from http://danielrasmus.com/what-is-an-information-worker/

Trupe, A. L. (2001). *Effective writing text: Discourse communities.* Retrieved June 10, 2013, from http://www.bridgewater.edu/~atrupe/ENG101 /Text/discom.htm

Webber, S. (2010, May 25–27). *Information literacy for the 21st century.* Paper presented at INFORUM 2010: 16th Conference on Professional Information Resources. Retrieved June 10, 2013, from http://www.inforum.cz/pdf/2010/webber-sheila-1.pdf

CHAPTER OUTLINE

Determining the Information You Need

LEARNING OBJECTIVES

By the end of this chapter, students will achieve the following objectives:

▶ Explain the need for a main research question and relevant, focused research questions.

▶ Develop effective main research questions and focused research questions.

▶ Distinguish between primary and secondary information sources.

▶ Explain various ways to present information.

▶ Explain various ways to access information.

▶ Identify and describe 21st-century information sources.

BE IN THE KNOW

Primary Source Analysis Tool

As you will learn in this chapter, the use of primary and secondary information sources will be critical to your research efforts as you go through school.

The Library of Congress (www.loc.gov) has devised a Primary Source Analysis Tool to help students review primary source materials and to assess their value as they pertain to the research topic. This tool can be accessed at www.loc.gov/teachers/primary-source-analysis-tool/.

Once you have completed your analysis online your results can be downloaded, printed, or e-mailed using the links at the bottom of the page.

The tool suggests several formats of information. Use the drop-down menu at the top of the page to choose from:

- Any Format
- Photographs and Prints
- Books and other Printed Texts
- Manuscripts
- Maps
- Motion Pictures
- Sound Recordings
- Oral Histories
- Political Cartoons
- Sheet Music and Song Sheets

Once you have chosen your format, there are three columns where you can enter information. These columns are:

- Observe
- Reflect
- Question

There is also space where you can record "Further Investigation" information.

If you are stumped by what to put into the columns (information can be put into the columns in any order and you can go back and forth as need be), there are questions you can access by clicking on the ? icon in each column. The questions change based upon the format chosen.

As you start research on a topic, consider using this handy tool online. It may just be the jumpstart your project needs.

SOLVING INFORMATION PROBLEMS: DEFINING THE NEED AND THE AUDIENCE

One of the most daunting tasks that college students face during their academic careers is writing research papers. Even if writing comes easily to you, there is still the matter of deciding on a topic (unless your instructor has already assigned one to you), identifying your audience, defining the need for your paper (in other words, what you want to accomplish by writing it), and deciding what writing style you will use based upon the need.

To be efficient, you first must clearly define the concepts relevant to your topic and the related information need. A need can be a problem that must be solved, a question that must be answered, or a task that must be performed. This need must be defined and communicated clearly.

THE RESEARCH PROCESS

On any given day, you consciously or subconsciously make decisions and solve problems. This involves a process. Research requires following a process to retrieve information on a specific topic, using reliable search tools to find the information, and being able to recognize the information as useful or irrelevant. Effective research employs the problem-solving skills discussed in Chapter 1.

Review the steps in effective research presented in Chapter 1. For now, our focus is on Step 1: Define the Need.

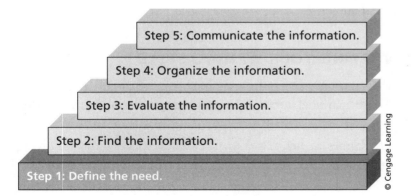

Research Process Step 1: Define the need. The first step of any research project should be to clearly define what is needed.

Step 5: Communicate the information.
Step 4: Organize the information.
Step 3: Evaluate the information.
Step 2: Find the information.
Step 1: Define the need.

© Cengage Learning

SELF-ASSESSMENT QUESTIONS

Think of situations you have been in that require information on subjects you know nothing about.

- What process did you use to learn more about the subject?
- Did you have a plan?
- What steps did you follow to find the information you needed?

2

© Steve Smith/Shutterstock.com

DEFINING A TOPIC

In school, your research topic most likely will be determined by its relevance to the assignment. Your instructor may assign a specific topic or give you a range of topics from which to choose. Examples of other criteria for selecting topics are current events or current needs in a field, organizational goals and priorities, market trends, or training needs. These topics are more relevant to the workplace and represent research that you might undertake later in your career. The criteria for selecting a topic will depend largely on your field, organizational needs, and audience.

IDENTIFYING YOUR WRITING STYLE

Now that you have successfully defined your research topic and the related informational need, it is important to establish the writing style that you will use for your paper.

Ann Raimes in her text *Keys for Writers*, suggests the following writing styles be used for research papers based upon the need.

▶ If the main purpose of your research paper is to inform or explain an idea to the reader, then use *informative (also known as expository) writing*.

▶ If your paper's goal is to persuade readers to see your point of view or to spur them into action, use a *persuasive writing* style.

▶ If you are writing about an experiment or laboratory results, or are describing a detailed process, then a *technical* or *scientific writing* style should be employed (Raimes, 2013).

DEFINING THE AUDIENCE

At this stage of the writing process, you should define your audience. In the workplace, there are many audiences for whom you may conduct research and provide results: your supervisor, clients, third-party vendors, other internal company departments, company publications or intranet sites, or the media, among others. In these cases, your audience has already been identified for you.

While you are in school, your instructor may dictate your audience to you, but other times you may be able to make that choice yourself. Raimes advocates asking yourself this question as you continue to frame how you will conduct research and present your information: "how will reading my paper change or affect how my audience thinks, feels, or understands my topic?" (Raimes, 2013).

By defining your topic and your audience and identifying the writing style best suited to both, you will be well on your way to solving an information problem.

THE MAIN RESEARCH QUESTION

One of the best ways to further define your topic is to formulate a main research question as a starting point for the research. The main research question should include the key terms or concepts that are relevant to your topic. An effective research question will not be too broad or you will have too much information to sort through, and will not be so narrow that you are confined in your research. It should direct your research appropriately for your topic and your audience. Time and effort spent on developing an effective research question will save time and effort later in the research process.

Review the following examples of effective and ineffective research questions.

Effective research questions:

1. What effect does divorce have on academic achievement in elementary school children?
2. How has global warming affected the size of the polar ice cap?
3. What are the differences between the various processors available for computers?

Ineffective research questions:

1. Who was Benjamin Franklin?
2. Should older people be allowed to drive?
3. Does the United States have a good foreign policy?

provable/credible

An effective research question poses a question that can be answered with verifiable facts. It is phrased in a way that avoids subjective responses or opinions. It is sufficiently specific to address the real need or purpose of the research. For example, effective research question #1 is specific. The answer to this question can be formed by searching electronic, library, and other information resources to find verifiable facts. If no information is available, a study can be conducted to compare the academic performance of children from divorced parents with the academic performance of children from two-parent families. If the study is conducted properly, using sound scientific investigative methods, the result should be useful information about how divorce affects academic performance in children.

By contrast, ineffective research question #1 (about Benjamin Franklin) is too broad to be useful in directing the research process. Benjamin Franklin's life has many facets. The best answer to this question depends on the purpose of the information. If you are collecting information on American statesmen, you would focus on the political life of Franklin. If you want information on inventors, you would describe Franklin by looking at his scientific endeavors. Perhaps your goal is to compile a general biography about influential Americans. Your perspective would be different, and you would seek different kinds of information from different information sources. Until the question is narrowed, you cannot search effectively for information or conduct research. You also would organize the information differently depending on which aspect of Benjamin Franklin's life is selected.

Now look at ineffective research question #2 (about older people driving). This question also is too vague to be effective and is phrased

2

in a way that solicits opinion, not fact. For example, if you were to ask this question to a group of older people (or related information sources), you might get an entirely different answer than if you were to ask the question to a group of individuals who have had loved ones injured or killed by an older driver. The question also lacks a definition of "older," as well as criteria for assessment. The question is closed-ended, meaning that it is phrased in such a way that solicits a brief yes-or-no response.

Ineffective research question #3 (about foreign policy) also is vague, broad, and subjective. What aspect of foreign policy is in question? From whose perspective should the question be answered? Which political party? Which country? What is the purpose of the question? When questions such as these are necessary to understand the research question, the question may be too general and broad. Answering the questions provides direction to your research project.

Opinion and judgment are different. Both are subjective in nature in that both require your ideas and thoughts. Judgment, however, is supported by facts and verifiable data, whereas opinion is not. In college and in the workplace, you may be asked for your judgment on a topic or issue. An example in school is a position paper in which you are asked to state and support your stance on a topic. A workplace example is you being asked to provide a recommendation for a course of action. In both cases, you are being asked, in a sense, for your opinion. To be considered a reliable researcher, you must use relevant facts to support your stance. Doing so distinguishes judgment from opinion and contributes to your credibility and professional advancement.

? CRITICAL THINKING QUESTIONS

▶ What are the differences between the effective and ineffective questions?
▶ How would you make the three ineffective research questions effective?
▶ How do the three effective research questions help in planning the research process?

● ● ● **questions to ask to define a research question**

- Is the research question specific enough?
- Does the question elicit fact or opinion?
- Can the research question be answered with verifiable facts?

2

FOCUSED RESEARCH QUESTIONS

Once you have formulated your main research question, the next step is to break down the main question into more detailed questions, called focused research questions. Focused research questions break down the main question by asking *who, what, where, when, why,* and *how.* These questions keep the research directed to the specifics of the topic and purpose of the question. They allow the researcher to develop a well-planned and efficient search strategy.

Review the focused research questions below, which have been developed for the following main research question.

Does exercise level positively or negatively impact food consumption in obese individuals?

Effective focused questions:

▶ What is the definition of an obese individual?

▶ What is the definition of exercise?

▶ How is exercise measured?

▶ Do obese individuals who increase their level of exercise increase or decrease their food intake measured in calories?

▶ What level of exercise shows a change in food intake?

These focused questions allow you to make a plan for researching the main question. They give you a start on identifying specific resources you can use to find the information. By answering the focused questions, you can begin to organize your thoughts, back up your ideas with information, and logically and reasonably answer the main research question.

SELF-ASSESSMENT QUESTIONS

Think about a research project you have completed in the past.

• What is an effective research question?

• What are good focused questions you could have asked for this project?

● ● ● questions to ask to define a focused research question

• Do my focused questions direct me to the specifics of the question?

• Do my focused research questions address the purpose of the question?

• Do my focused research questions organize my thoughts about the question and direct my research activity?

2

CASE IN POINT: LET ME ENTERTAIN YOU

Read the scenario below. Then, in groups or as a class, discuss the questions at the end.

As a recent college graduate, Rachael Burgess was eager to start her new job at a meeting and event management company as a meeting manager/administrative assistant. In her new position Rachel has been asked by her supervisor to research onsite entertainment for a client who was going to be holding a sales meeting at a nearby resort in six months.

Eager to impress her supervisor with a quick turnaround of information, and using her computer savvy, Rachel did an Internet search of entertainment options in the city where the resort was located, and presented the top three search results to her boss within 30 minutes of the request.

▶ Aside from using a search engine, what other sources of information could Rachael have used to locate the information her supervisor requested?

▶ What focused research questions could Rachael have asked about the client's request? How might asking focused research questions affect Rachael's search for information?

▶ How reliable and credible do you think information is that comes from being a top search item on the Internet?

▶ Do you think the quickest research results are always the best and most accurate?

PRIMARY AND SECONDARY INFORMATION SOURCES

Information sources can be categorized as primary or secondary. Primary information sources are those that are closest to the actual event, time period, or individual in question. The information in these sources has not been edited, interpreted, condensed, or evaluated, which might change the original information. Obviously, the more altered or manipulated the original information is, the more risk there is for error. Primary resources also present original thinking and observations, such as the original research used to write journal articles reporting on original scientific studies, experiments, or observations.

Secondary information sources are those that are removed from the primary source. Authors of secondary sources examine, interpret, or reflect on the primary source information to restate or reuse the information. Secondary sources also act as pointers to the primary sources by referencing the original sources. Secondary information sources are more widely available than primary sources, and sometimes easier to use, but they should be evaluated critically to ensure that care has been taken to maintain the integrity of the original information and that the author of a secondary source has not misinterpreted or altered the original information to support a specific opinion or viewpoint. Whenever possible, it is wise to locate the primary source using the references in the secondary source and to give credit to both in your citations.

Use of inaccurate or misleading secondary information can compromise your research. Keep in mind that all information has the potential to influence some behavior. Therefore, you must ensure that you use information that is accurate, credible, and complete. Chapter 4 further addresses ways to determine the credibility of information.

Examples of primary sources:

- memoirs
- diaries
- autobiographies
- interviews with people
- public records
- transcripts of speeches
- letters, e-mails, memos, electronic mailing lists, blogs, discussion threads, newsgroups, and other correspondences
- discussions and electronic discussions on the Internet
- meetings and minutes taken at meetings
- newspaper articles reporting at the time of the event
- surveys
- government documents
- artifacts
- photographs and works of art
- observations

❱ patents

❱ works of literature, such as fiction and poems

Examples of secondary sources:

❱ books and textbooks

❱ review articles from scholarly journals

❱ scientific reports (articles in scholarly journals that describe an original research study, experiment, or observation)

❱ technical reports

❱ conference papers and proceedings

❱ theses and dissertations

❱ handbooks

❱ databases

❱ catalogs and other indexing and abstracting tools used to locate information

❱ newspaper articles that analyze events

❱ dictionaries and encyclopedias

❱ magazine articles

❱ newspapers

❱ videotapes and audiotapes, CD-ROMs, DVDs, and online media sources that have been edited

LIBRARY INFORMATION SOURCES

Once you have thought about the information need and clearly defined the need in terms of a research question and appropriate focused questions, it is time to move to Step 2 in the information process, finding the information, which incorporates two different skills:

1. Being aware of the various sources of information available.

2. Knowing how to locate and access the information in the information source.

Identifying the sources of information that are useful in academic and workplace research is a critical step in conducting an effective information search. Knowledge of information sources available in libraries and on the Internet is the foundation of library literacy, an important component of information literacy.

? CRITICAL THINKING QUESTIONS

❱ Of the two types of information sources, primary and secondary, which do you think is more accessible? Why?

❱ What specific primary information sources might be available for your field of study? List as many examples as you can.

❱ What specific secondary information sources are available for your field of study? List as many examples as you can.

❱ What are potential issues with using any of these secondary information sources for your field of study?

SELF-ASSESSMENT QUESTION

• What types of primary source information would authors have at their disposal to research your life?

2

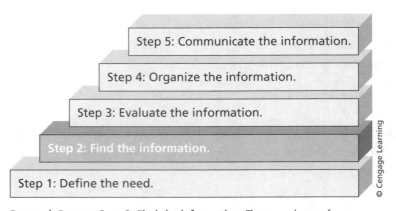

Step 5: Communicate the information.

Step 4: Organize the information.

Step 3: Evaluate the information.

Step 2: Find the information.

Step 1: Define the need.

© Cengage Learning

Research Process Step 2: Find the information. The second step of any research project should be to find the information efficiently.

BOOKS

Books are common and convenient sources of information. Books can be fiction (content that is based on imagination and not necessarily on fact) or nonfiction (information that is factual.). Books are

Christian Beirle González/Flickr Select/Getty Images

available on every subject of interest. Books are found in library stacks in most libraries.

Because of the significant time lapse between the time a book is written and its publication, certain types of information found in books may be outdated. For example, information in a book on human anatomy will be valid for years to come, as anatomy does not change quickly. Conversely, a book on computer software is likely to be outdated quickly because of the nature of the information and the rapidly changing technical world. When you select a book as a reference, you will have to use good judgment about the kind of information you are seeking. In the example of computer software, a better and more current choice would be technical documentation from the most recent version of the software you are researching.

Fiction

The primary purpose of a work of fiction is entertainment. Fiction gives the reader the opportunity to see problems and solutions through the actions of the character(s). The reader can live vicariously through the novel's characters and gain insight into "real-life" situations without repercussion. Figure 2-1 outlines the elements of fiction.

Historical fiction is based on an event or a sequence of events in history that actually occurred, with people who actually lived or are created within the author's imagination. The author re-creates action and emotion through imagination to tell the story of the event or of the characters.

Elements of a Fiction Novel	
Character(s)	Solution to the problem
Plot	Tone/mood
Theme	Symbolism
Setting	Imagery
Point of view	Figurative language
Basic problem	

© Cengage Learning

Figure 2-1   Elements of a Fiction Novel. Numerous elements in a fiction work differentiate it from nonfiction.

Elements of Nonfiction

Facts	Direct quotes
Characters (Real)	Illustrations
First person accounts	Timelines
Actual events	Maps
Actual places	Table of contents
Photographs	Bibliography
Archival material	Glossary
Charts	Index
Diagrams	

© Cengage Learning

Figure 2-2   Elements of Nonfiction. The elements commonly seen in nonfiction are more factual than creative.

Nonfiction

Nonfiction presents factual information. Nonfiction books are based on research and actual events that have occurred, and characters or objects that actually exist now or have existed in the past. Critical evaluation of the information given in a nonfiction resource is vital to the credibility of a research project. Elements that should be considered in light of the goal of your research include the author's background, purpose for writing the book, and attitude, and the audience for which the work is written. See Figure 2-2 for examples of elements of nonfiction. Evaluation of nonfiction information will be discussed in-depth in Chapter 4.

REFERENCE SOURCES

A library typically has a reference section or reference desk (or information desk) that is staffed by a reference librarian. Library patrons use reference services to get answers to questions or to receive assistance with their research needs. The professionally trained librarians who staff the reference desk will help you find the kind of information sources that best meet your needs by conducting a reference interview. In many libraries, you also can call, e-mail, or use online chat to get help.

Use the reference desk to:

- get help finding a library resource.
- get the answer to a specific, factual question.

▶ get assistance in using the online public access catalog (OPAC) or other library computer resources.

▶ access ready reference books that are commonly used.

▶ access rare or restricted items in the library.

▶ locate difficult-to-find information.

▶ put a library resource on hold when an item you need is temporarily unavailable (i.e., checked out by another patron); the librarian will notify you when the resource has been returned.

▶ access resources that instructors have set aside for a specific project or for a specific time period.

▶ discover items in the library that are not cataloged in the OPAC, such as old telephone books, college-course catalogs, and school yearbooks.

▶ sign up for use of library equipment, such as microform readers or computers.

▶ make a recommendation to the library that it purchase something for its collection.

▶ ask to be shown exactly where in the library a resource is located (most librarians will take you there).

▶ gain access to locked or reserved study or conference rooms.

▶ get recommendations on specific resources to meet a specific research need.

▶ get recommendations for useful web sites or advice on searching the Internet.

▶ get a referral to a different library that has additional resources to meet your needs.

▶ request a resource from another library through the interlibrary loan system.

A reference source is material from which information can be drawn. Reference sources are authoritative and frequently subject-specific. Reference resources include reference books, records from library catalogs, general or subject-specific indexes, and bibliographic databases. Many reference materials are available in both print and electronic formats and often are accessible through a local library computer system or via the Internet. Reference sources may provide actual information, or they may be used to find additional information sources. Some of the more commonly available and useful reference sources are described below. Typically, reference books cannot be checked out of the library and must be used in the library. In most cases, you can make copies of the information you need, provided that you observe copyright restrictions.

Encyclopedias

An encyclopedia is a collection of detailed articles on a wide range of subjects. Encyclopedias typically are used to find background information on a subject. They can be general (e.g., *World Book Encyclopedia*), covering a broad range of topics, or subject-specific (e.g., *Encyclopedia of Psychology*). Subject-specific articles contain detailed articles related to specific fields of study and are written by experts in that field.

Encyclopedias are basic tools that can be good starting points for research. Topics are arranged in alphabetical order and presented in short to medium-length essays. The articles sometimes include illustrations or other visual materials and may reference additional articles or suggest

Jupiter Images

Books are common and convenient sources of information.

related topics of interest. Encyclopedias also may supply keywords to help you narrow or broaden your search. Online encyclopedias can be accessed without charge or for a subscription fee.

Much of the information in encyclopedias, such as historical facts, does not change. Other information, such as medical interventions and technical data does change and requires frequent updating. To accommodate changes such as these, many encyclopedia publishers issue yearbooks, which are annual publications documenting recent changes and updates to information.

Stephen Simpson/Iconica/Getty Images

Examples of general encyclopedias:

▶ *World Book Encyclopedia*

▶ *Academic American Encyclopedia*

▶ *The Encyclopedia Britannica*

▶ *The Encyclopedia Americana*

▶ *The Random House Encyclopedia*

▶ *The New Lincoln Library Encyclopedia*

▶ *The New Book of Knowledge*

Examples of subject-specific encyclopedias:

▶ *World Book Encyclopedia of People and Places*

▶ *The American Civil War: A Multicultural Encyclopedia*

▶ *Famous First Facts, International Edition: A Record of First Happenings, Discoveries and Inventions in World History*

▶ *The Encyclopedia of Adoption*

▶ *U.X.L. Encyclopedia of Biomes*

▶ *The International Encyclopedia of Adult Education*

▶ *Advertising Age Encyclopedia of Advertising*

▶ *The Encyclopedia of Flight*

▶ *The Encyclopedia of Human Emotions*

Dictionaries

A dictionary is an alphabetical listing of words, used for a quick search of a word or topic to find the word's meaning, spelling, and pronunciation. Dictionaries also include information on parts of speech or word form and word origin. Some dictionaries are general in nature and are useful for basic writing tasks. Others, such as medical dictionaries, are specific to a field of study or topic area. These provide more detailed information similar to that found in an encyclopedia and often include illustrations and other reference-type information.

Additional examples of the hundreds of subject-specific dictionaries are computer-user and technical dictionaries, electronics dictionaries, and slang dictionaries. Numerous electronic dictionaries are available on the Internet without charge. In addition, many dictionaries are available in electronic format appropriate for electronic readers.

Examples of general dictionaries:

▶ *The Oxford English Dictionary*
▶ *The American Heritage Dictionary*
▶ *Merriam-Webster's Collegiate Dictionary*
▶ *The World Book Dictionary*
▶ *The Random House Dictionary of the English Language*
▶ *Collins English Dictionary*

Examples of specific dictionaries:

▶ *The New Dictionary of Cultural Literacy*
▶ *The Dictionary of Accounting Terms*
▶ *The Diabetes Dictionary*
▶ *The Cambridge Aerospace Dictionary*
▶ *The Historical Dictionary of Afghanistan*
▶ *The Agriculture Dictionary*
▶ *Webster's Biographical Dictionary*
▶ *Webster's Geographical Dictionary*

Directories

A directory is a collection of data organized in a way that allows users to access the information easily. Directories can be alphabetical listings of people, organizations, companies, or institutions. They include addresses, telephone and fax numbers, and other pertinent information. Organizational directories contain member information as well as dates and information for conferences and publications. Common directories are telephone and city directories and the

United States Zip Code Directory. Many directories are available online with search features that allow the information to be located easily.

Examples of directories commonly used in research:

▶ *College Blue Book*

▶ *Biographical Directory of the United States Congress*

▶ *Bowker's News Media Directory*

▶ *Martindale-Hubbell Law Directory*

▶ *Directory of Physicians in the United States*

▶ *Writer's Market*

▶ *Sports Market Place Directory*

▶ *U.S. Government Manual*

Almanacs

An almanac is a publication that provides statistics, lists, figures, tables, and specific facts in a variety of areas. Almanacs typically are published on an annual or other regular basis. Almanacs may be general or may be devoted to a specific topic area or field of study. Researchers use almanacs to find and compare current or historical information or statistics. Often, this information is in table form for ease of use. Some online almanacs can be accessed without charge, and others for a subscription fee.

Examples of general almanacs:

▶ *The World Almanac and Book of Facts*

▶ *The Encyclopedia Britannica Almanac*

▶ *Whitaker's Almanack*

▶ *Information Please*

Examples of subject-specific almanacs:

▶ *The African American Almanac*

▶ *Days to Celebrate: A Full Year of Poetry, People, History, Holidays, Fascinating Facts and More*

▶ *Farmer's Almanac*

▶ *Poor Richard's Almanac*

▶ *Peterson's College & University Almanac*

▶ *U.S. Immigration & Migration Almanac*

▶ *Almanac of American Education*

▶ *U.X.L. Hispanic American Almanac*
▶ *Plunkett's Automobile Industry Almanac*
▶ *Information Please Business Almanac*
▶ *Sports Illustrated Almanac*

Atlases

An atlas is a collection of geographical and historical information. Atlases incorporate maps, charts, descriptions, tables, demographic information, natural resources statistics, and data on the physical features of geographical areas. Researchers use atlases to locate places around the world and in outer space, as well as to gather information about the demographics of a region, the physical features of an area or a region, or distances between locations. Atlases also are used to plan travel and other recreational activities. Because the world is dynamic and political boundaries change, the user has to ensure that the information is the most current available.

Examples of atlases:
▶ *World Book Atlas*
▶ *National Geographic Atlas of the World Atlas of the World* (Oxford University Press)
▶ *Oxford New Concise World Atlas*
▶ *Collins World Atlas Gazetteer*
▶ *Atlas of World Affairs*
▶ *The Kingfisher Student Atlas*
▶ *Rand McNally Commercial Atlas & Marketing Guide*
▶ *Color Atlas of Low Back Pain*
▶ *Scholastic Atlas of Space*
▶ *Atlas of the Universe*

Indexes

An index is an alphabetical list that can be used to find information within a source. An index can be found at the end of a single-volume reference work or nonfiction book. In multivolume reference books, indexes usually are compiled in a separate volume and also may be subject-specific.

Another type of index, the periodical index, is a cumulative list of articles from periodicals. Contents are arranged alphabetically by author, title, or subject. An index entry is called a citation. Each citation in a periodical index contains information about the article, including the author, article title, and name, volume, issue, and page numbers of the periodical in which the article is published. Periodical indexes may be general in nature, or for a specific topic area, or may combine a group of related disciplines. More will be discussed in Chapter 3 about how to use periodical indexes.

Examples of indexes that may be useful in research:

▶ *Reader's Guide to Periodical Literature*
▶ *Children's Magazine Guide*
▶ *Wilson Humanities Index*
▶ *Education Index*
▶ *Social Science Index*
▶ *Art Index*
▶ *Music Index*
▶ *Alternative Press Index*
▶ *Business Periodical Index*
▶ *Book Review Digest*

Other Common Reference Sources

Often called ready reference sources, these materials usually are kept at or near the reference desk in a library because of their frequent use. In addition to the reference tools mentioned previously, other common ready reference sources include concordances, handbooks, thesauruses, manuals, and style manuals.

Concordance: an alphabetical list of the most pertinent words in a given text and a notation of where they might be found within that text. Concordances are used for in-depth study of a work or collection.

Examples of concordances:

▶ *A Concordance to Beowulf*
▶ *A Concordance of the Collected Poems of James Joyce*
▶ *Strong's Exhaustive Concordance of the Bible*

2

Handbook: a resource that provides concise data, usually in table or chart form, on a specialized subject area. A handbook is a useful reference for finding current statistics, procedures, instructions, or specific information on a topic.

Examples of handbooks:

▶ *Handbook of Recreational Games*
▶ *Boy Scout Handbook*
▶ *Brownie Girl Scout Handbook*
▶ *Young Person's Career Skills Handbook*
▶ *Handbook of Photography*

Thesaurus: a collection of synonyms, near-synonyms, antonyms (word opposites), phrases, and slang terms for words. A thesaurus can be arranged alphabetically or by idea or concept. As with other resources, specialized thesauruses include specialized expressions for a specific field, such as medicine or computer science. A thesaurus will help you find words to express an idea for which you want to find a different or an opposite word. A typical thesaurus has synonyms for thousands of words. Many thesauruses have unique and helpful features, and the greatest benefit is derived from the thesaurus you are using by being familiar with its features. Also, many words are not directly interchangeable. A thesaurus and a dictionary used together will ensure that you are using the correct word.

At first glance, a thesaurus can look complicated. Therefore, you should start by getting to know your specific thesaurus. Complete instructions typically are found in the introduction. The two main kinds of thesaurus are: (1) a Roget-type, which uses a categorization system, and (2) an A–Z type, which lists headwords alphabetically. In a Roget-type thesaurus, the user looks up the word in the index. The index lists the meaning under each word, and a page number next to the meaning selected for the word. Then the user goes to that page to find synonyms, antonyms, and other information pertaining to the word.

PUT IT TO USE Look at the word before and the word after each category to ensure that you have reviewed all the possible similar entries. Also, look at all parts of speech. You might see another word with a different part of speech that will broaden your word search.

In the A–Z listing type of thesaurus, each headword (typically bolded) is listed with its parts of speech (verb, noun, adjective, adverb, etc.) and a concise definition. Users will have to consult a dictionary for a more extensive definition. Synonyms are listed under the headword. Most words have several meanings. The words listed together under a headword share at least one meaning with the headword. Usually, the first words listed reflect the most common meanings of the word.

> **PUT IT TO USE** Different words have different connotations, or implied meanings. Be sure you understand the word and its connotation before using it, or you might be saying something you did not intend to say.

Examples of thesauruses:

▶ *Random House Roget's College Thesaurus*

▶ *The Thinkers Thesaurus: Sophisticated Alternatives to Common Words*

▶ *Roget's Descriptive Word Finder*

▶ *American Heritage Thesaurus for Learners of English*

Manual: similar to a handbook; provides detailed and sometimes "how to" information on specific topics.

Examples of manuals:

▶ *United States Government Manual*

▶ *Official Manual of the State of Missouri*

Style manual: a writing guide that provides guidelines for writing mechanics and documentation format for research papers and theses. Style manuals are updated continually to keep current with new forms of information. For example, style guides provide standard formats for references and resource citations. As information sources develop and are referenced in scholarly works, the guides must be updated so writers can reference their sources according to the guide. Different styles of citing information sources will be discussed in Chapter 6.

Examples of style manuals:

▶ *The Chicago Manual of Style*

▶ *New York Times Manual of Style and Usage*

2

▶ *MLA (Modern Language Association) Style Manual and Guide to Scholarly Publishing*

▶ *Publication Manual of the American Psychological Association (APA)*

▶ *Elements of Style*

PERIODICALS

A periodical is published on a regular or recurring basis—daily, weekly, monthly, bimonthly, quarterly, or annually. Among periodicals are scholarly journals, popular magazines, trade publications, and newspapers. Periodicals can be issued in print, microform, and electronic formats.

An important feature of a periodical is its currency. Because periodicals are published frequently, they are expected to provide up-to-date information on a topic. The different types of periodicals and the uses of each are summarized next. Evaluation of periodicals is discussed in Chapter 4.

Scholarly Journals

A scholarly journal typically is published by an educational institution or a professional association. The main goal of a scholarly journal is to disseminate information to professionals and researchers in the field in a timely manner. Scholarly journals often are peer-reviewed— sometimes termed refereed—which means that the content of the journal has been read with scrutiny and accepted by knowledgeable reviewers who are not on the journal's editorial staff but who work in the field or area discussed in the article. Scholarly journals present reports of original research, experiments, or studies, as well as commentaries, discussions on current issues or events, examinations or analyses of specific topic areas, and reviews of scholarly books or other media in the field of study.

A few examples of the many hundreds of scholarly journals:

▶ *Journal of the American Medical Association (JAMA)*

▶ *Harvard Law Review*

▶ *American Journal of Occupational Therapy (AJOT)*

▶ *The Journal of American Culture*

- *The Journal of Individual Society*
- *Community College Journal*
- *Journal of Sport Management*
- *Journal of Environmental Engineering*
- *School Library Journal*

Popular Magazines

A popular magazine provides information on topics of interest to the general public, including (but certainly not limited to) news, entertainment, lifestyles, popular culture, leisure reading, parenting, home, science and nature, self-improvement, and do-it-yourself projects. Although some of these magazines provide well-researched and documented information, many do not. The articles typically are short, lacking references or substantive information, often providing information of a sensational nature, and containing advertisements. The main goal of articles in popular magazines is to sell copies of the magazine itself.

A few examples of the many hundreds of popular magazines:

- *Good Housekeeping*
- *Redbook*
- *Vanity Fair*
- *People*
- *Time*
- *Newsweek*
- *U.S. News & World Report*
- *Vogue*
- *Sports Illustrated*
- *Popular Mechanics*

Trade Publications

A trade publication is a periodical intended for a specific industry or business, usually published by an association tied to the trade. The authors of articles in trade publications typically are practitioners or professionals in a specific field. The goal of these articles is to inform

2

others in the industry. Trade publications typically contain articles that provide applied information versus research.

A few examples of the many hundreds of trade publications:
- ▶ *Women's Wear Daily*
- ▶ *Valu-line*
- ▶ *Furniture World*
- ▶ *Hoard's Dairyman*
- ▶ *Aramco World*
- ▶ *Advertising Age*
- ▶ *Stores & Retail Spaces*
- ▶ *Chain Store Age*
- ▶ *Bobbin*
- ▶ *Booklist*

Newspapers

Newspapers are of a local, regional, national, or international venue and are general or topic-specific. They usually cover current news and events and come in both a paper and online format. Newspapers may be published by commercial enterprises, by individuals, or by professional organizations, to provide information to its members and the public.

A few examples of the many hundreds of newspapers:
- ▶ *New York Times*
- ▶ *Boston Globe*
- ▶ *USA Today*
- ▶ *Kansas City Star*
- ▶ *St. Louis Post Dispatch*
- ▶ *Wall Street Journal*
- ▶ *Al Jazeera*

More will be discussed in Chapter 4 on how to critically evaluate periodicals.

MULTIMEDIA

Information can be in a form other than print or electronic. Many libraries house or have access to a variety of graphic, audio, video, and film media sources of information. Among these are maps, videotapes, CD-ROMs, DVDs, 16-mm films, audiotapes, vinyl records, and so forth. Each library or library system has access to various media or can borrow a desired media resource from another library using the interlibrary loan system.

INFORMATION RETRIEVAL SYSTEMS

Information retrieval systems allow access to electronic resources and information. Electronic resources include online catalogs, databases, indexes, abstracts, and full-text articles in electronic journals, reference sources, and e-books that are stored in an electronic format and accessed by computer. Many forms of information are available electronically.

ONLINE PUBLIC ACCESS CATALOG (OPAC)

A library catalog is a register of all bibliographic items in a specific library or library system. A bibliographic item is any piece of information or information resource that is a library material. In the past, researchers located library holdings by searching a card catalog—a file cabinet containing individual cards with bibliographic information about specific items in the library. Since the mid-1980s, the physical card catalog most often has been replaced with a computerized catalog called an OPAC.

An online public access catalog (OPAC) is a computerized online catalog of all the materials held in a library and can be searched quickly and efficiently using a computer. An OPAC provides electronic records of materials that a library owns. OPACs can be searched using author, title, subject, call number, or keyword. The purpose of cataloging library resources is to help the library patron find the resource, to show what the library has available, and to provide enough information for the user to make a decision about selecting the resource. Many libraries have made their OPACs accessible via the Internet. Most OPACs are Windows-based and, to simplify the search, use pull-down menus, pop-up windows, dialog boxes, mouse operations, and graphical user interface components.

Library cataloging follows established cataloging rules that have been designed to ensure consistent cataloging of library materials.

Most cataloging rules are based on the International Standard Bibliographic Description (ISBD), produced by the International Federation of Library Associations (IFLA).

DATABASES

A database is a collection of digitized information organized for simplified, fast searching and retrieval. Databases are updated regularly and contain bibliographic citations or references for periodicals, books, reports, and other publications. Full-text databases contain these citations, as well as the full text of the periodical, book, or report. A database may be general or subject-specific.

Vendors of databases are called aggregators. An aggregated service simultaneously accesses information from several databases. Examples of those that provide this service are EBSCOhost, ProQuest, and Gale. Libraries subscribe to these resources to make information readily available to their staffs and library users. Librarians have access to literally hundreds of databases for all kinds of information. Electronic formats allow convenient searching of the resource, using techniques that narrow the search to pinpoint the exact data needed.

Examples of databases:

- *PsycINFO:* a database of more than three million records of peer-reviewed literature in the behavioral sciences and mental health areas.
- *Academic Search Premier:* a database that includes both scholarly and peer-reviewed journals dating back to 1975.
- *Business Source Premiere:* a database that indexes journals related to the many areas of business.

THE INTERNET

The Internet is a high-speed electronic network that connects personal computers and organizational computer facilities around the world. This network is connected by fiber optics such as telephone lines, cables, and communications satellites. The Internet is available to anyone with a computer, connections, and an Internet service provider (ISP) such as EarthLink or CenturyLink. Many cable companies, such as Comcast, also provide Internet service. The Internet has been called the "information superhighway" because this network connects millions of computers around the world, allowing users to communicate through e-mail and file transfers. A rich source of information, the Internet allows users to access a limitless amount of data if they have the skills to find this information.

The Internet is a massive information-retrieval system. The World Wide Web is an international network of Internet servers that allows access to documents written in HTML (hypertext markup language) and provides links to other documents, graphic files, audio files, video files, and many other forms of information. This means that you can move from one resource to another by clicking on links within a resource. Note that "Internet" is not synonymous with "World Wide Web." The World Wide Web is something that is available via the Internet, as are e-mail and other Internet services. Consider the World Wide Web to be a read–write information space for Internet resources such as images, text, videos, and other media.

A web site is made up of a collection of web pages that are stored in a single folder or within related subfolders of a web server. A web page is an electronic resource on the World Wide Web that is assigned a unique Internet address called a uniform resource locator (URL). It is displayed using a web browser such as Internet Explorer. Web pages can contain numerous types of information including text and graphics, audio and video, interactive multimedia, applets (subprograms that run inside the page), links, and downloadable files.

In some cases, the user has to download additional software modules, called plug-ins, and install them on the computer to run interactive elements and applets or to display specialized types of data. Hundreds of plug-ins are available on the Internet, downloadable free of charge. Most specialized software applications for graphics, video, and animation have their own specialized plug-ins that are required to view their specialized content. In most cases, the web page will have a link and instructions on how to locate and download the needed plug-ins. Other plug-ins serve specialized functions on a web page.

Examples of plug-ins for viewing elements and specialized plug-ins for web pages:

- *Flash:* allows viewing of rich-media content such as animations and interactive presentations
- *QuickTime:* enables viewing of video, sound, animation, text, graphics, and so forth

▶ *Acrobat Reader:* allows viewing of .pdf files

▶ *RealMedia:* enables viewing of video, sound, animation, and graphics including streaming audio and video

▶ *ieSpell:* adds a tool to Internet Explorer that spell-checks text input boxes on web pages

▶ *Adblock Plus:* blocks banner ads, popups, and any image source URLs for multiple browsers

Web pages also contain content that cannot be seen in a browser. For example, a web page contains scripts (often JavaScript) that add functionality to the page. When you roll the mouse over a place on a page and additional text appears, you are seeing the results of JavaScript. Another unseen element on a web page is a Cascading Style Sheet, which tells how the page is to be formatted. Meta tags provide hidden information about the page itself, providing information to search engines to help in categorizing the page for search purposes.

A home page is the main or first screen of a web site, with links to other pages on the site. This first page also is called an index page and may be described that way in the web page's address ending in index .html, or something similar. Many college and university libraries have home pages with links to various research resources, as do many other organizations that provide information to specific industries or to the public in general. On the home page, most libraries include links to online databases and their OPAC.

Many web pages include a navigation bar with links to other pages on the web site, or sometimes to entirely different web sites. Navigation bars can be horizontal or vertical, depending upon the web site design. Typically, the navigation bar is seen on all pages of the web site to make it easy to jump from one area to another. If you get to a page that does not have the navigation bar, you can simply click your browser's back button to go back to the page showing the navigation bar. The back button takes you, in order, to the pages visited previously.

Common links on the navigation bar are *About* (provides information about the sponsor of the web site), *Home* (takes you to the home page of the site), *Contact Us* (provides contact information), and *Resources* (provides additional resources or external links). Numerous other links might be to company departments, products and services, certificates, publications, and other relevant pages, depending on the purpose and design of the site.

Web Browsers

Although you can view most web pages with any software application that can read text documents, to view a web page as it is intended and to access all of the page's functionality, you must use special software called a web browser. The browser interprets the Internet files and puts them in a readable format. There are many different web browsers with different capabilities. Even different versions of the same web browser have different capabilities.

Examples of commonly used browsers:

▶ Google Chrome

▶ Mozilla Firefox

▶ Internet Explorer

▶ Opera

▶ Safari

Search Engines

Because there are millions of Internet sites, we must have an efficient way to search for the information and sites we need. Search engines use computer software that makes the World Wide Web searchable by using keywords or phrases. Search results may be listed by relevancy, by currency, or by some other method. The Internet has many different search engines that can be used to find information, but because each search engine allows searching through only those files in its specific database, using only one search engine provides only a small portion of the available sites on the Internet. To find a more complete list of Internet sites, meta-search engines search multiple individual search engines simultaneously. For extensive information, ratings, and tips on using search engines effectively, go to SearchEngineWatch on the Internet.

Examples of commonly used search engines:

▶ Yahoo

▶ Google

▶ Bing

? **Critical Thinking Questions**

- How do online search engines work?
- How might different search engines affect the results of a search? (This might take some research!)
- Is the large number of results from an Internet search a bad thing? Why or why not?
- Under what circumstances might you want to limit the number of results you receive?

- Ask
- AOL
- MyWebSearch
- Blekko
- Lycos
- Dogpile
- Webcrawler
- Info
- InfoSpace
- Search
- Excite
- GoodSearch

PUT IT TO USE   Keep in mind that when you are using a search engine, you are not searching the entire Internet; you are searching a portion of it.

Internet Information Resources

As stated earlier, many resources available in a physical library are now available on the Internet via virtual libraries, subject directories, and individual web sites. Many of the resources are free, and others are fee-based or subscription services. Some of the more useful Internet information sources are explored in more depth here.

INTERNET SUBJECT DIRECTORIES: An important tool on the Internet is a subject directory, a collection of links to a large number of Internet resources, typically organized by topic area. Commercial subject directories are general in nature and are much less selective. Academic and professional directories usually are maintained by experts and cater to professionals who need credible information.

Examples of Internet subject directories:

- INFOMINE (infomine.ucr.edu)
- The Internet Public Library (www.ipl.org)

ONLINE REFERENCE RESOURCES: Information-literate individuals can easily access online reference resources such as dictionaries, thesauruses, encyclopedias, almanacs, handbooks, directories, and so forth via the Internet. Fee structures for these resources vary from no charge to an annual or monthly subscription charge. Some sites are free but require a registration, and others allow free use of basic services while charging a fee for more advanced or expanded services.

Examples of useful reference resources on the Internet:

- Refdesk (www.refdesk.com)
- Questia (www.questia.com)
- Merriam-Webster Online (www.m-w.com)
- Encyclopedia.com (www.encyclopedia.com)
- Occupational Outlook Handbook (www.bls.gov/oco/home.htm)

> **PUT IT TO USE**   Though it is a convenient source of information, Wikipedia should not be used for academic research. Wikipedia is written and edited by its readers and sometimes contains misinformation, and it is not considered an authoritative source. You should look to other online sources that contain more consistent and edited information.

ONLINE PERIODICALS: As discussed earlier in the chapter, a single library does not subscribe to every available periodical. An alternative to using the library's periodicals is to find a full-text version of the article online. The general procedure to search for full-text articles is basically the same as that for a physical library. An online periodical index enables users to find the needed citation information. In many cases, the actual full-text article can be accessed directly from the citation. Some full-text articles are available free, and others must be purchased. Many online libraries and subject directories also link to periodical indexes and to the articles themselves.

Examples of periodical sites on the Internet:

- PubMed Central (www.pubmedcentral.nih.gov)
- HighBeam (www.highbeam.com)

2

❱ NewsLink (newslink.org)

❱ FindArticles (www.findarticles.com)

WEB PORTALS: A web portal, sometimes called a gateway, is a site on the Internet that provides links to many different kinds of information. Some portals are general in nature, and others provide links to information in a specific topic area, such as business, computers, law, or medicine. On a web portal, you can find industry-related information, products, news, periodicals, organizations, chat rooms, people finders, and almost anything else related to the industry and found on the Internet. Some web portals are maintained by Internet service providers (e.g., AOL and Yahoo), and others are maintained by states, professional organizations, or special interest groups. There are hundreds, if not thousands, of web portals for almost every industry.

Examples of web portals on the Internet:

❱ AOL (www.aol.com)

❱ About (www.about.com)

❱ Forbes (www.forbes.com)

❱ FirstGov (www.firstgov.com)

PROFESSIONAL AND TRADE ORGANIZATIONS

Professional and trade organizations are groups of professionals who have similar interests or positions. These organizations are excellent sources for current information in an industry, for trends and current practices, for licensure and certification information, and for networking with other professionals who have similar interests. Most organizations have some kind of online presence and offer excellent and credible information on their web sites. Information-literate individuals can stay current in their field by participating in professional organizations and by reviewing these web sites regularly. A good starting place to find appropriate professional organization web sites is with Google's directory listing for professional organizations.

Examples of professional organizations:

❱ The American Occupational Therapy Association (www.aota .org)

SELF-ASSESSMENT QUESTIONS

- What professional organizations are appropriate for your field?
- What information do these organizations maintain on their web sites?

- Information Technology Association of America (ITAA) (www .itaa.org)
- Computer Technology Industry Association (CompTIA) (www.comptia.org)
- American Health Information Management Association (AHIMA) (www.ahima.org)
- American Association of Medical Assistants (AAMA) (www .aama-ntl.org)

CHAPTER SUMMARY

Chapter 2 provided you with strategies for creating main and focused research questions and clarified the purposes of each. After establishing your research questions, you learned several information sources and how to access each.

POINTS TO KEEP IN MIND

- Main and focused research questions are important in directing your research and organizing your research information effectively.
- Main research questions should be specific and answered by verifiable facts.
- Focused research questions should direct your research and organize your information search strategies.
- Primary information sources are those that have not been altered or interpreted and are preferred for research.
- If you use secondary resources, it is best to find and reference the primary source as well as the secondary source.
- Know the resources that are best suited to answering your research question as well as how to select and access them.

apply it

Find printable activities on the companion web site for this book, accessed through www.cengagebrain.com.

Activity #1: Resource Exploration

STEP 1: Review your library resources, consult with the reference librarian at your local library or school library, and search the Internet to complete the Resource Table for your field of study.

STEP 2: Continue to add to the list as you find additional resources, and keep this table electronically for reference as you conduct research and locate additional resources.

RESOURCE TABLE

Resource Type	Resource Name	Resource Location and Access Instructions	Description
Primary Information Sources			
Secondary Information Sources			
Nonfiction Books			
General Encyclopedias			
Subject-Specific Encyclopedias			
General Dictionaries			
Subject-Specific Dictionaries			
Directories			
Almanacs			
Atlases			
Indexes			
Concordances			
Handbooks			

Thesauruses			
Manuals			
Scholarly Journals			
Popular Magazines			
Trade Publications			
Databases			

Activity #2: Database Exploration

STEP 1: Using your library's resources, explore the databases that are available. Usually these include a brief description of the database. Some libraries list databases in alphabetical order and by subject covered.

STEP 2: Thinking of your field of study, list the specific databases that are appropriate for your research.

Activity #3: Search Engine Comparison

STEP 1: Do a search for a limited topic of your choice using a search engine, and then do the same search using a metasearch engine.

STEP 2: Compare and contrast the results. What is the difference in the number of results of your search? What is the difference in the type of results or sites that are returned?

STEP 3: Note which search engine(s) best meets your needs.

Activity #4: Internet Resource Exploration

STEP 1: Explore the Internet to complete the Internet Resource Table for your field of study.

STEP 2: Continue to add to the list as you find additional resources, and keep this table electronically for reference as you conduct research.

continued

continued

INTERNET RESOURCE TABLE

Resource Type	Resource Name	Resource URL and Access Instructions	Description
Web Browsers			
Common Plug-ins for Your Browser			
Search Engines			
Internet Subject Directories			
Online Reference Resources			
Online Periodicals			
Web Portals			
Professional and Trade Organizations			

CHECK YOUR UNDERSTANDING

Visit www.cengagebrain.com to see how well you have mastered the material in Chapter 2.

SUGGESTED ITEMS FOR LEARNING PORTFOLIO

Refer to the "Developing Portfolios" section at the beginning of this textbook for more information on learning portfolios.

- Resource Table
- Database Exploration List
- Comparison of Search Engine Report

REFERENCES

Library of Congress. (n.d.). *Primary Source Analysis Tool.* Retrieved June 14, 2013, from http://www.loc.gov/teachers/primary-source-analysis-tool/

Raimes, A. & Miller-Cochran, S. (2013). *Keys for Writers (7/e).* Boston, MA: Wadsworth, Cengage Learning.

2

How Do You Find and Access Information?

LEARNING OBJECTIVES

By the end of this chapter, students will achieve the following objectives:

▶ Use several techniques to search for relevant information efficiently.

▶ Identify several common sources for information.

▶ Use library resources to find and access information.

▶ Use electronic resources to find and access information.

▶ Explain the importance of having a method for collecting information.

3

BE IN THE KNOW

The Library of Congress

The Library of Congress is the nation's oldest federal cultural institution and serves as the research arm of Congress. It is also the largest library in the world, with more than 155.3 million items on approximately 838 miles of bookshelves. The collections include more than 35 million books and other print materials, 3.4 million recordings, 13.6 million photographs, 5.4 million maps, 6.5 million pieces of sheet music, and 68 million manuscripts (Library of Congress, n.d.).

The Library of Congress occupies three buildings on Capitol Hill. The Thomas Jefferson Building (1897) is the original separate Library of Congress building. (The Library began in 1800 inside the U.S. Capitol.) The John Adams Building was built in 1938, and the James Madison Memorial Building was completed in 1981.

Major exhibitions of the library are also available online, as are selected prints and photographs, historic films, and political speeches. Find the Library of Congress Online Catalog at catalog2.loc.gov/. You can search these records by keyword or browse by authors/creators, subjects, name/titles, uniform titles, and call numbers. Browse lists also include searching aids such cross-references and scope notes (Library of Congress, n.d.).

Whether you visit in person or online, the Library of Congress is a national treasure and an invaluable reference tool. Use it!

SOLVING INFORMATION PROBLEMS: FIND THE INFORMATION

Even with an effective research question and several focused research questions that serve to narrow the research scope sufficiently, finding the right information can still be a daunting task. Reference the steps in the Research Process shown below. To complete Step 2: Find the Information, you first must understand how libraries have evolved to meet the demands of the digital age, how they are organized, how the materials in libraries and information on the Internet are cataloged and referenced, and how to access and efficiently use these reference tools.

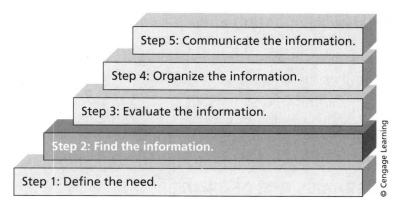

© Cengage Learning

Research Process Step 2: The second step of any research project should be to efficiently find the information.

THE EVOLUTION OF LIBRARIES

The use of libraries dates back to ancient times. Throughout their existence, libraries have always managed to remain adaptable to the needs of their users. This is no more evident than it is today.

If you are a member of Generation Y (born between 1977 and 1994) or Generation Z (born between 1995 and 2012), technology has always been a part of your life. You likely have always had instant access to nearly everything you have needed and have not known any other way to live.

In this digital age, the availability of and access to information has changed dramatically with the advent of the Internet and other communication avenues over the past 20 to 30 years, and will continue on. During this time, libraries have had to embrace these new technologies in order to meet the changing needs of their users. Libraries were not the inventors of these communication avenues, but they were early adopters of them. Libraries sensed the shifting needs of their audience and thus embraced how they could find, evaluate, and communicate information to users in new and meaningful ways to solve information problems, whether that be for a research paper, for finding a job, or to answer personal questions about taxes or medical issues, to name a few.

3

? CRITICAL THINKING QUESTION

▶ How do you see libraries collaborating within their communities?

Today, libraries fill an even greater role in the community by becoming collaborators with those they serve. Libraries are no longer seen as just loaners of books, but instead they are heralded as epicenters for providing a wide variety of services that help to fulfill a community's needs. Libraries and librarians are continually working to understand how patrons use information, and thus rely on input and feedback from those very users to improve their "product" of being information providers.

HOW LIBRARIES ARE ORGANIZED

Whether it is a public, national, school, academic, or special library (such as a law library, medical library, or museum library), all libraries organize their holdings using a library catalog, which is a log or register of all the items in the library. Materials in a library are referred to as bibliographic items. A library item can be any piece of information, such as a book, a graphic, a map, a DVD, an audiotape or a videotape, a computer file, and so on. Before the computer came into extensive use in the 1980s, libraries physically documented their library catalog using a card catalog. Pre-computer card catalogs were large sets of physical file cabinets holding a catalog record (small index cards) containing each library item's relevant information. Information on the catalog record included the call number, author, title, edition, publisher, brief physical description of the item, notes about the item's content, and a valid Library of Congress subject heading assigned to the item. The file cabinets were organized to enable searching using different types of information, such as by author, title, or subject.

Nearly all physical card catalogs have been replaced by a convenient computer system—the online public access catalog (OPAC). Although some libraries still retain their card catalogs, few libraries update these physical references. You might see a sign posted stating the last year the card catalog was updated. More current information then would reside on the OPAC. Some libraries have removed their card catalogs altogether to make space for additional book stacks or technology.

We discussed OPACs in-depth in Chapter 2. The following is a review of important points to keep in mind.

OPACs catalog the holdings of a specific library or library system. Each library or library system has access to various resources. Some libraries house information pertaining to a specific area, such as medicine or law. In other libraries the collection is designed for the general public. Educational libraries on college and university campuses contain holdings for both the general public and the school's specific programs of study and research.

OPACs do not catalog information within a specific library holding. In many cases, libraries lend materials to patrons of a different library through the interlibrary loan system. OPACs, including those that are Web-based, do not catalog all holdings everywhere, only holdings for that specific library or library system. For example, an OPAC will catalog a library's specific journal holding, such as the *Journal of the American Medical Association*. The library will not catalog a specific article published in that journal. To find specific articles, a periodical index is required. (Indexes will be discussed shortly.)

OPACs do not catalog all of the items in a library. Many libraries store informational items that are not cataloged. These items might include local historical documents, old phone books, school yearbooks, folders of newspaper clippings, manuscripts, photographs, map collections, pamphlets, and so forth. Different libraries have different holdings catalogs. In some cases, the library is in the process of cataloging holdings. (If you are looking for these kinds of items, ask the reference librarian.)

OPACs allow for searching using several criteria. These criteria include author of the work, title of the work, official designated subject heading, and keywords.

Many other resources are available outside a library or library system on the Internet. In addition to OPACs, which make searching for a library's resources convenient and efficient, many valuable information sources can be accessed via the Internet. Information-literate individuals understand both library and nonlibrary resources and how to locate and access these resources efficiently.

Throughout the course of your education or career, you likely have used many print resources such as books and periodicals. Libraries have many nonprint materials as well. Nonprint materials are items that are published in any format other than paper and may or may not be cataloged in the OPAC. To use any of these items, ask the reference librarian for help.

Nonprint Resources Commonly Found in a Library	
Computer files	BluRay
Sound recordings	CD-ROMs
Visual materials	Cassette tapes
Computer disks	Video tapes (videocassettes)
Video discs	Laserdiscs
DVDs	Vinyl records
Models	Motion pictures (film reels)
Slides	Photographs
Kits	Microform

USING DIGITAL LIBRARIES

In addition to OPACs, many schools and organizations are turning to creating and using digital (or online) libraries. This takes the online experience from a simple search (like Google) to accessing information and books that are stored online. You may find after searching for information that you've found the right book, but in order to access the content you must have access to a library. Digital libraries have many advantages over their traditional brick-and-mortar counterparts. These advantages include:

- ▶ **Convenient hours.** Unlike a conventional library, a digital library may be accessed 24/7/365.

- ▶ **Access from anywhere.** As long as you are logged on to a computer with Internet access and know the library's uniform resource locator (URL), you can be physically located anywhere in the world and tap into the library's resources.

- ▶ **Multiple users.** Digital libraries can accommodate multiple users (although likely far less than Google), and those multiple users can even be reviewing the same information at the same time.

- ▶ **Length of time the book can be "checked out."** With a traditional library, most books and other resources can only be checked out for a set length of time. With a digital library there may be a greater or even no time limit, and you can retrieve the same information over and over again.

- ▶ **Generally no fees.** Conventional libraries will charge a nominal fee per day if a book or resource is not returned by the due date. This, of course, is not the case with a digital library.

Some library sites may require you to establish a username and password before granting access. Other sites may charge a small fee to access their information.

▶ **Online chat capability.** This is a quick way to get your question answered by the online reference librarian.

There are a few disadvantages to a digital library:

▶ **No reference librarian at your side to help you make the most of your research effort.** You usually have to fill out a form and wait a certain period of time before you receive a response from an online librarian. This can be as little as a couple of hours or as long as a couple of days. If you know you are going to need help with your research, it is best to build in additional time to address your reference needs.

▶ **Not everything is online.** Some materials are only in print form, and therefore will not be available to you online. As technology continues to evolve, this may become less of an issue. But for now, do note that sometimes a walk to the library is in order.

WORKING WITH YOUR LIBRARIAN

One of the greatest resources available to students during their academic career is the school librarian. Librarians offer a wealth of expertise on finding and evaluating information in a digital environment that even the information-literate student may never acquire. Additionally, librarians are tech-savvy and are well schooled on the latest trends of how their users want to receive information. The information-literate learner recognizes that leveraging this additional expertise will aid in success in both the classroom and the workplace.

? CRITICAL THINKING QUESTIONS

▶ Do you think you utilize the librarians at your school as much as you should?
▶ What researching skills do you think you could learn from your librarians?

CASE IN POINT: THE SEARCH FOR RESEARCH

Read the scenario below. Then, in groups or as a class, discuss the questions at the end.

Danielle Watson has been given an assignment to write a research paper for her college history course. Her professor has allowed free choice on the selection

Continued

Continued

of topics. Danielle has learned about using the library and its resources, but this is the first time she has been instructed to write a paper that requires her to put this information to use. For this assignment, the professor stipulates that the students use specific resources, both primary and secondary sources. These required resources include:

- ▶ five nonfiction books
- ▶ five reference resources
- ▶ appropriate indexes
- ▶ two general databases
- ▶ two subject-specific databases
- ▶ four scholarly journals
- ▶ three credible web sites
- ▶ What plan does Danielle have to make to complete the assignment successfully?
- ▶ What should Danielle's first step be?
- ▶ Whom could Danielle consult as she begins her research?
- ▶ What kinds of information sources does Danielle need to begin her research?
- ▶ Where can she find these resources?
- ▶ How will Danielle search for the information within each resource?
- ▶ What information-gathering strategies can be used?

TYPES OF ELECTRONIC RESOURCES

Increasingly, reference materials can be found in electronic (or digital) form. The following items may be available to you through your school's library or perhaps the interlibrary loan system described earlier. Consider using any of these electronic sources of information as you seek to conduct research.

E-JOURNALS

Electronic journals, also known as e-journals or ejournals, are electronic versions of scholarly journals used for research. Oftentimes, e-journals are available via subscription through an Electronic Journals Service (EJS) such as EBSCOhost. Check with your school's library or Learning Resource Center to see if it has such a service available to you.

EBOOKS

Ebooks (sometimes referred to as e-books) are digitized versions of published books that contain both text and images and that are readable on a computer, e-reader, or smart phone. Some advantages of ebooks include generally lower cost (and sometimes free) than their printed counterparts, easier and lighter to transport, and immediate availability via download.

STREAMING VIDEOS

Streaming videos continue to gain in popularity. There is virtually no end to what one can watch via streaming video, including TV shows, news, sports, movies, and gaming. Popular sites include YouTube, Vimeo, and Hulu.

PODCASTING

Podcasting is the syndication and distribution of digital interactive media files (audio, video, and text) over the Internet. The content contained in a podcast can be virtually anything, from a song, to an educational lecture, to a political debate. There are hundreds of educational podcasts available online. Use a search engine and type in "educational podcasts" to access them. Your school's library may also have access to podcasts.

BLOGS

A blog, shortened from the word weblog, is a publication forum on the Internet where articles (called posts) are placed and where others can read and comment. Posts are usually listed in reverse chronological order, so that the most recent information or comments are seen first.

There are millions and millions of blogs in existence today on every subject imaginable. Blogs on a particular topic you are researching may provide useful information. Use a search engine to access blogs on a specific subject.

GRAPHICS AND IMAGES

Graphics and images can greatly enhance how information is presented. An Internet search of your research topic may yield many representations of your subject. Chapter 5 has additional information about how to organize graphics.

GOOGLE SCHOLAR

Google Scholar (scholar.google.com) searches a wide variety of scholarly publications from various content providers, including universities, academic publishers, and professional societies. Many campus libraries provide a direct link to Google Scholar from their intranet site.

WIKIS

A wiki is a web page that can be viewed and modified by anyone with a web browser and access to the Internet. Wikis urge collaboration and contribution by its users. Because *anyone*, expert or not, can place and alter information on a wiki, many schools do not consider information gleaned from a wiki a credible or reliable source. Be sure to check your school's policy on the use and citation of wiki information prior to starting your research project.

SOCIAL MEDIA

The use of social media for academic research is proliferating. The following are some examples of tools and resources that are being used today that help people find and share information in an educational setting.

- ▶ Social bookmarking, news, and social citation tools such as CiteULike, delicious, and Reddit.
- ▶ Social networking services including LinkedIn, Facebook, and Academia.edu.
- ▶ Blogging and microblogging tools such as Blogger, Tumblr, and Twitter.
- ▶ Presentation sharing tools including Scribd, SlideShare, and SlideRocket.

▶ Audio and video tools such as Flickr, Livestream, and SmugMug.

▶ Research and writing collaboration tools including Dropbox, Google Docs, and Wetpaint.

▶ Information management tools, for instance, iGoogle, and Netvibes.

▶ Project management, meeting, and collaboration tools, for example, Basecamp, Skype, and Huddle (C. Gray, 2011).

Check your school's policies on the use of social media for academic research before assuming that its use is acceptable.

SEARCHING FOR INFORMATION

As discussed in Chapter 2, search tools such as OPACs, databases, indexes, and so forth help researchers find information. Understanding basic search techniques is essential to be able to use these tools effectively. The first step in conducting a search for information is to know the types of information available for most library resources, which include the following four pieces of information:

1. Author

2. Title

3. Subject

4. Keyword

Specific strategies for searching using each of these types of information are described below.

AUTHOR SEARCH

An author search is used to locate works by the author. You have to know at least the author's last name. Any additional information, such as the first and middle name or initials, will help to limit the number of items you will find within your search. For example, to find writings by James Michener, you could search using any of the following names:

Michener

Michener, J

Michener, James

By providing as much information as you can, you make your search more efficient because you limit the number of results you have to sort through. In many cases, a work is authored by more than one person. If a work has more than one author, use all of the names to limit the search appropriately.

Authors can be people, groups of people, or organizations. When searching for materials published by an organization, you can search by the organization's name, part of the name, and often the acronym for the organization. For example, if you want to search for materials written or published by the American College of Sports Medicine, you could use any of the following terms to start your search:

> American
>
> American College
>
> American College of Sports
>
> American College of Sports Medicine
>
> ACSM

Obviously, the more accurately you describe the organization by using all of the words in the name, the more limited your search results will be, making the search more efficient.

TITLE SEARCH

A title search is used to locate specific titles of books, references, periodicals, and other resources. If you know the title or part of the title of the book or material for which you are searching, a title search is appropriate. For example, if you are searching for the book *The DaVinci Code,* you could use the following search terms to locate the book quickly:

> The DaVinci Code
>
> DaVinci Code
>
> DaVinci

Keep in mind that the more accurate and complete the information you use for your search terms, the fewer will be the number of items appearing in your search results. Many books and other materials have DaVinci in the title. By supplying the full title—The

DaVinci Code—you will limit your search results significantly and save time that otherwise would be required to sort through all of the results to find exactly what you want.

> **PUT IT TO USE** Most catalogs ignore the initial articles "A," "An," and "The."

SUBJECT SEARCH

A subject search is used to find materials on a specific topic. Standardized subject headings are assigned by the Library of Congress, and these subject headings are listed in the *Library of Congress Subject Headings (LCSH)* publication. This multivolume set, typically found at the reference desk of the library, provides synonyms for the subject, as well as related terms to narrow or broaden your search. The *LCSH* also provides references that will direct you to the specific subject heading that is used for a general topic.

For example, if you are searching for "farming," the LC subject information would state "see Agriculture," directing you to search under the general topic of "Agriculture." If you were to search for "musicians," you would be directed to use a more specific category related to that term. The *LCSH* listing might provide the information, "see Jazz Musicians" or "see American Musicians."

In addition, the *LCSH* organizes large subjects logically into categories directing you to the correct subject listing. Sample subject headings for "medicine" include:

Animal equality

Animal ethics

Animal experimentation

Animal rights

Animal rights activists

An author can be a subject as well as the author of a work. The more information you provide, the more accurate the search results will be. To find items *about* an author, you would treat the author as a subject and search by the author's last name, as in:

Shakespeare, William

Dickinson, Emily

Thoreau, Henry David

An examination of the *Library of Congress Subject Headings* information will provide insight into how the headings are used. Referring to Figure 3-1, the subject for this entry is "Mental Illness." The listing provides a brief description of the kinds of information that might be found under the "Mental Illness" subject, then gives several abbreviations to help you find additional subject headings that might be more appropriate for your search.

LCSH abbreviations include the following:

▶ *May Subd Geog:* This notation indicates that the subject may be geographically subdivided, meaning that other subject listings may be related more closely to your specific search subject. The hyphens indicate a subdivision, for example, Mental Illness-Australia.

▶ *UF:* This abbreviation denotes *unauthorized headings.* The common subjects listed here are not used in the *LCSH* subject list, and you will waste your time using these search terms to look for your resources. In the example of "Mental Illness" in Figure 3-1, the common terms of "Diseases, Mental," "Madness," "Mental disorders," and "Mental diseases" would not be effective search terms.

▶ *BT:* This abbreviation stands for *broader topic,* a more general topic. This notation gives subject listings that are broader than "Mental illness." If "Mental illness" has too few resources, you can try the subject headings in the BT list. In this example, you might look under the subjects of "Diseases," "Psychiatry," or "Psychology, Pathological."

▶ *RT:* This abbreviation means *related topic.* The subjects under the RT abbreviation are associated with the main subject but fall outside of the main term's hierarchy. If you are not finding what you want using "Mental illness," you might try "Mental health" in this example.

▶ *NT:* This abbreviation means *narrower topic.* The subjects listed under the NT notation are search terms that can be used that are more specific. If you find too many resources under the

---

Mental illness (*May Subd Geog*)

Here are entered popular works and works on social aspects of mental disorders. Works on the legal aspects of mental illness are under Insanity. Works on clinical aspects of mental disorders, including therapy, are entered under Psychiatry.

UF	Diseases, Mental
	Madness
	Mental disorders
	Mental diseases
BT	Diseases
	Psychiatry
	Psychology, Pathological
RT	Mental health
NT	Dual diagnosis
	Genius and mental illness
	Insanity
	Neurobehavioral disorders

— **Alternative treatment**

— **Diagnosis**

      BT Psychodiagnostics

      NT Psychiatric disability evaluation

— **Epidemiology**

      USE Psychiatric epidemiology

— **Prevention**

— **Surgery**

      USE Psychosurgery

— **Treatment** (May Subd Geog)

— **Evaluation**

      NT Psychiatric rating scales

© Cengage Learning

Figure 3-1 *LCSH* **Subject Entry.** An *LCSH* subject entry helps a researcher to narrow down a larger topic to specifically locate a library resource by how it is classified.

main subject of "Mental illness," you might narrow your search by using one of the subjects under the NT notation.

▶ *SA:* This abbreviation (not seen in the Figure 3-1 example) stands for *see also*. Subjects under the SA notation cover similar subjects.

▶ *USE:* This notation gives information about the correct subject heading in the *LCSH* listing. For example, if you see, under the subject "Mental Illness," that you might want to look up

SELF-ASSESSMENT QUESTION

- What are some synonyms for the topic "Mental Illness" that you could use as an alternative search term?

SELF-ASSESSMENT QUESTION

- What key terms or term combinations could you use for a topic that you might be asked to research in your job or a course? Write down at least ten key terms or term combinations that you could use to conduct a keyword search.

"surgery," the *USE* notation tells you that Psychosurgery is the appropriate heading for subjects about surgery and mental illness. Understanding this notation could save a significant amount of time by pointing you in precisely the right direction.

▶ *Hyphens:* All of the subject headings noted with a hyphen are subdivisions of the major listing to help you focus on the exact area of mental illness you want to explore.

KEYWORD SEARCH

If you do not know an author or title, you can conduct a keyword search. The difference between a keyword and a subject is that the subject is limited to the specific Library of Congress subject heading assigned to the item, whereas a keyword is any word or word combination in the record.

A keyword search looks for specific keywords in all fields in a record and is used when you would like to look for a word or a combination of words simultaneously. In an OPAC, the keyword could be in the title, the author's name, the subject, or other places in the record. On the Internet, a keyword search brings up results that have that word or word combination anywhere in the document.

BOOLEAN OPERATORS

Boolean operators include the words "and," "or," and "not." These terms can be used in combination with keywords to broaden or narrow the search results by specifying exactly how you want the search to be conducted. Boolean operators can be used with most search engines, databases, and OPACs. A clear understanding of how these simple operators work can save a lot of time in using electronic searching tools.

Boolean operators work like a Venn diagram with words. A Venn diagram uses circles that stand alone or overlap to show logical relationships between concepts or ideas. Suppose you want to conduct a search using the search terms "film" and "theater." Each Boolean operator will narrow or broaden your search using keywords.

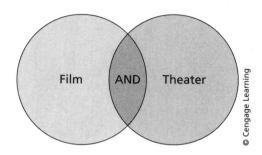

Figure 3-2   Boolean Searching Using "AND". Using the Boolean operator "and" gives the results that include both search terms.

Figure 3-2 shows the use of the Boolean operator "AND". The operator "AND" is used to search for information on both film *and* theater. The results using these two keywords and the operator "AND" will bring up information that includes both film and theater. The correct notation you would use as your search terms would be *film AND theater*. The results would fall into the middle shaded area created by the overlapping of the film and theater circles. There would be no results for only film and no results for only theater. This operator obviously narrows the search by finding results that include both film and theater.

Figure 3-3 shows the use of the Boolean operator "NOT". The "NOT" operator is used when you want to bring up information with one of the keywords, but you do not want information that includes the other keyword. In this example, searching for *film NOT theater* results in information about film only and does not bring up information about theater. Any results about film but also including

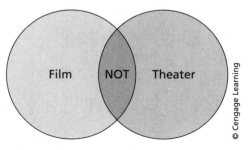

Figure 3-3   Boolean Searching Using "NOT". Using the Boolean operator "not" gives the results that include one search term but not the other.

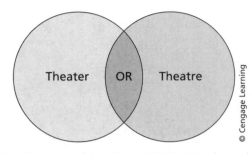

Figure 3-4   Boolean Searching Using "OR". Using the Boolean operator "or" gives results that include one search term or the other search term, or both.

SELF-ASSESSMENT QUESTIONS

Go back to your own workplace research example.
- Using the keywords you listed and other appropriate terms, how could you narrow or broaden your search using only one operator?
- How can you combine your search terms using the Boolean technique to broaden your search? To narrow your search?

the term "theater" will be omitted. This obviously narrows the search significantly, saving time that might be wasted in sorting through information on film that also includes theater.

Figure 3-4 shows the Boolean operator "OR", which can be used to broaden a search. For example, "theater" has the accepted alternate spelling of "theatre." If you want to make sure that the search returns information using both spellings, you would use the Boolean operator "OR", as in *theater OR theatre*. This will return information that includes both spellings of the word.

Combining Boolean operators can be useful at times. For example, if you want to search for information about film and either spelling of theater, you could use the "AND" operator combined with the "OR" operator, as *in film AND (theater OR theatre)*, as illustrated in Figure 3-5.

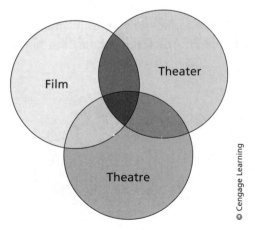

Figure 3-5   Boolean Searching Using "AND" and "OR". Using the Boolean operator "or" in combination with "and" expands your search.

Implied Boolean operators include + in front of a word to retrieve results when the word is included and a − in front of the word to retrieve results where the word is excluded—similar to AND and NOT operators. Quotation marks around phrases sometimes are used to retrieve results when the specific phrase is included. On the Internet, most search engines have an "Advanced Search" link that provides a way to focus or narrow the searches. These advanced search tips and tools explain the specific search language used by that specific search tool.

INDEXES

OPACs reference library print and nonprint holdings, including periodicals; however, they do not reference individual articles within newspapers, journals, or magazines. To access these types of materials, you must have an index or online database.

Book Indexes

Like the OPAC, an index tells you the "address" or location of information within a specific resource. In nonfiction books, the index usually is located at the back of the book. A book's index is an alphabetical list of subjects, referenced by page numbers, showing where you can find that subject mentioned within the text. In a multivolume reference set, each volume may have its own index. Often, the index is a stand-alone index volume. Each subject in the alphabetical list in the index references the volume number and page number where the subject is mentioned in the resource.

For example, in a multivolume resource where the volumes are referenced by a separate index and volumes are separated alphabetically, "Abraham Lincoln" would be referenced as follows: Lincoln, Abraham L:259. The L is the volume letter, and 259 is the page number where the article about Abraham Lincoln begins.

Some indexes use only numbers. For example, in a multivolume reference set where the volume is referenced by volume numbers, information on Abraham Lincoln would be referenced as follows: Lincoln, Abraham 10/259. The number on the left is the volume number. The number on the right is the page number where the article begins.

In many cases, Abraham Lincoln is discussed in multiple places. Additional references would be listed after the main subject listing, indented.

Lincoln, Abraham L:259

Booth, John Wilkes B:300

Gettysburg Address G:128

Grant, Ulysses S. G:238

Periodical Indexes

A periodical index is a cumulative list of articles from a set of periodicals arranged in alphabetical order by author, title, or subject, and typically within a specified date range. The entries or citations provide all the information needed to find a specific article.

An important difference between a library's catalog or OPAC and a periodical index is that a periodical index does not reflect the specific periodicals to which a specific library subscribes. Periodical indexes are published by commercial entities and index a preestablished set of periodicals whether a specific library does or does not subscribe to all of the periodicals referenced in the index. Once you find an article you want to read in a periodical index, you have to check the OPAC of the library you are in to see if the library actually subscribes to that periodical. If so, you can go to the periodical area of the library, locate the periodical and specific volume, and read the article.

Typically, periodicals cannot be checked out of the library; however, you can make a photocopy of the article—if you adhere to copyright restrictions. In larger libraries, periodicals often are separated by current (periodicals recently received) and bound (periodicals bound together by volume or by time period). Older periodicals may even be in a different place entirely in the library, such as in the basement, as they are not used often and can take up a lot of space.

PUT IT TO USE   Carefully read the signs posted in your library to see where the periodicals are located and how they are organized.

If the library does not subscribe to the periodical you want, you have three options:

1. Find a library that does subscribe to the periodical, and go there physically and read or copy the article.

2. Request that a copy of the article be sent to the home library through the library's interlibrary loan system. This usually involves a fee of a few dollars per page for copying, and often takes a few days to receive.

3. Access the article electronically using a full-text resource available either through the library or on the Internet. To find the article electronically, use an electronic version of the periodical index. Clicking on the title of the article typically brings up the full text of the article, if it is available. In many cases, the abstract, or short summary, of the article can be read, even if the full-text version is not available. Many online resources provide full-text articles either without charge or for a single-use or subscription fee.

Thousands of periodical indexes cover more than 150,000 individual periodicals. Before you can begin searching for an article, you must find the appropriate index in which to search. General periodical indexes cover a broad range of topics in scholarly journals, popular magazines, and newspapers. Subject-specific periodical indexes cover articles in selected scholarly journals related to a broad topic or subject area.

As examples, the *Business Periodicals Index* references articles in the business arena and the *Index to Legal Periodicals* references legal-related articles. To find the most appropriate periodical index for your area of research, consult with your librarian. Figure 3-6 shows an example of a citation and the information you need to find the article in the actual periodical.

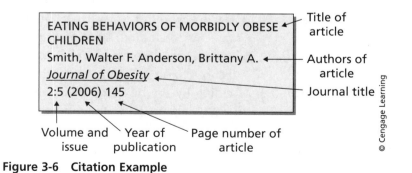

Figure 3-6 Citation Example

? CRITICAL THINKING QUESTIONS

Select a topic that you might want to research for one of your classes or for your career. Answer the following questions:

▶ In what subject area does my topic belong? (e.g., art, education, business, science)

▶ Do I need articles from professional journals or from popular magazines?

▶ Should I include both primary and secondary resources? Which would be best for my topic?

▶ Will my topic be covered in a general index, or should I look in subject-specific indexes?

▶ What indexes cover my subject or topic, and are they available at my library? In print? Electronically?

▶ How current does my information have to be?

▶ What indexes cover the necessary time periods?

success steps: using a periodical index

- Develop a list of keywords and subject headings for your topic.

- Determine the specific periodical index to use.

- Use the search word list and periodical index to find the exact citation for the article you want to read.

  - Read the introductory material in a printed periodical index to see exactly how to use the periodical.

  - Use the search tool in an electronic index and Boolean operators to narrow or broaden your search as needed.

- Go to the location in the library for the periodicals, and use the title of the periodical, the volume and page numbers listed in the citation, and the actual title of the article to find the article you want to read.

- Make a copy of the article, if needed.

If your library does not subscribe to the periodical you need, use the interlibrary loan system to have a copy of the article sent to your library.

DATABASES

A database is a collection of digitized information organized for simplified, fast searching and retrieval. Like an OPAC, databases can be searched by subject, author, title, and keyword. Boolean operators typically can be utilized with databases, too, to broaden or narrow a search. A database may contain just a citation, or a citation and abstract, or a citation and full-text article that includes the abstract. When you are searching in a database, you can limit your search in numerous ways, including searching by the type of publication, by the date of the publication, by the publication itself, and so forth. You can print portions of a database, save the database to be accessed later, or e-mail the database.

COLLECTING INFORMATION

Once you have developed your search statement and research questions, determined where to find the information, and accessed the information, the next step is to collect the information from the information source. You can use several methods to collect your information.

SCANNING AND SKIMMING

Scanning and skimming are techniques for researchers who are exploring or seeking specific information. Scanning usually comes first and involves moving through material quickly to see if it contains what you need. If the scanning provides sufficient reason to do so, the researcher can go back and skim the information further. Use both scanning and skimming when you want to determine if an article is relevant to your research. Both scanning and skimming are good techniques when you have a lot of material to cover in a short time or if you have a lot of information to consolidate into a manageable amount.

Scanning is used to search for headings, keywords, ideas, or a specific piece of information. This technique is used when you know exactly what you are looking for and are concentrating on finding specific information. For example, when you are looking for a number or a name in a telephone book, you are scanning.

success steps: skimming through a document

- Read the first and last paragraphs of the text.
- Read the titles, headings, and subheadings within the text.
- Read the first sentence of each paragraph.
- Look for names, dates, and places.
- Review nonfiction elements such as graphs, tables, charts, diagrams, and captions.
- Look for other organizational clues such as italicized words, bold print, and bulleted lists.
- Read any questions that may appear at the end of a text.

SELF-ASSESSMENT QUESTIONS

Select a chapter of a textbook that you are required to read for class in the next day or so. Scan the chapter, then skim the chapter. Then read the chapter fully.

- How much information do you think you got out of the chapter before you read it fully?
- Do you think that the scanning and skimming helped you in comprehending the information?

Skimming typically follows scanning but is equally important. Skimming is used to quickly determine the main idea in text by reading subheadings and the first sentences of sections and paragraphs. It allows the researcher to cover a great deal of information quickly and efficiently. It also gives the researcher an opportunity to determine whether more in-depth reading is necessary.

ONLINE HIGHLIGHTING

Highlighting is a technique that researchers use to mark important words, phrases, or passages of text for future use. Highlighting also can be used to discriminate between important information and interesting information. *Important information* is that which answers initial research questions or solves initial problems. *Interesting information* is that which the author uses to clarify the main points. As a researcher, you must be able to differentiate the two types of information and not be distracted by extraneous text. Excessive highlighting minimizes its effectiveness by obscuring the main ideas, so you should highlight only major concepts and key phrases.

If you conduct much of your research digitally, using online highlighting can be a very effective and time-saving tool. In addition to the ability to highlight text and images, some tools offer bookmarking and sticky note capabilities.

Some popular online highlighting tools include:

- Awesome Highlighter (www.awesomehighlighter.com)
- Diigo (www.diigo.com)
- I-Lighter (www.ilighter.com)

KEEPING AND ORGANIZING INFORMATION ON THE COMPUTER

With all of the information that you are gathering for your research projects, it is important that you keep your files organized into some logical pattern on your computer or tablet so that you do not waste time searching for items.

One very handy tool that can help you make and keep sense of all of your information is an open-source bibliographic management tool called Zotero (www.zotero.org). Zotero allows users to collect, organize, cite, and share all of their research sources. You can collect PDFs, images, audio and video files, and parts of web pages, to name a few. It also automatically indexes the full-text content of what you have captured so you can find the files you are looking for quickly and easily.

Zotero allows you to create bibliographies and citations and you can choose which publication format (such as MLA or APA style) to use. It can be downloaded for free and it is compatible with Mac, Windows, and Linux.

CHAPTER SUMMARY

This chapter addressed several key issues as they pertain to finding and accessing information. You learned that in order to find information, you must first understand how libraries are organized, how the materials in libraries and on the Internet are cataloged and referenced, and how to access and efficiently use these reference tools.

Chapter 3 also focused on the importance of understanding basic search techniques for finding information in libraries. Finally, you learned several effective techniques for collecting information from the information source.

POINTS TO KEEP IN MIND

In this chapter, several main points were discussed in detail:

- ▶ It is important to use librarian expertise when conducting research.
- ▶ There are many types of electronic resources that can be used to find information.

3

❱ Most library resources include four pieces of information: author, title, subject, and keyword. Each can be used to search for information.

❱ Boolean operators are a type of search method that include the words "and," "or," and "not." The use of these words can broaden or narrow a search.

❱ Types of library indexes include book indexes and periodical indexes.

❱ A database is a collection of digitized information organized for simplified, fast searching and retrieval.

❱ Three techniques for collecting information include scanning and skimming, online highlighting, and organizing information on the computer.

apply it

Find printable activities on the companion web site for this book, accessed through www.cengagebrain.com.

 Activity #1 Reviewing and Revising the Search Process

Select or create a research project. Use the Research Skills Worksheet in Figure 3-7 as a road map for research or problem solving. Write your response in the spaces provided. Then answer the following questions:

1. How did following this process help you find and access the information you needed?

2. As a result, do you think you were more efficient in your research?

3. What are the most difficult steps in this process? Why?

 Activity #2 Searching Practice: Part 1

Use the topic "computer literacy in the classroom" and a search engine on the Internet (www.google.com, www.bing.com,

Research Process	Task	Your Response
What is the problem or question to be addressed?	Write out clearly the specific assignment.	
What is the topic to be researched?	Write down your specific search statement.	
What questions have to be answered?	Write four research questions to accompany search statement.	
What key concepts have to be addressed?	Identify and write down two or three key concepts.	
What synonyms can be used for key concepts?	Write four to eight synonyms for key concepts.	
What perspective should be used to address the questions?	Determine the point of view—subjective, objective, multiple perspectives.	
How current does your information have to be?	Look at the questions and decide the importance of currency of the resource.	
What resources should be utilized?	List four to six specific resources to be used.	
Where are these resources located and accessed?	Write down call numbers for print resources, and access procedures for electronic resources.	
What means of information collection will be used?	Determine note-taking style, and record information.	
What information is needed to cite these sources?	Record the needed information for each source.	

Figure 3-7   Research Skills Worksheet

or www.yahoo.com) to practice searching for appropriate information.

> **1.** What keywords should you use for this topic?
>
> **2.** What are some synonyms for the keywords?

Type the words or phrases, and examine your results.

continued

continued

3. What words or phrases might you not want to include in your keywords?

4. How can you combine your search terms using Boolean operators to narrow or broaden your results?

 Activity #3 Searching Practice: Part 2

Using the OPAC, find one *book* on a topic related to this class.
Title: _____

Author: _____ Call Number: _____
Will this be a good source for the topic? Why or why not?

Find one article from a scholarly journal on the topic, using a periodical index.

Article Title: _____

Author: _____ Publication Date: _____

Periodical Title: _____

Periodical Index Utilized: _____

Will this be a good source for the topic? Why or why not?

CHECK YOUR UNDERSTANDING

Visit www.cengagebrain.com to see how well you have mastered the material in Chapter 3.

SUGGESTED ITEMS FOR LEARNING PORTFOLIO

Refer to the "Developing Portfolios" section at the beginning of this textbook for more information on learning portfolios.

▶ Completed Research Skills Worksheet

REFERENCES

Gray, C. (2011). *Social media: a guide for researchers*. Retrieved June 28, 2013, from http://www.rin.ac.uk/our-work/communicating-and -disseminating-research/social-media-guide-researchers

Library of Congress. (n.d.). *About the Library*. Retrieved July 2, 2013, from http://www.loc.gov/about/

3

Evaluating Information

LEARNING OBJECTIVES

By the end of this chapter, students will achieve the following objectives:

▶ Use a set of criteria to evaluate information and information sources.

▶ Identify specific criteria that should be used to evaluate web pages for credibility and appropriateness.

BE IN THE KNOW

Evaluate This!

Did you know that you can have a professional career as an evaluator? According to the American Evaluation Association (www.eval.org), an evaluator is someone who assesses the strengths and weaknesses of programs, personnel, policies, products, or organizations to improve their efficiency (American Evaluation Association, n.d.). Their web site lists evaluation/evaluator/research job openings on its career page.

The following is a sampling of job titles associated with evaluation:

- Monitoring and Evaluation Consultant
- Manager, Research, and Evaluation
- STEM Education and Evaluation Manager
- Senior Evaluation
- Evaluation Assistant
- Public Health Evaluator
- Senior Evaluation Officer
- Online Course Development Evaluator
- Director of Research and Evaluation
- Evaluation Analyst

Learning to properly evaluate information is one component of becoming information-literate. And who knows, it may end up becoming your career!

SOLVING INFORMATION PROBLEMS: EVALUATE THE INFORMATION

Information-literate individuals critically analyze information and its sources to ensure that it is useful. Critical analysis is applying rational and logical thought while deconstructing information to assess its value. Lack of critical analysis increases the risk of using inaccurate and inappropriate information, making poor decisions based on poor information, and losing time. Critical analysis applies to print materials and resources, multimedia resources, and information on

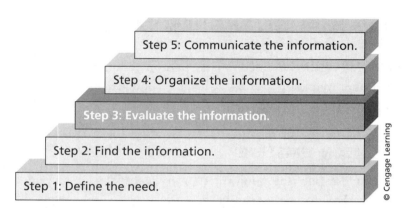

Research Process Step 3: Evaluate the Information. The third step of any research project should be to critically evaluate the information found.

the Internet. This chapter suggests several criteria you can use to analyze information and information sources as the next step in the research process. We will look first at criteria that can be applied to all information and then discuss tips that apply specifically to critiquing information found on the Internet. After you read this chapter, you should be able to apply critical analysis in asking questions about information sources, as well as provide criteria for evaluating information sources.

4

EVALUATING THE RESOURCE

Evaluating information is based in large part on common sense. Still, to understand evaluation criteria, it helps to understand how information is published and communicated.

PUBLICATION TIMELINE

The timeline for publishing information influences the content and defines how the information can be used effectively. Thus, the publication timeline becomes one of several criteria for evaluation. When an event occurs, radio and news agencies such as CNN may be able, via satellite systems, to give live reports of the event. Newspapers and magazines, however, take much longer to report the facts of the same event. You may read the facts in a newspaper by the next day's edition, but a magazine may take weeks or even months to publish the report. The timeline for publication of information in scholarly journals and books is even longer, because of more complex review and publication processes. Large-volume resources, such as encyclopedias, directories, and handbooks, may not publish the information for many months, if not years.

Even though Internet technology allows almost instantaneous publication of the information, a person must update the web site constantly. Other than news web sites, information on the Internet is outdated quickly. Figure 4-1 provides a general timeline of currency of the information.

Different kinds of information are needed for different purposes. Following are examples of the best formats for various types of information, based on information flow and timing:

▶ *History.* History is an example of a topic that does not necessarily require up-to-the-minute information. For some information projects, however, understanding historical facts is necessary. For example, if you are writing a report about an event in history, understanding the context in which that event occurred might be critical to the effectiveness of your finished project. You might want to know about the geographical area, the society and its culture, the political environment, the time period, and the area's demographics. Because this information

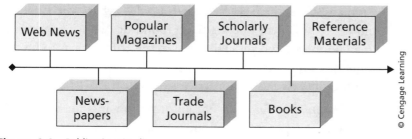

Figure 4-1   Publication timeline

does not change from the past, a book or an encyclopedia might be an excellent source of the information. Historical sites on the Internet would provide the same type of data. Conversely, if you are seeking a contemporary perspective on a historical event, a more recent information source would be more appropriate.

▶ *Technology.* Technology provides an example opposite from that of history. Because changes in technology occur rapidly, the information a book contains about a given technology is likely to be outdated by the time the book is published. Take the example of a book describing a computer software program. An updated version of the software is likely to be available by the time the book is published. A better resource for this type of information would be a help manual published with the software or documentation from the web site of the company that publishes the software.

▶ *Behind-the-scenes information.* In some cases, an understanding of what occurred just before an event is important. This kind of information may be in the form of personal correspondence (e.g., memos, e-mails, letters, electronic mailing lists), various types of documentation (e.g., diaries, journals, logs, personal notes, lab notes of an experiment), and other media (e.g., newsletters, conference programs). This information is not always easy to find or access, but it can help to explain why an event occurred or to document the chronology of events.

▶ *Immediate information.* Live news information sources, such as those found on the Internet, provide immediate information.

4

In many cases, the facts of the event (who, what, where, when, how) are provided, but the background or "why" of the event may not be known yet. This kind of information has to be critiqued carefully, as live reporting may be inaccurate when there is little time to check the facts.

▶ *Current information.* Current information includes information that is reported a few hours to a few days after an event. TV and radio reporting, newspaper reporting, and Internet reporting all provide this type of information. There may have been time to research the background of the event and to check the facts. The content may also include analysis, statistics, interviews, historical context, and other relevant information.

▶ *Older information (weeks).* Magazines provide information several days to weeks after an event. Because these information sources take longer to publish the content, they allow sufficient time to check facts, research the background and historical context, find supporting data, conduct interviews, and enhance the information. Often these information sources report for a specific purpose, so the content must be critiqued for bias or a specific slant. The information is less current than live or next-day reports, and although there is time to check facts, accuracy is not guaranteed.

▶ *Older information (months to years).* Information that is several months, or even years, old is published in scholarly journals, conference papers, research reports, and books. These information sources require time to conduct detailed studies or analyses of data or events, review by peers or editors, and physical publication of the resources. Journals and conference papers that are found online adhere to the same process, so the time requirement is similar. An advantage is that these resources can provide more detailed, thorough, and accurate information.

▶ *Older information (years).* Information that is several years old typically is published in book form. Researching and writing a book may take months to years, followed by additional time for review, editing, and production. This type of resource can provide accurate and detailed information with supporting background, analysis, and commentary. Typically, books provide much more information than the information forms previously described. They can support one perspective or provide numerous viewpoints. Currency of the information is sacrificed for volume and depth.

▶ *Reference resources.* Publications such as encyclopedias, handbooks, and statistical compilations all provide factual and typically unbiased information. These information sources sacrifice currency for detail and accuracy. They require time to check the facts and ensure accuracy, compile the information, and publish the resource. Sometimes these kinds of resources can be found on the Internet, but, like online journals, they require time for gathering and organizing the information, and additional time to input the data into a database.

TYPES OF RESOURCES

Journals and magazines are common sources of information. The three basic types of journals and magazines are: (1) scholarly journals, (2) trade publications, and (3) popular magazines. Each of these types has a different purpose and target audience. Collectively, they hold a wealth of useful information, but it is important to recognize the differences between and among them to critically evaluate the appropriateness of their content.

Scholarly Journals

Scholarly journals are written by authorities in a topic area or field of study and include research reports and other academic or factual information. The main purpose of a scholarly journal is to report original, current research data to individuals in the scholarly and professional arenas. Scholarly research means that scientists and researchers have conducted highly structured studies using accepted methods and have made educated, justifiable conclusions about the results. These scientists and researchers typically work for educational institutions, such as colleges and universities, or for private research organizations, such as research labs, think tanks, hospitals, and non-profit groups. In their articles, they use the language and technical terminology associated with the specific field. They also employ a structured format and follow accepted guidelines for studying a specific topic. The research results in qualitative data, which describe

zhang bo/E+/Getty Images

4

4

the characteristics or observations of something, or quantitative data, which measure something.

In many cases, the articles are sent out to reviewers who are specialists in the field. The reviewers critically analyze the information, methods, results, and conclusions that the authors have drawn. The reviewers make recommendations to the publisher that the manuscript be accepted, revised in some way, or rejected because of poor study design or invalid conclusions. The review provides expert appraisal, and although the review does not guarantee accuracy, it does provide a check on the content, adding to the information's credibility. Poor research or inaccurate content has less chance of being accepted for publication in a scholarly journal than in other, less structured types of journals or magazines. A journal that uses this review system is called a refereed or peer-reviewed journal. Journals that employ this level of rigor are typically highly credible.

Examples of the many hundreds of scholarly journals are:

▶ *Journal of the American Medical Association* (commonly called *JAMA*)
▶ *Journal of Geology*
▶ *Reviews of Modern Physics*
▶ *Journal of Infectious Disease*
▶ *Journal of Computer Information Systems*
▶ *Journal of International Business Studies*
▶ *Journal of Interior Design*
▶ *The American Professional Constructor*

Authors whose articles are published in scholarly journals are required to follow a structured format for organizing and publishing an article. Each scholarly journal has a set of guidelines informing authors how their manuscript should be submitted. These guidelines can be found in the journal itself or obtained from the publisher or the journal's web site. Editors of the scholarly journal assess the quality and appropriateness of each article against these guidelines to determine appropriateness for publication.

To illustrate how reviews and manuscript guidelines are used, consider the following examples: The *Journal of Nutrition Education and Behavior* sends three reviewers a manuscript addressing the topic

? CRITICAL THINKING QUESTIONS

▶ What are five refereed journals that apply to your field of study? How do you know they are refereed? (Consider using www.google.com or another online search engine, or talk to your reference librarian, to find at least five examples that might be useful in your research activities. Many journals have web sites describing their publications.)

▶ What are five journals that are not refereed? How do you know they do not use a peer review process?

of food behavior. These reviewers might be university professors who teach in nutrition programs and who have completed research and published their own articles on a nutrition behavior topic. Other appropriate reviewers could be nutritionists who are familiar with food behaviors and psychologists who specialize in this area.

Regardless of their professional position, all reviewers are selected based on their expertise in nutrition behavior theories and the kinds of studies they have completed in the past. The reviewers also have access to the journal's guidelines, so they are knowledgeable about how the manuscript should be organized. The reviewers know how sound behavior studies should be organized and how to objectively evaluate the assumptions and conclusions from the data. They have a high level of education and have had substantial training in the topic area and in research design.

As reviewers of articles, their goal is to critically and objectively evaluate the assumptions, methods, and conclusions to ensure that only sound information is published. The reviewers often make suggestions to the authors, who then have the opportunity to implement the suggestions and thereby improve the quality of the article before publication.

This peer review process maintains the credibility of scientific investigation and reporting. A goal of scientific researchers is to publish articles about their research. Publishing an article lets the scientific community know what they are doing. The scientific community then reports the results of the study to the general population. Standards for activities such as manufacturing and legislation are based on current published and accepted research. Without publication, researchers' efforts go unrecognized and the information does not get implemented into daily life. If the researchers do not conduct sound research and use the data appropriately, their studies do not get published. The entire system provides an important check and balance for all of us.

A close look at the organization of a scholarly journal article and the purpose of each part of the article will help you develop your ability to gain useful information. A review of the *Guidelines for Authors* available for almost every scholarly journal will show that articles in these journals are required to be structured in a similar fashion. Most accounts of research are presented in a format similar to what is described next.

Abstract. An abstract is a brief synopsis of the article. In business proposals and other documents, the abstract is commonly called the executive summary. An abstract typically is limited to a specified length (e.g., 500 words) and must include the basic components or facts of the article. It provides the context and reasons for doing the study or writing the article. A good abstract explains briefly how the study was accomplished, identifies the major results, and states the conclusion. It also may state briefly why the study is important. Reading the abstract of a scholarly journal article before delving into the entire article can save a significant amount of time by revealing whether the information is appropriate for your purpose. If you determine that the article is appropriate, you then can read the article in its entirety for more details.

Keywords. Many scholarly journals include a list of words that help to identify the main concepts in the article. These keywords show how the article has been categorized in various search engines and library indexes. In the example of the behavior change article, keywords might include: *behavior change theory*, *nutrition behavior*, *eating behavior*, *weight loss*, and *obesity*. These keywords can be used to search for articles on similar topics in journal indexes and search engines.

Introduction. Most journal articles begin with an introduction explaining why the authors have conducted the study or written the article and why the information is important. For example, in our nutrition behavior article, the author may start with a brief discussion of obesity as a significant problem in the United States, partially caused by poor nutrition. Most introductions end in some kind of purpose statement or thesis statement for the article. These statements explicitly state the intent of the study or article. In formal scientific studies, the purpose statement is replaced by a hypothesis, in which the authors make a statement that they will attempt to support with the results of their specific study.

Literature review. The literature review comes after the introduction and provides a brief overview of the relevant studies or articles that support or provide background information on the current study. The purpose of the literature review is to provide a solid foundation for the topic, using published information. One of the goals of scientific research is to add to the scientific body of knowledge in the field. Demonstrating the relationship of the current study to existing research clarifies that correlation and summarizes the scientific body of knowledge that relates specifically to the topic of the current study. The author must objectively review highlights, relevant findings, issues, controversies, successes, or failures of previous research.

For example, in the behavior change article, a thorough and informative literature review would highlight several behavior change theories or studies, including those that did not succeed. The author would be careful not to skew the perception to support the purpose of the study. Excellent literature reviews start out with a broad scope, then narrow the focus specifically to the need for the current study or article.

Some articles are written for the sole purpose of discussing previous literature. These are called review articles. In the nutrition behavior example, a review article might highlight the major nutrition behavior theories studied in the past. Review articles do not include a methods section or a results section as described next. The review article is an excellent starting place for researching a scientific topic.

Methods. After the context and need for the study have been discussed in the introduction and the highlights from relevant previous studies have been summarized, the author explains in detail how the current study was conducted. Sound research methods contribute to the validity and reliability of the study. In addition, if another researcher wants to re-create the study, he or she could follow the methods described in the article. The description of the methods also allows the article's reviewers to determine if the study was conducted in a logical manner and if sound research standards and procedures were followed. If a tool, such as a questionnaire, was used, it should be included as an exhibit at the end of the article. If it is not included, readers should be able to contact the authors to gain access to the tool that was used.

Results. This section logically follows the methods section. Here, the author presents the results of the study in an objective, logical manner. Visual representations of data, such as tables, charts, graphs, diagrams, or photographs, are used frequently to illustrate the information. Establishing a direct correlation between the methods section and the results is vital to the study's credibility. The charts or tables should be labeled clearly and organized so readers can easily understand what is being communicated without reading the text of the article. Presenting information graphically whenever possible and appropriate adds to the clarity of the information.

Discussion. The next section in the article consists of a discussion of the results. Here, the author explains the results, discusses any problems that arose during the study that might have influenced the results, presents any unexpected event or finding, and relates the results back to the original findings in the literature. In some cases, the findings are supported by the literature review. In other cases, the findings contradict previous findings. In the event of a discrepancy, the author typically provides an explanation of the contradiction to the best of his or her ability. In most cases, the author makes an educated assumption about the findings, regardless of whether the findings supported or contradicted previous research.

Conclusions. Finally, the conclusions section explains the major inferences that can be drawn logically from the study and outlines why the findings are important to the industry or the general population. Authors often make recommendations for future research, including other topics that can be studied formally to help answer the research question or expand on the findings. A conclusion must be supported directly by results of the study versus the author's opinion.

References. Authors of articles in scholarly journals are required to state in their articles exactly where they get any information or facts. The source of a fact is indicated in the text of the article where the fact occurs and is called a citation. The complete source for the citation is provided in the reference list at the end of the article. Each journal provides its own style guide, including, among other requirements, specifically how to cite sources. Information on style guides is presented in Chapter 6.

Citing references appropriately credits authors of original work and is essential to avoid plagiarism (stealing information or ideas from others). Plagiarism is highly unethical, illegal, and can lead to being reprimanded, fired, or sued. Using information that has been verified by others is acceptable and necessary to substantiate new research, but the original author or source of the information must be given proper credit.

Trade Publications

Trade publications (sometimes called trade journals) can be excellent sources of information, but they must be viewed critically for accuracy, credibility, and appropriateness. Authors of trade publications typically are specialists or practitioners in a given field. They write their articles for others in the same industry who face the same issues and have the same informational needs. Most information in trade publications is practical in nature, reporting on issues such as procedures, materials, technology, equipment, events, and policies or processes.

Typically, trade publications have no formal review process other than the basic editorial review, which ensures that the article is well-written and does not contain grammatical and typographical errors. In these publications, authors use the technical language of the field because the article is written for other industry professionals. Information is presented in charts, graphs, diagrams, and photographs, as appropriate. Although the authors often mention where they acquired their information, some do not cite their resources formally, in which case it may be difficult to find the original or primary source of the information.

A few examples of the many hundreds of trade publications are:

▶ *Advertising Marketing and Research Reports*
▶ *Industrial Equipment News*
▶ *Concrete Products*
▶ *Building Design and Construction*
▶ *Business Solutions*
▶ *Computer Graphics World*
▶ *Veterinary Practice News*
▶ *Hospitality Technology*

? CRITICAL THINKING QUESTIONS

▶ What trade publications are available in your field?
▶ How can you use the information from these types of publications appropriately?

Popular Magazines

Popular magazines are the least useful type of journal/magazine for credible research. The main purpose of the articles in popular magazines is entertainment, to get readers to purchase the magazine, or perhaps to sway the reader to a specific way of thinking or point of view. Authors of the articles in popular magazines are writers on staff with the magazine and rarely are specialists in the topic area. In addition, freelance writers, who typically are not specialists in any one area, sell their articles to the magazine for a fee. Freelance writers conduct research and interviews to find the information needed for a specific article. They are writers, not authorities, with a goal of entertaining or informing the general population, resulting in increased sales and profits for the publication.

The language of the article typically is not as technical, because the target audience is usually the general public. As is the situation with trade journals, popular magazines have no review process other than the editorial review to ensure that the articles are well-written and free of grammatical and typographical errors. Even though some authors mention their sources of information, they rarely cite these sources formally, as is required in a scholarly journal. Often, numerous photographs are used instead of the charts and graphs presenting quantitative data.

You should be cautious in using information from popular magazines. There is no guarantee that the information is accurate, unbiased, or appropriate, and it can be difficult to verify facts or find the original or primary source of information in the absence of formal resource citations. Still, popular magazines are useful in some areas of research and for some types of information. For example, an interior designer can use popular magazines to keep up with current and geographical trends in design, materials, and techniques. Popular magazines also commonly include interviews with leaders in the field, provide current news and discussion of issues, and follow market trends.

A few examples of the hundreds of popular magazines are:

- *Men's Health*
- *Smithsonian*
- *National Geographic*
- *Entrepreneur Magazine*
- *Popular Science*
- *Wired*
- *PC Magazine*

Guido Mieth/Flickr/Getty Images

4

▶ *Sports Illustrated*

▶ *Scientific American*

▶ *The New Yorker*

? CRITICAL THINKING QUESTIONS

▶ What popular magazines publish information related to your field?

▶ How can you use the information from these popular magazines appropriately?

● ● ● questions to ask about evaluating resources

- When did the actual event occur?

- How current is the information in your source?

- How much time is required to transfer the information into the format of this resource?

- What kind of information is needed? What is the purpose of the information?

- How current should the information be?

- What is the best source of information based on the publication's timeframe?

- Do you have to find the original or primary sources of information?

- What is the purpose of the publication you are using for your research?

- Has the publication put its articles through a formal peer review?

EVALUATING AUTHORITY

After determining the kind of resource you want to use, the next step in evaluating your information is to determine the authority of its author. Evaluating the authority means to look critically at the author of the information, as well as the sponsor or owner of the specific resource, such as the publisher or owner of a web site. Your goal is to determine if those who write the information are qualified to do so and whether they provide credible information. Several elements should be evaluated when considering the author and the publisher of a book or article, or the sponsor or owner of a web site.

AUTHOR

In many information sources, the author's name is displayed prominently—on the front and title page of a book, on the first page of journal articles, and as a byline of newspaper and magazine articles. Some information sources, such as encyclopedias and reference materials, have a number of authors, as well as a group of contributors or an editorial board that oversees the information submitted.

Several clues will help you determine an author's authority, which will give you an idea about the credibility of the information:

▶ *Expertise:* Look for signs that the author is an expert in the topic area and brings knowledge to the material. Expertise can come from academic degrees, work experience, previous publications, and extensive research. Consider conducting an Internet search using the author's name to find any organizations with which the author is associated, other publications he or she has written, news stories about the author, or other references. For some fields, biographical references provide information about many experts in a variety of fields. For example:

▶ *Contemporary Authors*, by Thomson-Gale Publishers, provides biographical and bibliographical information on fiction and nonfiction authors.

▶ Marquis *Who's Who* publishes biographical references in many different professional fields and geographical areas.

▶ *Academic background and credentials.* Look for evidence that the author has a credible academic background and qualifications for writing on the topic. Self-proclaimed experts or those who are merely impassioned about a topic may not be qualified to write about it. In research, a credible author might have a Ph.D. (or at least a Master's degree) in a related field, signifying that he or she conducts research or teaches in the area. In medically related areas, the author might be an M.D. or other medical professional with a qualified background pertaining to the topic.

▶ *Work-related or other experience.* In the business world, clues to credibility might be evident in work experience rather than academic credentials. Many credible web sites have "Biography" sections listing the author's work-related experience. You also could conduct an Internet search to see if the author's name is associated with a company or professional organization. In most search engines, putting the name in quotes facilitates the search. For example, try a search for "Bob Smith" in www.google.com. The company or organization's web site can provide additional information about the author. If the author is a professor at a university, for example, you might find out past and current research topics, courses taught, and committees on which the author serves.

▶ *Licensure or certification.* In some areas, an author might have a license or certification in a specific area, such as an MCSE (Microsoft Certified Systems Engineer), which indicates that he or she has passed an examination in Microsoft operating systems. If you find a credential and want to see if it is valid, conduct a search using the credential's name or letters to find the sponsoring organization and the explanation of the specific credential. Most organizations state exactly what the certified individual must know to gain and maintain certification and also may provide a list of currently certified individuals in a directory. For some professions, such as those in healthcare or financial fields, professionals are often licensed or otherwise regulated by the state. Maintaining a state credential frequently requires meeting continuing education or other professional certification requirements. Searching a database of state credentialed professionals in a specific field can provide information regarding an individual's credibility.

▶ *Affiliation.* Look for the author's affiliations, such as with academic institutions, professional organizations, government agencies, and other professional groups. Authors who are affiliated with recognized organizations tend to be more credible. In many fields of study, professionals are expected to maintain membership in professional organizations. Also, check the affiliation itself. For example, Texas International University and the American Heart Disease Association sound credible, but they are not real, even though the names are similar to authentic and highly credible organizations. Research the organization if you are not familiar with it and its purpose.

▶ *Other publications.* In some cases it is useful to find out what other publications to which the author has contributed or produced. A simple search using the author's full name in quotes on www.google.com may turn up additional publications. Books typically have an "About the Author" page or information on the book jacket that provides a list of the author's previous publications. Too, reputable authors often are cited by other scholars.

▶ *Contact information.* In many publications, information about the author is available so you can contact the author either directly or through the publisher of the resource. Look for telephone numbers, mailing addresses, and e-mail addresses.

? CRITICAL THINKING QUESTIONS

▶ Think about your field of study. What credentials would you expect for authors of credible information?

▶ What academic background, work experience, academic degree, license, or affiliations would you expect? Why?

4

PUT IT TO USE   When using these biographical resources, be aware that they may list authors in some fields but do not cover all areas of study. Also, these references may not list individuals with significant expertise and who could offer valuable resources.

PUT IT TO USE   An e-mail address with no other information is not sufficient for assessing an author's credibility. Anyone can easily create an e-mail address. If this is the only piece of information available, consider e-mailing the author to see if you can obtain additional information.

PUBLISHER

Another significant component of authority is the publisher of the resource. The publisher is responsible for the actual publication or web site in which the information is located. Resources can be published by a university press, a trade press, a governmental agency, a not-for-profit organization, a specialized press, or an individual. Academic print products often are published by university presses, which tend to be scholarly and highly reputable. These publishers put their materials through a formal and rigorous screening to ensure that they meet the standards and goals of the publishing organization. The content often undergoes a peer review, which gives it high credibility. Trade presses publish trade journals and magazines, which tend to be less formal in their review of information and typically do not require a peer review of their content.

Information published by a government agency is generally credible. For example, the U.S. Government Printing Office (GPO) publishes numerous materials to keep Americans informed about the activities of the three branches of government. You can find information published by the GPO at its web site (www.gpo.gov) on the Internet. Among the numerous materials published by the GPO are, for example, the 9/11 Commission Report, the Budget of the United States Government, congressional bills, economic indicators, and the United States Code. Just about anything you want to know about the government that is available to the public can be found here.

Another type of publisher is the subsidy publisher. Also known as a vanity press, these publishers charge authors a fee to publish their work. In contrast to a traditional publisher, which accepts the risk of publication and ensures high-quality materials by providing editorial services and marketing or distribution of the product, the role of the subsidy publisher usually is limited to actual production of a book. The editorial and marketing tasks are the author's responsibility. Products from joint venture publishers can be of excellent quality, and many well-received books have come from these publishers. As with any resource, however, you must assess the accuracy, quality, and credibility of the information.

SPONSOR OR OWNER

In addition to researching the author and publisher, you should investigate the sponsor or owner of the resource. This is especially important when assessing web sites. A sponsor may be an organization or an individual. A large and reputable organization, such as the American Heart Association, tends to be more credible than an unknown individual. Also, determine if the sponsor advocates a

? CRITICAL THINKING QUESTIONS

▶ Go to the U.S. Government Printing Office at www.gpoaccess.gov. Think carefully about your area of study. What are 10 different information sources published by the GPO that you might find useful in your job or academic courses?

▶ Who are the best known publishers of information in your area of study?

? CRITICAL THINKING QUESTIONS

▶ Visit the web site of a subsidy publisher. What guidelines are required for publishing something?

▶ What services does the publisher provide to the author?

⌐ SELF-ASSESSMENT QUESTIONS

• Why would someone want to publish his or her materials through a subsidy press?

• What advantages and disadvantages would this kind of publishing have?

4

4

? CRITICAL THINKING QUESTIONS

▶ When researching information in your field, what kind of sponsor or owner would you expect to be credible? Why? Give some examples.

▶ When researching information in your field, what kind of sponsor or owner would you be highly suspicious of? Why? Give some examples.

specific viewpoint or philosophy. This information usually can be found in the "Home" or "About Us" portion of a web site or on promotional print materials.

When evaluating sponsors, look carefully at *why* they are presenting the information. This is important for print and Internet resources alike. Does the sponsor have a mission associated with the content? For example, the mission statement of the American Heart Association is "to build healthier lives, free of cardiovascular diseases and stroke" (American Heart Association, 2013). You would expect credible information on health, disease, and related information from this association. Because it is a not-for-profit agency, it does not have the ulterior motive of selling products or making money from sponsoring this information. In contrast, a manufacturer of a healthcare product is in the business of making money by selling that product. Therefore, information sponsored by this kind of organization should be evaluated more critically to determine the accuracy and credibility of the content.

PUT IT TO USE   Just because an entity sells a product or makes money from the information does not mean that the information is biased or inaccurate; it only means that you should check out the information carefully and keep in mind the purpose of the organization.

● ● ● **questions to ask about evaluating authority**

- Who is the author?
- What are the author's academic credentials related to the topic?
- What is the author's experience related to the topic?
- What kind of credential(s) does the author have (such as a license or certificate)?
- What is the author's affiliation?

- What else has the author published?

- Is the author well-known in the field?

- Is information provided so you can contact the author?

- Who is the publisher, and what kinds of materials are published?

- Who is the sponsor or owner (especially of web sites), and is that sponsor stable?

- What is the sponsor's philosophy?

- Is the sponsor suitable to address this topic?

- Did the author prepare this information as a part of his or her professional duties or have some other relationship with the sponsor?

EVALUATING CURRENCY

Currency refers to the timeliness of the information. For a print product, currency is determined by date of publication. As you will recall, different types of publications require different timelines. To review—newspapers are published a few hours after the event. Books can take months or even years to get the information into print, so the date of publication must be viewed in light of the type of information resource. Although web pages can take much less time to publish information, it is difficult sometimes to determine the currency of the information. Recall as well that an information-literate individual understands how current the information has to be for the specific purpose. For some needs, the information must be as up-to-date as possible. For other purposes, such as historical research, currency is not important.

Additional clues can be found within the information itself. Look carefully at the references the author uses. A journal article that has been published recently but uses references from 10 years ago is not likely to be as current as one that uses more recent references. In the scientific community, many changes and advancements can happen in a short time. Also, look for clearly dated information. For example, if the article refers to a statistic about computer use in public schools,

> ● ● ● **questions to ask about**
> **evaluating currency**
>
> - How current does the information have to be?
> - What is the date of publication of the resource?
> - What is the edition of the resource?
> - Can you determine the currency of the original source of the information by looking at the references?
> - Is the sponsoring organization stable, meaning that it is a viable organization that will probably be around for a while?

check the date of the original source. If that statistic is from 1980, it is not relevant today. Some information that is older may be fine depending on the type of information that it is. The important part is that you carefully evaluate the type of information you are using and make a judgment on its currency and relevance to your topic.

DATE AND EDITION OF A PUBLICATION

In a print product, look for the copyright date on the reverse side of the title page. Determine if the date is appropriate for the topic. Many information sources are revised periodically with minor changes for reprinting, or new editions are published with more significant changes. More than one edition indicates that the material has been updated to reflect new information and to correct mistakes. Multiple editions suggest a more reliable resource because the publisher chooses to continue to publish the book's subsequent versions.

EVALUATING THE CONTENT

After you have evaluated the resource itself, the authority of the author of the content, and the currency, you will evaluate various aspects of the content itself. When looking critically at the content, you should evaluate for whom the material was written, purpose and scope of the information, objectivity of the information, and its accuracy and verifiability. Examining these characteristics in-depth will illustrate their importance in the evaluation process.

? CRITICAL THINKING QUESTIONS

- Think about a specific research project that you have had to do in school or in your job. How current did this information have to be?
- For this project, what kinds of information sources would be best to use? Specifically, how would you determine the currency of the information?

4

INTENDED AUDIENCE

A first step is to determine the intended audience for whom the information was written. In general, information is written for specialists in the field, practitioners, a general audience or the general public, an educated audience, or some kind of specialized group. On the one hand, information that is highly technical is intended for clinicians, physicians, technicians, or practitioners. It may be too technical for laypersons or for an overview of a topic. On the other hand, information that is too general and is written for the general public may not be useful to a practitioner or researcher who requires detailed, technical information. The intended audience of the information and the information source dictate the type, depth, and focus of the content. In general, you should ask if the content is sufficiently scholarly to meet your goal but not so technical that it is too difficult to understand.

PURPOSE AND SCOPE

The next step is to look at the information to try to understand its purpose. Why was the information written or produced in the first place? Was the goal to inform, entertain, trick, sell, persuade, or damage? Some sources are created to provide new information; other sources are created to update existing information. In many cases, content is written so it provides only one side or view of an issue. Other resources provide a balanced treatment of all sides of an issue.

SELF-ASSESSMENT QUESTIONS

- Who are the various intended audiences for information in your field of study?
- For each audience, what is the level and focus of the writing and content?

SELF-ASSESSMENT QUESTION

- Think about a topic that you might research in your field of study. For the topic you select, what information would be considered as background or an overview? What information would provide more focused details?

4

● ● ● questions to ask about evaluating content

- Who constitutes the intended audience?
- Is the tone and treatment of the information appropriate for the intended audience?
- Are the terms and concepts too technical to understand?
- Are the terms and concepts too simplified to be useful?
- Are the depth and detail sufficient for the needs of the audience?

● ● ● **questions to ask about evaluating content**

- What is the purpose of the information?
- Do you detect ulterior motives, such as selling, persuading, damaging, and so forth?
- Is the information a primary source or a secondary source?
- What is the scope of the information?

Scope refers to how broad or narrow the topic is. An overview topic typically is broad in scope, with few details. A narrowly focused treatment of the topic gives details on a small portion of a larger topic. This is why you have to thoroughly understand your need for the information, and then decide how in-depth the information has to be. For scholarly journals, review articles give an overview of the major findings of a topic. Each article referenced in the overview article follows with details on a narrow subtopic. In many research projects, broadly scoped sources are sufficient for describing the context or background of a topic. Then, more narrowly focused sources are used to detail the main topic of the project.

OBJECTIVITY

When evaluating content, you will have to determine whether information is fact or opinion. Facts are things that can be proven to have happened or to exist. Opinions are statements or judgments or beliefs, which may or may not be true. Facts should be backed up by a credible source and should be verifiable. You could go to a primary source to find the same information. Keep in mind, though, that opinions can be written to look as if they are facts.

PUT IT TO USE   You should look at the facts the author provides, as well as facts the author does not provide. For example, an author may provide accurate facts about the benefits of taking a specific medication for a disease but leave out the serious side-effects of taking the medication. Another author might alert you to the possible side-effects as well as the benefits.

Information is presented from a specific point of view. In a neutral point of view, only the facts are presented, without bias. Bias means that the facts are presented with prejudice. An information source should be critiqued to see if it has any prejudice or bias in the way it is presented. For example, if a health food store publishes a newsletter highlighting the benefits of taking the vitamins sold in the store but fails to discuss any research suggesting that taking the vitamins has no benefits or negative consequences, the newsletter has a biased point of view. Opinion pieces, commentaries, and book reviews are all written with a specific point of view.

Most news agencies are said to have one point of view or another (e.g., conservative or liberal). You will have to study the content to determine the point of view. Content should be evaluated based on whether the author conveys personal emotions or prejudices, makes unjustified claims or excessive claims of certainty, or distorts facts to support a point of view.

? CRITICAL THINKING QUESTIONS

▶ In your area of study, how might information-providers be biased? Give specific examples.

▶ What are controversial topics or issues in your field about which authors might show emotion or have extreme views?

PUT IT TO USE   Biased information is not necessarily bad information, but it is essential to recognize biased information and then seek out the opposite viewpoint so you will have a clear understanding of the entire issue or topic.

PUT IT TO USE   Credible scientists do not use the word "prove." Instead, they frame their findings as "the research suggests . . ." or "there is a correlation between. . . ."

● ● ● questions to ask about evaluating content

- Is the information presented fairly and from a neutral point of view?
- Is there a specific motive for presenting the information?
- Are all sides of a story presented?

continued

continued

- Who is the author, and why is he or she presenting the information?
- What is the purpose of the information?
- Are facts and statements justified and backed up with sound research or primary sources?
- Is the author moderate or extreme in presenting the views?
- Is there a conflict of interest?
- If there is advertising, is it appropriate and separate from the objective information?

ACCURACY AND VERIFIABILITY

Along with objectivity, you will have to determine if the information is accurate and whether it can be verified with another credible resource. Accuracy covers a wide scope including:

- accurate facts
- accurate reference to other resources
- no typographical errors
- no grammatical or punctuation errors
- logical assumptions
- logical flow of information
- logical conclusions based on information
- accurate visual aids, such as charts, graphs, and diagrams
- appropriate coverage of material.

PUT IT TO USE   Look to see if the author can be contacted to verify facts or answer clarifying questions.

Verifiable means that the information is based on facts that can be authenticated by another credible source or several credible sources.

The best information cites the original or primary resource. The resources have to be available for checking to verify that they exist and actually support the statements and facts in the content. On a web page, check the links to see if they go to where they say they will go and if the linked source is also credible. For print references, consider checking the listed references to ensure that they support what has been stated. Also, compare the facts or statements made in one source with what is generally accepted.

For example, consumption of high-fat foods and lack of exercise are generally recognized as increasing the risk for heart disease. A resource that states otherwise goes against what is accepted to be true in the scientific community. Though new uses of technology and discoveries can result in changes to generally accepted ideas, these statements must be evaluated critically before accepting them.

PUT IT TO USE If an information resource does not enable you to readily check the references, be suspicious of the information.

OVERALL QUALITY

In addition to accuracy of the information, the overall quality has to be evaluated, assessing the structure of the document and how the information is arranged. High-quality information is arranged in a logical and consistent manner. The information is broken down into logical sections or parts and is well laid out. Headings describe the content accurately. Visual aids, such as graphs, photos, charts, and tables, provide additional information and do not distract readers from the material. Visual aids are able to stand alone; you can understand the information from the graphic without requiring explanation from the text. Chapter 5 includes a discussion of organizational strategies for various types of information. These strategies can be used to organize your own material, as well as assess the quality of information resources.

● ● ● **questions to ask about the content**

- What is the subject? Is it consistent with the title of the document or resource?
- Is the information free from grammatical, typographical, and punctuation errors?
- Are the assumptions, the flow of information, and the conclusions logical?
- Are the visual aids accurate?
- Are facts and statements justified and supported with sound research or primary sources?
- Can the references be verified?
- Do the statements agree with what is generally accepted as being true?
- Is the information complete, or are data missing that, if provided, might change the interpretation of the document or resource?
- For Internet information, is the information available in another format, such as a printed product in a library?

SELF-ASSESSMENT QUESTIONS

4

- What impact does lack of editing (demonstrated by typographical and grammatical errors) have on the information you read?
- What impact does an illogical arrangement of information have on the resources you use?

In addition to the actual content, copyright issues must have been addressed and dealt with legally and ethically. More will be said in Chapter 6 about the ethical and legal issues surrounding information.

● ● ● **questions to ask about evaluating content**

- Is the information presented in a logical manner?
- Is the presentation consistent?
- Do the visual aids help to comprehend the material?
- Can the visual aids stand alone?

CASE IN POINT: NUTRITIONAL VALUE

Read the scenario below. Then, in groups or as a class, discuss the questions at the end.

Sheryl Fraser is a medical assistant working for a large physician practice. Her supervisor has asked her to develop some nutrition pamphlets to hand out to patients, encouraging them to change poor eating behaviors in favor of a diet within recommended dietary guidelines. The nutrition books in the office are outdated, so Sheryl decides to seek the needed information on the Internet. She types the search term "nutrition" using www.google.com—which indicates about 402,000,000 web sites.

As she looks through the first few sites, she finds contradictory information. One site suggests eating a 10-day diet of grapefruit to lose weight rapidly. Another site recommends a high-protein, low-carbohydrate diet. A third site informs her that the only way to be healthy is to avoid all meat and dairy products and adhere to a vegetarian diet. Though Sheryl did learn basic nutrition principles in her training as a medical assistant, she wants to be able to refer to credible resources to support the information in her pamphlet.

- How will Sheryl begin to sort through the vast number of web sites devoted to nutrition?
- Realizing the contradictory information on nutrition presented on the Internet, how will Sheryl determine which information is credible and which is not?
- How well do you think Sheryl will be able to judge which information she finds is accurate and which is inaccurate?
- How will Sheryl find data she can translate into information that her patients will understand, knowing that most of her patients have limited backgrounds in health-related topics, especially nutrition?

EVALUATING WEB SOURCES

You can find just about anything you want on the Internet: scholarly resources, full-text documents, directories, virtual libraries, university web sites, academic research, information portals, silly and joke sites, advertisements, trade sites and information, scams, personal pages, illegal activities, music, videos, and about anything else you can dream of. On the one hand, some of this information is excellent—reliable, verifiable, accurate, credible, and legal. On the other hand, much of the information on the Internet is not useful or appropriate—inaccurate, false, slanted, and sometimes illegal. Unfortunately, telling the difference from appearances alone can be difficult. The information-literate individual must know how to distinguish the good information from the bad. Train yourself to view web resources critically, even to the point of taking on a suspicious attitude toward each site you visit. This attitude will keep you critically analyzing the information that you find.

> **PUT IT TO USE**   Do not accept everything you read just because it is found online. Anyone can write and post anything for any purpose on the Internet.

EVALUATING WEB SITE AUTHORITY

When evaluating authority for web sites, the three most critical criteria to examine are author, owner or sponsor, and web address.

Author

As you have learned, in many information sources, the author's name is displayed prominently—on the front and title page of a book, on the first page of journal articles, and as a byline of newspaper and magazine articles.

When using web sites, finding the author may take a bit more effort. A web site is created for a specific purpose. For example, some web sites sell products or services. Others convey information on a narrow topic area. Others attempt to persuade readers to adopt a specific viewpoint or opinion. Still other sites are intended for entertainment. Some web pages are even created to damage another individual or group. With this in mind, you can gain a great deal of information on the credibility of a web site by evaluating the authorship or the person or organization that created and maintains the site. You must think critically about the purpose of the site. Holding the author or owner of a web site to the same standard as that of an author of a printed document is critical to his or her credibility.

In some cases, especially on reputable web sites, information about the author is easily found on the web site itself. Look for "Contact Us," "About," "Background," "Philosophy," "Who Am I?" or "Biography" on the site. Most web sites give names, addresses, phone numbers, or e-mail addresses inviting you to contact the site's owner or administrator. The goal is to try to find someone who is responsible for the site in terms of the information and its accuracy.

Sponsor or Owner

On a web site, in addition to "About Us" or "Home," look at the header or footer for a distinctive watermark or branding on the page to find information about the sponsor or owner. Try to determine if sponsors or owners are stable and durable, indicating that they are reliable and will be around for the long term. A large professional organization tends to be more stable and durable than an individual. A URL ending in .edu designates that the sponsorship is an academic institution. A URL ending in .gov indicates that the sponsor is a government agency. These sources are likely to be more credible than commercial or organizational sites. Keep in mind that anyone can publish anything on the Internet and web sites can be taken down at any time. Also, look to see if you can contact the webmaster of the site, and you can use www.whois.net to find information about the owner of the domain name for websites.

Web Address

Some information found on a web site gives clues about the author, publisher, and sponsor or owner. By understanding the clues, you can more readily make an informed decision about the quality of the information and the site itself. Figure 4-2 provides a fictitious URL—Universal Resource Locator—that serves as the example for the following discussion.

In our example, the top-level domain name is .edu, meaning that the server resides at an academic institution. The Internet Corporation for Assigned Names and Numbers (ICANN) is the entity responsible for approving these accredited top-level domains. Figure 4-3 provides a partial list of other common types of server locations that you should know.

? CRITICAL THINKING QUESTIONS

▶ Conduct an Internet search for a topic in your field of study. What is an example of a web site that has each of the following goals?
- Selling a product or service
- Informing readers of objective facts
- Persuading readers to a specific way of thinking or supporting one side of an issue

▶ How did you determine the goal of each site?

4

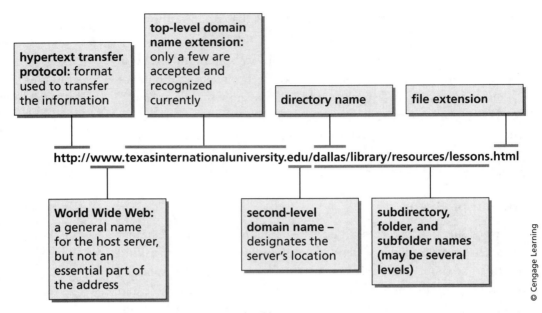

Figure 4-2 Fictitious Web Address

ICANN continues to add accredited domain-name registrars to its top-level domains list as technology and business developments warrant. In addition, each country has its own two-letter code that often is used in conjunction with the top-level domain name. For a complete list of country codes, go to the International Organization for Standardization (ISO) (www.iso.org). As examples, the ISO code for the United Kingdom is .uk and the ISO code for Botswana is .bw. When the ISO is used in the domain name, it signifies that the server is located in that country.

PUT IT TO USE Typically, you can rely on the .gov and .edu sites as being reliable and presenting relatively accurate information. The government or educational entity behind the site usually is bound by a code of ethics and is watched by many different individuals or agencies. The other top-level domain name extensions may not afford the same level of confidence because these may have vested interests or may be created by individuals who have personal or organizational agendas.

Extension	Type of Organization	Description
.edu	Educational institution	The .edu extension tells that the web site is sponsored by an educational institution, usually a college or university. These sites are often more reliable and credible than commercial or personal web sites.
.com	Commercial organization	The .com extension tells that the web site is a commercial site. These sites typically give information about a company, promote and advertise the company's products and services, and sometimes allow for online purchasing. The information is typically reliable, but is not scholarly.
.gov	Government agency	The .gov extension is reserved for governmental agencies and owned by the United States Federal Government. The information on these sites is typically viewed as credible.
.mil	Military entities	The .mil extension is reserved for military entities—Army, Navy, Air Force, Marines, and so forth.
.net	Internet service providers	The .net extension is sponsored by an Internet service provider.
.org	Organizations	The .org extension is reserved for organizations such as not-for-profit, religious, lobby, and charitable organizations. Information on these sites is typically credible; however, organizations exist for a purpose. Look carefully at the mission of the organization as you review the information.
.aero	Air transportation industry	The .aero extension is newly authorized and is sponsored by the air transportation industry.
.biz	Businesses	The .biz extension is reserved for large and small businesses.
.coop	Cooperatives	The .coop extension is newly authorized and is sponsored by the National Cooperative Business Association (NCBA) for cooperatives.
.info	Information	The .info extension is sponsored by the Afilias Global Registry Services and developed for information sites.
.museum	Museums	The .museum is sponsored by the Museum Domain Management System and is reserved for museums.
~	Personal web page on a server	A "tilde" ~ often denotes a personal web page on the server. In our example in Figure 4-2, adding /~BSmith after the .edu extension might signify a professor's personal web site on this server. Review personal web pages carefully, as they may not be monitored as closely as pages created for institutions or departments of institutions.

Figure 4-3   URL Extensions

EVALUATING WEB SITE CURRENCY

The currency of a web site is critical if you plan to use that site as a resource in your research. On web sites, the date of the last revision often is found on the bottom of the first page or on every page. A reputable web site typically gives the last date the site was updated.

In some cases, each page includes a date, indicating the currency of the information. For example, if an organization's web site has a page for the Board of Directors and the page has a current date, you can assume with some certainty that the information is current. Although not true in every case, a current date usually is an indicator of currency, but be aware that a site could indicate an update and still contain outdated information.

Obviously, not all information requires the same attention to currency. A web site pertaining to the ancient history of Greece does not require the same currency as a site that provides the latest state regulations on Medicare and Medicaid. A site that provides state regulations on Medicare and Medicaid from 1997 is of little use except for historical reference. In some cases, you might want the information posted on the site near the time the incident actually occurred. News web sites often archive their periodicals so that you can see the stories as they were written at the time.

Web Site Stability

Unlike a print product, a web site can be changed in a moment, and viewers may or may not be informed of the changes. The site can even be moved to a different web address with no forwarding information, making it difficult to locate, or deleted from the Internet altogether. A good clue to determine the stability of the site typically lies in the sponsorship. A nationally recognized organization (e.g., American Red Cross), a governmental agency, or an academic institution (e.g., a college or university), or a large corporation (e.g., AT&T) probably is not going anywhere—at least not without making national news. The main web sites usually can be relied upon to remain stable. The consequences of an established organization's moving its web site can be significant. Conversely, an individual's personal web site might move with little or no serious repercussions.

Keep in mind that a regular registration fee is required to maintain ownership of the web address, and some time and effort to maintain the site itself. Clues to web sites that are not maintained include broken or dead links (links that do not go to the intended site on the Internet), outdated links (links that go to old information

4

? CRITICAL THINKING QUESTIONS

▶ Suppose an article you read suggests an information source from the Internet. You want to verify the facts by going to that information source, but the web page had been discontinued. What will you do?

▶ What will you want the author of that content to have done to help you in your research?

▶ What kinds of issues might cause a web site to be ignored or deleted from the Internet?

when it appears that they should be going to current information), and information that does not match other resources you have determined to be current.

> **PUT IT TO USE**   Although you cannot be guaranteed that a site is stable and will be there when you want to return to it, it is best to try to use information from relatively stable sources. When you cite your references in a document and someone wants to review your sources of information, you may run into difficulties if the site you have referenced is no longer accessible.

EVALUATING WEB SITE CONTENT

Many web sites have host advertisements to support the web site. Although the presence of advertising does not negate the credibility of the information, it should cause you to take notice. Evaluate the advertisements carefully to determine if the relationship with the products or services being advertised influences the objectivity of the information. On web pages, advertising should be clearly separate from objective material. Web sites should be straightforward, clearly differentiating advertisements from objective facts or statements.

Tips for recognizing biased content:

▶ excessive claims of certainty
▶ appeal to emotion
▶ personal attacks
▶ too good to be true
▶ something for sale
▶ associated cost or fee
▶ unsupported claims of fact
▶ ignoring or omitting contradictory facts or views
▶ appeals to popular opinion
▶ before-and-after testimonials

- suggestive or negative innuendos
- magnification or minimization of problems
- presentation of information out of context
- sarcastic or angry tone
- advertisements

EVALUATING MULTIMEDIA

So far, our focus has been on evaluating print and Internet resources. Multimedia resources include graphics, video resources, audio resources, simulations, animations, clip art, photographs, vodcasts, podcasts, and software. These resources can provide valuable information in an interesting delivery format. As with print and Internet resources, however, this type of information must be evaluated critically to determine if it is appropriate, credible, and useful for your purposes.

All information should be evaluated in a similar way, regardless of how it is delivered or presented. Apply the same criteria as you would for a print or an Internet resource:

1. Evaluate the resource.
2. Evaluate the authority.
3. Evaluate the currency of the resource and information.
4. Evaluate the content itself.

Additional criteria for evaluating multimedia resources include the following.

- **FUNCTIONALITY.** How well do multimedia work within the environment in which they are being viewed? For many multimedia choices, technical aspects determine how or if the information can be viewed. If viewing multimedia from a CD-ROM or DVD, the application should work without error on the computer. Multimedia viewed on the Internet should load relatively quickly and should state clearly if any additional plug-ins or software is needed for viewing. For Internet multimedia, viewers often are required to download a special application, such as QuickTime, Java, ActiveX, or Acrobat Reader.

In most cases, these plug-ins are free and easily accessible on the Internet. A good web site has a link to the pages where the software can be downloaded.

▶ **USABILITY.** Usability means that the multimedia are easy to use, or "user friendly." This criterion is especially notable with software, animations, simulations, audio objects, and video objects. Layout should be logical and consistent throughout the object. The navigation should be intuitive and easy to find and follow. Any instructions should be clear and complete. Links should be functional, and if they are not, there should be a mechanism for reporting nonfunctional links to a webmaster.

Multimedia objects should download quickly, even at slower Internet speeds, and downloading instructions should be clear. If the tool is complicated, as with certain software, a Help tool should be available to answer common questions or provide instructions for all actions.

▶ **ACCESSIBILITY.** Many features make a multimedia object accessible to individuals who have various disabilities. An example of a design feature of a web page is an ALT tag for links and images to assist sight-impaired viewers. A complete list of standards for accessible design can be found on the Americans with Disabilities Act web site at www.ada.gov.

? CRITICAL THINKING QUESTION

▶ What kinds of multimedia might be useful in your field? Give several examples of multimedia you might be required to evaluate.

4

● ● ● **success steps for evaluating multimedia resources**

- Evaluate the resource
- Evaluate the authority
- Evaluate the currency
- Evaluate the content
- Evaluate the functionality
- Evaluate the usability
- Evaluate the accessibility

CHAPTER SUMMARY

This chapter summarized how to evaluate information. You learned that information-literate individuals critically analyze information and its sources to ensure that it is useful. You also learned that while evaluating information is based in large part on common sense, several components should be reviewed to assess the quality of the information. These include evaluating the resource, evaluating the authority, and evaluating the currency of the information. Additionally, you learned that evaluating web sites for authority, currency, and content is important to determine if the web site is a credible source of information. Finally, you learned that it is equally as important to evaluate information retrieved from a multimedia source as it is from print and Internet sources.

POINTS TO KEEP IN MIND

In this chapter, several main points were discussed in detail:

- Evaluating information using critical analysis applies to print materials and resources, multimedia resources, and information on the Internet.

- The publication timeline is one of the criteria for evaluating a resource.

- Journals and magazines are common sources of information. These include scholarly journals, trade publications, and popular magazines. Each of these forms has a different purpose and target audience.

- Evaluating the authority means to look critically at the author of the information, as well as the sponsor or owner of the specific resource, such as the publisher or owner of a web site.

- Currency refers to the timeliness of the information. In a print product, this includes the date and edition of the publication. For web sites, the date of the last revision is considered.

▶ When evaluating the content of the information, factors to take into account include the intended audience, the purpose and scope, the objectivity, the accuracy and verifiability, and the overall quality of the content.

▶ In addition to the criteria for evaluating information for print and Internet resources, multimedia adds functionality, usability, and accessibility to the list.

apply it

Find printable activities on the companion web site for this book, accessed through www.cengagebrain.com.

 Activity #1: Information Checklist

GOAL: To review and organize the criteria for evaluating information and information sources and to create a checklist for this evaluation.

STEP 1: Review the various criteria for evaluating information resources and the content.

STEP 2: Develop a checklist to ensure that you complete a thorough evaluation when you conduct your research.

 Activity #2: Information Resource Comparison

GOAL: To emphasize the importance of understanding the type of resource and how to evaluate credibility and timing.

STEP 1: Every person in the group should select one topic and then bring in one example of each of the following types of information sources:

a. a refereed scholarly journal

b. a trade publication

c. a popular magazine

STEP 2: Present your examples to the group and compare the characteristics of each that you would assess as you evaluate the resource.

continued

4

continued

Activity #3: Web Research

GOAL: To develop a full understanding of the various kinds of information found on the Internet.

STEP 1: Conduct an Internet search to find examples of the following types of web sites:

   a. an excellent web page that provides highly credible information

   b. a questionable web page that provides information for which you cannot easily determine the credibility

   c. a web page designed to sell you something

   d. a web page designed to influence your opinion on a controversial issue by using emotion and extreme remarks

   e. a web page designed as a hoax or to mislead purposely the reader for some aim

STEP 2: Print out a copy of each web page, and clearly identify the characteristics that give you clues about the type of information the page provides.

CHECK YOUR UNDERSTANDING

Visit www.cengagebrain.com to see how well you have mastered the material in Chapter 4.

SUGGESTED ITEMS FOR LEARNING PORTFOLIO

Refer to the "Developing Portfolios" section at the beginning of this textbook for more information about learning portfolios.

   ▶ Checklist for Evaluating an Information Resource and Information

   ▶ List of information resources that are useful in your field of study, categorized by type of resources

REFERENCES

American Evaluation Association. (n.d.). *Welcome to the American Evaluation Association*. Retrieved June 13, 2013, from http://www.eval.org/

American Heart Association. (2013). *About us: Our mission*. Retrieved June 13, 2013, from http://www.heart.org/HEARTORG/

4

Cavan Images/Photonica/Getty Images

5

Organizing Information

LEARNING OBJECTIVES

By the end of this chapter, students will achieve the following objectives:

▶ Explain the purpose and importance of effective information organization.

▶ Describe methods of organizing verbal and visual information.

▶ Select and apply an appropriate method for organizing information.

▶ Describe the uses of information and considerations when organizing information for each use.

5

BE IN THE KNOW

Time Management

As you will read in this chapter, the effective organization of the information you have found is critical to properly presenting that information in whatever form (report, proposal, letter, etc.) you choose. But what happens if you, as the organizer of said information, is not organized yourself?

Between school, work, and life in general, you are a busy person. One of the best skills you can learn that will help carry you through life is that of time management. The following are some suggestions for effective time management:

- **Focus on one thing at a time.** Multitasking can dilute your attention and may not be as efficient as concentrating on one task at a time. Complex tasks require concentrated attention.

- **Prioritize your tasks.** There will be times when all tasks simply cannot be completed in the amount of time that you have available. In those cases, prioritizing and completing the most pressing tasks first is necessary.

- **Assess the amount of time each task requires.** Schedule the task when you have the appropriate amount of time for it, and reserve the time for that task. Determine the tasks and task components that are essential and eliminate nonessential elements.

- **Don't procrastinate unenjoyable tasks.** Get them done in a timely manner and reward yourself for the accomplishment. One suggestion is to complete less enjoyable tasks first to get them out of the way. Your motivation to complete them is getting to the more enjoyable tasks.

- **Make a realistic daily schedule and to-do list based on the amount of time needed for each task.** Print out the list each day and refer to it as needed to stay focused on what must be completed. Periodically, check your progress and adjust the schedule as needed. Identify specific times for phone calls, meetings, and other duties. If a task is not completed, move it to your list for the following day.

- **Establish a weekly game plan.** Determine projects and goals on a weekly basis and then break them down into daily tasks.
- **Determine your most productive time of day.** Use that time to complete the most important tasks. Routine tasks should be accomplished during lower-energy periods.

Will you look at the time!

SOLVING INFORMATION PROBLEMS: ORGANIZE THE INFORMATION

Step 4 of the research process involves organization. Many elements contribute to effective organization of information. The goal of your task will define whether you are preparing a proposal, a technical report, or some other type of presentation. Selecting the appropriate document and preparing it in a way that communicates your message and accomplishes your goal are critical to your success.

Once you have determined the appropriate type of document, you must present your information in a logical and coherent manner that holds your audience members' attention and brings them to a logical conclusion. The way in which you organize facts and figures, as well as the format in which they are presented, largely determines the response you will receive.

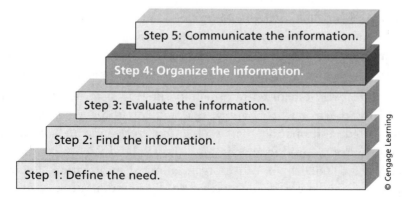

Step 5: Communicate the information.

Step 4: Organize the information.

Step 3: Evaluate the information.

Step 2: Find the information.

Step 1: Define the need.

© Cengage Learning

Research Process Step 4: Organize the Information

This chapter will introduce you to organizational methods, as well as presentations commonly used in professional settings that you may be asked to complete at some time in your career—proposals, technical reports, tables, charts, and multimedia. General concepts of organization will be applied to each, and considerations specific to each of the formats will be discussed. Many of the concepts presented here can be applied to other documents and reports that you may encounter.

THE IMPORTANCE OF EFFECTIVE ORGANIZATION OF INFORMATION

Think of a time when you were attempting to understand a piece of information or a document that was poorly organized. Recall the frustration and difficulty you might have felt as you attempted to sort through and use that information. Compare that situation to a time when you used information that was organized methodically and efficiently. Chances are that you experienced less stress, used your time more efficiently, and completed your task more easily and effectively. The manner in which you organize and present information can have the same effect on your audiences.

Information typically is presented to achieve a goal. For example, a researcher who is applying for a grant is seeking funding to complete his or her research activities. The information the researcher presents in the grant application must convince the funding agency that the research is necessary, beneficial, and cost-effective. As another example, a student is asked to write a position paper on a controversial topic. The student will have to provide background information on the issue, compare various positions on the topic, state his or her position with supporting reasoning and explanation, and draw a conclusion. The goal for each of these projects calls for different organizational strategies.

Effectively organized information allows you to be understood, and for the recipient to apply, question, or utilize what you have presented. Information that is organized and presented effectively contributes to productive communication. Productivity on the job also is facilitated by effective organization of information. Reports, proposals, and other documents that clearly communicate relevant facts contribute to efficient completion of tasks and projects. Well-organized

SELF-ASSESSMENT QUESTIONS

- Based on your experience, what is an example that demonstrates effective organization of information?
- Compare that example with an example of ineffective organization of information. What are the differences between the two situations?
- How did each of these situations affect you?

5

information in professional reports and presentations will contribute to the success of your organization as well as your professional development and advancement.

ORGANIZATIONAL STRATEGIES

You are more likely to be understood when you organize your information and communication effectively. Material that is organized in a logical and meaningful fashion is more readily used and applied than random, disorganized data (Huitt, 2003). By organizing information systematically, you will maximize the opportunity for your audience to receive an accurate message. For example, a criminal justice student who is describing the events leading up to a crime might choose to organize the information chronologically because this type of organization best conveys the sequence of events leading to the crime. If the same student wants to explore the motives for the crime, however, the information might be organized according to possible cause and effect.

As a presenter of information, you have choices in how information is arranged. Huitt (2003) discusses organization of information as it pertains to learning, and Stucker (2006) and Wurman (2000) approach organization of information from an applied perspective. Consider the following organizational strategies based on the work of these researchers.

> **PUT IT TO USE**   Consider the goal you wish to achieve by presenting your information. Organize this information in a way that will logically lead to your goal. Explore *concept mapping* and *mind mapping* by completing an Internet search using these as your search terms. Consider how mind or concept mapping can help you organize you information.

ORGANIZATION BY CATEGORY OR CONCEPT

Separate ideas that combine to produce a concept must be understood individually before their synthesis makes sense. This calls for organization by category or concept. For example, if a student of early childhood education wants to describe a positive classroom environment for kindergarten students, she first might discuss the physical classroom

? CRITICAL THINKING QUESTIONS

- What information in your field would be organized most effectively by concept or category? Would you organize this information using synthesis or analysis strategies? Why?
- Consider a presentation or assignment that you completed recently. How did you implement the concepts? How might you have implemented them further to improve your presentation or assignment?
- Consider an assignment that you currently are completing or will be starting in the near future. How can you implement organization by category or concept to benefit the assignment? Conversely, why might this method not be appropriate for this assignment?

5

environment, types of activities available to the children, characteristics of the teacher, and a schedule appropriate for this age group. Each element of the positive classroom is discussed in terms of its attributes, why these attributes are important for kindergartners, and techniques for developing each attribute in the classroom. She then pulls together the individual elements and describes a typical day in the kindergarten class. The discussion includes how the separate concepts blend and interact to produce a positive classroom environment. Effectively organized information has provided a clear description of each element and enabled the audience to synthesize them into a coherent concept.

Organization by category or concept also is effective when constructing a case to support a premise. Consider the example of a student in a healthcare management class who is involved in a debate over private versus government-sponsored health insurance coverage. In this example the student is promoting government-sponsored health programs. He discusses individual themes such as the financial burden of illness and uninsured individuals, the cost-effectiveness of implementing preventive health measures, and strategies for implementing government-sponsored programs. He supports his statements with reliable data that he has researched and evaluated for credibility. The student then brings together his ideas to provide a convincing case for a government-sponsored health program. In this scenario, well-organized information makes the student's case more compelling. Both of these examples use the synthesis of ideas to create a concept.

A variation on organization by concept is to begin with a major concept and break it down into the elements that form the central idea. Continuing with the example of the early childhood education student, consider that she is presenting information on playground-management strategies. In this example, playground management is the major concept. Within that concept, she might talk about setting behavior expectations appropriate to kindergartners, structuring group activities, and safety considerations. This application of organization by concept uses analysis of a concept by breaking it down into its respective parts.

CHRONOLOGICAL ORGANIZATION

Organization according to time, called chronological organization, is used when the sequence of events influences an outcome. A common example is found in the instructions for assembling something such as

? CRITICAL THINKING QUESTIONS

- What information in your field would be most effectively organized chronologically? How would you include transitional information?
- Consider a presentation or an assignment that you recently completed. How did you implement these concepts? How might you have implemented them further to improve your presentation or assignment?
- Consider an assignment that you are currently completing or will be starting in the near future. How might you implement chronological organization to benefit this assignment? Conversely, why might this organization not be effective for this assignment?

5

a model or a piece of furniture. Information provided out of sequence would lead to failure and frustration. And consider the example of a computer technology student who, in a practical exam, is explaining and demonstrating the steps involved in repairing a computer. To be successful, the steps must be explained and executed in a specific sequence. Likewise, the allied health student who is describing or demonstrating a treatment procedure must organize the information in the proper sequence or the treatment is likely to be ineffective.

Often, chronological organization of information is necessary for a sequence of events to make sense and explain an outcome. Consider how effective your next joke would be if you were to give the punch line first and then tell the details of the joke randomly! The example of the criminology student describing the events leading to a crime provides an example of effectively leading to and explaining an outcome using chronological organization.

Certain information that is organized chronologically involves transition from one phase to the next. In these situations, recipients of the information have to understand the progression between steps or stages. For example, a physical therapist assistant student describing the progression of a patient through treatment must organize treatment steps in sequence and also must clarify the relationship of one phase of treatment to the next.

In another example, the student in a human development class is describing the sequence of development in an infant. The developmental stages must be described sequentially, and the information organized and explained to demonstrate the continuity of development. Each of these cases illustrates the importance of information that explains the relationship between the chronological phases.

HIERARCHICAL ORGANIZATION

Hierarchical organization is used when information is best conveyed in a specific order, such as from most to least important or least complex to most complex. Bloom's taxonomy, which you first read about in Chapter 1, is an example of a hierarchical arrangement beginning with the least complex concepts and progressing to the most complex. Another example is the computer technology student who is describing the process of diagnosing a computer problem. He starts by looking for simple

? CRITICAL THINKING QUESTIONS

- What information in your field would be most effectively organized hierarchically?
- Consider a presentation or an assignment that you recently completed. How did you implement these concepts? How might you have implemented them further to improve your presentation or assignment?
- Consider an assignment that you currently are completing or will be starting in the near future. How might you implement a hierarchical organization to benefit this assignment? Conversely, why might hierarchical organization be ineffective for this assignment?

? CRITICAL THINKING QUESTIONS

- What information in your field would be organized most effectively alphabetically?
- Consider a presentation or assignment that you recently completed. How did you implement these concepts? How might you have implemented them further to improve your presentation or assignment?
- Consider an assignment that you currently are completing or will be starting in the near future. How can you implement an alphabetical organization to benefit the assignment? Conversely, why might it not be appropriate for this assignment?

5

problems, such as a poorly connected cable, and describes progressing to more complex problems, such as examining the processor. A graphic design student uses hierarchical organization when she creates a brochure for a product and lists the various models of the product, beginning with the model that has the fewest features and lowest cost and progressing to the model with the most features and highest cost.

ALPHABETICAL ORGANIZATION

Obvious examples of alphabetical organization are dictionaries and telephone directories. Alphabetical organization is appropriate when the reader knows the information he or she is looking for and must locate it by a keyword. Glossaries and directories are additional examples of situations in which alphabetical organization is effective and appropriate.

In some circumstances, you will be presenting pieces of information as equivalent and nonhierarchical in nature. Presenting the information alphabetically is a method of organization that does not imply any type of order based on any attribute or characteristic. For instance, if you are crediting individuals who contributed to a project, listing them alphabetically avoids the implication that one individual contributed more than another. Or consider the pharmacy technician student who is describing, as part of an assignment, the characteristics

● ● ● **questions to ask to select a method of organizing information**

- What am I trying to accomplish by presenting this information? What is my goal?
- What organizational method best supports my goal?
- Is my information best organized according to ideas or concepts that build to a logical conclusion?
- Is my information best organized according to time or in a sequential order?
- Is my information best organized in a hierarchical fashion to show the relative importance of the information pieces?
- Is my information best located by a keyword or inappropriate for hierarchical organization?

of various medications. By ordering the medications alphabetically, the student avoids any implied hierarchy and makes the list usable because the names of the medications are easily located alphabetically.

Table 5-1 summarizes the strategies discussed for organizing information. Table 5-2 reviews and summarizes Bloom's concepts and suggests how each level of the cognitive domain can be used to guide the information-organization process. Keep these concepts in mind, as the organizational strategies discussed here will be described according to Bloom's cognitive domain.

Organization Method	Description
Organization by Category or Concept	Separate ideas are combined to produce a concept. The synthesis of individual ideas produces a logical conclusion. Conversely, a concept can be presented in its entirety and subsequently analyzed into its parts.
Chronological Organization	Chronological organization is organization according to time. The sequence of events influences or explains an outcome.
Hierarchical Organization	Hierarchical organization is used when information is best conveyed in a specific order. It indicates the relative significance of information, as from most to least important or from least complex to most complex.
Alphabetical Organization	Alphabetical organization is appropriate when the reader knows the information he or she is looking for and has to locate it by a keyword. It is used to organize information in a manner that does not suggest a hierarchy.

© Cengage Learning

Table 5-1   Summary of Information Organization Strategies

Bloom's Level	Definition	Uses
Knowledge	Provides facts and figures	Presenting factual background information, often as a foundation for more complex ideas
Comprehension	Compares, summarizes, shows an understanding of concepts	Providing examples and explanations of facts and background information
Application	Relates an example or a set of rules to an authentic situation	Explaining how something is done; applying a procedure to a set of circumstances
Analysis	Breaks down a concept into its components	Simplifying a complex concept; showing the components of a complex idea
Synthesis	Creates a new idea or concept from single facts or components	Presenting a new idea; explaining how individual elements combine to create a new concept
Evaluation	Makes a judgment about the effectiveness or appropriateness of an idea or concept	Defending or advocating a position or idea; presenting a solution

© Cengage Learning

Table 5-2   Applying Bloom's Taxonomy as a Strategy for Organizing Information

CASE IN POINT: REPORT IT

Read the scenario below. Then, in groups or as a class, discuss the questions at the end.

Anna Hensley graduated from college 6 months ago. Recently she accepted a position as a research assistant for a human resources firm, where her duties include accessing, organizing, and presenting information on hiring trends, salaries, industry growth, and other topics related to the human resources field. She also is responsible for preparing funding proposals for various projects. Anna must be able to locate relevant information, organize it logically into a document appropriate to her purpose, and present it effectively.

During her orientation period she was guided by her supervisor's expertise. Now Anna has received the first major assignment that she is to complete independently. Although she is adept at locating and collecting information that supports her research goals, she is less sure of her ability to organize and present the information effectively. She is concerned about selecting the appropriate type of report or document, what information to include, how to organize it, and how to present it in a way that her audience will understand and that will achieve the project goals.

▶ How familiar are you with various types of documents and reports and their uses?

▶ For each type of document or report, how logically could you organize the information?

▶ How would you go about selecting an organizational plan?

▶ How would you select your presentation method? When would you use a verbal format? When would you use a visual format? When would you consider other media?

▶ If you decide to use a table or chart, how would you present its content logically and clearly?

▶ If you select another presentation medium (such as Microsoft PowerPoint), what considerations would you make during preparation?

PRESENTING INFORMATION EFFECTIVELY

Information can be presented verbally (orally or written), graphically, or through multimedia. Your choice of presentation media depends on several factors including your audience, the type of information you are conveying, and the presentation environment.

Be aware that some standards apply to use of all information regardless of the format in which it is presented. For all formats, keep in mind the following considerations, many of which review information from earlier in this chapter as components of organizing information.

Selecting your presentation medium carefully will maximize the effectiveness of your information.

▶ *Organization of the presentation.* The visual organization of your presentation is as important as the way in which the information itself is structured. For example, written documents must be formatted to maximize legibility. Graphics and multimedia must be easy to see and clearly understand. Electronic information, such as that presented on web pages, must be navigated intuitively.

▶ *Ethical and legal considerations.* All information must be referenced properly and the sources cited. Information must be used in a way that applies information rather than simply repeats someone else's work. Plagiarism is illegal and unethical in all presentation formats. (Plagiarism and appropriate referencing will be addressed in Chapter 6.)

▶ *Credibility considerations.* Information must come from credible, current, and reliable sources. The evaluation methods discussed in Chapters 1 and 4 must be applied to all information used in any presentation.

● ● ● questions to ask to present information effectively

- Who is my audience?
- What is the purpose of my presentation?
- What is the presentation environment?
- Does the organization of my presentation maximize its legibility?
- Are my information sources properly cited and referenced?
- Have I ensured that my information comes from current, credible, and reliable sources?

5

ORGANIZING WRITTEN DOCUMENTS

Written presentations include documents such as reports, proposals, needs assessments, and others. As part of effective organization, written work must be presented professionally and in a manner that reflects the standards of your field.

The first step in creating an effective document or presentation is to organize the information in a way in which you can use it. After you have implemented your research strategy, you are likely to have an extensive amount of information. Organizing the material in a way that is useful to you provides the foundation for creating an effective end product. Consider the following suggestions for organizing the information that you have retrieved. You may find that a combination of these strategies will best meet your needs.

PUT IT TO USE While researching information, implement a method or methods for organizing your data that fits your style and preferences.

▶ *Know the organization strategy you have selected.* Understanding how you are going to arrange your information will allow you to organize your resources accordingly. For example, if you have decided that chronological organization is most appropriate for your topic, you can sort your resources in an accurate sequence. If you are organizing information by concept, you may choose to sort your data into folders labeled for each main idea.

▶ *Use a format that works for you.* Do you find yourself buried in piles of paper on your desk? Do you cringe at the thought of reading documents on the computer screen? Collect your resources in a format that works for you. Some individuals read printed copies more effectively and benefit from taking notes on them, highlighting important points. Other people prefer to read documents electronically and take brief notes as they read from the computer screen. Be aware, though, that some information may be available in only one format, so you will have to be flexible. For example, if some of your material is available only in a book and you prefer the electronic documents, you necessarily will have to adapt your preferred method to that format.

▶ *Use a cataloging system that works for you.* A cataloging system is the system you use to physically organize material. Examples of cataloging systems are note cards, binders, electronic folders, and various types of files. Each has its advantages and shortcomings. For example, individual file folders allow you to easily separate documents into categories that support individual concepts. Your choice will depend on your personal preference and style. Table 5-3 summarizes the advantages and disadvantages of various cataloging systems and gives suggestions for using each.

The manner in which a document is prepared contributes to its organization. Compare a document that uses graphics effectively to a document that uses graphics randomly and haphazardly. Thoughtful and effectively placed graphics add to the clarity and meaning of the document whereas misused graphics can distract and confuse the reader. Consider the following factors when preparing written documents.

▶ *Follow the recommended style.* Guidelines for writing style come from various sources. Style guides such as *The Chicago Manual of Style, Publication Manual of the American Psychological Association (APA)*, and the *Modern Language Association (MLA) Style Manual* provide standards for language use and citation of references. Each profession and field tends to adopt one style consistently. For example, the social science fields generally use the APA style in research papers and journal articles. Preparing and organizing documents in the style used in your field provides readers with a recognized format. Style guides also provide consistent formatting elements such as spacing, margins, treatment of graphics, tables, and charts, and other elements. Consistent formatting allows the reader to recognize and locate information more easily.

▶ *Use language and level of complexity appropriate to your audience.* As much as possible, know who will be reading your finished document or listening to your presentation. For general audiences, use simple language and define terms when necessary. For professional audiences or groups with more advanced knowledge, use more technical language and terminology. Choosing the level of language appropriate to your audience is related closely to selecting an appropriate level of resources for

Cataloging System	Advantages	Disadvantages	Suggested Uses
Note cards	• Convenient for recording one idea or fact per card. • Small size allows opportunity to sort and rearrange information.	• Numerous cards can be difficult to manage.	• Arrange events chronologically. • Arrange information hierarchically. • Arrange information alphabetically. • Elaborate on a single idea or concept per card to effectively organize information.
Binders	• Documents can be stored and reviewed in original form. • All information is kept in one place. • Addition of divider tabs allows efficient organization of information.	• Sorting information by individual facts is more difficult in full document form.	• Create a section of information for each concept or idea.
Electronic folders	• Use of paper is minimized. • Information can be retrieved and reorganized with relative ease.	• May not be readily accessible without a computer. • If documents are bookmarked, will require Internet access.	• Sort information by concept or idea. • Rearrange and duplicate information to meet a different need.
Individual file folders	• Documents can be stored and reviewed in original form. • Information can be easily rearranged as needed and to serve various purposes.	• Can be challenging to keep multiple individual folders together. • Create a separate folder for a designated time period, and organize information chronologically.	• Create a folder for each idea or concept.
Expandable files	• Documents can be stored and reviewed in original form. • Information can be kept in one place.	• Can be bulky.	• Use in ways similar to individual files.
Visual organizers	• Effective for visual and kinesthetic learners. • Information can be easily rearranged. • Provides a view of the "big picture."	• Not easily transported. • May be less effective for verbal learners. • Difficult to include in-depth detail.	• Show relationships between concepts. • Create as a timeline.

© Cengage Learning

Table 5-3   Information Cataloging Systems. Some of the more commonly used techniques for cataloging information are summarized here, and you may be aware of others.

Digital Vision/Getty Images

Keeping information organized as you work is critical to presenting information effectively.

5

the type of project you are completing. For general audiences, you are more likely to use language and organizational strategies based on the less complex levels of Bloom's taxonomy, for example, and with more seasoned professionals, organization based on more advanced levels of the taxonomy is appropriate.

You probably will agree that a presentation for new graduates should be more basic than a presentation for seasoned professionals. New members of a profession tend to need straightforward facts and information as they learn about the field. Facts, examples, and other

? CRITICAL THINKING QUESTIONS

Imagine that you are preparing to give two presentations. One will be for new graduates just getting started in your field, and the other will be for seasoned professionals.

▶ What differences would you make in the two presentations?

▶ How could you use Bloom's taxonomy to organize the information in each of the presentations?

information that provide a foundation for learning are appropriate for individuals who are learning about a field. Based on Bloom's taxonomy, you would organize your information according to the lower levels of the cognitive domain and use the knowledge, comprehension, and possibly application levels.

More advanced members of the profession can be expected to have the foundational knowledge and to be using it to assess situations, solve problems creatively, and evaluate circumstances. For these professionals, you likely would organize information based on the higher levels of Bloom's taxonomy—analysis, synthesis, and evaluation. As might be expected, more experienced professionals are able to use information in a more complex manner. Thus, you can use Bloom's taxonomy to organize information differently, in a way that meets the needs of your audience.

Language use also must be considered in terms of your audience. If you use highly technical language, you probably will lose an audience of people who are inexperienced in your field. Consider the example of a physician explaining a complex medical issue to a patient. Unless the patient is a medical professional with the appropriate background, the physician will have to use language that the patient can understand if he or she is to understand and comply with treatment. Conversely, language that is too simple may not hold the interest of a more knowledgeable audience and may be insulting to their level of expertise. The following are guidelines for organizing a presentation to communicate effectively to a specific audience.

▶ *Organize information from simple to complex.* Organizing information from simple to complex provides a foundation on which the recipient of the information can build more complex concepts. Suppose you are teaching someone to drive. Before starting the ignition, you will provide basic information about the car, including where the various controls are located and activated, how to adjust the mirrors and seat, and basics about steering, turning, and other factors in controlling the car. Next, you might ask the learner to review the information you have provided and repeat what you have described to indicate understanding. All of this is done before asking the new driver to actually drive the car.

After the learner has actually driven the car, you might ask him or her to compare the actual driving experience to what he or she thought it would be like and to consider how this insight will contribute to the learning experience. As the learner practices and further develops driving skills, you will ask him or her to solve problems commonly encountered on the road and to assess his or her progress. By organizing the information from simple to complex, you have led the learner from the basics of driving to being able to problem-solve and to evaluate various driving situations. Table 5-4 illustrates how this example reflects Bloom's taxonomy.

Level in Bloom's Taxonomy	Step of Teaching How to Drive a Car	Explanation
Knowledge	The learner receives basic information about the car, such as where the controls are located, how to adjust the mirrors and seat, and basics about steering, turning, and other factors in controlling the car.	The new driver learns the facts that are foundational to maneuvering the car effectively and safely.
Comprehension	The learner reviews or summarizes the information provided and gives some examples.	The new driver translates the basic knowledge into his or her own words and, in doing so, explains and demonstrates an understanding of the concepts.
Application	The learner actually drives the car.	The new driver puts the newly learned concepts to use.
Analysis	The learner compares the actual driving experience to what he or she thought it would be like.	The new driver compares and contrasts the experience with his or her expectations, and assesses each element of the driving experience.
Synthesis	The learner considers how this insight will contribute to the learning experience.	The new driver integrates what he or she has learned with his or her own ideas and develops new concepts about the driving experience. The learner combines concepts to formulate solutions to problems.
	The learner solves problems commonly encountered on the road.	The new driver integrates what he or she has learned with his or her own ideas and develops new concepts about the driving experience. The learner combines concepts to formulate solutions to problems.
Evaluation	The learner assesses his or her progress.	The new driver compares his or her proficiency to acceptable standards of skill and safety and makes an assessment of the skills he or she needs to develop.

© Cengage Learning

Table 5-4 Simple-to-Complex Organization Related to Bloom's Taxonomy

▶ *Follow conventional language, spelling, and grammar standards.*
Professionals should avoid slang as well as unorthodox spelling
and grammar. Using recognized language standards contributes
to the perception of well-organized information. Imagine that
you were reading a document containing slang from the 1950s
and 1960s. Although you might be entertained and amused,
how seriously would you take the information? Of course,
using an occasional slang word for emphasis can be an effective tool. Generally, however, language should follow standard
guidelines. Guidelines for language conventions, as we said,
can be found in the style guide (APA, MLA, etc.) used in your
field. Finally, you should respect elements of diversity and
incorporate them appropriately in the context of your document or presentation.

▶ *Check for accuracy.* In organizing information, you must
ensure its accuracy to maximize the usefulness of the information and minimize the chances of misquoting sources. Information that is clear and correct contributes to a well-received
document or presentation and supports your credibility as an
information provider.

▶ *Use graphics that are clear and enhance the content of the document.* Thoughtfully selected graphics can enhance the clarity of
information, in contrast to randomly placed graphics, which
detract from your message. When considering the use of graphics in the overall organization of your document or presentation, you first must consider how the graphics mesh with the
written text.

5

PUT IT TO USE   Use Bloom's taxonomy to determine
the appropriate level of complexity of information for
your audience. Generally, audiences with less experience
will benefit from information structured at the lower
levels of the taxonomy, while more experienced audiences
are likely to benefit from information organized at the
higher levels.

Jupiter Images

Graphics should be clearly related to the information in the text, convey an accurate message, and effectively communicate without having to read the text.

ORGANIZING GRAPHICS

Graphics—figures, tables, charts—must be appropriate to the content of your document or presentation and accurately convey the message you are sending. After you have determined where a graphic would be appropriate in your overall organizational plan, you must effectively organize the information represented in the graphic. Any documentation or sources for the data must be included in full. Graphics that contribute to the clarity of your document or presentation have the following characteristics, based on the work of Klass (2002):

▶ *The reader can easily understand the graphic.* The graphic must clearly communicate a message. If the graphic is comparing or explaining data, the type of data must be stated clearly and the relationships among the data illustrated clearly.

▶ *The graphic elaborates on the information in the document or presentation.* There must be a clear relationship between the graphic and the information that you are conveying. For example, if you are comparing two sets of data, a good choice might be a graph that clearly illustrates the differences between the two sets.

5

▶ *The image is selected for its ability to convey an accurate message.* Your choice of a graphic will depend on the type of information you want to convey. For example, a pie chart, which illustrates the relationship of parts to the whole, could be the best way to show the percentages of religious groups represented in the United States. (Examples of commonly used charts, tables, and other graphics and their uses are outlined in the subsequent discussion of "Types of Graphics.")

▶ *A table, chart, or graphic is able to stand alone.* The reader should be able to understand the information presented in a table or chart without referring to the text of the document for additional explanation. The meaning of data represented must be defined clearly. The table or chart should allow the reader to form conclusions from the data.

▶ *A table or chart simplifies information.* A value of tables, charts, and figures is that they simplify information that would be confusing if it were explained only in the text. As an example, review the information in Table 5-4 and imagine how long and convoluted the information could be if it were presented in sentence format. To determine whether the information is best expressed in a table or chart, write out the information in sentences. If this is confusing to read, or if you become frustrated in writing it, chances are that it would be represented best in a table or a graphic. If the information can be expressed effectively in text, though, a graphic may be unnecessary.

▶ *An effective graphic is as simple as possible.* The graphic takes the simplest form that conveys the data accurately. Extraneous colors, lines, and other embellishments can detract from meaningfulness of the data.

▶ *Data are presented in relationship to a context.* Context adds to the meaning of data by showing how the data relate to a standard, category, or other framework. A graphic should provide information that explains the context to which the data relate.

▶ *Pictures or cartoons illustrate ideas in the text.* Some information has more impact when it is conveyed in an image. The political cartoons on the editorial page of the newspaper, for example, generally would not be as entertaining if their message were described in text. Like tables, charts, and other graphics, images (pictures and cartoons) are used most effectively when they simplify a concept or emphasize a point that has been discussed in the text.

success steps for organizing graphics effectively

Organize graphics so:

- the reader can easily understand the graphic,

- the graphic elaborates on the information in the document or presentation,

- the image is selected for its ability to convey an accurate message,

- the table or chart or figure is able to stand alone,

- the table or chart or figure simplifies information,

- the graphic is as simple as possible,

- data are presented in relationship to a context, and

- pictures or cartoons illustrate ideas in the text.

TYPES OF GRAPHICS

Of the many types of graphics that can be used in documents and presentations, each has its advantages for conveying various kinds of information. Consider the following examples of graphics that are available:

- **Bar charts** (also called column charts or histograms) compare data by varying the length of the columns or bars. Bar charts can be drawn vertically or horizontally. Figure 5-1 provides an example of a bar chart. Variations of bar charts include simple column charts, stacked column charts, and 100% stacked bar charts. Electronic programs such as Microsoft Excel allow users to apply 3-D effects, color, labels, and legends to bar charts.

- **Line charts** typically display a trend over time. Typically, time is represented on the X axis of the graph and the element being measured over time is represented on the Y axis. Figure 5-2 is an example of a line chart. In addition to simple line charts, variations on line charts include stacked line charts and 100% stacked

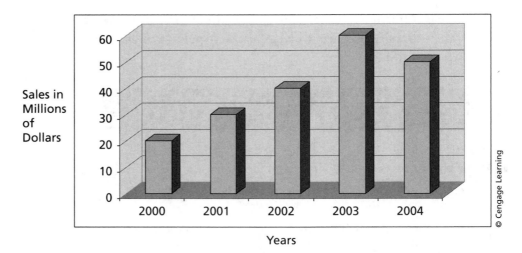

Figure 5-1   Example of a Bar Chart. This bar chart shows the sales of a company over the course of five years. By comparing the length of the bars, the reader can easily compare the sales between years.

line charts. As in the case of bar charts, computer programs such as Microsoft Excel allow the user to apply 3-D effects, along with markers at each data point, color, and legends.

▶ **Pie charts** show the contribution of each value to a total, allowing the reader to understand the relationship of parts to

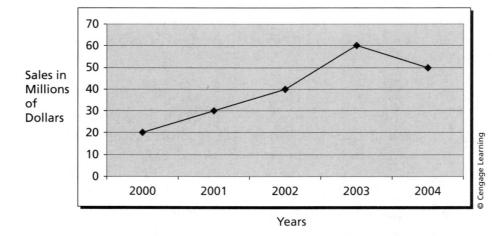

Figure 5-2   Example of a Line Chart. This line chart shows the same sales of a company represented in Figure 5-1. Instead of comparing the length of the bars, the reader can easily track the sales over time. The line connecting the data points clearly indicates the trend over time.

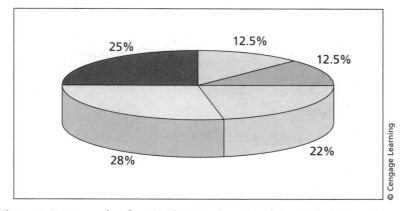

Figure 5-3   Example of a Pie Chart. Each section of this pie chart shows the percentage of various elements that make up the whole. Note that the visual size of each slice accurately represents the numbered percentages noted on the chart. This representation portrays a three-dimensional pie chart, but the same information could be represented in a simple two-dimensional chart.

the whole. An example of a pie chart is provided in Figure 5-3. Types of pie charts include the simple pie chart, an exploded pie chart, and a bar of a pie chart. As with other types of charts, you can add 3-D effects, color, labels, and legends, as desired.

▶ **Scatter charts** (sometimes called scatter plots) compare pairs of values under the same situations. A scatter chart is illustrated in Figure 5-4.

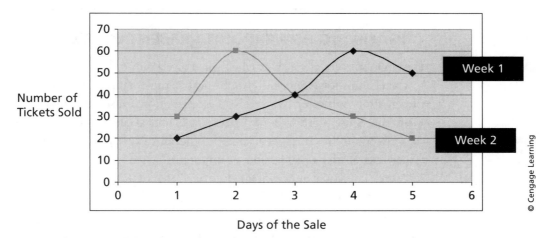

Figure 5-4   Example of a Scatter Chart. This scatter chart compares the number of tickets sold on each day of a two-week period. The lines have been added using Microsoft Excel.

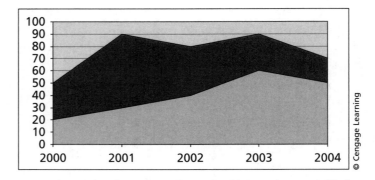

Figure 5-5   **Example of an Area Chart.** On this area chart, each filled area represents a value over time. The peak of each filled area represents the value (on the Y axis) of the categories represented on the X axis.

▶ **Area charts** display trends and their magnitude over time, as illustrated in Figure 5-5. Area charts are similar to line charts, except that the area below the line is filled in. You can add 3-D effects, color, legends, labels, and animation to this type of chart, using Microsoft Excel.

> **PUT IT TO USE**   When using a graphic to present information, select the simplest graphic that communicates your message effectively. For various types of graphs, explore the types of graphs available in Microsoft Excel.

ORGANIZING POWERPOINT PRESENTATIONS

Presentation software such as Microsoft PowerPoint offers opportunities to create impressive and fairly sophisticated presentations. When using presentation software, two levels of organization must be considered. First, the content must be organized in a logical and understandable manner, using the concepts discussed earlier in this chapter. In addition, visual and spatial organization is important when using presentation software. The visual appeal of an electronic presentation has a significant impact on audience members and their response to the presentation.

The suggestions presented here are only general guidelines, and straying from the rules can increase the impact of your presentation at times. For example, black, orange, and lime green typically are not recommended as a good color combination for an entire PowerPoint presentation, but if you use these colors on one slide that refers to the pop culture of the 1960s, they can emphasize your message. Good judgment in considering your topic, audience, and other factors is always essential to creating effective presentations. Consider the following recommendations for creating an effective PowerPoint presentation (Montecino, 1999).

▶ *Select colors thoughtfully.* Color choice can have a significant effect on how viewers receive your presentation. For example, text that is difficult to read because of low contrast with the background may cause your viewers to "tune out" your presentation because it is too difficult to follow. Keep in mind the following points about color in your presentations.

- Select color combinations that provide enough contrast to facilitate reading but are not so high-contrast that they become distracting. Select colors that promote legibility.

- Avoid colors that clash or form an unusual combination. Unorthodox color combinations can be effective if used sparingly and to support a specific theme but should not be used consistently or for an entire presentation.

- Review Figure 5-6 for various examples of effective color choices.

© Cengage Learning

Slide 1: Low-contrast colors are difficult to read.

Figure 5-6   Examples of Use of Color in PowerPoint. Effective PowerPoint slides should use basic colors with enough contrast for viewers to see the slide elements clearly. These examples show how color can be used on slides to advantage or disadvantage.

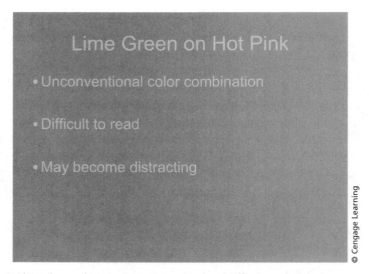

Slide 2: This color combination is unconventional and difficult to read.

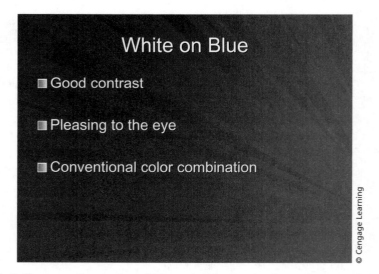

Slide 3: The conventional colors of blue and white are pleasing to the eye and are easily read.

Figure 5-6   (*Continued*)

▶ *Use legible fonts.* The text in a presentation must be legible to all members of the audience, yet not overwhelming. To maximize legibility, consider font size and style. Figure 5-7 provides examples.

  • The recommended font size in a presentation is 22–48 points. Smaller font sizes become difficult to read, and larger font sizes may become overwhelming and be difficult to fit on the slide.

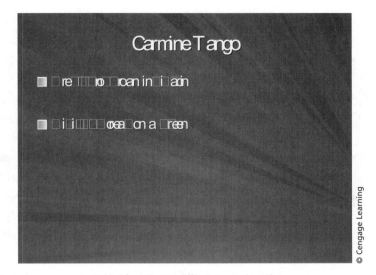

Slide 1 shows an embellished font that is difficult to read on the screen.

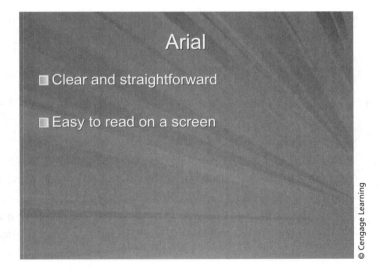

Slide 2 shows a plain font that is easily read on the screen.

Figure 5-7   Examples of Fonts in PowerPoint. Compare Slide 1 with Slide 2, which are different fonts of the same size.

- Fonts should be of a standard and plain style, such as Arial or Times Roman. Intricate and embellished fonts are difficult to read on a screen.

▶ *Present information clearly and concisely.* Slides are only one part of the overall presentation. In addition, you will be explaining and possibly demonstrating the main points represented on the slides. Therefore, you should consider the slides as a supplement to guide viewers through the information you are presenting. To use the slides effectively, consider the following recommendations:

- Set a limit of six lines per slide and six words per line. Capture the main idea, and state it succinctly. Expand on each idea orally.

- Use phrases versus sentences. Again, these are main ideas to guide the viewer. Your explanation will provide the details.

- Use a larger font to state main ideas. PowerPoint automatically adjusts the font size as the levels of text decrease. Keeping that in mind, state the main idea on the higher levels of the PowerPoint outline and supporting ideas underneath. The main idea will be in larger font and the supporting ideas in smaller font.

- Limit punctuation and avoid abbreviations that might be unclear to viewers.

- Do not use all capitals or all lowercase letters. Do use conventional grammar rules.

▶ *Create visual appeal.* The general organization and appearance of your presentation have an impact on your audience. The following are suggestions for creating an effective and professional presentation.

- Select a plain or simple background that does not compete with your message. A solid color or a watermark background that supports your theme is appropriate. Bold and busy backgrounds make the text difficult to read and detract from your message.

- Avoid distracting slide transitions, text appearances, and sounds. If you do choose to use one of the custom features available in PowerPoint, select one that is subtle and that is consistent with the tone and message of your presentation.

- Be consistent. If you do choose to use a custom feature, use it throughout the presentation.

- As with written documents, use graphics only if they support the text and the theme of the presentation. Limit graphics to one or two per slide.

5

? CRITICAL THINKING QUESTIONS

▶ What is the best PowerPoint presentation you have seen? What made it effective?

▶ What is the worst PowerPoint presentation you have seen? Why was it ineffective?

> **PUT IT TO USE**   Watch your PowerPoint presentation yourself before presenting to an audience. Evaluate it for legibility, clarity, and visual appeal. View the presentation from various perspectives to ensure that it is clearly visible from all vantage points.

PREZI: THE ZOOMING PRESENTATION EDITOR

Although PowerPoint is the most popular presentation software, there are alternatives that can make your presentations more distinct. One of these is Prezi, which you can access in a free and basic version at www.prezi.com. Unlike a PowerPoint presentation that contains many slides, a Prezi presentation consists of one slide that contains all of your text and graphics. On that one slide you can focus your viewer's attention wherever you wish. You can move the focus of attention up, down, left, or right from topic to topic, called *panning*. Or you can also move the focus in and out from the topics and details, called *zooming*. Panning and zooming with Prezi can make your presentations stand out and be more effective, but you must avoid common mistakes.

- *Use panning to show relationships between topics.* Arrange your topics on the slide in a way that illustrates your point. For example, if you are telling a story or describing an event, you may wish to place your topics in a line from left to right to show their sequence. Or you may place them in a list from top to bottom to indicate importance.

- *Use grouping to avoid panning too much.* Quickly panning from one side of your presentation to the other can be distracting to your viewers, even disorienting. To avoid panning too much, place related topics fairly close to each other in groups.

- *Use zooming to show relationships between a topic and its supporting details.* PowerPoint presentations usually list the topic in the title and the details in bullets below on the same slide. Prezi allows you to focus first on the topic, zoom in to view the details, and then zoom in further to see more details if you wish.

5

▶ *Use layering to make zooming more effective.* When viewing a topic, make sure that the details are close to the topic, yet not quite big enough to be read. Zoom in to let your viewers read the details when you are ready. This technique, called *layering*, helps your viewers to focus first on the topic and then on the details while maintaining the connection between them.

OTHER PRESENTATION SOFTWARE

While PowerPoint is considered the standard bearer of presentation software and Prezi is continuing to gain acceptance, there is other software available with which you may come into contact (and therefore will need to become proficient at) in the workplace.

▶ **GoAnimate.** GoAnimate is a do-it-yourself animated video web site. And while the product is not considered strictly presentation software, it has significant business applications. One of the best features is that it allows the user to concentrate on the narrative, which can help in selling a product or a concept to others. There is an extensive content library where you can choose (and manipulate) characters, backgrounds, and other information to make a customized video in minutes. The finished product can then be downloaded, shared, or published on YouTube or Facebook.

▶ **Google Docs.** Google Docs is free and can be accessed if you have a Google account. Presentations can be customized with text, images, videos, or imported slides. Google Docs utilizes distributed (cloud) computing, so documents can be shared with other people. This is especially helpful if you are working on a group project. The final presentation can be downloaded as a PowerPoint file or embedded or shared through a link.

▶ **SlideSnack.** SlideSnack is an online presentation sharing tool that allows you to upload a presentation (such as PowerPoint, Keynote, or Word) as a .pdf file. From there you can create a *slidecast,* which is presentation plus voice. The presentation can then be shared over any social media site or downloaded as video and distributed over YouTube, Vimeo, or other video sharing service (Hung, 2013).

5

SELF-ASSESSMENT QUESTIONS

- How proficient do you think you are using PowerPoint?
- What features do you think might make Prezi the more desirable presentation software to use?
- What other uses might you find for Google Docs?

APPLICATION AND USES OF ORGANIZED INFORMATION

Organized information has several standard uses in the professional world. Proposals, grants, and technical reports are standard documents that are common to many fields. Each has a standard format and uses information in specific ways. Understanding how each report or document uses various types of information will maximize your effectiveness in preparing or reviewing these documents. You may encounter other types and applications of information in the workplace. Proposals, grants, and technical reports are covered here.

PUT IT TO USE Parts of the following formats for professional papers also can apply to assignments that you complete in school. Although there is no standard structure for school assignments, relevant parts of the following standard report formats can be incorporated into your assignments based on your instructor's requirements. Select those that support your assignment goals, and use them as your guidelines.

Roy Mehta/Riser/Getty Images

Using a standard format for thoughtful preparation of grants, proposals, and technical reports maximizes the effectiveness of your presentation.

5

PROPOSALS AND GRANTS

Proposals typically are written to suggest a program or an action. Grants are written to obtain funding for research or a project. Proposals and grants are covered together here, as their organization and the information they contain are similar. Specific elements of a grant or proposal will vary depending on the situation. General components and the information contained in each are presented here. The components used as an example here are based on guidelines from the *Catalog of Federal Domestic Assistance* (n.d.).

▶ *Summary:* Typically, the Summary of a proposal is brief (several paragraphs) and provides an overview of the proposed project. Because a summary is the first page of a proposal, it makes the first impression. Therefore, effective organization of information and presentation of the primary objectives of the project are critical.

▶ *Introduction:* The Introduction in a proposal is its foundation and plays a significant role in establishing your credibility. The introduction provides general information about participants in the project, the organization, organizational goals, and a history of the organization's activities. Use Bloom's *knowledge* level of the cognitive domain to organize the introduction.

▶ *Statement of Problem and Purpose:* This statement clearly describes the problem or issue being addressed, as well as the benefits the program will provide. Other issues that typically are addressed in this section include a brief history of the problem, current programs that address it, and how the current proposal supplements these programs. Also important is to present alternatives for continuing the program when current funding is depleted. Bloom's stage of *analysis* and critical thinking skills are applied in this phase.

▶ *Objectives:* The Objectives portion states what the project is intended to achieve and the methods that will be used to meet the goals. Goals must be measurable and realistic, and the project will be evaluated based on how effectively the stated goals are met. Creating feasible and meaningful goals requires the synthesis of needs, reality, and creative thinking and ideas.

▶ *Action Plan:* The Action Plan in the proposal relies heavily on Bloom's level of *synthesis*. This plan outlines the sequence of activities that will lead to achievement of the goals. Graphics such as a flowchart or a table can be used to effectively explain the sequence of project events.

▶ *Evaluation:* The Evaluation phase of a project covers evaluation of the final product as well as the process leading to it. Projects typically are evaluated on how well they met the objectives and goals, how closely the plans were followed, and how the project met the needs stated at the beginning of the project. Bloom's *evaluation* stage from the cognitive domain is a way to think about organizing information for this last stage of a proposal.

TECHNICAL REPORTS

Technical reports are common in the workplace, to communicate the results of a project or research. Technical reports typically contain the following elements and are organized accordingly (Sherman, 1996), with some variation, depending on your situation.

▶ *Title:* The title should be concise, yet describe the content of the report.

▶ *Author information:* The author's name, title, professional affiliation, and contact information should be provided.

▶ *Abstract:* The abstract is a brief yet thorough overview of the report's contents. The abstract summarizes the findings and results and can be used as a concise version of the entire paper. Writing an effective abstract requires strong analysis and synthesis skills.

▶ *Keywords:* The keywords provide parameters of the report and may be used to search for additional information on the topic.

▶ *Body of the report:* The body of the report contains all the relevant information. Depending on the type of information, the written body of the report can be organized in a variety of ways, as described in this chapter. For example, a research project might be organized chronologically. The body of the report requires skills related to Bloom's levels of *application*, *analysis*, and *synthesis* as you explain what you did, your findings, your interpretations, and explanation of new ideas that emerge from your work.

5

▶ *Acknowledgements:* Here, you recognize and express appreciation to individuals who helped or supported you in your project.

▶ *References:* The sources referred to are documented according to the guidelines in the recommended style book.

▶ *Appendices:* Documents that support your report but did not flow with the body of the report are included as appendices. Appendices should be referenced in the text according to your style book.

> **PUT IT TO USE**   If you are required to develop a specialized report, follow the guidelines provided to you. Additional information may be found online by conducting a search using as your search term the type of report you are doing.

CHAPTER SUMMARY

In Chapter 5 you learned the importance of organizing information that conveys your message effectively to your specific audience. To do so, you learned that information must be prepared effectively, using methods such as alphabetical, hierarchical, or others. The method selected depends on the type of information. In addition, the presentation format must be appropriate for the audience and type of information and may include visual organizers, various types of reports, or other formats.

POINTS TO KEEP IN MIND

▶ Effective organization of information is a critical part of information literacy.

▶ Effective organization of information, both in the preparation and presentation phases, is essential to your credibility.

▶ Information should be organized and presented according to its type, your goal, and the intended audience.

apply it

Find printable activities on the companion web site for this book, accessed through www.cengagebrain.com.

 Activity #1: Creating a Visual Organizer

GOAL: *To create and use a visual organizer to organize information.*

STEP 1: Select a topic for which you would like to organize information. The topic should be fairly complex, and you should have a genuine need to organize the information related to the topic.

STEP 2: Research visual organizers on the Internet. Suggested search terms are "visual organizers" and "concept maps."

STEP 3: Select a visual organizer that suits your needs and learning style. Use it to organize the information related to your topic. You may want to try several organizers to see which is most helpful to you.

 Activity #2: Selecting the Best Way to Present Data

GOAL: *To select the most effective presentation methods for various types of information.*

STEP 1: Distribute three small index cards to each group member. Ask each group member to record one type of data on each of the cards. The data should be representative of an aspect of your field.

STEP 2: Randomly select from the completed cards. As a group, decide which graphic would best convey the information. Support your choice with a rationale.

STEP 3: Create the graphic you have chosen. Make sure that it meets the criteria for an effective graphic. Decide on the type of graphic, color choice, added effects, labels and legends, and so forth. Explain how your choices enhance the presentation of the information.

STEP 4: Complete as many versions of steps 2 and 3 as possible.

continued

5

continued

Activity #3: Creating a PowerPoint Presentation

GOAL: To apply suggested practices for creating an effective PowerPoint presentation.

STEP 1: Select a topic that is of interest to you and that you would like to present in a PowerPoint presentation.

STEP 2: Create a PowerPoint presentation on your topic according to the guidelines recommended in this chapter. Seek additional information if needed.

STEP 3: Present your PowerPoint slides to an audience. Ask viewers to give a constructive critique of your work.

Activity #4: Web Page Exploration

GOAL: To develop an awareness of effective web page design and organization.

STEP 1: Review as many web pages as possible related to a topic of interest.

STEP 2: Evaluate each web site according to the criteria listed in the chapter. Print the page, and record your observations directly on the page.

STEP 3: Review your observations and determine which sites were appealing and why. Compile a reference of web page design tips and ideas that you can use in the future.

CHECK YOUR UNDERSTANDING

Visit www.cengagebrain.com to see how well you have mastered the material in Chapter 5.

SUGGESTED ITEMS FOR LEARNING PORTFOLIO

Refer to the "Developing Portfolios" section at the beginning of this textbook for more information on learning portfolios.

REFERENCES

Catalog of Federal Domestic Assistance. (n.d.). *Developing and writing a grant proposal.* Retrieved June 17, 2013, from https://www.cfda.gov/?static=grants&s=generalinfo&mode=list&tab=list&tabmode=list

Huitt, W. (2003). The information processing approach to cognition. *Educational Psychology Interactive.* Valdosta, GA: Valdosta State University. Retrieved June 17, 2013, from http://www.edpsycinteractive.org/topics/cognition/infoproc.html

Hung, A. (2013). *The 6 best business presentation software alternatives to PowerPoint.* Retrieved June 17, 2013, from http://goanimate.com/video-maker-tips/6-best-business-presentation-software-and-powerpoint-alternatives/

Klass, G. (2002). *Presenting data: Tabular and graphic display of social indicators—constructing good tables.* Retrieved June 17, 2013, from http://lilt.ilstu.edu/gmklass/pos138/datadisplay/sections/goodtables.htm

Montecino, V. (1999). *Creating an effective PowerPoint presentation.* Retrieved June 17, 2013, from http://mason.gmu.edu/~montecin/powerpoint.html

Sherman, A. (1996). *Some advice on writing a technical report.* Retrieved June 17, 2013, from http://www.csee.umbc.edu/~sherman/Courses/documents/TR_how_to.html

Stucker, C. (2006). *Organizing information the way people use it.* EzineArticles.com. Retrieved June 17, 2013, from http://ezinearticles.com/?Organizing-Information-the-Way-People-Use-It&id=113311

Wurman, R. S. (2000). LATCH: *The five ultimate hattracks.* Retrieved June 17, 2013, from http://www.informit.com/articles/article.aspx?p=130881&seqNum=6

Legal and Ethical Issues Related to Information

LEARNING OBJECTIVES

By the end of this chapter, students will achieve the following objectives:

▶ Explain how privacy and security can be breached and protected in both print and electronic environments.

▶ Define and describe intellectual property, copyright, and fair use of copyrighted material and how they relate to using information legally and ethically.

▶ Define plagiarism and discuss ways to avoid plagiarizing another's work.

▶ Explain how to cite various information sources.

▶ Describe the importance of information literacy in the workplace.

BE IN THE KNOW

Teamwork

You may have heard the expression "There is no *I* in team." While this statement is both literally and figuratively true, there are several "I" statements of which you should be aware as they pertain to being a successful team member in both the classroom and the workplace. As you will read later on in this chapter, employers place high value on an employee's ability to be a fully participative member of a team and the importance of and its relationship to information literacy.

Consider the following points. Read them and put yourself in a team situation. Do you agree with these statements as they apply to you? What actions might you take to make yourself a better team member?

- *I* need to be accountable to my team members to complete the work I have been assigned.

- *I* am as valued as a team member as anyone else on the team.

- *I* value the contributions of all team members.

- *I* fully participate in discussions and decisions that affect the outcome of the project.

- *I* am a team leader and other team members look to me to fill that role.

- *I* weigh all suggestions equally before coming to a conclusion.

- *I* care about the success of the project as much for my team members as I do for myself.

- *I* meet or exceed deadlines and provide quality work that positively affects that outcome of the project.

- *I* voice my opinions and concerns to the team in order to make the project as successful as possible.

- *I* recognize that different team members bring different skills to the team.

What other "I" statements can you think of as they relate to being a successful team member? GO TEAM!

SOLVING INFORMATION PROBLEMS: COMMUNICATE THE INFORMATION

As we have discussed so far, an information-literate individual knows how to define the need for research, find the information in the library or on the Internet, evaluate the information, and organize the information. The last critical component of information literacy is the ability to use information legally and ethically and communicate it effectively to others—Step 5 in the research process. Legal and ethical aspects of information include the concepts of intellectual property, copyright, plagiarism, and fair use. Additional legal and ethical considerations involve privacy and security issues when communicating information.

This chapter addresses these aspects of communicating the information found during the research process. It is not meant to provide legal counsel or advice but is intended only to discuss the types of issues that you, as an information-literate professional, should consider.

Commercial Eye/Iconica/Getty Images

In face-to-face situations, people both see and hear you.

6

INTELLECTUAL PROPERTY

Intellectual property refers to anything created by the mind, such as literary works (books, poems, essays), artwork (drawings, paintings), inventions, ideas, logos or symbols, names, designs, and images or photographs. In general, the concept of intellectual property treats anything created by the mind (or intellect) the same as any material property and gives to owners of intellectual property rights similar to those of material property owners. When conducting research and using information, then, the intellectual property of others, or things others have thought of, must be respected. Likewise, if you create something, your own creation becomes your intellectual property that others must respect.

The two major areas of intellectual property are industrial property and copyright. Industrial property refers to intellectual property created in the line of conducting business or for business purposes, such as inventions, trademarks, and industrial and business designs. An invention is any idea or concept that is new, useful, and not obvious. A patent is a legal protection of the invention and gives the inventor exclusive rights to develop and sell the invention commercially to make a profit for a designated period of time. An inventor must apply for and receive a patent. A trademark is a legal protection by which businesses distinguish their products and services from one another, through logos, names, symbols, or other identifying elements, and retain the rights to use the element exclusively in the

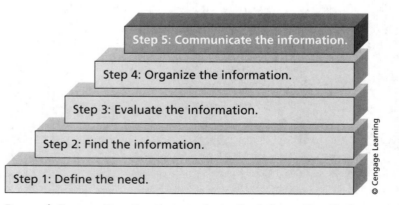

Research Process Step 5:   Communicate the Information. The last step of a research project should be to effectively communicate the information.

course of their business. Industrial design rights protect the aesthetics or appearance, design, or style of the originator.

Copyright protects other forms of intellectual property, such as literary works, artwork, music, audio and video productions, photographs, and newspaper articles. All of these protections of intellectual property can be bought, sold, and transferred or licensed to third parties. The purpose of intellectual-property protection laws is to encourage creation and innovation for the public good by protecting the producing individuals, businesses, and organizations from exploitation. Other types of intellectual property apply to specific purposes, such as materials related to geographical indication, personality rights, plant breeders' rights, trade secrets, and others. Most relevant to the discussion in this chapter is copyright and its implications in the use and communication of information.

SELF-ASSESSMENT QUESTIONS

- What intellectual property have you created yourself that you would not like others to use without your permission?
- How would you feel if other people were to present your intellectual creations as their own? Write down your feelings.

COPYRIGHT

Copyright reflects the rights given to creators of some forms of expressions of intellectual property, such as literary and artistic works. Copyrights are protected by copyright laws. Ideas are not copyrighted; only the expression of those ideas in some documented format can be copyrighted. Ideas in the form of procedures, methods, facts, techniques, styles, and mathematical concepts cannot be copyrighted. Figure 6-1 provides examples of expressions covered by copyright law.

▪ novels	▪ films
▪ poems	▪ paintings
▪ plays	▪ drawings
▪ reference works	▪ photographs
▪ articles in periodicals	▪ sculptures
▪ computer programs	▪ architecture
▪ databases	▪ advertisements
▪ musical compositions	▪ maps
▪ choreography	▪ technical drawings
▪ applets	▪ songs
▪ Web pages	▪ images

© Cengage Learning

Figure 6-1   Examples of Copyrighted Materials

6

The goal of a copyright is to protect the original creators of the work (and their heirs). Copyright assures that the original creator of the work can do with the work whatever he or she wants. The original creators have the right to authorize someone else to use the work, prohibit others from using their work, or sell their copyright to someone else. This means that they can give up their rights (usually for a negotiated fee) to someone else, who then becomes the copyright owner. This new owner becomes protected by copyright law, as was the original owner.

Copyright law is founded in the Intellectual Property Clause of the U.S. Constitution, initially enacted as the Copyright Act of 1790 (Patry, 1994, 2000). The Copyright Act of 1976 is the basis of current copyright law (United States Code, 2003). Advances in technology and the Internet result in the law being revised continually to reflect current needs and issues. The information-literate professional stays updated on changes in the law that affects the use of information.

Copyright law regulates more than just "copying" the work. It also controls translating the material into another language, performing the material (as in a play), copying electronic versions of a work (as in music or movie CD or DVD), and broadcasting it (on radio, TV, or over the Internet). In short, copyright covers reproducing a work in any way. Copyright laws protect creators of original works by assuring that they receive their due recognition and economic rewards associated with their creation.

Once an individual or a group creates an original work, this work is considered to be copyrighted simply by its existence. Although copyright is not dependent upon registration, creators of original material can document their ownership by registering a work with the United States Copyright Office. The copyright symbol © is used to identify a copyrighted work. Copyright protection is documented, for a fee, to the originator of the expression for a specified time limit, such as life of the originator plus several years to allow the originator's heirs the benefit of gaining benefit from the copyrighted work (University System of Georgia Board of Regents, n.d. [a]). Documenting a copyright protects the owner of the work by allowing him or her to sue another individual who uses the work without appropriate permission. The exact copyright terms can be complicated and depend on several factors, including when the work was published and created.

When a copyright expires, the work is transferred into the public domain. The time after which a copyright expires depends on the type of work, its publication date, and other factors. When the work moves to the public domain, it no longer is protected by copyright and anyone can use it. Information-literate individuals ensure that they do not have to obtain permission to use originally copyrighted materials by checking with the United States Copyright Office to get a specific copyright expiration date for the material in question. And regardless of copyright status, it is courteous and professional to credit the original creator (University System of Georgia Board of Regents, n.d. [b]).

Fair use means that in some cases you can copy and distribute copyrighted materials without permission from or payment to the copyright holder. In general, fair use allows some limited copyrighted materials for educational, research, and other purposes. Fair-use laws are complicated and not defined clearly. Information-literate individuals seek clarification of the law when they are uncertain.

PLAGIARISM

Using someone else's original work without acknowledging the original creator is termed plagiarism. The work can be an idea, actual language, or some other original material. Plagiarism is a growing problem in educational and professional settings, and information-literate individuals take care to avoid this unethical and illegal practice.

Examples of plagiarism are:

- copying another person's work and submitting it as your own
- presenting work completed by someone else as their own
- taking an idea from someone else and submitting it as your own
- copying text into an original document without indicating the text with quotation marks or correctly acknowledging the original creator of the work
- paraphrasing someone else's work too closely and submitting it as your own

6

- writing down words spoken by someone else in a face-to-face, telephone, or electronic discussion and submitting them as your own without acknowledging the original source
- copying diagrams, photographs, images, charts, tables, clip art, and similar items as your own without obtaining permission and giving proper credit
- reusing any media that is in electronic form, such as audio files, video files, applets, and software programs, without obtaining permission and giving proper credit to the original creator

Regardless of the type of material, if the work of others is presented without giving them proper credit or citing the source of the work properly, this constitutes plagiarism.

You do not have to document anything that is your original creation or idea. Examples of things you do not have to document are:

- your own experiences, observations, insights, thoughts, and conclusions
- your own results from personal observation of an experiment or study
- your own artistic or literary creations such as prose, poems, diagrams, artwork, audio recordings, video recordings, and photographs
- facts that are generally accepted as being true
- common knowledge or observations considered to be common sense
- historical events, myths, and legends

STRATEGIES FOR AVOIDING PLAGIARISM

To avoid plagiarizing someone else's information, several strategies are outlined as follows:

- *Quote.* Using another's exact words is acceptable, but you must copy the exact words, use quotation marks around the quoted words, and cite the source properly. Quotation marks should be used whether the copied words are spoken or written. When adding your own words to quoted text, you must put your words in brackets to distinguish them from the quoted material. Adding your own words is necessary sometimes to put the quote in context or to fill in missing words so the entire message can be understood more easily.

▶ *Paraphrase.* Paraphrasing means rephrasing the words of someone else. It is acceptable as long as the meaning is not changed and the originator is credited properly with a citation. The paraphrase must be accurate, and the source properly cited. Paraphrasing involves more than rearranging the order of words or changing minor elements of a passage. Read the original material and, without looking at it, rewrite the content using your own words. If you have to intersperse exact phrases from the original, place these words within quotation marks. The paraphrase is followed by a statement giving credit to the original author. An example of a paraphrase is:

> According to Smith, when children eat too much sugar, they display abnormal behavior for several minutes and then show significant signs of fatigue and irritation.

▶ *Summarize.* Summarizing requires condensing a significant amount of someone else's work into a shorter statement or paragraph. As is the case with paraphrasing, this is acceptable as long as the meaning is not changed and the originator is given proper credit with a citation. To accomplish this, read the original information and then try to condense the content without looking. If you have used any exact text, place it within quotation marks. Also, place quotation marks around any special words taken from the original text.

▶ *Take effective notes.* To reduce the likelihood of plagiarism, it is a good idea to take careful notes so you can remember exactly which ideas are yours and which are someone else's ideas. One way to keep track is to develop a note-taking strategy that includes a notation or symbol for your idea (such as *MINE*) and a notation or symbol for the ideas of the author of the work (such as *AU*). Put all direct quotes in quotation marks. When you take notes, designate *AU* next to facts, quotes (with quotation marks), paraphrased sentences, and summaries of

6

the author's work. When you write down your own insights and thoughts, use *MINE* (or whatever designation you choose). And be sure to clearly label the source of the information on each page of your notes.

▶ *Save your work.* You can take several measures to maintain the security of your own work. To prevent others from plagiarizing your work, keep copies of your draft work in separate files. For example, rather than revising your original file, save the first draft as draft 1, your second draft as draft 2, and so forth. This will be a reminder that you actually did the work yourself. Save copies of your files in separate places, and make at least one hard copy of your work. Do not allow others to access your computer files.

You can protect your computer and original work by saving documents as protected files that require a password for access. Use the search feature on the "Help" menu to learn the steps for creating a password to protect your documents, using your particular software. There is an option to password-protect the document. Of course, you will have to remember the password so you can open your file. This procedure works in most Microsoft Office applications. Other applications have similar features.

▶ *Use plagiarism detection software.* The advent of the Internet has made plagiarism easier than ever. Cyber-plagiarism, as it is known, has seen a dramatic rise in recent years, especially by students and content writers (bloggers, writers, and other professionals). Schools, colleges, and universities now routinely check for plagiarism using plagiarism-detection software, such as Turnitin. In addition, content plagiarized from web sites usually can be identified easily by performing a search using the first line of the material as the search term, which pulls up the document for review. You can avoid a costly mistake by downloading free software that will detect any plagiarism in your work. An information-literate person knows that unintentional plagiarism is still plagiarism.

▶ *Manage your time.* Plan your studying and assignments so that you have time to plan, research, and write your work effectively. Leave time to read and write with careful attention

6

to citing sources and representing other authors' works in an acceptable manner.

▶ *Read and rewrite.* An effective way to avoid plagiarizing is to read the original source, put it away, and complete your writing based on your reading. When your writing is complete, return to the original work and check your facts for accuracy. Cite references appropriately.

▶ *Apply the information.* Discuss the information you are using in the context of your assignment. Expand on ideas. Apply the information in a unique way to the topic at hand. Refer to the original thought or fact, but apply it creatively to your project using your own original ideas.

▶ *Cite your sources appropriately.* Sources should be referenced in the text as well as in the reference list. There are several acceptable styles of source citation and reference, and you should follow the style prescribed by your instructor.

In addition to upholding your own responsibility for being honest, it is important to participate in helping to make your learning environment one of high integrity. Honest students need to report any possible cheating and plagiarism that may be occurring. Personally confronting a classmate may or may not be an option, but reporting the episode is critical so that the situation can be properly addressed.

PUT IT TO USE There should be no difference when considering the intellectual property rights for electronic sources and other resources. The same consideration should be given to intellectual property found on the Internet as with any other information source.

POTENTIAL CONSEQUENCES OF PLAGIARIZING

Plagiarizing another's work and getting caught for doing so comes with dire consequences. If you are in the workforce, the chances of getting fired, or at least being formally warned and written up in your personnel file, are very real.

6

Being accused of plagiarizing while in school is no less consequential. All institutions of higher learning regard cheating and plagiarism very seriously. Academic policies and procedures clearly spell out rules about academic honesty and integrity, and schools place this information in college catalogs and online on the school's web site.

Oftentimes course syllabi will address the school's use of Turnitin or other plagiarism detection software as a standard operating procedure. As reading and adhering to syllabi is a course requirement, the mention of the use of such software by the institution puts you on further notice that plagiarism will not be tolerated.

The information-literate person recognizes what constitutes plagiarism and the resulting penalties that follow. Be sure you are that person.

CITING INFORMATION SOURCES

As discussed, to avoid plagiarism and infringement on someone else's intellectual property, you will have to properly cite and document the sources of information in your materials. Even if you do not quote or paraphrase the source directly, if the source contributed significantly to your document, you should cite it properly. In addition to crediting the author appropriately, proper citation allows the reader or viewer of your material to go to your sources to obtain additional information or verify your facts. It also shows that you actually conducted sound research rather than randomly providing or fabricating information.

There are many acceptable ways to cite information sources in your writing. Methods for writing citations and reference lists are available in guidelines contained in writing style guides. These style guides prescribe exact formats for writing, punctuating, referencing sources within text, and citing sources in reference areas and are revised and updated regularly. Many professions, businesses, and academic institutions prefer or require use of one style over another, and some publishers specify the style you are to use. You should become familiar with the style and follow it consistently.

Common style guides and examples of citations according to each are outlined below. Each of these guides specifies exactly how various types of citations are to be structured, including punctuation and use of italics, and how the elements are ordered. The style guides give specific styles for the many different types of resources—books, chapters in books, journals, articles in journals, magazines and magazine articles, newspapers and newspaper articles, review articles, online resources, web sites, and most other sources of information. Examples of specific styles are as follows.

APA STYLE

The *Publication Manual of the American Psychological Association* (www.apastyle.org) is the style prescribed by the American Psychological Association (APA). This style typically is used in the fields of psychology, health, and social sciences:

Publication Manual of the American Psychological Association, 6th ed. (2009). Washington, DC: American Psychological Association.

Correct APA style for citation of a book, ebook, or chapters with one author:

Author, A.B. (year). *Title of book with one author: Subtitle of book.* Location of publisher: Publisher.

Correct APA style for citation of an article of a journal:

Author, A. B. (year). Title of article within the journal. *Title of Journal, Volume number*, page number range.

Correct APA style for citation of a web page:

Author, A. B. (year). *Title of document.* Retrieved Month day, year, from http://web address. (Note: No punctuation follows the web address, to ensure accuracy in retrieving.)

Correct APA style for citation of a video:

Producer, A. A. (Producer). (Year). *Title of video* [Mode]. Country of origin: Studio.

6

Correct APA style for citation of an online video:

Name (Producer). (Year). *Title of video* [Mode]. Available Date of access, from complete URL.

Correct APA style for citation of motion pictures:

Producer, A. A. (Producer), & Director, B. B. (Director). (Year). *Title of motion picture* [Motion picture]. Country of origin: Studio.

Correct APA style for citation of music recordings:

Writer, A. (Copyright year). Title of song [Recorded by B. B. Artist if different from writer]. On *Title of album* [Medium of recording: CD, record, cassette, etc.] Location: Label. (Date of recording if different from song copyright date).

Correct APA style for citation of photographs:

Photographer's Last Name, First Initial. Date of composition (if unknown use n.d.)). *Title of work*. Museum or collection, City of collection or museum. Retrieved from Name of database.

Correct APA style for citation of online photographs:

Photographer's Last Name, First Initial. (Date of composition (if unknown use n.d.)). *Title of work*. Museum or collection, City of collection or museum. Retrieved Date of access, from complete URL of web site.

Correct APA style for citation of archived personal communication (i.e., oral histories):

Last Name, First Initial. Middle Initial. of person interviewed. (Date of Interview). Interview by First initial. Middle initial. Last Name [mode of medium]. Project title, Project sponsor. Location of archive, city.

Correct APA style for citation of magazines:

Author's Last Name, First Initial. Middle Initial. (Date of Publication). Title of article. *Name of Magazine*, volume, pages.

6

Correct APA style for citation of magazines
from electronic sources:

Author's Last Name, First Initial. Middle Initial. (Date of Publication). Title of article. *Name of Magazine*, volume, pages. (If retrieved from a Database, then citation should look like a print citation.)

Author's Last Name, First Initial. Middle Initial. (Date of Publication). Title of article. *Name of Magazine*, volume, pages. Retrieved from complete URL.

Correct APA style for citation of newspapers:

Author's Last Name, First Initial. Middle Initial. (Date of Publication). Article title. *Newspaper Title*, edition, section, pages (p./pp.).

MLA STYLE

The *MLA Style Manual and Guide to Scholarly Publishing* is the style guide of the Modern Language Association of America (MLA) (www .mla.org). This style typically is used in the fields of arts, literature, and humanities:

Gibaldi, J. *MLA Handbook for Writers of Research Papers*. 7th ed. New York: Modern Language Association of America, 2009.

Correct MLA style for citation of a book, ebook,
or chapters with one author:

Author, A. B. Title of book with one author. Location of publisher: Publisher, year.

Correct MLA style for citation of an article of a journal:

Author, A. B. "Title of article within the journal." *Title of the Journal*, Volume. issue. (year): page number range.

Correct MLA style for citation of a web page:

Author, A. B. "Title: Subtitle of web page." *Title of web page*. Sponsoring/publishing Agency, if available. Additional description

6

information. Date of electronic publication or date of last revision. Day Month Year of access http://web page address.

Correct MLA style for citation of a video:

Title of video. Dir. First Name Last Name. Distributer, Year of Production. Medium. Year of Release if different from Production date.

If citing a person's role in the video, then start with the person's name.

Correct MLA style for citation of an online video:

Title of video. Dir. First Name Last Name. Distributer, Year. *Name of database or web site.* Web. Date of access.

If citing a person's role in the video, then start with the person's name.

Correct MLA style for citation of motion pictures:

Title of motion picture. Dir. First Name Last Name. Studio, Year. Medium.

If you are citing the contribution of an individual, begin with that person's name.

Correct MLA style for citation of music recordings:

Last Name, First Name. (Composer, conductor, ensemble, or performer, depending on emphasis) *Title of recording.* Artist or Artists. Manufacturer, year of issue (n.d. if not known.). Medium.

Correct MLA style for citation of photographs:

Photographer's Last Name, First Name. *Title of work.* Date of composition (if unknown use n.d.). Museum or collection (if unknown, then use Private Collection without city). City of collection or museum.

Correct MLA style for citation of online photographs:

Photographer's Last Name, First Name. *Title of work.* Date of composition (if unknown use n.d.). Museum or collection (if unknown, then use Private Collection without city). City of collection or museum. *Name of database or web site.* Web. Date of access.

Correct MLA style for citation of personal interview:

If you did the interview, list who you interviewed and how the interview was done.

Last Name, First Name. Type of Interview. Date of Interview.

Correct MLA style for citation of letter, memo, or e-mail:

A LETTER THE RESEARCHER RECEIVED: TS (typescript) is machine-typed; MS (manuscript) is handwritten.

Last Name, First Name Middle Initial. Letter to author. Date of letter. TS/MS.

E-MAIL: Last Name, First Name Middle Initial. "Subject heading." Message to author. Date of message. Medium of delivery.

Correct MLA style for citation of magazines:

Author's Last Name, First Name Middle Initial. "Title of Article." *Name of Magazine* Day Month Year: Pages. Print.

Correct MLA style for citation of magazines from electronic sources:

MLA MAGAZINE ARTICLE CITATIONS FROM A DATABASE: Author's Last Name, First Name Middle Name or Initial. "Title of Article." *Name of Magazine* Day Month Year: pages. *Name of database*. Web. Date of access.

MLA MAGAZINE ARTICLE CITATIONS FROM ONLINE MAGAZINE: Author's Last Name, First Name Middle Name or Initial. "Title of Article." *Name of Magazine*. Name of sponsor/publisher, date of publication. Web. Date of access.

Correct MLA style for citation of newspapers:

Author's Last Name, First Name Middle Initial. "Article Title." *Newspaper Title* Date of Publication, ed., sec.: pages. Print.

NEWSPAPER ARTICLE WITH NO EDITION OR SECTION: Author's Last Name, First Name Middle Initial. "Article Title." *Newspaper Title* Date of Publication: Pages. Print.

6

NEWSPAPER ARTICLE WITH AN EDITION: Author's Last Name, First Name Middle Initial. "Article Title." *Newspaper Title* Date of Publication, ed.: Pages. Print.

NEWSPAPER ARTICLE WITH A SECTION: Author's Last Name, First Name Middle Initial. "Article Title." *Newspaper Title* Date of Publication, sec.: Pages. Print.

NEWSPAPER ARTICLE WITH AN EDITION AND SECTION: Author's Last Name, First Name Middle Initial. "Article Title." *Newspaper Title* Date of Publication, ed., sec.: Pages. Print.

Correct MLA style for citation of newspapers from a database:

Author's Last Name, First Name Middle Name or Initial. "Article Title." *Newspaper title* Date of publication: pages. *Name of Database.* Web. Date of access.

Correct MLA style for citation of online newspapers:

Author's Last Name, First Name Middle Name or Initial. "Article Title." *Newspaper title.* Name of sponsor, date of publication. Web. Date of access.

CHICAGO STYLE

The Chicago Manual of Style (www.press.uchicago.edu) is published by the University of Chicago Press. This style guide has the widest use overall, including the fields of history and other humanities. The official publication is:

The Chicago Manual of Style. 16th ed. 2010. Chicago: University of Chicago Press.

Correct Chicago style for citation of a book with one author:

Author's Last Name, First Middle. Date. *Title of Book with One Author: Subtitle of Book.* Location of publisher: Publisher.

Correct Chicago style for citation of an article of a journal:

Author's Last Name, First Middle. "Title of Article." *Title of Journal* Volume, no. (year): page number range.

6

Correct Chicago style for citation of a web page:

Author's Last Name, First Middle. "Title of web page." Location: sponsor, n.d. (means no date on the web page) http://web address (accessed Month day, year).

Correct Chicago style for citation of film, television, and other recorded mediums:

First Name Last Name, *Title of Work*, Format, directed/performed by First Name Last Name (Original release year; City: Studio/Distributor, Video release year.), Medium.

? CRITICAL THINKING QUESTIONS

▶ What citation style is used or required at your institution?
▶ What citation style does your profession use?

PUT IT TO USE See the respective style manuals for correct citations of other types of information sources. Check for free downloads or PDFs of style manuals as well.

INFORMATION AND PRIVACY ISSUES

For the general public, privacy means keeping private information out of public view or access. For celebrities and otherwise famous (or infamous) people, privacy means keeping their personal lives out of public view. Enormous controversy abounds over privacy today, especially when national security is involved. Do the privacy rights of individuals supersede the collective rights of the general public to be safe? Or is it the other way around?

Privacy and information literacy means that individuals using information should maintain the privacy of other individuals' personal information. The HIPAA (Health Insurance Portability and Accountability Act of 1996) protects your medical information in a variety of ways. The actual act and extensive information concerning its implementation can be found at the Health and Human Services web site (www.hhs.gov). Similarly, other types of privileged information, such as legal information, are protected by laws.

The Privacy Act of 1974 also provides many rights to U.S. citizens. For more information, see the U.S. Department of Justice web site (www.usdoj.gov).

6

? CRITICAL THINKING QUESTIONS

▶ Why might public access to your personal medical information be a problem? How could someone else use this information against you?

▶ Should the personal rights of individuals be sacrificed for the public right to security? Why or why not?

▶ How could someone use your personal information (other than medical information) against you?

Privacy rights are becoming increasingly important because the Internet makes a large amount of information available to anyone who wants to access it. In using a computer, you leave behind a large amount of information about yourself. For example, your computer logs your movement through the Internet, storing information in your browser's history. The cached history reveals every web page you visit. You can erase this information to some extent on your own computer, but if you are connected to a server, the record is maintained, typically without user access. In addition, web sites collect a large amount of information from you when you access the site. In general, your computer's information and other demographic information are freely available to anyone who chooses to collect it. Information-literate individuals are aware of this reality and take precautions accordingly. Running spyware software regularly to detect unwanted intrusions into your privacy is a "must" in today's electronic world.

INFORMATION AND SECURITY ISSUES

In addition to understanding and abiding by the legal and ethical uses of information, information-literate people follow legal and ethical guidelines associated with receiving, viewing, and transmitting information related to security. Information-literate individuals are aware of the following common security issues facing information users.

COMPUTER SECURITY

Because much of what professionals do with information takes place on a computer and the Internet, these systems must be kept as secure as possible. Maintaining security and following security guidelines help to ensure that the information received and sent is free of harmful software and does not infringe upon others' privacy or copyright rights.

Some guidelines for computer security are the following:

▶ *Maintain current security protection on your computer.* Protecting your computer and the network alike from incoming viruses (e.g., worms, Trojan horses, malware) and other

6

In many workplace situations, information is presented in small group meeting formats.

destructive software programs (e.g., spyware) is vital to your privacy and safety and that of others. Security is achieved by installing and continually renewing security software, keeping operating systems updated with the latest security patches, and staying current on the latest security issues related to computers and the Internet. Operating systems and security programs have features that automatically look for updates on a scheduled basis so you are alerted to updates and issues regularly and promptly. In addition, both spyware and virus programs can be set to check your system for problems regularly. Set updates and checks for both spyware and virus programs to run frequently and regularly.

▶ *Practice safe e-mailing procedures.* E-mail can bring viruses and other destructive software programs to your computer, especially in attached files. Never open an attached file in an e-mail if you are not sure who sent it to you, or if it looks suspicious in any way. Hackers can send destructive programs through other people's e-mail addresses—even people you know. If you are not expecting an e-mail with an attachment from someone

6

you know, confirm that this person indeed sent it to you before you open it.

▶ *Protect your computer when using wireless technology.* Many laptop users access the Internet via wireless technology. You must secure your system to protect you from hackers who try to access the information on computers or attempt to read Instant Messages or e-mail by tapping into a wireless network. This is especially easy to do in a public-access wireless hotspot, such as a coffee shop, hotel, or airport. Hackers can access shared files and read anything on a computer. They also can see the information being transmitted over the Internet. For example, if you are using an unsecured wireless access point in a coffee shop to make a banking transaction and a hacker is sitting at the table next to you, you may be giving up your passwords, account numbers, and other confidential information.

▶ *Practice safe and ethical networking.* Never access an account except the one assigned to you. Also, never access another person's folders or files without his or her permission.

▶ *Do not use your work's computer resources for personal activities.* This policy often is enforced in businesses and schools. Whatever you do on an organization's computer system can be viewed and retrieved by system administrators, even if you have deleted the material.

▶ *Never send or make available on a computer obscene, vulgar, rude, derogatory, discriminatory, or slanderous materials.* This practice is potentially illegal, as well as highly unethical and unprofessional. In addition, you are wise not to send or distribute unsolicited e-mail, also known as SPAM, even if it is cute, humorous, informative, touching, or harmless. SPAM takes up a lot of time and server space and has no place in the work setting.

▶ *Do not violate copyright laws.* This means that you should not make copyright material available for others to see on a network or send copyrighted materials to others without appropriate permissions. The exception is when the use falls within the fair-use guidelines for certain research and educational activities.

6

▶ *Do not violate privacy laws.* If you were to access or make available the private information of others, you would be violating privacy laws. This also means that you should never transmit audio or video clips of others or publish individuals' pictures without their written permission.

▶ *Use secure passwords.* Passwords help to secure network and computer access, as well as access to individual folders and files. Be smart about your password selection. Passwords should be difficult to guess. For example, a password consisting of your son's name and birthday may be easily guessed. A password consisting of meaningless random letters and numbers, such as ffg62thk, is a better choice. Although random passwords are more difficult to remember, they are much more secure. Also, select passwords with both numbers and letters to increase the difficulty of guessing. In many systems (though not all), special characters (e.g., $, %, &) can be used to increase the difficulty. Change passwords regularly and at any time you think someone has discovered your password. Never leave your password list on your computer or in an easily located area.

▶ *Back up your files.* Even the most diligent, safety-conscious computer users are susceptible to a computer crash. Electronic equipment eventually breaks down. To ensure that a computer crash or system virus infection does not become a crisis for you, back up your important computer files in a safe way, and store the backup files in a different and safe location. You can back up files using flash drives; however, this media is susceptible to damage and may not last as long as you need the files. Data backup software is inexpensive (and, in some cases, free) and is a more reliable option. You also can purchase inexpensive Internet storage space from third-party vendors that allows you to upload and store your files on their servers. Be sure to check the credibility of the vendor, though.

Whatever method you use, store your backup files in a location different from that of your computer or network so if some disaster strikes your building, both your computer and your backups will not be there. For extremely important documents, consider making a hard copy of the file and storing it in a safe place.

6

SELF-ASSESSMENT QUESTIONS

- How secure is your own computer system and the network you use daily?
- What specific security steps do you take currently?
- How could you improve your security?
- What security steps or policies are taken at your school? (You may have to do some research.) Are these adequate? Do you feel protected?
- Can you think of any policies you would recommend to your school?

Be sure to back up your files often when you are working on a document, and save the drafts of your work as separate files. This procedure will protect you in case your file becomes infected with a virus or gets degraded in some way, in addition to documenting that the work is yours if someone steals (plagiarizes) the material.

▶ *Be aware of Internet scams.* Internet scams consist of any activity in which someone tries to sell you products fraudulently, tries to gain personal information from you, or attempts to get you to invest in some illegal or nonexistent project. Common Internet scams include illegal online auctions, money offers, work-at-home plans, get-rich-quick schemes, travel and vacation offers, and prizes and sweepstakes. Some of these activities are called "phishing" expeditions, with the goal of getting your money, personal information (e.g., social security card number or credit card numbers), and other private information such as usernames and passwords. An example is the unsolicited e-mail that makes an offer and requests your credit card number in return.

? CRITICAL THINKING QUESTION

▶ How might a lack of security in regard to those with whom you work impact you personally? List as many ways as you can.

PUT IT TO USE   Go to www.ftc.gov/bcp/conline/pubs/online /dotcoms.htm to view the Top Ten List of fraudulent activities. This government web site helps to keep the American public informed about fraudulent Internet activities and is updated on a regular basis.

CASE IN POINT: IT'S NOT WHAT YOU KNOW BUT WHO YOU KNOW

Read the scenario below. Then, in groups or as a class, discuss the questions at the end.

Lily Scala recently graduated from a school in North Carolina as a computer science major. Her first job is working at a software company that specializes in accounting and finance. In her daily interactions with clients Lily hears various accounting and finance terms with which she is not familiar, and she finds it frustrating that she does not know the language and thus finds it difficult to interact with her clients.

Lily was offered initial training when she first started her job, but much of it was of a human resources nature and not specific to her job description. When she needs to provide information to her clients she often does a Google search but finds that many times Google only provides general information and nothing that is specific to her organization.

▶ Aside from a Google search, what are some other ways that Lily can find the information she needs to do her job and help her clients?

▶ What types of resources might Lily use to help her understand the industry in which she works?

Image 100 Ltd./Getty Images

Most professionals are required to make presentations to large groups of people at some time in their career.

6

THE IMPORTANCE OF INFORMATION LITERACY IN THE WORKPLACE

As you have learned, information literacy is comprised of many components. These include:

- Critical thinking, creative thinking, problem solving, and higher-order thinking
- Effective communication and organizational skills
- Digital, computer, library, media, visual, and technology literacy

As an information worker in the digital age, you are called on to use all of these components in some fashion and to some degree to solve information problems.

Transitioning to the workplace will require you to use these skills in a variety of combinations and in ways that you might not have imagined. As stated earlier, the way you use information in school supports your own learning goals. In the workplace, however, the information environment supports the goals of the organization. Here is your opportunity to show your employer that you are an information-literate employee by positively contributing to the company's goals through your use of your literacy skills to solve information problems.

SELF-ASSESSMENT QUESTIONS

- Using the listed components of information literacy, in what areas do you feel you are the strongest?
- What might you do to strengthen the areas that you have identified as being weak points?

WHAT EMPLOYERS SEEK

Any more, employers have certain expectations of their new hires, especially recent graduates. While they are looking for technical skills that apply directly to the job and the organization, they also seek fundamental and foundational skills in their employees that can be applied across all industries and job titles.

In a recent (2012) study by the group Project Information Literacy (projectinfolit.org), employers were asked to identify their expectations and provide an assessment of their new college hires' ability to solve information problems. The following list addresses the competencies that employers seek but that recent college hires seldom demonstrate:

- **Asking others on the team to help with research.** Employers found that recent hires tended to conduct research on their own, much as they did in college, as opposed to turning to others in the organization to help them solve information problems. Employers further commented that new hires failed to grasp the importance of collaboration with others as a way to research answers and solve problems. Workplace research is considered interdependent and structured, thus observed organizational behaviors are as important, if not more important, than mere facts and figures.

▶ **Going beyond a cursory Google search.** This competency speaks directly to finding information beyond what is available online. College students tend to do all of their research online and consider that sufficient. In the workplace, employers expect that new hires will go beyond the computer and seek answers using non-digitized materials such as company reports, manuals, books, and most importantly, human capital. New hires often do not consider their colleagues as valuable sources of information, and yet those very people have organizational experience and knowledge that goes well beyond what the new hire has learned to date.

▶ **Fitting pieces of the information puzzle together.** This involves higher-order thinking. Recall Bloom's Taxonomy from Chapter 1. Thinking involves six levels: knowledge (lowest), comprehension, application, analysis, synthesis, and evaluation (highest). Employers noted that college hires often failed to properly analyze, synthesize, or evaluate information and to find correlations and patterns among information bits, or to be able to find the value in or the importance of those bits of information.

▶ **Adopting a wide-ranging research approach to finding information.** College students, while conducting research online (and only using online sources), tend to search for information as quickly as possible and assume that the first (or second or third) informational nugget that they find is the best. In the workplace, employers need employees who can conduct a comprehensive search for information using myriad sources, and then use critical and creative thinking skills to solve information problems on behalf of the organization (Head 2012).

WHAT GRADUATES BRING

The same Project Information Literacy (2012) study also queried recent college graduates about the differences between conducting research to complete college work and using information to solve

6

information problems in the workplace. Not surprisingly, these new hires relied on their tried-and-true way of conducting online research but struggled with the transition between school and work. For example, new hires no longer had access to their campus libraries (or librarians), there were no faculty office hours to get questions answered or get direction, and no syllabi that neatly outlined the workload on a week-by-week basis.

When interviewed, participants noted three major challenges in transitioning from college to the workplace. All three challenges related to their abilities to solve information problems in the workplace based upon the skills and strategies they learned while conducting course-related research in school. These challenges include:

▶ **Embracing a "get it done now"attitude.** New college hires struggled with the immediacy of needing to find and communicate information. Gone were the days of having an entire semester to work on a project, when and where they wanted. Participants said this sense of urgency left them with feelings of vulnerability, being replaceable, and being constantly hurried.

▶ **No clear sense of direction is given.** Despite some initial training when they were hired, participants said that this formal training was not ongoing and that change was constant within the organization. With less direction on how to solve information problems in the workplace, those interviewed expressed feelings of disorientation and fear.

▶ **Finding information must be done within the framework of the organization and its people.** Conducting research while in college is typically not considered a social activity. Even if you work on a project as part of a team, the chances are great that you are still finding and evaluating the information you need on your own and bringing it back to the larger group. That is generally not the case in the workplace, however. Colleagues, supervisors, and trusted coworkers can all have the information you are seeking when a quick Google search cannot yield the answer. Participants noted that using traditional forms of research, such as seeking the expertise of colleagues, was a remarkably efficient and productive way of solving information problems in the workplace (Head 2012).

? CRITICAL THINKING QUESTION

▶ Do you think that finding and using information is social? Why or why not?

Digital Vision/Getty Images

Many professionals are required to use information to teach or train someone else.

6

STRATEGIES FOR BEING A PROFESSIONAL INFORMATION WORKER

So how do you go about transitioning how you find and evaluate information from the classroom to the workplace? Research suggests that early on in their careers college graduates must modify how they operate as an information worker to fit into the "information culture" of their organization (Head 2012). This, coupled with entering a fast-paced workplace, makes doing information work seem challenging, if not daunting. Head (2012) offers some strategies that can be employed to help you make that transition as suggested by interviews with recent graduates in the Project Information Literacy study.

▶ **Use your supervisor as an information source to build knowledge.** Your supervisor is privy to organizational decisions that you are likely not as a new employee and understands why those decisions are being made. He or she is fully entrenched in the "information culture" of your organization and thus becomes a valuable and valued resource.

▶ **Seek out relationships with trusted coworkers.** While it may be quickest and easiest to seek out information from your supervisor, oftentimes coworkers can be a reliable source of information. This person may or may not be a part of your immediate team. Take the time to get to know others in the organization who can provide you with guidance and make a point of learning from them.

▶ **Go online first, then ask a coworker for additional information.** As a recent graduate, your first reaction to solving an information problem may be to look online. Generally, there is nothing wrong to this approach, but online sources may not give you the answers you are seeking. Google and other search engines do not know the ins and outs of your organization and thus cannot provide you with the contextualized information that you need. If searching online can give you background information on a topic, that is a valid approach. Take that information to a coworker and ask for help in filling in the gaps to solve the information problem that is unique to your organization.

6

SELF-ASSESSMENT QUESTIONS

- How comfortable are you seeking out information from relative strangers in the workplace?
- What strategies might you employ to gain confidence in speaking to those whom you do not know at work?

? CRITICAL THINKING QUESTION

- What are some strategies you might use to help build your "social network" at work?

▶ **Use networked knowledge and Internet sources to find experts.** This is an especially helpful approach if the information problem you are solving is very technical in nature. Online forums can help you find the information that you need if you cannot get the answers from someone at work.

Clearly there is no single "best" way to solve information problems in the workplace. Your most successful strategy for doing so will be your ability to build your own professional "social network" comprised of your supervisor, trusted coworkers, and outside experts who can guide you in completing your daily tasks. In this way, you will become a professional information worker in the digital age.

CHAPTER SUMMARY

In this chapter, you learned about the importance of using information legally and ethically and how to communicate it effectively to others. This includes the concepts of intellectual property, copyright, plagiarism, and fair use. You also learned about the need to properly cite and document the sources of information in your materials. Of additional concern is how information and privacy issues interact, as well as information privacy and security issues. You learned about aspects of communicating information so it is understood and used for some purpose in the most legal, ethical, and effective ways. Finally, you learned about the importance of being information-literate in the workplace, the information literacy skills you should learn while in school and bring with you to work, and strategies for being a professional information worker.

POINTS TO KEEP IN MIND

In this chapter, several main points were discussed in detail:

▶ Intellectual property refers to anything created by the mind, such as literary works, artwork, inventions, logos or symbols, names, designs, and images or photographs.

6

▶ Copyright reflects the rights given to creators of some forms of expressions of intellectual property. Copyrights are protected by copyright laws.

▶ Plagiarism and cyber-plagiarism are unethical and illegal practices. They are a growing problem in educational and professional settings.

▶ Style guides are used to properly cite information sources. Standard style guides, among others, include the APA Style, the MLA Style, and the Chicago Style.

▶ Privacy related to information literacy means that individuals using information should maintain the privacy of other individuals' personal information.

▶ Securing information on a computer is an increasingly important topic. Guidelines for how to protect information housed on a computer aid in protecting that information.

▶ Employers seek recently graduated new hires with a wide variety of information literacy skills.

▶ Preparing to become a professional information worker will support your success in the workplace.

apply it

Find printable activities on the companion web site for this book, accessed through www.cengagebrain.com.

 Activity #1: Personal Note-taking Procedure

GOAL: To develop a personal note-taking procedure that avoids plagiarism when conducting research.

STEP 1: Think carefully about how you can take notes during the research process. Develop a plan of action for your note-taking procedure to help you formalize how you take notes.

continued

6

continued

STEP 2: Write this plan in a step-by-step procedure format, and place your plan in your portfolio. If you find it useful, create a checklist that will help you follow the plan during any research activity.

Activity #2: Computer Security Evaluation

GOAL: To emphasize the importance of computer security and to evaluate the current level of your computer's security.

STEP 1: Develop a checklist for your computer security. Include all relevant steps, programs, and procedures to ensure safe computing in your personal home office and workspace, as well as in your workplace.

STEP 2: Use your checklist to evaluate the security level of your current situation.

STEP 3: Develop a plan to optimize your security situation in any place where you use your computer.

Activity #3: Citation Exploration

GOAL: To demonstrate an understanding of how to cite information sources properly.

STEP 1: Determine the acceptable style used in your institution or workplace for citing information sources.

STEP 2: Search the Internet for information on using this style.

STEP 3: Acquire the official style guide and implement use of this style in each assignment, research task, and other written document.

CHECK YOUR UNDERSTANDING

Visit www.cengagebrain.com to see how well you have mastered the material in Chapter 6.

SUGGESTED ITEMS FOR LEARNING PORTFOLIO

Refer to the "Developing Portfolios" section at the beginning of this textbook for more information on learning portfolios.

◗ Personal Note-taking Plan

◗ Computer Security Evaluation Checklist

REFERENCES

Head, A. (2012). *Learning curve: how college graduates solve information problems once they join the workplace.* Retrieved June 21, 2013, from http://projectinfolit.org/pdfs/PIL_fall2012_workplaceStudy _Without_Appendix_Revised.pdf

Patry, W. F. (1994, 2000). *Copyright law and practice.* Retrieved June 18, 2013, from http://digital-law-online.info/patry/patry5.html

United States Code. (2003). *Copyright law of the United States of America and related laws contained in Title 17 of the United States Code.* Retrieved June 18, 2013, from http://www.copyright.gov /title17/

University System of Georgia Board of Regents. (n.d. [a]). *Giving credit where credit is due.* Retrieved June 18, 2013, from http://www.usg .edu/galileo/skills/ unit08/credit08_09.phtml

University System of Georgia Board of Regents. (n.d. [b]). *Public Domain.* Retrieved June 18, 2013, from http://www.usg.edu/galileo/skills /unit08/ credit08_10.phtml

6

Andresr/Shutterstock.com

CHAPTER OUTLINE

Financial Literacy Defined

The Importance of Financial Literacy at Any Age

Personal Values and Personal Responsibilities

The Seven Levels of Maslow's Hierarchy of Needs

Getting Started on Your Financial Journey and How Technology Can Help

7

Introduction to Financial Literacy

THE BIG PICTURE

This chapter lays the foundation for understanding the many aspects of financial literacy. It also provides a context for applying the information presented in subsequent chapters.

LEARNING OBJECTIVES

By the end of this chapter, you will achieve the following objectives:

▶ Define *financial literacy*.
▶ Explain the importance of being financially literate at any age.
▶ Distinguish between personal values and personal responsibilities.
▶ Identify the seven levels of Maslow's Hierarchy of Needs.
▶ Explain how technology aids in achieving financial literacy.

CHAPTER 7 CASE IN POINT

Lauren Bishop is an incoming freshman at a college one state away from where she grew up. This is her first time away from home without the daily guidance of her parents.

While still in high school, Lauren worked part-time at a local gourmet shop assisting customers and stocking merchandise. Although her earnings were relatively small, Lauren's parents insisted that she open a checking account at the local bank so that she could learn "the ropes" of managing her money and how to use a debit card. While she is at school, Lauren's parents are going to use that checking account to give Lauren a monthly budgeted amount to fund items that are not paid for by other means.

During freshman orientation on campus, Lauren noticed a hub of activity at the student union where vendors were peddling a variety of services, among them several credit card companies offering such incentives as a free T-shirt, a Frisbee, or 10 percent off their first purchase, simply by filling out a credit card application. Enticed by that 10-percent discount and the notion of being an "adult" with a "real" credit card, Lauren filled out the application and waited for her card to arrive in the mail.

When the credit card arrived in her dorm mailbox a short time later, she immediately went to the local mall to purchase a sweater like the ones so many young women on campus were wearing that fall. She figured that she could pay her credit card bill from her checking account when the statement arrived 30 days later and not tell her parents about it.

Unfortunately for Lauren, when the card statement arrived, she did not have enough money in her checking account to cover the cost of the sweater. In addition, the credit card company had tacked on a twenty-five-dollar annual fee that Lauren had not anticipated. Lauren decided that the best thing to do would be to pay the minimum amount required that month while hoping she would have sufficient funds next month to bring the balance to zero.

Imagine yourself to be in Lauren's position. Thoughtfully and honestly answer the following questions:

▶ How dependent are you on others for your financial well-being?

▶ How well do you think you manage your personal finances?

continued

▶ Do you take full responsibility for your financial situation?

▶ How do you decide if a purchase is something you need or want?

▶ How do you rate yourself when it comes to understanding the use of credit cards?

▶ From whom do you seek financial advice?

FINANCIAL LITERACY DEFINED

In these tough and uncertain economic times, many Americans find themselves struggling to make ends meet, often living paycheck to paycheck. The average citizen confronts mounting debt, is unclear about how to make important financial decisions, and will experience a later and less secure retirement. Financial problems such as these can lead to health issues, emotional stress, and decreased productivity (Shorb, n.d.). While this current phenomenon has many causes, a major contributing factor is that many Americans are *financially illiterate.*

Financial illiteracy in this country is not unique to one gender, socioeconomic group, age, or race. It impacts Americans in a variety of ways, all of them negatively. Consider the following:

▶ **LACK OF SAVINGS AND DEBT.** A failure to save, or save sufficiently, can affect one's financial circumstances. Using credit, and thus carrying debt, to "fix" financial problems leads to even greater financial consequences.

▶ **BANKRUPTCY AND FORECLOSURE.** Financial illiteracy has led many Americans down the unfortunate path of severe financial problems, including bankruptcy and foreclosure.

▶ **INCREASE IN EXPENSES.** A lack of financial literacy causes people to make misinformed choices that can cost large amounts of money in terms of interest payments over time.

moshimochi/Shutterstock.com

Learning the ropes of financial literacy now will bode well for you the rest of your life.

▶ **WORKPLACE ISSUES.** Financial stress at home can find its way into the workplace, thus impacting productivity and creating increased emotional stress.

▶ **HEALTH AND RELATIONSHIPS.** Money issues can creep into other aspects of our lives, often negatively, potentially affecting one's health, employment, and relationships (Shorb, n.d.).

WHAT IS FINANCIAL LITERACY?

So, then, what can we do as Americans to remove ourselves from the path of the oncoming train that is financial illiteracy? The answer, of course, is to become financially literate. But what does that term mean, and how does one go about becoming financially literate?

In the *2008 Annual Report to the President* as authored by the President's Advisory Council on Financial Literacy, the Council defines **financial literacy** as "the ability to use knowledge and skills to manage financial resources effectively for a lifetime of financial well-being." Further, the Council defines **financial education** as "the process by which people improve their understanding of financial products, services, and concepts, so they are empowered to make informed choices, avoid pitfalls, know where to go for help and take other actions to improve their present and long-term financial well-being" (Department of the Treasury, 2008).

As a college student, you are a possible candidate for accumulating debt through the use of student loans, credit cards, and making financial missteps that can cause you real financial harm, now and well into your adult life. As you transition from college into the workplace, you will be exposed to numerous choices of financial services and products, more so than you are now, and mistakes at this level can have significant ramifications, including job loss, a poor credit rating, bankruptcy, and even homelessness.

If you haven't started already, *now* is the time to begin your financial education so that you can achieve financial literacy that will serve you at present and well into your future.

THE IMPORTANCE OF FINANCIAL LITERACY AT ANY AGE

As you embark on your journey to financial literacy, it's important to establish a baseline of what you know you know, what you think you know, what you think you might not know, and what you know you don't know about personal finances and money management. In this way, you can target the areas in which you need to shore up your financial education.

Let's begin with a simple "Financial Aptitude Test," as provided by the Federal Deposit Insurance Corporation (FDIC) that will help you to gauge your financial education.

1. It's always smart to send in the minimum payment due on a credit card bill each month and stretch out the card payments as long as possible instead of paying the bill in full. *True or False?*

2. Your credit record (your history of paying debts and other bills) can be a factor when you apply for a loan or a credit card but cannot affect noncredit decisions such as applications for insurance or an apartment. *True or False?*

3. While one or two late payments on bills may not damage your credit record, making a habit of it will count against you. *True or False?*

4. There's no harm in having many different credit cards, especially when the card companies offer free T-shirts and other special giveaways as incentives. The number of cards you carry won't affect your ability to get a loan; what matters is that you use the cards responsibly. *True or False?*

5. A debit card may be a good alternative to a credit card for a young person because the money to pay for purchases is automatically deducted from a bank account, thus avoiding interest charges or debt problems. *True or False?*

6. It makes no sense for young adults to put money aside for their retirement many years away. People in their 20s should focus entirely on meeting monthly expenses and

saving for short-term goals (such as buying a home or starting a business) and not start saving for retirement until their 40s at the earliest. ***True or False?***

7. If you receive an e-mail from a company you've done business with asking you to update your records by reentering your Social Security number or bank account numbers, it's safe to provide this information as long as the e-mail explains the reason for the request and shows the company's official logo. ***True or False?***

8. The best way to avoid a "bounced" check—that is, a check that gets rejected by your financial institution because you've overdrawn your account—is to keep your checkbook up to date and closely monitor your balance. Institutions do offer "overdraft-protection" services, but these programs come with their own costs. ***True or False?***

9. All checking accounts are pretty much the same in terms of features, fees, interest rates, opening balance requirements, and so on. ***True or False?***

10. Let's say you put money in a savings account paying the same interest rate each month, and you don't take any money out. Even though your original deposit and the interest rate remain unchanged, the amount of money you will earn in interest each month will gradually increase. ***True or False?*** (Federal Deposit Insurance Corporation, 2005).

Note: Answer key to Financial Aptitude Test is located on page 29.

Obviously this "test" is not all encompassing, nor was it designed to be. But it should give you an indication of topic areas where you might want to put some additional thought or do some research on your own.

Activity #1: Self-Analysis: Grading Your Financial Acumen, found at the end of this chapter, will help guide you in assessing your strengths and weaknesses when it comes to your financial education.

IT'S NOT TOO EARLY TO START SAVING

Ideally, the road to financial literacy should start at an early age and continue as a lifelong journey. Unfortunately, most of us do not start on this road until we are adults; oftentimes we do not save enough to be financially secure, let alone enjoy a comfortable retirement.

As a young college student, you should be aware that one of the first tenets of sound financial decision making is to abide by the concept of "pay yourself first." By this we mean automatically putting some money into a savings account or other investments such as a U.S. Savings Bond before you are tempted to spend it. Start small, even if it's just twenty-five or fifty dollars a month. If you have those funds automatically deducted from your paycheck and placed into savings, you won't miss them. "The important thing is to start saving as early as you can—even saving for retirement when that seems light years away—so you can benefit from the effect of compound interest," states Donna Gambrell, of the FDIC's Division of Supervision and Consumer Protection (Federal Deposit Insurance Corporation, 2005). **Compound interest** is when interest on an investment (such as money in a savings account) itself earns interest.

Another way to save money is by not falling into the trap of common mistakes that young adults tend to make with their money. Certainly everyone makes financial mistakes at one or more points in their lives, but the trick is to keep those mistakes at a minimum, and, even more important, to learn from them. This is a significant facet of your financial education and one that you are wise to learn from sooner rather than later.

The following list includes top financial mistakes that many young people make and what you can do to avoid making those mistakes from the start:

▶ **PURCHASING ITEMS YOU DON'T NEED AND PAYING EXTRA FOR THEM IN INTEREST.** Think back to the Case in Point at the beginning of this chapter. Lauren Bishop used her credit card to pay for a sweater, only to find out that she didn't have enough money in her checking account to pay off the balance. Only paying the minimum amount guarantees that Lauren will incur finance charges in the coming month (and perhaps for many months to follow). So how do you avoid Lauren's situation? Consider the following:

• Really assess if you "need" the item versus "want" the item. Try not to bow to peer pressure or to reward yourself if things are going well or not so well. Impulse buying can make you feel good for the moment, but it won't make you feel so great when that credit card statement comes calling. Waiting a day or two, or even just a few hours, before you purchase (and be mindful of how quick and easy it is to shop online) may prevent you from making a costly decision that you will come to regret.

- Research major purchases and comparison shop before you buy. Doing so will not only get you the best deal for your money; it also might sway your decision against making the purchase at all.

- If you do use a credit card to pay for a major purchase, be smart about how you repay. If available, take advantage of offers of "zero-percent interest" on credit card purchases for a certain number of months. Be mindful, however, of when and how interest charges begin and what that does to your monthly payment amount. Always pay as much as you can before interest charges kick in so that you are paying interest on a lower balance than the purchase price.

▶ **GETTING TOO DEEPLY INTO DEBT.** Sure, this seems obvious. Don't spend what you don't have. That's simple, right? Unfortunately, our ability to borrow (via credit cards and other means) is all too easy these days. And borrowing helps us get what we want, when we want it. With this reality comes the fact that millions of adults of all ages find themselves struggling to pay their loans, credit cards, and other bills. Learn to be a good money manager and to recognize the warning signs of a serious debt problem. Some of these warning signs include the following:

- Borrowing money to make payments on loans you already have

- Getting payday loans. A **payday loan** (also called a **paycheck advance**) is a small, short-term loan that is intended to cover a borrower's expenses until his or her next payday.

- Deliberately paying your bills late

- Putting off doctor visits or other important life activities because you don't have enough money

▶ **TARNISHING YOUR FINANCIAL REPUTATION.** The simplest way around this is to pay your bills on time, every month. While one or two late payments on your loans or other regular financial obligations (rent, for example) will probably not hurt you in the long run, a pattern of late bill payment can adversely affect your **credit score**s and **credit report**. Here's how that can happen:

- **Credit bureau**s are companies that prepare credit reports used by lenders, employers, insurance companies, and others to assess your financial reliability, generally based on your track record of paying bills and debts. They produce credit scores that evaluate a person's credit record based on a point system. If your credit scores are low and your credit report is damaged by your inability to pay your bills on time, you will likely be charged a higher interest rate on your credit card(s) or on a loan that you really want and need. You could also be turned down for employment or renting an apartment. Even your auto insurance may be negatively impacted.

▶ **YOU OWN A FISTFUL OF CREDIT CARDS.** The general rule of thumb is that two to four credit cards are a sufficient amount for most adults. These include any cards from department stores, oil companies, and any other retailers. Why shouldn't you carry more than this suggested amount?

- Temptation, plain and simple. The more cards you have, the more tempted you may be to use them to fuel costly impulse buying.

- Each card you own, even if you don't use it, represents money that you *could* borrow up to the card's **spending limit**. For each new card you acquire, you are seen as someone who could potentially get into greater debt. And that could mean qualifying for a smaller or costlier loan.

▶ **NOT TRACKING YOUR EXPENSES.** It's easy to overspend in some areas, most likely for the things you want (not necessarily need), and to shortchange other areas, including that savings account that you were so good about opening. Devising a tracking/budget system that works for you is your best bet for setting and sticking to your financial limits.

▶ **WATCH OUT FOR THOSE FEES.** Financial institutions love to charge noncustomers anywhere from one dollar to four dollars for using their automated teller machines (ATMs). They are also quick to charge for **bounced check**s, that is, writing checks for more than you have in your account. These fees can range from 15 to 30 dollars for *each* check. You can take the following steps to mitigate these unwanted fees:

- Whenever possible, use your financial institution's ATMs (including branches) or ATMs that are a part of an ATM network to which your bank belongs.

- To avoid bounced check fees, keep your checkbook balanced and up to date, including recording all debit card transactions. This task becomes easier with the use of online and phone banking, both of which are free services. In addition, be sure to record those ATM withdrawal slips within your check register or cross-reference them online. If not closely monitored, those unrecorded $20 ATM transactions can result in your account being overdrawn (Federal Deposit Insurance Corporation, 2005).

We will discuss all of these suggestions for minimizing financial mistakes throughout the remainder of this textbook.

SEEKING FINANCIAL ADVICE

Ultimately, it is you who must take charge of your finances. But as we have already seen, successfully managing one's financial situation can be a daunting task, with many risks (and rewards, it is hoped!) associated with it. The good news is that even though you hold final responsibility for your finances, there are people, companies, and government agencies that can help you in your financial decision making, now and well into your future.

People get their money advice from myriad sources. At your age, your main source of financial advice may come from your parents. Studies corroborate that most young adults today rely on their parents as the main source of financial knowledge (Shorb, n.d.). The good news is that parents are seen as a trusted source of information. The bad news is that if parents exhibit bad financial habits, those habits most likely are passed down to the next generation.

Here are some resources you can tap into to get financial advice:

▶ **FAMILY, FRIENDS, AND COWORKERS.** The caveat here is that while you trust and admire these people, they really might not be very financially literate themselves.

▶ **YOUR FINANCIAL INSTITUTION.** Every bank and credit union has people on staff who can give you advice on the services they offer that best meet your financial needs, including the merits of online banking. They can also provide you with written materials on a variety of topics that you can use for reference. Their web sites also contain useful information.

▶ **YOUR SCHOOL.** Check with the Financial Aid office for information on student loans, grants, scholarships, loan repayment information, **exit counseling**, and other financial information. The Career Services office has both onsite and online resources available to you, including data on internships, job searches, networking, and other career counseling information. (Read more about the Financial Aid office in Chapter 5 of this textbook.)

▶ **GOVERNMENT AGENCIES.** Many federal and state government agencies are dedicated to financial information geared to consumers. Most of the information is available via agency web sites. Some of the most useful ones include the following:

• **The Federal Deposit Insurance Corporation (FDIC)** web site at www.fdic.gov/consumers. The FDIC Consumer Protection page provides a wealth of financial information to educate and protect consumers on a wide variety of topics, including banking and your money, loans and mortgages, identity theft and fraud, and updated consumer news.

• **The Financial Literacy and Education Commission** web site at www.mymoney.gov. MyMoney.gov is the U.S. government's web site dedicated to teaching all Americans the basics about financial education. The site houses important information from 20 federal agencies and bureaus designed to help consumers make smart financial choices.

• **360 Degrees of Financial Literacy** web site at www.360financialliteracy.org. Sponsored by the American Institute of Certified Public Accountants, the site is

7

intended to help Americans understand their personal finances through every stage of life. This site has a page dedicated to college students.

- **Your state's official** web site. Most state governments offer assistance and publish useful information for its citizens, including how to start a business, labor and employment information, and tax information.

▶ **YOUR EMPLOYER.** Many employers, especially larger ones, offer investment opportunities through stock purchase plans, 401K programs, and the like. The Human Resources department generally has printed materials and might offer classes to help you make informed investment decisions.

▶ **THE MEDIA.** The Internet, newspapers and magazines, television, and radio are filled with information about financial matters. When accessing information via the Internet, bear in mind that anyone can put anything up on the World Wide Web, and not all sources are reliable or trustworthy. Generally, you can rely on the .gov and .edu web sites as being reliable and presenting relatively accurate information. The government or educational entity behind the site is usually bound by a code of ethics and is watched by many different individuals or agencies. Regardless, be sure to verify your source(s) before moving forward with any financial decisions or taking the information as truth.

▶ **EDUCATIONAL OPPORTUNITIES.** Consult your local library, schools, community college, and other educational resources for personal finance classes, seminars, and the like. Financial institutions and those in the "money business" (investment bankers, brokers, financial advisors, and so on) often sponsor discussions on different financial vehicles and investment opportunities.

▶ **FINANCIAL PLANNER.** A **financial planner** is an investment professional who helps individuals set and achieve their long-term financial goals. The role of a financial planner is to find ways to increase the client's net worth and help the client accomplish all of their financial objectives. As a college student, you might not need this level of financial advice, but you might want to seek the advice of such a person as you enter the workforce, purchase a home, start a family, and so on. Note that using a financial planner costs money.

---

success steps for seeking financial advice

- Enlist the help of family, friends, and coworkers.
- Speak to staff members at your financial institution.
- Tap into resources at your school.
- Check the web sites of federal and state government agencies that provide financial guidance.
- Consult with your employer on retirement and investment opportunities.
- Use different media outlets to conduct research on financial issues.
- Take advantage of any financial educational opportunities in your area.
- Seek out the counsel of a financial planner.

PERSONAL VALUES AND PERSONAL RESPONSIBILITIES

Thinking about and discovering what you want out of life gives you guidance for what to do to lead a satisfying life. Understanding yourself enables you to make key life decisions. One of the significant steps in this process is to identify your personal values.

Personal values are the principles, standards, or qualities individuals consider worthwhile or desirable. Values provide a basis for decisions about how to live and serve as guides we can use to direct our actions. For something to be of value, it must be prized, publically affirmed, chosen from alternatives, and acted on repeatedly and consistently. Values are not right or wrong or true or false; they are personal preferences.

People may place value on family, friends, helping others, religious commitment, honesty, pleasure, good health, material possessions,

The financial road you choose to travel says much about your understanding of financial literacy.

iQoncept/Shutterstock.com

financial security, and a satisfying career. Examples of conflicting values are family versus satisfying career, religious beliefs versus pleasure, and material possessions versus financial security (Garman and Forgue, 2010). If you are unsure of, or lose sight of your values, you fall into the trap of making choices out of impulse or instant gratification rather than on sound reasoning and responsible decision making (Hereford, n.d.).

Closely aligned with personal values is the concept of responsibility and personal responsibility. "Responsibility means being accountable for what we think, say, and do. **Personal responsibility** involves working on our own character and skill development rather than blaming others for situations and circumstances. It means choosing to design a life that honors our values and purpose," states professional life success coach Steve Brunkhorst. Accepting personal responsibility is what moves you from childhood into adulthood. It is part of the maturation process that you are undergoing at this stage of your life. Personal responsibility does not stand alone, however. It influences your successes, achievements, motivation, happiness, and self-actualization. By accepting that you are wholly responsible for yourself and that no one—neither your parents, your teachers, nor your friends—is coming to your rescue, signals that you have become an adult (Tracy, n.d.).

RESPONSIBILITIES VERSUS EXCUSES

On the other end of the spectrum are excuses, the polar opposite of personal responsibility. Excuses allow you to blame others for what's happening in your life. They rob you of your ability to achieve your goals, and they steal your self-esteem and quality of life (Bowman, n.d.).

Excuses are also habit forming. If you get into the habit of making excuses, you have also fallen into the trap of avoiding responsibility at the same time. It's easy to set a goal or objective for yourself and even easier to create an excuse as a "just-in-case" fallback in the event that it is too hard for you to accomplish that goal (Tracy, n.d.).

PERSONAL VALUES VERSUS FINANCIAL GOALS

So far in this book, we have seen several examples of how people tend to be financially illiterate, and we've identified many common financial mistakes that young adults make. One of the most important steps you can take as you journey down the road to financial literacy is to understand the relationship between your personal values and your financial goals.

As we have seen, values provide a basis for decisions about how to live and serve as guides we can use to direct our actions. **Goals** are the vehicle for putting those actions into motion.

Successful financial planning evolves from your financial goals. **Financial goals** are the specific short-, medium-, and long-term objectives that you want to attain through financial planning and management efforts. Financial goals should be consistent with your personal values (Garman and Forgue, 2010). As a young adult, you may define short-, medium-, and long-term goals in these time frames:

- ▶ **SHORT-TERM.** Goals that can be accomplished in three months or fewer. As an example of this, you might want to save $100 to buy an e-reader in three months.

- ▶ **MEDIUM-TERM.** Goals that will take between three months and one year to achieve. For example, you might like to save for six months to take a trip with friends next summer.

- ▶ **LONG-TERM.** Goals that take more than one year to accomplish. One of your long-term goals following graduation could be to pay off your student loans early by paying an extra $150 per month (CashCourse, 2011[b]).

Setting goals helps you visualize the gap between your current financial status and where you want to be in the future. Examples of financial goals include the following:

▶ Finish a college education.

▶ Pay off education loans.

▶ Take a vacation.

▶ Own a home.

▶ Meet financial emergencies.

▶ Accumulate funds to send children through college.

▶ Be financially independent at retirement.

None of these goals, however, is specific enough to guide financial behavior. Specific goals should be measurable, attainable, realistic, and time-bound (Garman and Forgue, 2010).

Consider the following acronym when goal setting. Turn your goals into SMART goals. SMART goals are Specific, Measurable, Attainable, Realistic, and Time-bound. This provides you with a plan that has a sequence of achievable small steps that will lead to you reaching your goals, financial or otherwise.

Let's say one of your medium-term goals is to go with your friends to Colorado next July for a week. Make this a SMART goal by doing the following:

▶ **SPECIFIC:** A specific goal is, "I want to spend a week next summer in Colorado with three friends." A vague goal, for comparison, is more like stating, "I want to do something fun next summer."

▶ **MEASURABLE:** You need $500 for your share of gas money for the drive to Colorado and back, your share of the split hotel room cost, and food for the week. This is more concrete than "I will need money for the trip."

▶ **ATTAINABLE:** It's February, so you have about five months to save for your trip in July, and you'll save the money from your campus bookstore job. You need to save $100 per month, or $25 per week, to go on the trip. You are more apt to see results with this goal than if you say, "I'll save any money that's left over at the end of the month."

▶ **REALISTIC:** You and your friends will drive the 1000 miles in 15 hours, splitting driving time among the four of you. A vague goal is more like saying, "We'll make the trip in a day."

▶ **TIME-BOUND:** You'll have 75 percent of the money saved by May. A vague goal would be to say, "I'll have the money by mid-Spring" (CashCourse, 2011[a]).

Setting your own financial goals is not rocket science, but it is on the critical path to achieving financial literacy. Take the time now to write down your goals, revisit them often, accomplish them, and then create new goals to help ensure your financial well-being now and well into the later stages of your life.

THE SEVEN LEVELS OF MASLOW'S HIERARCHY OF NEEDS

Abraham Maslow was a psychologist who in the 1940s introduced the concept of a "hierarchy of needs" as an explanation of a person's growth and development as that person works to achieve their full potential. Usually presented as a pyramid (see Figure 7-1), the hierarchy suggests that people are motivated to fulfill the most basic of needs first before moving on to other needs (Cherry, n.d.).

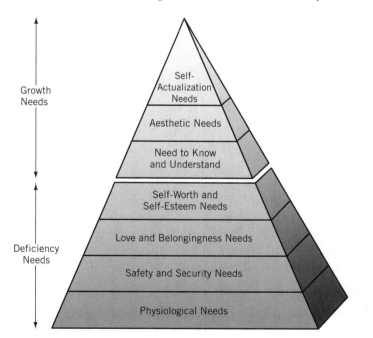

Figure 7-1 Maslow's Hierarchy of Needs.

Source: Text Material adapted from D. Martin and K. Joomis, *Building Teachers: A Constructivist Approach to Introducing Education*, (Belmont, CA: Wadsworth, 2007), pp. 72-75

TYPES OF NEEDS

As you can see, the lowest levels of the pyramid comprise a person's most basic needs, while the top of the pyramid denotes more complex needs. Maslow believed that a person's needs are similar to instincts and that they play a significant role in motivating human behavior (Cherry, n.d.). The lowest four needs—physiological, safety and security, love and belongingness, and self-worth and self-esteem—are considered deficiency needs (also known as D-needs), essential for a person's well-being. These needs must be satisfied before the person is motivated to seek experiences that pertain to the upper levels (Martin and Joomis, 2007).

The top three layers of the pyramid—the need to know and understand, aesthetic needs, and the need for self-actualization—are considered growth needs (sometimes referred to as being needs or B-needs). Growth needs can never be satisfied completely. Contrary to the deficiency needs, for which motivation diminishes when a need is satisfied, as growth needs are met, people's motivation to meet additional growth needs increases. The more these needs are satisfied, the more people want to pursue them. For example, the more one comes to understand, the more one's motivation to learn more increases (Martin and Joomis, 2007). Detailed information on each of the seven levels follows:

▶ **PHYSIOLOGICAL NEEDS.** Maslow suggested that the first and most basic need people have is the need for survival: their physiological requirements for food, water, and shelter. People must have food to eat, water to drink, and a place to call home before they can think about anything else. If any of these physiological necessities is missing, people are motivated above all else to meet that missing need.

▶ **SAFETY AND SECURITY NEEDS.** After their physiological needs have been satisfied, people can work to meet their needs for safety and security. (But the physiological needs must be met first.) Safety is the feeling people get when they know no harm will befall them physically, mentally, or emotionally; security is the feeling people get when their fears and anxieties are low.

▶ **LOVE AND BELONGINGNESS NEEDS.** After the physiological needs and the needs for survival and for safety and security have been met, an individual can be motivated to meet the needs represented at higher levels of the pyramid. The third level of the pyramid represents needs associated with love and belonging. These needs are met through satisfactory relationships—relationships with family members, friends, peers, classmates, teachers, and other people with whom individuals interact. Satisfactory relationships imply acceptance by others. Having satisfied their physiological and security needs, people can venture out and seek relationships from which their need for love and belonging can be met.

▶ **SELF-WORTH AND SELF-ESTEEM NEEDS.** Once individuals have satisfactorily met their need for love and belonging, they can begin to develop positive feelings of self-worth and self-esteem and act to foster pride in their work and in themselves as people. Before they can work toward self-esteem, however, they must feel safe, secure, and part of a group such as a class in school.

▶ **NEED TO KNOW AND UNDERSTAND.** The fifth level of Maslow's pyramid represents an individual's need to know and understand. According to Maslow's hierarchy, this motivation cannot occur until the deficiency needs have been met to the individual's satisfaction.

▶ **AESTHETIC NEEDS. Aesthetics** refers to the quality of being creatively, beautifully, or artistically pleasing; aesthetic needs are the needs to express oneself in pleasing ways. People are motivated to meet this need only after the previous five needs have been met.

▶ **NEED FOR SELF-ACTUALIZATION.** At the top of the pyramid is the need for **self-actualization**, which is a person's desire to become everything he or she is capable of becoming—to realize and use his or her full potential, capacities, and talents. This need can be addressed only when the previous six have been satisfied. It is rarely met completely; Maslow (1968) estimated that fewer than 1 percent of adults achieve total self-actualization (Martin and Joomis, 2007).

7

DISTINGUISHING BETWEEN NEEDS AND WANTS

One of the hardest things we learn as we grow up is how to under-stand the difference between a "need" and a "want." A **need** is something that is a necessity in life, such as food, water, and shelter. A **want** is something that is not a necessity but is desired to increase the quality of life. As you move into adulthood, it's very important that you have a clear understanding of these two terms and how they directly impact your financial well-being.

To look at it another way, a need is a "have to have" and a want is a "nice to have." So, for example, you may need a new pair of sneakers, but wanting the athlete-endorsed pair at three times the cost of a regular pair can get you into financial trouble, especially if it is at the expense of some of your identified needs. That's where so many young adults get into debt. The *want factor* overrides the *need factor*, and so out comes the credit card, or the failure to pay established bills, or dipping into savings (if there *are* savings), all of which are used to fulfill a want, not a need.

As Maslow's hierarchy of needs points out, motivation in life is key. When the first four levels of the pyramid, the deficiency needs, are met, motivation diminishes. You have food and shelter, you are safe and secure, you are loved and feel a part of a larger circle, and you have a measure of self-worth and self-esteem. It's all good, as they say. It's the status quo.

As a young person embarking on your adult life, now is the time for your growth needs (the top three levels of the pyramid) to come into play. Here's your opportunity to become motivated to reach your very greatest potential. Here's your chance at becoming financially literate.

GETTING STARTED ON YOUR FINANCIAL JOURNEY AND HOW TECHNOLOGY CAN HELP

As you will see in subsequent chapters in this book, technology is at the forefront of how we handle (but not necessarily successfully man-age) our finances. Paychecks are automatically deposited. Debit cards take the place of carrying cash. Online bill payment is the monthly

tanewpix/Shutterstock.com

Use technology to your advantage when it comes to managing your finances.

norm. Balances can be checked online from virtually any electronic device. It's quick. It's convenient. And it's easy. But "buyer beware."

Technology allows us to save time and headaches when tracking our funds. The only thing we seem to lose when using technology is the hands-on approach to our money—balancing our checkbook, getting cash to pay expenses, and the like (Jacobs, 2011). What often gets lost in all this technology is the ability to create and adhere to a budget, and that's where the trouble begins.

Each of the next five chapters in this book addresses the topics and skills you will need to lead you to becoming a financially literate person.

CASE IN POINT REVISITED

In the Case in Point presented at the beginning of this chapter, Lauren Bishop made the costly error of signing up for a credit card on campus and using it as soon as she received it. She allowed her desire for a new sweater to outweigh the financial burden its purchase would cost her, thus misinterpreting her needs from her wants.

Realizing after the first credit card statement came that she was in over her head financially, she decided to get an on-campus job two nights a week that would give her sufficient income to pay off her credit card as well as some extra money that she could use for the things she really wanted. She also decided to take the credit card out of her wallet and tuck it away in a drawer so she wouldn't be tempted to use it again.

CHAPTER SUMMARY

Chapter 7 introduced you to the concept of financial literacy. You are now familiar with what you need to do to be a financially literate individual and why being financially literate is important to your success. Conversely, you are aware of the challenges that can face an individual who is not financially literate.

POINTS TO KEEP IN MIND

- ▶ Financial literacy is the ability to use knowledge and skills to manage financial resources effectively for a lifetime of financial well-being.
- ▶ The financially literate person recognizes the pitfalls of poor financial management and seeks to avoid them.
- ▶ Identifying one's personal values helps clarify one's personal responsibilities when it comes to making financial decisions.
- ▶ It is important to distinguish between needs and wants.
- ▶ The use of technology can be of benefit when it comes to managing one's money.

CRITICAL THINKING QUESTIONS

1. What financial mistakes have you made at this stage in your life? How do you plan to correct them?

2. What are the advantages of "paying yourself first?"

3. From whom might you seek financial advice?

4. How do your personal goals affect your personal responsibilities when it comes to your finances?

5. How complete is your understanding of Maslow's hierarchy of needs? What level do you think you have reached on the pyramid? What changes can you make to reach the next level?

6. In what (desirable) ways might you express yourself aesthetically at home or in the classroom?

7. Do you use technology to your advantage when it comes to your finances? If so, how? In what areas might you improve?

8. Define *financial literacy*.

9. Name the specific knowledge required for an individual to be a financially literate student or professional.

10. Explain the importance of identifying one's personal values and personal responsibilities in terms of becoming financially literate.

11. Outline the challenges facing an individual who does not possess financial skills in school and in the workplace.

7

apply it!

 Activity #1: Self-Analysis: Grading Your Financial Acumen

GOAL: Critically assess where you stand in your "financial education" and generate a list of areas for improvement.

Using the following rating table, rate yourself in each area, using a scale from 1 to 4, where

1 = what you know you don't know

2 = what you think you might not know

3 = what you think you know

4 = what you know you know

Be honest.

RATING TABLE	
Area	**Rating 1–4**
Creating, Adhering to, and Adjusting a Budget	
Saving While in College	
Saving for a Big Purchase	
Saving for Emergencies	
Saving for the Future	
Responsible Use of Credit Cards	
Good Debt Versus Bad Debt	
Avoiding Credit Card Fraud and Identity Theft	
Types of Bank Accounts and Banking Services	
How Online Banking Works	
Options for Financial Aid	
Getting and Paying Off Student Loans	
Obligations and Responsibilities for Paying Taxes	
Identifying Types of Taxes You Might Need to Pay	
Ways of Filing Taxes	
Consequences of Not Paying Taxes	

The remaining chapters in this book will address all the areas listed in the table.

Activity #2: Identifying Your Personal Values

GOAL: Identify your personal values and why these values are important to you.

STEP 1: Using the following table, identify the 10 personal values that are most important to you. A list of personal value examples has been provided for your use, or you may use your own.

MY PERSONAL VALUES	
Value	**Why This Value is Important to Me**

Personal value examples include the following:

Ambition, competency, individuality, equality, integrity, service, responsibility, accuracy, respect, dedication, diversity, improvement, enjoyment and fun, loyalty, credibility, honesty, innovativeness, teamwork, excellence, accountability, empowerment, quality, efficiency, dignity, collaboration, stewardship, empathy, accomplishment, courage, wisdom, independence, security, challenge, influence, learning, compassion, friendliness, discipline and order, generosity, persistency, optimism, dependability, flexibility

7

CHECK YOUR UNDERSTANDING

Visit www.cengagebrain.com to see how well you have mastered the material in Chapter 7.

REFERENCES

Bowman, M. (n.d.). *It's all about responsibility.* Retrieved October 20, 2011, from http://www.bowmansmoneycollege.com/Articles/Financial_responsibility.htm

Brunkhorst, S. (2005). *12 reflections on personal responsibility.* Retrieved November 3, 2011, from http://www.boxingscene.com/motivation/29761.php

CashCourse (2011[a]). *Accomplishing financial goals.* Retrieved October 26, 2011, from http://www.cashcourse.org/oregonstate//articles/id/1808/categoryid/113/accomplishing-financial-goals

CashCourse (2011[b]). *Defining financial goals.* Retrieved October 26, 2011, from http://www.cashcourse.org/oregonstate//articles/id/1807/categoryid/113/defining-financial-goals

Cherry, K. (n.d.). *Hierarchy of needs. The five levels of Maslow's hierarchy of needs.* Retrieved October 20, 2011, from http://psychology.about.com/od/theoriesofpersonality/a/hierarchyneeds.htm

Department of the Treasury (2008). President's Advisory Council on Financial Literacy. *2008 annual report to the president.* Retrieved October 26, 2011, from http://www.jumpstart.org/assets/files/PACFL_ANNUAL_REPORT_1-16-09.pdf

Federal Deposit Insurance Corporation (Spring 2005). FDIC Consumer News. Special Guide for Young Adults. Retrieved October 26, 2011, from http://www.fdic.gov/consumers/consumer/news/cnspr05/spring_05_bw.pdf

Garman, E. and Forgue, R. (2010). *Personal Finance, 10th ed.* Mason, OH: South-Western Cengage Learning.

Hereford, Z. (n.d.). *Have a personal value system.* Retrieved October 20, 2011, from www.essentiallifeskills.net/personalvaluesystem.html

Jacobs, D. (2011). *Has technology killed our ability to manage our money?* Retrieved October 20, 2011, from http://moneyhealthcentral.com/has-technology-ended-the-family-budget/

Martin, D. and Joomis, K. (2007). *Building Teachers: A Constructivist Approach to Introducing Education,* Belmont, CA: Wadsworth. Retrieved November 4, 2011, from http://academic.cengage.com/resource_uploads/downloads/0495570540_162121.pdf

Schmansky, R. (2010). *Building your financial foundation: watch out for money complacency.* Retrieved October 26, 2011, from http://blog.fpaforfinancial-planning.org/2010/07/27/building-your-financial-foundation-watch-out-for-money-complacency/

Schmansky, R. (2010). *Unsure of what to do next? Know where you stand in your financial life cycle.* Retrieved October 21, 2011, from http://blog.fpaforfinancialplanning.org/2010/07/12/unsure-of-what-to-do-next-know-where-you-stand-in-your-financial-life-cycle/

Shorb, V. (n.d.). National Financial Educators Council. *Financial literacy and the revival of the American dream.* Retrieved October 26, 2011, from http://www.financialeducatorscouncil.org/pdf/bonus/financial_literacy.pdf

Tracy, B. (n.d.) *Taking personal responsibility.* Retrieved November 2, 2011, from http://www.successmethods.org/brian_tracy-a19.html

Answer key for Financial Aptitude Test on p. 8

1. False
2. False
3. True
4. False
5. True
6. False
7. False
8. True
9. False
10. True

Managing Change

Use this **Master Student Map** to ask yourself

HOW I CAN USE THIS CHAPTER . . .

• Connect with the natural learner within me.
• Discover a way to interact with books that multiplies their value.
• Use a journal to translate personal discoveries into powerful new behaviors.

WHAT IF . . .

• I could use the ideas in this book to more consistently get what I want in my life?

CRITICAL THINKING EXERCISE 1

Textbook reconnaissance

Start becoming a master employee this moment by doing a 15-minute "textbook reconnaissance." First, read this book's Table of Contents. Do it in 3 minutes or less. Next, look at every page in the book. Move quickly. Scan headlines. Look at pictures. Notice forms, charts, and diagrams.

Look especially for ideas you can use. When you find one, write the page number and a short description of the idea here. You also can use sticky notes to flag pages that look useful. (If you're reading *From Master Student to Master Employee* as an ebook, you can flag pages electronically.)

_____
_____
_____
_____
_____
_____
_____
_____
_____
_____

© Ruslan Ivantsov/Shutterstock.com

POWER process

Discover what you want

Imagine a person who walks up to a counter at the airport to buy a plane ticket for his next vacation. "Just give me a ticket," he says to the reservation agent. "Anywhere will do."

The agent stares back at him in disbelief. "I'm sorry, sir," she replies. "I'll need some more details. Just minor things—such as the name of your destination city and your arrival and departure dates."

"Oh, I'm not fussy," says the would-be vacationer. "I just want to get away. You choose for me."

Compare this person to another traveler who walks up to the counter and says, "I'd like a ticket to Ixtapa, Mexico, departing on Saturday, March 23, and returning Sunday, April 7. Please give me a window seat, first class, with vegetarian meals."

Now, ask yourself which traveler is more likely to end up with a vacation that he'll enjoy.

The same principle applies in any area of life. Knowing where we want to go increases the probability that we will arrive at our destination. Discovering what we want makes it more likely that we'll attain it.

Okay, so the example about the traveler with no destination is far-fetched. Before you dismiss it, though, do an informal experiment: Ask three other students what they want to get out of their education. Be prepared for hemming and hawing, vague generalities, and maybe even a helping of pie in the sky à la mode.

This is amazing, considering the stakes involved. Students routinely invest years of their lives and thousands of dollars, with only a hazy idea of their destination in life.

Now suppose that you asked someone what she wanted from her education and you got this answer: "I plan to get a degree in journalism with double minors in earth science and Portuguese so that I can work as a reporter covering the environment in Brazil." The details of a person's vision offer clues to their skills and sense of purpose.

Another clue is the presence of "stretch goals"—those that are big *and* achievable. A 40-year-old might spend years talking about his desire to be a professional athlete some day. Chances are, that's no longer achievable. However, setting a goal to lose 10 pounds by playing basketball at the gym 3 days a week is another matter. That's a stretch—a challenge. It's also doable.

Discovering what you want helps you succeed in higher education. Many students quit school simply because they are unsure about what they want from it. With well-defined goals in mind, you can look for connections between what you want and what you study. The more connections, the more likely you'll stay in school—and get what you want in every area of life.[1]

You're One Click Away...
from accessing Power Process media online and finding out more about "Discovering what you want."

iStockphoto.com/mathieukor

8

Master student
qualities

This book is about something that cannot be taught. It's about becoming a master student and master employee.

Mastery means attaining a level of skill that goes beyond technique. For a master, work is effortless; struggle evaporates. The master carpenter is so familiar with her tools that they are part of her. To a master chef, utensils are old friends. Because these masters don't have to think about the details of the process, they bring more of themselves to their work.

COLLABORATIVE
CRITICAL
RESPONSIBLE
CREATIVE
Willing to change
COMMUNICATIVE
willing to work
WILLING TO TAKE RISKS
SELF directed

Oliver Cleve/Getty Images

Mastery can lead to flashy results: an incredible painting, for example, or a gem of a short story. In basketball, mastery might result in an unbelievable shot at the buzzer. For a musician, it might be the performance of a lifetime, the moment when everything comes together. You could describe the experience as "flow" or being "in the zone."

Often, the result of mastery is a sense of profound satisfaction, well-being, and timelessness. Distractions fade. Time stops. Work becomes play. After hours of patient practice, after setting clear goals and getting precise feedback, the master has learned to be fully in control.

At the same time, he lets go of control. Results happen without effort, struggle, or worry. Work seems self-propelled. The master is in control by being out of control. He lets go and allows the creative process to take over. That's why after a spectacular performance by an athlete or performer, observers often say, "He played full out—and made it look like he wasn't even trying."

Likewise, the master student is one who makes learning look easy. She works hard without seeming to make any effort. She's relaxed *and* alert, disciplined *and* spontaneous, focused *and* fun-loving.

You might say that those statements don't make sense. Actually, mastery does *not* make sense. It cannot be captured with words. It defies analysis. Mastery cannot be taught. It can only be learned and experienced.

By design, you are a learning machine. As an infant, you learned to walk. As a toddler, you learned to talk. By the time you reached age five, you'd mastered many skills needed to thrive in the world. And you learned all these things without formal instruction, without lectures, without books, without conscious effort, and without fear.

Shortly after we start school, however, something happens to us. Somehow we start forgetting about the master student inside us. Even under the best teachers, we experience the discomfort that sometimes accompanies learning. We start avoiding situations that might lead to embarrassment. We turn away from experiences that could lead to mistakes. We accumulate a growing list of ideas to defend, a catalog of familiar experiences that discourages us from learning anything new. Slowly, we restrict our possibilities and potentials.

However, the story doesn't end there. You can open a new chapter in your life, starting today. You can rediscover the natural learner within you. Each chapter of this book is about a step you can take on this path.

Master students share certain qualities. These are attitudes and core values. Though they imply various strategies for learning, they ultimately go beyond what you do. Master student qualities are ways of *being* exceptional.

Following is a list of master student qualities. Remember that the list is not complete. It merely points in a direction.

As you read the following list, look to yourself. Put a check mark next to each quality that you've already demonstrated. Put another mark, say an exclamation point, next to each quality you want to actively work on possessing. This is not a test. It is simply a chance to celebrate what you've accomplished so far—and start thinking about what's possible for your future.

☐ **Inquisitive.** The master student is curious about everything. By posing questions, she can generate interest in the most mundane, humdrum situations. When she is bored during a biology lecture, she thinks to herself, "I always get bored when I listen to this instructor. Why is that? Maybe it's because he reminds me of my boring Uncle Ralph, who always tells those endless fishing stories. He even looks like Uncle Ralph. Amazing! Boredom is certainly interesting." Then she asks herself, "What can I do to get value out of this lecture, even though it seems boring?" And she finds an answer.

☐ **Able to focus attention.** Watch a two-year-old at play. Pay attention to his eyes. The wide-eyed look reveals an energy and a capacity for amazement that keep his attention absolutely focused in the here and now. The master student's focused attention has a childlike quality. The world, to a child, is always new. Because the master student can focus attention, to him the world is always new too.

☐ **Willing to change.** The unknown does not frighten the master student. In fact, she welcomes it—even the unknown in herself. We all have pictures of who we think we are, and these pictures can be useful. But they also can prevent learning and growth. The master student is open to changes in her environment and in herself.

☐ **Able to organize and sort.** The master student can take a large body of information and sift through it to discover relationships. He can play with information, organizing data by size, color, function, timeliness, and hundreds of other categories. He has the guts to set big goals—and the precision to plan carefully so that those goals can be achieved.

☐ **Competent.** Mastery of skills is important to the master student. When she learns mathematical formulas, she studies them until they become second nature. She practices until she knows them cold, then puts in a few extra minutes. She also is able to apply what she learns to new and different situations.

☐ **Joyful.** More often than not, the master student is seen with a smile on his face—sometimes a smile at nothing

in particular other than amazement at the world and his experience of it.

☐ **Able to suspend judgment.** The master student has opinions and positions, and she is able to let go of them when appropriate. She realizes she is more than her thoughts. She can quiet her internal dialogue and listen to an opposing viewpoint. She doesn't let judgment get in the way of learning. Rather than approaching discussions with a "Prove it to me and then I'll believe it" attitude, she asks herself, "What if this is true?" and explores possibilities.

☐ **Energetic.** Notice the student with a spring in his step, the one who is enthusiastic and involved in class. When he reads, he often sits on the very edge of his chair, and he plays with the same intensity. He is determined and persistent. He is a master student.

☐ **Well.** Health is important to the master student, though not necessarily in the sense of being free of illness. Rather, she values her body and treats it with respect. She tends to her emotional and spiritual health as well as her physical health.

☐ **Self-aware.** The master student is willing to evaluate himself and his behavior. He regularly tells the truth about his strengths and those aspects that could be improved.

☐ **Responsible.** There is a difference between responsibility and blame, and the master student knows it well. She is willing to take responsibility for everything in her life—even for events that most people would blame on others.

For example, if a master student takes a required class that most students consider boring, she chooses to take responsibility for her interest level. She looks for ways to link the class to one of her goals. She sees the class as an opportunity to experiment with new study techniques that will enhance her performance in any course. She remembers that by choosing her thoughts and behaviors, she can create interesting classes, enjoyable relationships, fulfilling work experiences, or just about anything else she wants.

☐ **Willing to take risks.** The master student often takes on projects with no guarantee of success. He participates in class dialogues at the risk of looking foolish. He tackles difficult subjects in term papers. He welcomes the risk of a challenging course.

☐ **Willing to participate.** Don't look for the master student on the sidelines. She's in the game. She is a team player who can be counted on. She is engaged at school, at work, and with friends and family. She is willing to make a commitment and to follow through on it.

☐ **A generalist.** The master student is interested in everything around him. In the classroom, he is fully present.

Outside the classroom, he actively seeks out ways to deepen his learning—through study groups, campus events, student organizations, and team-based projects,. Through such experiences, he develops a broad base of knowledge in many fields that can apply to his specialties.

☐ **Willing to accept paradox.** The word *paradox* comes from two Greek words, *para* ("beyond") and *doxen* ("opinion"). A paradox is something that is beyond opinion or, more accurately, something that might seem contradictory or absurd yet might actually have meaning.

For example, the master student can be committed to managing money and reaching her financial goals. At the same time, she can be totally detached from money, knowing that her real worth is independent of how much money she has. The master student recognizes the limitations of the mind and is at home with paradox. She can accept that ambiguity.

☐ **Courageous.** The master student admits his fear and fully experiences it. For example, he will approach a tough exam as an opportunity to explore feelings of anxiety and tension related to the pressure to perform. He does not deny fear; he embraces it. If he doesn't understand something or if he makes a mistake, he admits it. When he faces a challenge and bumps into his limits, he asks for help. And, he's just as willing to give help as to receive it.

☐ **Self-directed.** Rewards or punishments provided by others do not motivate the master student. Her desire to learn comes from within, and her goals come from herself. She competes like a star athlete—not to defeat other people but to push herself to the next level of excellence.

☐ **Spontaneous.** The master student is truly in the here and now. He is able to respond to the moment in fresh, surprising, and unplanned ways.

☐ **Relaxed about grades.** Grades make the master student neither depressed nor euphoric. She recognizes that sometimes grades are important. At the same time, grades are not the only reason she studies. She does not measure her worth as a human being by the grades she receives.

☐ **Intuitive.** The master student has an inner sense that cannot be explained by logic alone. He trusts his "gut instincts" as well as his mind.

☐ **Able to communicate.** Human beings are sending messages every second that they're awake. These messages are verbal and nonverbal, intellectual and emotional, clear and confused. The master student communicates at all these levels by transforming the raw material of words and gestures into a chorus of shared meaning. And when conflict occurs between people, the master student sees it as a chance to create a new level of understanding.

☐ **Able to collaborate.** The master student knows that when people passionately share a goal, they can accomplish more by acting as a group than acting alone. When team members polarize around two competing points of view, the master student seizes the power of the "third force"—a new option that includes the best elements of everyone's ideas.

☐ **Able to think creatively.** Where others see dull details and trivia, the master student sees opportunities to create. She can gather pieces of knowledge from a wide range of subjects and put them together in new ways. The master student is creative in every aspect of her life.

☐ **Able to think critically.** Not all ideas are created equal. The master student has the rare ability to remain open-minded and skeptical at the same time. She can analyze, evaluate, and apply ideas with a keen eye for logic, evidence, and usefulness.

☐ **Willing to be uncomfortable.** The master student does not place comfort first. When discomfort is necessary to reach a goal, he is willing to experience it. He can endure personal hardships and can look at unpleasant things with detachment.

☐ **Optimistic.** The master student sees setbacks as temporary and isolated, knowing that he can choose his response to any circumstance.

☐ **Willing to laugh.** The master student might laugh at any moment, and his sense of humor includes the ability to laugh at himself. While going to school is a big investment, with high stakes, you don't have to enroll in the deferred-fun program. A master student celebrates learning, and one of the best ways of doing that is to laugh now and then.

☐ **Hungry.** Human beings begin life with a natural appetite for knowledge. In some people it soon gets dulled. The master student has tapped that hunger, and it gives her a desire to learn for the sake of learning.

☐ **Willing to work.** Once inspired, the master student is willing to follow through with sweat. He knows that genius and creativity are the result of persistence and work. When in high gear, the master student works with the intensity of a child at play.

☐ **Caring.** A master student cares about knowledge and has a passion for ideas. She also cares about people and appreciates learning from others. She collaborates on projects and thrives on teams. She flourishes in a community that values win-win outcomes, cooperation, and love. ■

✓ CRITICAL THINKING EXERCISE 2

The master student in you

The purpose of this exercise is to demonstrate to yourself that you truly are a master student. Start by remembering a time in your life when you learned something well or demonstrated mastery. This experience does not have to relate to school. It might be a time when you aced a test, played a flawless soccer game, created a work of art that won recognition, or burst forth with a blazing guitar solo. It might be a time when you spoke from your heart in a way that moved someone else. Or it might be a time when you listened deeply to another person who was in pain, comforted him, and connected with him at a level beyond words.

Describe the details of such an experience in your life. Include the place, time, and people involved. Describe what happened and how you felt about it.

_____

_____

_____

_____

_____

_____

Now, review the article "Master student qualities" and take a look at the master student qualities that you checked off. These are the qualities that apply to you. Give a brief example of how you demonstrated at least one of those qualities.

_____

_____

_____

_____

_____

_____

Now think of other qualities of a master student—characteristics that were not mentioned in the article. List those qualities here, along with a one-sentence description of each.

_____

_____

_____

_____

_____

JOURNAL ENTRY 1
Discovery Statement

Declare what you want

Review the "Power Process: Discover what you want" on page 2. Then, writing on separate paper, brainstorm possible ways to complete the following sentence. When you're done, choose the ending that feels best to you and write it below.

I discovered that what I want most from my education is . . .

_____

_____

_____

_____

_____

This book is worthless—
if you just read it

iStockphoto.com/Franck-Boston

The first edition of this book began with the sentence *This book is worthless*. Many students thought beginning this way was a trick to get their attention. It wasn't. Others thought it was reverse psychology. It wasn't that either. Still others thought it meant that the book was worthless if they didn't read it. It meant more than that.

This book is worthless *even if you read it*—if reading it is all you do. What was true of that first edition is true of this one as well. Until you take action and use the ideas in it, *From Master Student to Master Employee* really is worthless.

The purpose of this book is to help you make a successful transition to higher education by setting up a pattern of success that will last the rest of your life. You probably won't take action and use the ideas in this book until you are convinced that you have something to gain. That's the reason for this introduction—to persuade you to use this book actively.

Before you stiffen up and resist this sales pitch, remember that you have already bought the book. Now you can get something for your money by committing yourself to take action—in other words, by committing yourself to From Master Student to Master Employee. Here's what's in it for you.

Pitch #1: You can save money now and make more money later. Start with money. Your college education is one of the most expensive things you will ever buy. You might find yourself paying $100 an hour to sit in class. (See Critical Thinking Exercise 13: "Education by the hour," on page 106, to come up with a specific figure that applies to your own education.)

As a master student, you control the value you get out of your education, and that value can be considerable. The joy of learning aside, higher levels of education relate to higher lifetime income and more consistent employment.[2] It pays to be a master student.

Pitch #2: You can rediscover the natural learner in you. Joy is important too. As you become a master student, you will learn to gain knowledge in the most effective way possible—by discovering the joyful, natural learner within you.

Children are great natural students. They quickly master complex skills, such as language, and they have fun doing it. For young children, learning is a high-energy process involving experimentation, discovery, and sometimes broken dishes. Then comes school. For some students, drill and drudgery replace discovery and dish breaking. Learning can become a drag. You can use this book to reverse that process and rediscover what you knew as a child—that laughter and learning go hand in hand.

Sometimes—and especially in college—learning does take effort. As you become a master student, you will learn many ways to get the most out of that effort.

Pitch #3: You can choose from hundreds of techniques. *From Master Student to Master Employee* is packed with hundreds of practical, nuts-and-bolts techniques. And you can begin using them immediately. For example, during the "Textbook reconnaissance," on page 1, you might find three powerful learning techniques in one exercise. Even if you doze in lectures, drift off during tests, or dawdle on term papers, you'll find ideas in this book that you can use to become a more effective student.

Not all of these ideas will work for you. That's why there are so many of them in *From Master Student to Master Employee*. You should experiment with the techniques. As you discover what works, you will develop a unique style of learning that you can use for the rest of your life.

Pitch #4: You get the best suggestions from thousands of students. The concepts and techniques in this book are here not just because learning theorists, educators, and psychologists say they work, but because tens of thousands of students from all kinds of backgrounds have tried them and agree that they work. These are students who dreaded giving speeches, couldn't read their own notes, and fell behind in their course work. Then they figured out how to solve those problems. Now you can use their ideas.

Pitch #5: You can learn about yourself. The process of self-discovery is an important theme in *From Master Student to Master Employee*. Throughout the book, you can use Journal Entries for everything from organizing your desk to choosing long-term goals. Studying for an organic chemistry quiz is a lot easier with a clean desk and a clear idea of the course's importance to you.

Pitch #6: You can use a proven product. The previous editions of this book have proved successful for hundreds of thousands of students. Student feedback has been positive. In particular, students with successful histories have praised the techniques in this book.

Pitch #7: You can learn the secret of student success. If this sales pitch still hasn't persuaded you to use this book actively, maybe it's time to reveal the secret of student success.

(Provide your own drum roll here.)

The secret is . . . there are no secrets. The ultimate formula is to give up formulas, keep experimenting, and find strategies that actually help you meet your goals.

The strategies that successful students use are well-known. You have hundreds of them at your fingertips right now, in this book. Use them. Modify them. Invent new ones. You're the authority on what works for you.

However, what makes any technique work is commitment—and action. Without them, the pages of *From Master Student to Master Employee* are just 2.1 pounds of expensive mulch.

Add your participation to the mulch, and these pages become priceless. ■

Master Employees
IN ACTION

"*I had a lot of difficulties in interviews, especially when an interviewer would ask me to describe myself. Looking back now, I realize that I was lucky I wasn't hired for any of those positions. It forced me to stop and be more critical about the type of person I was, and the type of job that would truly suit me. When I finally found a job opening that interested me, I discovered that I didn't have any problem in the interview.*"

—*Matt Carle,*
Graphic Designer

You're One Click Away...
from watching a video about Master Students in Action online.

© iStockphoto.com/kryczka

✓ CRITICAL THINKING EXERCISE 3

Commitment

This book is worthless unless you actively participate in its activities and exercises. One powerful way to begin taking action is to make a commitment. Conversely, if you don't make a commitment, then sustained action is unlikely. The result is a worthless book. Therefore, in the interest of saving your valuable time and energy, this exercise gives you a chance to declare your level of involvement up front. From the options below, choose the sentence that best reflects your commitment to using this book. Write the number of the sentence in the space provided at the end of the list.

1. "Well, I'm reading this book right now, aren't I?"
2. "I will skim the book and read the interesting parts."
3. "I will read the book, think about it, and do the exercises that look interesting."
4. "I will read the book, do some exercises, and complete some of the Journal Entries."
5. "I will read the book, do some exercises and Journal Entries, and use some of the techniques."
6. "I will read the book, do most of the exercises and Journal Entries, and use some of the techniques."
7. "I will study this book, do most of the exercises and Journal Entries, and use some of the techniques."
8. "I will study this book, do most of the exercises and Journal Entries, and experiment with many of the techniques in order to discover what works best for me."
9. "I promise myself that I will create value from this course by studying this book, doing all the exercises and Journal Entries, and experimenting with most of the techniques."
10. "I will use this book as if the quality of my education depended on it—doing all the exercises and Journal Entries, experimenting with most of the techniques, inventing techniques of my own, and planning to reread this book in the future."

Write the sentence number that best describes your commitment level and today's date here:

Commitment level _____ Date _____

If you selected commitment level 1 or 2, you probably won't create a lot of value in this class, and you might consider passing this book on to a friend. If your commitment level is 9 or 10, you are on your way to terrific success in school. If your level is somewhere in between, experiment with the techniques and learning strategies in this book. If you find that they work, consider returning to this exercise and raising your level of commitment.

Get the most out of this book

Get used to a new look and tone. This book looks different from traditional textbooks. *From Master Student to Master Employee* presents major ideas in magazine-style articles. There are lots of lists, blurbs, one-liners, pictures, charts, graphs, illustrations, and even a joke or two.

Rip 'em out. The pages of *From Master Student to Master Employee* are perforated because some of the information here is too important to leave in the book. For example, Journal Entry 2 asks you to list some important things you want to get out of your education. To keep yourself focused on these goals, you could rip out that page and post it on your bathroom mirror—or some other place where you'll see it several times each day.

You can rip out pages and reinsert them later by sticking them into the spine of the book. A piece of tape will hold them in place.

Skip around. Feel free to use this book in several different ways. Read it straight through. Or pick it up, turn to any page, and find an idea you can use right now. For example, if you want to learn how to set and achieve goals, skip directly to the article on this topic in Chapter 3.

You might find that this book presents similar ideas in several places. This repetition is intentional. Repetition reinforces key points. Also, a technique that works in one area of your life might work in others as well.

If it works, use it. If it doesn't, lose it. If there are sections of this book that don't apply to you at all, skip them—unless, of course, they are assigned. In that case, see if you can gain value from those sections anyway. When you commit to get value from this book, even an idea that seems irrelevant or ineffective at first can turn out to be a powerful tool in the future.

Listen to your peers. Throughout this book you will find features titled Master Employees in Action. These are short quotations from people in the workforce who are using the ideas presented in this text. As you dig into the following chapters, think about what you would say if you could add your voice to theirs.

Own this book. Determine what you want to get out of school, and create a record of how you intend to get it by completing the Journal Entries throughout this book. Every time your pen touches a page, you move closer to mastery.

Do the exercises. Action makes this book work. To get the most out of this book, do most of the critical thinking exercises. (It's never too late to go back and do the ones you skipped.) Exercises invite you to write, touch, feel, move, see, search, ponder, speak, listen, recall, choose, commit, and create. You might even sing and dance. Learning often works best when it involves action.

CRITICAL THINKING EXERCISE 19

Take your thinking to another level

Recall an idea or suggestion from the chapter that you'd like to explore in more detail. Summarize it, and include the page number where it appears.

You've just done some thinking at **Level 1: Remembering**—Now, take your thinking about this idea or suggestion to **one** of the higher levels:

Level 2: Understanding—Explain this idea in your own words and give examples from your own experience.

Level 3: Applying—Use the idea to produce a desired result.

Level 4: Analyzing—Divide this idea into parts or steps.

Level 5: Evaluating—Rate the truth, usefulness or quality of the idea—and give reasons for your rating.

Level 6: Creating—Invent something new based on the idea.

Demonstrate your higher-level thinking by writing a brief paragraph in the space below. If you want to show your thinking in another way, then check with your instructor. In either case, clearly state your intended level of thinking (For example, "To apply this idea, I would . . .")

Learn about learning styles. Check out the Learning Styles Inventory and related articles in Chapter 2. This material can help you discover your preferred learning styles and allow you to explore new styles. Then, throughout the rest of this book, you'll find suggestions for applying your knowledge of learning styles. The modes of learning can be accessed by asking four basic questions: *Why? What? How?* and *What if?*

Master Employees
IN ACTION

❝ *The budgeting work that I do in the office has made me a better money manager in my own life. It has taught me that money is just a way to ascribe value, and not a value in and of itself. I've been better able to evaluate the things I care about and the things I can do without.* ❞

—*Bill White, Construction Manager*

You're One Click Away...
from a video about Master Students in Action.

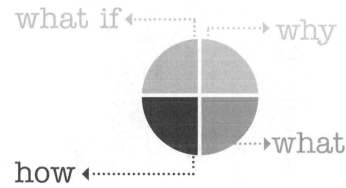

what if ← ·········· → why

how ← ·········· → what

Navigate through learning experiences with the Master Student Map. You can orient yourself for maximum learning every time you open this book by asking those same four questions: *Why? What? How?* and *What if?* That's the idea behind the Master Student Map included on the first page of each chapter, which includes sample answers to those questions. Remember that you can use the four-part structure of this map to effectively learn anything.

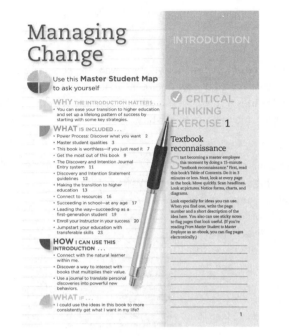

Experience the power of the Power Processes. A *Power Process* is a suggestion to shift your perspective or try on a new behavior. Look for this feature on the second page of each chapter. Users of *From Master Student to Master Employee* often refer to these articles as their favorite part of the book. Approach them with a sense of play and possibility. Start with an open mind, experiment with the ideas, and see what works.

Link to the Web. Throughout this book, you'll notice reminders to visit the College Success CourseMate for *From Master Student to Master Employee*. There you'll discover ways to take your involvement with this book to a deeper level. For example, access the Web site to do an online version of the Discovery Wheel exercise. Also look for videos, additional exercises, articles, PowerPoint slides, practice tests, and forms.

You're One Click Away...

To get access, visit
CengageBrain.com

© Cengage Learning 2013

Read the sidebars. Look for sidebars—short bursts of words placed between longer articles—throughout this book. These short pieces might offer insights that transform your experience of higher education.

Rewrite IN this book

Some books should be preserved in pristine condition. This book isn't one of them.

Something happens when you interact with your book by writing in it. *From Master Student to Master Employee* is about learning, and learning results when you are active. When you make notes in the margin, you can hear yourself talking with the author. When you doodle and underline, you see the author's ideas taking shape. You can even argue with the author and come up with your own theories and explanations. In all of these ways, you can become a coauthor of this book. Rewrite it to make it yours.

While you're at it, you can create symbols or codes that will help you when reviewing the text later on. You might insert a "Q" where you have questions or put exclamation points or stars next to important ideas. You could also circle words to look up in a dictionary.

Remember, if any idea in this book doesn't work for you, you can rewrite it. Change the exercises to fit your needs. Create a new technique by combining several others. Create a technique out of thin air!

Find something you agree or disagree with on

Focus on developing the "five Cs." One of the major goals of this book is to assist you in gaining skills that are valued in the workplace. In particular, you can benefit from developing the "five Cs"—character, creative thinking, critical thinking, communicating, and collaborating. For more details, see "Jumpstart your education with transferable skills" on page 23 and the Five Cs for Your Career articles near the end of each chapter. Use this material to make a seamless transition from success in school to success on the job. ■

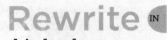

See character as a career asset. At the end of every workday, character boils down to two ideas that are weaved throughout this book: Define your values and align your actions. Another word for acting in alignment with your values is *integrity*, and it is a personal quality that your employers, clients, or customers will come to value.

When people know that they can count on you to make commitments and follow through, they'll be more willing to work with you over the long term. Integrity is more than an abstract word. It's also a practical strategy for surviving layoffs and increasing job security.

Think creatively about mistakes. Recall a mistake you made at work and then write about it. In a Discovery Statement, describe what you did to create a result you didn't want ("I discovered that I tend to underestimate the number of hours projects take"). Then write an Intention Statement describing something you can do differently in the future ("I intend to keep track of my actual hours on each project so that I can give more accurate estimates"). Doing these two things will help you mine valuable lessons and graduate from the school of hard knocks—with honors.

Thinking critically about your successes. You can also use journal entries to think critically about things that go well in your work life. Throughout your career, keep track of the positive outcomes you produce at work, including financial successes. Summarize these results in a sentence or two and add them to your résumé as well. Whenever you deliver a project on time and on budget, write Discovery Statements about how you created that result. Follow up with Intention Statements about ways to be even more effective on your next project.

Stay in communication about trends that will affect your career. Keep up to date with breaking changes in the job market

leaders and major players in your industry on social networks such as Twitter, Facebook, and LinkedIn.

Periodicals. Read the business sections of the *New York Times* and the *Wall Street Journal*, for example. Most newspapers also have online editions, as do magazines such as *Wired* and *Business Week*.

Professional associations. People in similar jobs like to band together and give each other a heads up on emerging trends—one reason for professional associations. These range from the American Medical Association to the Society of Actuaries. There's bound to be one for people in your field. Ask colleagues and search the Internet. *Note:* Many associations maintain Web sites and publish newsletters or trade magazines.

Conferences and conventions. Many professional associations sponsor annual meetings. Here's where you can meet people face to face and use your networking skills. Print and online publications are powerful sources of news, but sometimes nothing beats plain old schmoozing. Ask people at work what professional organizations they have joined.

Use the Power Processes to become a rock-star collaborator. They're full of ideas for producing results *and* building relationships.

Take the "Power Process: I create it all," for example. Before blaming a snafu on a coworker, look for any ways that you might have contributed to the problem. Even if you did *not* contribute to the problem, look for ways that you can contribute to the solution. Write Intention Statements to clarify what you will think, say, and do in the future to create a more positive work environment. In the workplace, problem solvers are valued.

By the way, one of the ideas behind "I create it all" is to create a gap between stimulus and response. See if you can fill this gap

The *Discovery and Intention Journal Entry* system

Using the Discovery and Intention Journal Entry system is a little like flying a plane. Airplanes are seldom exactly on course. Human and automatic pilots are always checking an airplane's positions and making corrections. The resulting flight path looks like a zigzag. The plane is almost always flying in the wrong direction, but because of constant observation and course correction, it arrives at the right destination.

As a student, you can use a similar approach. Journal Entries throughout this book are labeled as Discovery Statements, Intention Statements, or Discovery/Intention Statements. Each Journal Entry contains a short set of suggestions that involve writing.

Hello Author I Agree :)

Through Discovery Statements, you gain **awareness** of "where you are." These statements are a record of what you are learning about yourself as a student—both your strengths and your weaknesses. **Discovery Statements can also be declarations of your goals, descriptions of your attitudes, statements of your feelings, transcripts of your thoughts, and chronicles of your behavior.**

Sometimes Discovery Statements chronicle an "aha!" moment—a flash of insight that results when you connect a new idea with your prior experiences, preferred styles of learning, or both. Perhaps a solution to a long-standing problem suddenly occurs to you. Or a life-changing insight wells up from the deepest recesses of your mind. Don't let such moments disappear. Capture them in Discovery Statements.

Intention Statements can be used to alter your course. These statements are about your **commitment** to take action based on increased awareness. An intention arises out of your choice to direct your energy toward a specific task and to aim at a particular goal. The processes of discovery and intention reinforce each other.

Even simple changes in behavior can produce results. If you feel like procrastinating, then tackle just one small, specific task related to your intention. Find something you can complete in 5 minutes or less, and do it *now*. For example, access just one Web site related to the topic of your next assigned paper. Spend just 3 minutes previewing a reading assignment. Taking "baby steps" like these can move you into action with grace and ease.

The purpose of this system is not to get you pumped up and excited to go out there and try harder. In fact, Discovery and Intention Statements are intended to help you work smarter rather than harder.

The process of discovery, intention, and action creates a dynamic and efficient cycle. First, you write Discovery Statements about where you are now. Next, you write Intention Statements about where you want to be and the specific steps you will take to get there. Finally, you follow up with action—the sooner, the better.

Then you start the cycle again. Write Discovery Statements about whether or how you act on your Intention Statements—and what you learn in the process. Follow up with more Intention Statements about what you will do differently in the future. Then move into action and describe what happens next.

This process never ends. Each time you repeat the cycle, you get new results. It's all about getting what you want and becoming more effective in everything you do. This is the path of mastery— a path that you can travel for the rest of your life.

Sometimes a Discovery or Intention Statement will be long and detailed. Usually, it will be short—maybe just a line or two. With practice, the cycle will become automatic.

Don't panic when you fail to complete an intended task. Straying off course is normal. Simply make the necessary corrections. Consider the first word in the title of this book—*becoming*. This word implies that mastery is not an end state or final goal. Rather, mastery is a process that never ends.

Miraculous progress might not come immediately. Do not be concerned. Stay with the cycle. Give it time. Use Discovery Statements to get a clear view of your world. Then use Intention Statements to direct your actions. Whenever you notice progress, record it.

The following statement might strike you as improbable, but it is true: It can take the same amount of energy to get what you *don't* want in school as it takes to get what you *do* want. Sometimes getting what you don't want takes even more effort. An airplane burns the same amount of fuel flying away from its destination as it does flying toward it. It pays to stay on course.

You can use the Discovery and Intention Journal Entry system to stay on your own course and get what you want out of school. Start with the Journal Entries included in the text. Then go beyond them. Write Discovery and Intention Statements of your own at any time, for any purpose. Create new strategies whenever you need them, based on your current situation.

Once you get the hang of it, you might discover you can fly. ∎

Discovery and Intention Statement Guidelines

Writing Journal Entries helps you to develop self-awareness, self-direction, and other master student qualities. Use the following guidelines as a checklist. Consider removing this page from the book and posting it in a prominent place where you'll typically be writing your responses to the Journal Entries.

DISCOVERY STATEMENTS

☐ **Record the specifics about your thoughts, feelings, and behavior.** Notice your thoughts, observe your actions, and record them accurately. Get the facts.

Thoughts include inner voices. We talk to ourselves constantly in our heads. When internal chatter gets in your way, write down what you are telling yourself. If this seems difficult at first, just start writing. The act of writing can trigger a flood of thoughts.

Also notice how you feel when you function well. Use Discovery Statements to pinpoint exactly where and when you learn most effectively.

☐ **Use discomfort as a signal.** When you approach a daunting task, such as a difficult math problem, notice your physical sensations. Feeling uncomfortable, bored, or tired might be a signal that you're about to do valuable work. Stick with it. Write about it. Tell yourself you can handle the discomfort just a little bit longer. You will be rewarded with a new insight.

☐ **Suspend judgment.** When you are discovering yourself, be gentle. Suspend self-judgment. If you continually judge your behaviors as "bad" or "stupid" or "galactically imbecilic," sooner or later your mind will revolt. Rather than put up with the abuse, it will quit making discoveries. For your own benefit, be kind to yourself.

☐ **Tell the truth.** Suspending judgment helps you tell the truth about yourself. "The truth will set you free" is a saying that endures for a reason. The closer you get to the truth, the more powerful your Discovery Statements. If you notice that you are avoiding the truth, don't blame yourself. Just tell the truth about it.

INTENTION STATEMENTS

☐ **Make intentions positive.** The purpose of writing Intention Statements is to focus on what you want rather than what you don't want. Instead of writing "I will not to fall asleep while studying chemistry," write, "I intend to stay awake when studying chemistry." Also avoid the word *try*. Trying is not doing. When we hedge our bets with *try*, we can always tell ourselves, "Well, I *tried* to stay awake." We end up fooling ourselves into thinking we succeeded.

☐ **Make intentions observable.** Rather than writing "I intend to work harder on my history assignments," write, "I intend to review my class notes, and I intend to make summary sheets of my reading." Then, when you review your progress, you can determine more precisely whether you have accomplished what you intended.

☐ **Make intentions small and achievable.** Give yourself opportunities to succeed by setting goals you can meet. Break large goals into small, specific tasks that can be accomplished quickly. If you want to get an A in biology, ask yourself, "What can I do today?" You might choose to study biology for an extra hour. Make that your intention.

☐ **Set time lines.** For example, if you are assigned a paper to write, break the assignment into small tasks and set a precise due date for each one: "I intend to select a topic for my paper by 9 A.M. Wednesday."

Time lines are especially useful when your intention is to experiment with a technique suggested in this book. The sooner you act on a new idea, the better. Consider practicing a new behavior within four hours after you first learn about it.

☐ **Anticipate self-sabotage.** Be aware of what you might do, consciously or unconsciously, to undermine your best intentions. If you intend to study differential equations at 9 p.m., notice when you sit down to watch a two-hour movie that starts at 8 p.m. Also be careful of intentions that depend on others. If you write that you intend for your study group to complete an assignment by Monday, then your success depends on the other students in the group.

☐ **Include rewards.** When you meet your goal on time, reward yourself. Rewards that are an integral part of a goal are powerful. For example, your reward for earning a degree might be the career you've always dreamed of. External rewards, such as a movie or an afternoon in the park, are also valuable. These rewards work best when you're willing to withhold them. If you plan to take a nap on Sunday afternoon whether or not you've finished your chemistry assignment, the nap is not an effective reward.

☐ **Move from intention to action.** IIntention Statements are of little use until you act on them. If you want new results in your life, then take action. Life responds to what you *do*. ■

Andresr/Shutterstock.com

You share one thing in common with other students at your vocational school, college, or university: Entering higher education represents a major change in your life. You've joined a new culture with its own set of rules, both spoken and unspoken.

MAKING THE TRANSITION TO higher education

Whether you've just graduated from high school or have been out of the classroom for decades, you'll discover many differences between secondary and post-secondary education. The sooner you understand such differences, the sooner you can deal with them. Some examples of what you might face include the following:

- **New academic standards.** Once you enter higher education, you'll probably find yourself working harder in school than ever before. Instructors will often present more material at a faster pace. There probably will be fewer tests in higher education than in high school, and the grading might be tougher. Compared to high school, you'll have more to read, more to write, more problems to solve, and more to remember.

- **A new level of independence.** College instructors typically give less guidance about how or when to study. You may not get reminders about when assignments are due or when quizzes and tests will take place. You probably won't get study sheets before a test. Overall, you might receive less consistent feedback about how well you are doing in each of your courses. Don't let this tempt you into putting off work until the last minute. You will still be held accountable for all course work. And anything that's said in class or included in assigned readings might appear on an exam.

- **Differences in teaching styles.** Instructors at colleges, universities, and vocational schools are often steeped in their subject matter. Many did not take courses on how to teach and might not be as interesting as some of your high school teachers. And some professors might seem more focused on research than on teaching.

- **A larger playing field.** The institution you've just joined might seem immense, impersonal, and even frightening. The sheer size of the campus, the variety of courses offered, the large number of departments—all of these opportunities can add up to a confusing array of options.

- **More students and more diversity.** The school you're attending right now might enroll hundreds or thousands more students than your high school. And the range of diversity among these students might surprise you.

In summary, you are now responsible for structuring your time and creating new relationships. Perhaps more than ever before, you'll find that your life is your own creation. You are free to set different goals, explore alternative ways of thinking, change habits, and expand your circle of friends. All this can add up to a new identity—a new way of being in the world.

At first, this world of choices might seem overwhelming or even frightening. You might feel that you're just going through the motions of being a student or playing a role that you've never rehearsed.

That feeling is understandable. Use it to your advantage. Consider that you *are* assuming a new role in life—that of being a student in higher education. And just as actors enter the minds of the characters that they portray, you can take on the character of a master student.

When you're willing to take responsibility for the quality of your education, you can create the future of your dreams. Keep the following strategies in mind.

Decrease the unknowns. To reduce surprise, anticipate changes. Before classes begin, get a map of the school property and walk through your first day's schedule, perhaps with a classmate or friend. Visit your instructors in their offices and introduce yourself. Anything you can do to get familiar with the new routine will help. In addition, consider buying your textbooks before class begins. Scan them to get a preview of your courses.

Admit your feelings—whatever they are. School can be an intimidating experience for new students. People of diverse cultures, adult learners, commuters, and people with disabilities may feel excluded. Anyone can feel anxious, isolated, homesick, or worried.

Those emotions are common among new students, and there's nothing wrong with them. Simply admitting the truth about how you feel—to yourself and to someone else—can help you cope. And you can almost always do something constructive in the present moment, no matter how you feel.

If your feelings about this transition make it hard for you to carry out the activities of daily life—going to class, working, studying, and relating to people—then get professional help. Start with a counselor at the student health service on your campus. The mere act of seeking help can make a difference.

Allow time for transition. You don't have to master the transition to higher education right away. Give it some time. Also, plan your academic schedule with your needs for transition in mind. Balance time-intensive courses with others that don't make as many demands.

Find resources. A supercharger increases the air supply to an internal combustion engine. The resulting difference in power can be dramatic. You can make just as powerful a difference in your education if you supercharge it by using all of the resources available to students. In this case, your "air supply" includes people, campus clubs and organizations, and school and community services.

Of all resources, people are the most important. You can isolate yourself, study hard, and get a good education. However, doing this is not the most powerful use of your tuition money. When you establish relationships with teachers, staff members, fellow students, and employers, you can get a *great* education. Build a network of people who will personally support your success in school.

Meet with your academic advisor. One person in particular —your academic advisor—can help you access resources and make the transition to higher education. Meet with this person regularly. Advisors generally know about course requirements, options for declaring majors, and the resources available at your school. Peer advisors might also be available.

When you work with an advisor, remember that you're a paying customer and have a right to be satisfied with the service you get. Don't be afraid to change advisors when that seems appropriate.

Learn the language of higher education. Terms such as *grade point average (GPA)*, *prerequisite*, *accreditation*, *matriculation*, *tenure*, and *syllabus* might be new to you. Ease your transition to higher education by checking your school catalog or school Web site for definitions of definitions of these words and others that you don't understand. Also ask your academic advisor for clarification.

Show up for class. In higher education, teachers generally don't take attendance. Yet you'll find that attending class is essential to your success. The amount that you pay in tuition and fees makes a powerful argument for going to classes regularly and getting your money's worth. In large part, the material that you're tested on comes from events that take place in class.

Showing up for class occurs on two levels. The most visible level is being physically present in the classroom. Even more important, though, is showing up mentally. This kind of attendance includes taking detailed notes, asking questions, and contributing to class discussions.

Research on college freshmen indicates a link between regular class attendance and academic success.[3] Succeeding in school can help you get almost anything you want, including the career, income, and relationships you desire. Attending class is an investment in yourself.

Manage out-of-class time. For students in higher education, time management takes on a new meaning. What you do *outside* class matters as much—or even more than—what you do in class. Instructors give you the raw materials for understanding a subject while a class meets. You then take those materials, combine them, and *teach yourself* outside of class.

To allow for this process, schedule two hours of study time for each hour that you spend in class. Also, get a calendar that covers the entire academic year. With the syllabus for each of your courses in hand, note key events for the entire term—dates for tests, papers, and other projects. Getting a big picture of your course load makes it easier to get assignments done on time and prevents all-night study sessions.

Experiment with new ways to study. You can cope with increased workloads and higher academic expectations by putting all of your study habits on the table and evaluating them. Don't assume that the learning strategies you used in the past—in high school or the workplace—will automatically transfer to your new role in higher education. Keep the habits that serve you, drop those that hold you back, and adopt new ones to promote your success. On every page of this book, you'll find helpful suggestions.

Take the initiative in meeting new people. Introduce yourself to classmates and instructors. Just before or after class is a good time. Realize that most of the people in this new world of higher education are waiting to be welcomed. You can help them and help yourself at the same time.

Make peace with new technology. Turn back the clock just one decade. Google was just getting started. There was no Facebook, no Twitter, no iPad, and no iPhone.

Today, you can get a job in some companies as director of social media. Tablets and smartphones are as popular in the workplace as in higher education. And when people ask you to research the topic on the Internet, they tell you to "just Google it."

If you don't feel comfortable with the latest technology, welcome to the club. Many people who are going back to school will admit the same thing. Students in higher education are asked to engage with technology at a level that has no precedent in our history.

To make the transition to this world, remember two things. First, it's OK to admit the truth whenever you're outside of your comfort zone. Second, it's also OK to get help. Go to your academic advisor and ask about "help desks," technology workshops, classes, and other campus resources for getting up to speed with technology. One way to overcome fear of change is to get hands-on experience with digital tools as soon as possible.

Become a self-regulated learner. Reflect on your transition to higher education. Think about what's working well, what you'd like to change, and ways to make those changes. Psychologists use the term *self-regulation* to describe this kind of thinking.[4] Self-regulated learners set goals, monitor their progress toward those goals, and change their behavior based on the results they get.

From Master Student to Master Employee promotes self-regulation through the ongoing cycle of discovery, intention, and action. Write Discovery Statements to monitor your behavior and evaluate the results you're currently creating in any area of your life. Write about your level of commitment to school, your satisfaction with your classes and grades, your social life, and your family's support for your education.

Based on your discoveries, write Intention Statements about your goals for this term, this year, next year, and the rest of your college career. Describe exactly what you will do to create new

Rewrite
this book

Some books should be preserved in pristine condition. This book isn't one of them.

Something happens when you interact with your book by writing in it. *From Master Student to Master Employee* is about learning, and learning results when you are active. When you make notes in the margin, you can hear yourself talking with the author. When you doodle and underline, you see the author's ideas taking shape. You can even argue with the author and come up with your own theories and explanations. In all of these ways, you can become a coauthor of this book. Rewrite it to make it yours.

While you're at it, you can create symbols or codes that will help you when reviewing the text later on. You might insert a "Q" where you have questions or put exclamation points or stars next to important ideas. You could also circle words to look up in a dictionary.

Remember, if any idea in this book doesn't work for you, you can rewrite it. Change the exercises to fit your needs. Create a new technique by combining several others. Create a technique out of thin air!

Find something you agree or disagree with on this page, and write a short note in the margin about it. Or draw a diagram. Better yet, do both. Let creativity be your guide. Have fun.

Begin rewriting now.

results in each of these time frames. Then follow through with action. In this way, you take charge of your transition to higher education—starting now. ■

You're One Click Away...
from finding more strategies for mastering the art of transition online.

Connect to
RESOURCES

EDHAR/Shutterstock.com

As a student in higher education, you can access a world of student services and community resources. Any of them can help you succeed in school. Many of them are free.

Name a problem that you're facing right now or that you anticipate facing in the future: finding money to pay for classes, resolving conflicts with a teacher, lining up a job after graduation. Chances are that a school or community resource can help you. The ability to access resources is a skill that will serve you long after you stop being a student. In addition, taking advantage of services and getting involved with organizations can lead you to new experiences that expand your learning styles.

Resources often go unused. Following are examples of what you can find. Check your school and city Web sites for more options. Remember that you can connect with many of them online as well as in person.

Academic advisors/counselors can help you select courses, choose a major, plan your career, and adjust in general to the culture of higher education.

Arts organizations connect you to local museums, concert venues, clubs, and stadiums.

Athletic centers often open weight rooms, swimming pools, indoor tracks, basketball courts, and racquetball and tennis courts to all students.

Child care is sometimes made available to students at a reasonable cost through the early childhood education department on campus or community agencies.

Churches, synagogues, mosques, and temples have members who are happy to welcome fellow worshippers who are away from home.

Computer labs on campus are places where students can go to work on projects and access the Internet. Computer access is often available off-campus as well. Check public libraries for this service. Some students get permission to use computers at their workplace after hours.

Consumer credit counseling can help even if you've really blown your budget. And it's usually free. Do your research, and choose a reputable and not-for-profit consumer credit counselor.

Counseling centers in the community can assist you with a problem when you can't get help at school. Look for career-planning services, rehabilitation offices, outreach programs for veterans, and mental health clinics.

The **financial aid office** assists students with loans, scholarships, work-study, and grants.

Governments (city, county, state, and federal) often have programs for students. Check the government listings in your local telephone directory.

Hotlines offer a way to get emergency care, personal counseling, and other kinds of help via a phone call. Do an Internet search on *phone hotlines* in your area that assist with the specific kind of help you're looking for, and check your school catalog for more resources.

Job placement offices can help you find part-time employment while you are in school and a full-time job after you graduate.

Legal aid services provide free or inexpensive assistance to low-income people.

Libraries are a treasure on campus and in any community. They employ people who are happy to help you locate information.

Newspapers published on campus and in the local community list events and services that are free or inexpensive.

The **school catalog** lists course descriptions, and tuition fees, requirements for graduation, and information on everything from the school's history to its grading practices.

School security agencies can tell you what's safe and what's not. They can also provide information about parking, bicycle regulations, and traffic rules.

Special needs and disability services assist college students who have learning disabilities or other disabilities.

Student health clinics often provide free or inexpensive counseling and other medical treatment.

Student organizations present opportunities for extracurricular activities. Explore student government, fraternities, sororities, service clubs, religious groups, sports clubs, and political groups. Find women's centers; multicultural student centers; and organizations for international students, disabled students with disabilities, and gay, lesbian, bisexual, and transgender (GLBT) students.

Support groups exist for people with almost any problem, from drug addiction to cancer. You can find people with problems who meet every week to share suggestions, information, and concerns about problems they share.

Tutoring is usually free and is available through academic departments or counseling centers and is often free or low cost. ■

Succeeding in school— at any age

David Buffington/Getty Images

David Buffington/Getty Images

Being an adult learner puts you on a strong footing. With a rich store of life experiences, you can ask meaningful questions and make connections between course work and daily life. Any abilities that you've developed to work on teams, manage projects, meet deadlines, and solve problems are assets. Many instructors will especially enjoy working with you.

Following are some suggestions for adult learners who want to ease their transition to higher education. If you're a younger student, commuting student, or community college student, look for useful ideas here as well.

Acknowledge your concerns. Adult learners might express any of the following fears:

- *I'll be the oldest person in all my classes.*
- *I've been out of the classroom too long.*
- *I'm concerned about my math, reading, and writing skills.*
- *I'm worried about making tuition payments.*
- *How will I ever make the time to study, on top of everything else I'm doing?*
- *I won't be able to keep up with all the new technology.*

Those concerns are understandable. Now consider some facts:

- College classrooms are more diverse than ever before. According to the U.S. Census Bureau, 37 percent of students in the nation's colleges are age 25 and older. The majority of these older students attend school part-time.[5]
- Adult learners can take advantage of evening classes, weekend classes, summer classes, distance learning, and online courses. Also look for classes in off-campus locations, closer to where you work or live.
- Colleges offer financial aid for students of all ages, including scholarships, grants, and low-interest loans.

- You can meet other students and make new friends by taking part in orientation programs. Look for programs that are targeted to adult learners.

- You are now enrolled in a course that can help boost your skills at math, reading, writing, note taking, time management, and other key skills.

Ease into it. If you're new to higher education, consider easing into it. You can choose to attend school part-time before making a full-time commitment. If you've taken college-level classes in the past, find out if any of those credits will transfer into your current program.

Plan ahead. By planning a week or month at a time, you get a bigger picture of your multiple roles as a student, an employee, and a family member. With that awareness, you can make conscious adjustments in the number of hours you devote to each domain of activity in your life. For example:

- If your responsibilities at work or home will be heavy in the near future, then register for fewer classes next term.

- Choose recreational activities carefully, focusing on those that relax you and recharge you the most.

- Don't load your schedule with classes that require unusually heavy amounts of reading or writing.

For related suggestions, see Chapter 3: Time & Money.

Delegate tasks. If you have children, delegate some of the household chores to them. Or start a meal co-op in your neighborhood. Cook dinner for yourself and someone else one night each week. In return, ask that person to furnish you with a meal on another night. A similar strategy can apply to child care and other household tasks.

Get to know other returning students. Introduce yourself to other adult learners. Being in the same classroom gives you an immediate bond. You can exchange work, home, or cell phone numbers and build a network of mutual support. Some students adopt a buddy system, pairing up with another student in each class to complete assignments and prepare for tests.

In addition, learn about student services and organizations. Many schools have a learning assistance center with workshops geared to adult learners. Sign up and attend. Meet people on campus. Personal connections are key to your success.

Find common ground with traditional students. Traditional and nontraditional students have many things in common. They seek to gain knowledge and skills for their chosen careers. They desire financial stability and personal fulfillment. And, like their older peers, many younger students are concerned about whether they have the skills to succeed in higher education.

Consider pooling resources with younger students. Share notes, edit one another's papers, and form study groups. Look for ways to build on one another's strengths. If you want help with using a computer for assignments, you might ask a younger student for help. In group projects and case studies, you can expand the discussion by sharing insights from your experiences.

Enlist your employer's support. Let your employer in on your educational plans. Point out how the skills you gain in the classroom will help you meet work objectives. Offer informal seminars at work to share what you're learning in school. You might find that your company reimburses its employees for some tuition costs or even grants time off to attend classes.

Get extra mileage out of your current tasks. Look for ways to relate your schoolwork to your job. For example, when you're assigned a research paper, choose a topic that relates to your current job tasks. Some schools even offer academic credit for work and life experience.

Review your subjects before you start classes. Say that you've registered for trigonometry and you haven't taken a math class since high school. Consider brushing up on the subject before classes begin. Also, talk with future instructors about ways to prepare for their classes.

"Publish" your schedule. After you plan your study and class sessions for the week, write up your schedule and post it in a place where others who live with you will see it. If you use an online calendar, print out copies to put in your school binder or on your refrigerator door, bathroom mirror, or kitchen cupboard.

Enroll family and friends in your success. School can cut into your social life. Prepare friends and family members by discussing this issue ahead of time. See Chapter 9: Communicating for ways to prevent and resolve conflict.

You can also involve your spouse, partner, children, or close friends in your schooling. Offer to give them a tour of the campus, introduce them to your instructors and classmates, and encourage them to attend social events at school with you. Share ideas from this book, and from your other courses.

Take this process a step further, and ask the key people in your life for help. Share your reason for getting a degree, and talk about what your whole family has to gain from this change in your life. Ask them to think of ways that they can support your success in school and to commit to those actions. Make your own education a joint mission that benefits everyone. ■

You're One Click Away...
from finding more strategies for adult learners online.

Leading the way— succeeding as a first-generation student

8

American history confirms that people who are the first in their family to enter higher education can succeed. Examples range from the former slaves who enrolled in the country's first African-American colleges to the ex-soldiers who used the GI Bill to win advanced degrees. From their collective experience, you can take some life-changing lessons.

REMEMBER YOUR STRENGTHS

The fact that you're reading this book right now is a sign of your accomplishments. You applied to school. You got admitted. You've already taken a huge step to success: You showed up.

Celebrate every one of your successes in higher education, no matter how small they seem. Every assignment you complete, every paper you turn in, and every quiz question you answer is a measurable and meaningful step to getting a degree.

Discover more of your strengths by taking any fact that others might see as a barrier and looking for the hidden advantage. Did you grow up in a family that struggled to make ends meet financially? Then you know about living on a limited budget. Did you work to help support your family while you were in high school? Then you know about managing your time to balance major commitments. Did you grow up in a neighborhood with people of many races, religions, and levels of income? Then you already have an advantage when it comes to thriving with diversity.

Put your strengths in writing. Write Discovery Statements about specific personal, academic, and financial challenges you faced in the past. Describe how you coped with them. Then follow up with Intention Statements about ways to meet the challenges of higher education.

Also keep showing up. Going to every class, lab session, and study group meeting is a way to squeeze the most value from your tuition bills.

EXPECT CHANGE—AND DISCOMFORT

Entering higher education means walking into a new culture. At times you might feel that all the ground rules have changed, and you have no idea how to fit in. This is normal.

When you walked into your first class this semester, you carried your personal hopes for the future along with the expectations of your parents, siblings, and other relatives. Those people might assume that you'll return home and be the same person you were last year.

The reality is that you will change while you're in school. Your beliefs, your friends, and your career goals may all shift. You might feel critical of people back home and think that some of their ideas are limited. And in turn, they might criticize you.

First-generation students sometimes talk about standing between two worlds. They know that they're changing. At the same time, they are uncertain about what the future holds.

This, too, is normal. Education is all about change. It can be exciting, frustrating, and frightening—all at once. Making mistakes and moving through disappointments is part of the process.

ASK FOR SUPPORT

You don't have to go it alone. Your tuition buys access to many services. These are sources of academic and personal support. You'll find examples listed in "Connect to Resources" on page 16. Ask your school about any programs geared specifically to first-generation students.

The key point is to *ask for help right away*. Do this as soon as you feel stuck in class or experience conflict in a relationship.

Also keep a list of every person who stands behind you— relatives, friends, instructors, advisors, mentors, tutors, and counselors. Remind yourself that you are surrounded by people who want you to succeed. Furthermore, thank each of them for their help.

PAY IT FORWARD

You are an inspiration to your family, friends, and fellow students. Several people you know might apply to school on the strength of your example. Talk to these people about what you've learned. Your presence in their lives is a contribution. ■

Enroll your instructor
in your SUCCESS

Faced with an instructor you don't like, you have two basic choices. One is to label the instructor a "dud." When you make this choice, you endure class and complain to other students. This choice gives your instructor sole responsibility for the quality of your education and the value of your tuition payments.

There is another option. Don't give away your power. Instead, take responsibility for your education.

The word *enroll* in this headline is a play on words. Usually we think of students as the people who enroll in school. Turn this idea on its head. See whether you can enlist instructors as partners in getting what you want from higher education.

Research the instructor. When deciding what classes to take, you can look for formal and informal sources of information about instructors. One source is the school catalog. Alumni magazines or newsletters or the school newspaper might run articles on teachers. At some schools, students post informal evaluations of instructors on Web sites. Also talk to students who have taken courses from the instructor you're researching.

Or introduce yourself to the instructor. Set up a visit during office hours, and ask about the course. This conversation can help you get the flavor of a class and the instructor's teaching style. Other clues to an instructor's style include the *types* of material he presents (ranging from theory or fact) and the *ways* that the material is presented (ranging from lectures to discussion and other in-class activity).

Show interest in class. Students give teachers moment-by-moment feedback in class. That feedback comes through posture, eye contact, responses to questions, and participation in class discussions. If you find a class boring, recreate the instructor through a massive display of interest. Ask lots of questions. Sit up straight, make eye contact, take detailed notes. Your enthusiasm might enliven your instructor. If not, you are still creating a more enjoyable class for yourself.

Release judgments. Maybe your instructor reminds you of someone you don't like—your annoying Aunt Edna or a rude store clerk. Your attitudes are in your own head and beyond the instructor's control. Likewise, an instructor's beliefs about politics, religion, or feminism are not related to teaching ability. Being aware of such things can help you let go of negative judgments.

Instructors are a lot like you. They have opinions about politics, sports, and music. They worry about their health, finances, and career path. They're sometimes in a good mood and sometimes sad or angry. What distinguishes them is a lifelong passion for the subject that they teach.

© Ron Chapple/Getty Images

Get to know the instructor. Meet with your instructor during office hours. Teachers who seem boring in class can be fascinating in person. Prepare to notice your pictures and let them go. An instructor that someone told you to avoid might become one of your favorite teachers. You might hear conflicting reports about teachers from other students. The same instructor could be described by two different students as a riveting speaker and as completely lacking in charisma. Decide for yourself what descriptions are accurate.

Students who do well in higher education often get to know at least one instructor outside of class. In some cases, these instructors become mentors and informal advisors.

Open up to diversity. Sometimes students can create their instructors by letting go of pictures about different races and ethnic groups. According to one picture, a Hispanic person cannot teach English literature. According to other pictures, a white teacher cannot have anything valid to say about African music, and a teacher in a wheelchair cannot command the attention of a hundred people in a lecture hall. All of those pictures can clash with reality. Releasing them can open up new opportunities for understanding and appreciation.

Separate liking from learning. You don't have to like an instructor to learn from her. See whether you can focus on content instead of form. *Form* is the way something is organized or presented. If you are irritated at the sound of an instructor's voice, you're focusing on form. When you put aside your concern about her voice and turn your attention to the points she's making, you're focusing on *content*.

Seek alternatives. You might feel more comfortable with another teacher's style or method of organizing course materials. Consider changing teachers, asking another teacher for help outside class, or attending an additional section taught by a different instructor.

If you cannot change instructors, then take charge of your learning. Actively use the suggestions in this article. You can also learn from other students, courses, tutors, study groups, books, and DVDs. Be a master student, no matter who teaches your classes. Your education is your own creation.

Avoid excuses. Instructors know them all. Most teachers can see a snow job coming before the first flake hits the ground. Accept responsibility for your own mistakes, and avoid thinking that you can fool the teacher.

Submit professional work. Prepare papers and projects as if you were submitting them to an employer. Imagine that your work will determine whether you get a promotion and raise. Instructors often grade hundreds of papers during a term. Your neat, orderly, well-organized paper can stand out and lift a teacher's spirits.

Accept criticism. Learn from your teachers' comments about your work. It is a teacher's job to give feedback. Don't take it personally.

Use course evaluations. In many classes, you'll have an opportunity to evaluate the instructor. Respond honestly. Write about the aspects of the class that did not work well for you. Offer specific ideas for improvement. Also note what *did* work well.

Communicate effectively by phone and e-mail. Ask your instructors how they prefer to be contacted. If they take phone calls, leave a voice mail message that includes your first and last name, course name, section, and phone number.

If your instructor encourages contact via e-mail, then craft your messages with care. Start by including your name, course title, and section number in the subject line. Keep the body of your message brief and get to the point immediately.

Remember that the recipient of online communication is a human being whose culture, language, and humor may have different points of reference from your own. Write clearly, and keep the tone positive. Do not type in FULL CAPS, which is equivalent to shouting.

If there's a problem to solve, focus on solutions rather than blame. For example, avoid: "Why do you grade so unfairly?" Instead, write, "I'd like to understand your criteria for grading our assignments so that I can raise my scores."

Also proofread your message carefully and fix any errors. Write with full words and complete sentences. Avoid the abbreviations that you might use in a text message.

Finally, remember that instructors are busy people with personal lives. Don't expect them to be online at the same time as you.

Take further steps, if appropriate. Sometimes severe conflict develops between students and instructors. In such cases, you might decide to file a complaint or ask for help from an administrator.

Be prepared to document your case in writing. Describe specific actions that created problems. Stick to the facts—events that other class members can verify. Your school has grievance procedures to use in these cases. Use them. You are a consumer of education and have a right to fair treatment. ▓

You're One Click Away...
from discovering more ways to create positive relationships with instructors online.

Meeting with
YOUR INSTRUCTOR

Meeting with an instructor outside class can save hours of study time and help boost your grade. Instead of trying to resolve a conflict with an instructor in the few minutes before or after class, schedule a time during office hours. During this meeting, state your concerns in a respectful way. Then focus on finding solutions. To get the most from these meetings, consider doing the following:

- Schedule a meeting time during the instructor's office hours. These are often listed in the course syllabus and on the instructor's office door.

- If you need to cancel or reschedule an appointment, let your instructor know well in advance.

- During the meeting, relax. This activity is not graded.

- Come prepared with a list of questions and any materials you'll need. During the meeting, take notes on the instructor's suggestions.

- Show the instructor your class notes to see whether you're capturing essential material.

- Get feedback on outlines that you've created for papers.

- Go over items you missed on exams.

- Get overall feedback on your progress.

- Ask about ways to prepare for upcoming exams.

- If the course is in a subject area that interests you, ask about the possibilities of declaring a major in that area and the possible careers associated with that major.

- Avoid questions that might offend your instructor—for example, "I missed class on Monday. Did we do anything important?"

- Ask whether your instructor is willing to answer occasional short questions via e-mail or a phone call.

- When the meeting is over, thank your instructor for making time for you.

- Remember that meeting during office hours is something that you do in addition to attending class regularly.

Choosing your purpose

Success is a choice—your choice. To *get* what you want, it helps to *know* what you want. That is the purpose of this two-part Journal Entry. You can begin choosing success by completing this Journal Entry right now. If you choose to do it later, then plan a date, time, and place and then block out the time on your calendar.

Date: _____ Time: _____ Place: _____

Part 1

Select a time and place when you know you will not be disturbed for at least 20 minutes. (The library is a good place to do this exercise.) Relax for two or three minutes, clearing your mind. Next, complete the following sentences—and then keep writing. When you run out of things to write, stick with it just a bit longer. Be willing to experience a little discomfort. Keep writing. What you discover might be well worth the extra effort.

What I want from my education is . . . *to use my knowledge towards my career.*

When I complete my education, I want to be able to . . . *be successful within my career and further my education*

I also want . . . *to further my education and become a Doctor hopefully*

Part 2

After completing Part 1, take a short break. Reward yourself by doing something that you enjoy. Then come back to this Journal Entry.

Now, review the list you just created of things that you want from your education. See whether you can summarize them in one sentence. Start this sentence with "My purpose for being in school is. . . ." Allow yourself to write many drafts of this mission statement, and review it periodically as you continue your education. With each draft, see whether you can capture the essence of what you want from higher education and from your life. State it in a vivid way—in a short sentence that you can easily memorize, one that sparks your enthusiasm and makes you want to get up in the morning.

You might find it difficult to express your purpose statement in one sentence. If so, write a paragraph or more. Then look for the sentence that seems most charged with energy for you. Following are some sample purpose statements:

- My purpose for being in school is to gain skills that I can use to contribute to others.

- My purpose for being in school is to live an abundant life that is filled with happiness, health, love, and wealth.

- My purpose for being in school is to enjoy myself by making lasting friendships and following the lead of my interests.

Write at least one draft of your purpose statement here:

my purpose for furthering my education is to increase my blessings and happiness.

Jumpstart your education with
transferable skills

One dictionary defines *skill* as "the ability to do something well, usually gained by training or experience." Some skills—such as the ability to repair fiber-optic cables or do brain surgery—are acquired through formal schooling, on-the-job training, or both. These abilities are called *work-content skills*. People with such skills have mastered a specialized body of knowledge needed to do a specific kind of work.

However, there is another category of skills that we develop through experiences both inside and outside the classroom. These are *transferable skills*. Transferable skills are abilities that help people thrive in any job—no matter what work-content skills they have. You are developing these skills right now, even before you take your next job.

Perhaps you've heard someone described this way: "She's really smart and knows what she's doing, but she's got lousy people skills." People skills—such as *listening* and *negotiating*—are prime examples of transferable skills. Transferable skills are key to building the career you want over the long-term.

SUCCEED IN MANY SITUATIONS

Transferable skills are often invisible to us. The problem begins when we assume that a given skill can be used in only one context, such as working at a particular job. Thinking in this way places an artificial limit on our possibilities.

As an alternative, think about the things you routinely do to succeed in school. Analyze your activities to isolate specific skills. Then brainstorm a list of jobs where you could use the same skills.

Consider the task of writing a research paper. This calls for the following skills:

- *Planning*, including setting goals for completing your outline, first draft, second draft, and final draft.

- *Managing time* to meet your writing goals.

- *Interviewing* people who know a lot about the topic of your paper.

- *Researching* using the Internet and campus library to discover key facts and ideas to include in your paper.

- *Writing* to present those facts and ideas in an original way.

- *Editing* your drafts for clarity and correctness.

Now consider the kinds of jobs that draw on these skills.

For example, you could transfer your skill at writing papers to a possible career in journalism, technical writing, or advertising copywriting.

You could use your editing skills to work in the field of publishing as a magazine or book editor.

Interviewing and research skills could help you enter the field of market research. And the abilities to plan, manage time, and meet deadlines will help you succeed in all the jobs mentioned so far.

Use the same kind of analysis to think about transferring skills from one job to another. Say that you work part-time as an administrative assistant at a computer dealer that sells a variety of hardware and software. You take phone calls from potential customers, help current customers solve problems using their computers, and attend meetings where your coworkers plan ways to market new products. You are developing skills at *selling*, *serving customers*, and *working on teams*. These skills could help you land a job as a sales representative for a computer manufacturer or software developer.

The basic idea is to take a cue from the word *transferable*. Almost any skill you use to succeed in one situation can *transfer* to success in another situation.

The concept of transferable skills creates a powerful link between higher education and the work world. Skills are the core elements of any job. While taking any course, list the specific skills you are developing and how you can transfer them to the work world. Almost everything you do in school can be applied to your career—if you consistently pursue this line of thought.

Getting past the "I-don't-have-any-skills" syndrome means that you can approach job hunting with more confidence. As you uncover these hidden assets, your list of qualifications will grow as if by magic. You won't be padding your résumé. You'll simply be using action words to tell the full truth about what you can do.

Identifying your transferable skills takes a little time. And the payoffs are numerous. A complete and accurate list of transferable skills can help you land jobs that involve more responsibility, more variety, more freedom to structure your time, and more money. Careers can be made—or broken—by the skills that allow you to define your job, manage your workload, and get along with people.

Transferable skills help you thrive in the midst of constant change. Technology will continue to develop. Ongoing discoveries in many fields could render current knowledge obsolete. Jobs that exist today may disappear in a few years, only to be replaced by entirely new ones.

In the economy of the twenty-first century, you might not be able to count on job security. What you *can* count on is "skills security"—abilities that you can carry from one career to another or acquire as needed. Even though he only completed eight years of formal schooling,[6] Henry Ford said, "The only real security that a person can have in this world is a reserve of knowledge, experience, and ability. Without these qualities, money is practically useless."[7]

ASK FOUR QUESTIONS

To experiment further with this concept of transferable skills, ask and answer four questions derived from the Master Student Map.

Why identify my transferable skills? Identifying your transferable skills takes a little time. And the payoffs are numerous. A complete and accurate list of transferable skills can help you land jobs that involve more responsibility, more variety, more freedom to structure your time, and more money. Careers can be made—or broken—by the skills that allow you to define your job, manage your workload, and get along with people.

***What* are my transferable skills?** Discover your transferable skills by reflecting on key experiences. Recall a time when you performed at the peak of your ability, overcame obstacles, won an award, gained a high grade, or met a significant goal. List the skills you used to create those successes.

For a more complete picture of your transferable skills, describe the object of your action. Say that one of the skills on your list is *organizing*. This could refer to organizing ideas, organizing people, or organizing objects in a room. Specify the kind of organizing that you like to do.

***How* do I perform these skills?** You can bring your transferable skills into even sharper focus by adding adverbs—words that describe *how* you take action. You might say that you edit *accurately* or learn *quickly*.

In summary, you can use a three-column chart to list your transferable skills. For example:

Verb	Object	Adverb
Organizing	Records	Effectively
Serving	Customers	Courteously
Coordinating	Special events	Efficiently

Add a specific example of each transferable skill to your skills list, and you're well on the way to an engaging résumé and a winning job interview.

***What* if I could expand my transferable skills?** In addition to thinking about the skills you already have, consider the skills you'd like to acquire. Describe them in detail. List experiences that can help you develop them. Let your list of transferable skills grow and develop as you do.

FOCUS ON THE FIVE Cs

Throughout much of the nineteenth and twentieth centuries, people with basic skills in reading, writing, and arithmetic—the "three R's"—could expect to find entry-level jobs. The economy of the twenty-first century changes that. According to the *AMA 2010 Critical Skills Survey,* conducted by the American Management Association, employers are now looking for people with a specific set of transferable skills—the "four Cs." These include:

- **Creative thinking**—creating ideas for new products and services, presenting those ideas to others, and working with teams to refine and implement them. People who think creatively see failures as opportunities to learn and look for results over the long-term.

- **Critical thinking**—stating questions precisely, examining a variety of possible answers, testing the logical accuracy of and evidence for each answer, and using the results to make effective decisions and solve problems.

- **Communication**—creating and sharing meaning through speaking, listening, writing, and reading. Skilled communicators stay aware of their purpose—to inform, instruct, or persuade—and choose ways to meet that purpose with a variety of audiences.

- **Collaboration**—working effectively with diverse teams to set shared goals and to meet them. Skilled collaborators respect their peers, stay open to new ideas, manage conflict, and bring projects to completion.

Most of the employers included in the AMA Survey said that they evaluate current employees based on the four Cs. In addition, skills in thinking, communication, and collaboration are key factors in deciding who gets hired when a job opening occurs.

This edition of *From Master Student to Master Employee* adds a fifth and equally important "C" that employers seek:

- **Character**—demonstrating a positive attitude, commitment, flexibility, willingness to learn, and trustworthiness.

Character takes skills, such as the four Cs, and embeds them in a larger context. While skills are about what you can *do*, character is about who you *are*. When employers talk about a *professional work ethic*, they're referring to character. Many of the master student qualities related to character as well.

You can use the articles, exercises, and journal entries in this book to develop a variety of transferable skills. Chapters 1, 8, 9, and 10 in particular deal with the five Cs. Also look for *Five Cs for Your Career* at the end of every chapter for ways to develop these crucial qualities now—and take them with you into the workplace. ■

 You're One Click Away...
from learning more about transferable skills online.

60 transferable skills

There are literally hundreds of transferable skills. Start with the following list, which is organized by the chapter topics in this book. To learn more transferable skills, check out O*Net OnLine, a Web site from the federal government at online.onetcenter.org. There you'll find tools for discovering your skills and matching them to specific occupations. Additional information on careers and job hunting is available through CareerOneStop at www.careeronestop.org.

Self-management

1. Assessing your current knowledge and skills.
2. Seeking out opportunities to acquire new knowledge and skills.
3. Choosing and applying learning strategies.

4. Showing flexibility by adopting new attitudes and behaviors.

5. Persisting in order to meet goals.

For more information about self-management skills, see Chapter 1 of this book.

Self-discovery

6. Assessing your current knowledge and skills.

7. Seeking out opportunities to acquire new knowledge and skills.

8. Choosing and applying learning strategies.

9. Showing flexibility by adopting new attitudes and behaviors.

10. Changing habits.

For more information about self-discovery skills, see Chapter 2.

Time and money management

11. Scheduling due dates for project outcomes.

12. Scheduling time for goal-related tasks.

13. Monitoring income and expenses.

14. Raising funds.

15. Preparing budgets.

For more information about time and money skills, see Chapter 3.

Memory

16. Focusing attention to learn new information and ideas.

17. Selecting key information and ideas to remember.

18. Associating new information and ideas with prior knowledge.

19. Discovering meaningful ways to organize new information and ideas.

20. Encoding new information and ideas in ways that appeal to the senses.

For more information about memory skills, see Chapter 4.

Reading

21. Reading for key ideas and major themes.

22. Reading for detail.

23. Reading to synthesize ideas and information from several sources.

24. Reading to discover strategies for solving problems or meeting goals.

25. Reading to understand and follow instructions.

For more information about reading skills, see Chapter 5.

Note taking

26. Taking notes on material presented verbally, in print, or online.

27. Creating pictures, graphs, and other visuals to summarize and clarify information.

28. Organizing information and ideas in digital and paper-based forms.

29. Researching by finding information online or in the library.

30. Gathering data through field research or working with primary sources.

For more information about note-taking skills, see Chapter 6.

Test taking and related skills

31. Assessing personal performance at school or at work.

32. Using test results and other assessments to improve performance.

33. Working cooperatively in study groups and project teams.

34. Managing stress.

35. Using mathematics to do basic computations and solve problems.

For more information about test-taking skills, see Chapter 7.

Creative and critical thinking

36. Thinking to create new ideas, products, or services.

37. Thinking to evaluate ideas, products, or services.

38. Evaluating material presented verbally, in print, or online.

39. Making decisions.

40. Solving problems.

For more information about thinking skills, see Chapter 8.

Communication

41. Listening fully (without judgment or distraction).

42. Interpreting and responding to nonverbal messages.

43. Writing.

44. Editing.

45. Speaking to diverse audiences.

For more information about communication skills, see Chapter 9.

Collaboration

46. Leading and participating in project teams.

47. Assigning and delegating tasks.

48. Giving people feedback about the quality of their performance.

49. Preventing and resolving conflict.

50. Managing multiple projects at the same time.

For more information about collaboration skills, see Chapter 10.

Health

51. Changing habits that affect health.

52. Making health-related decisions based on sound information.

53. Maintaining reserves of energy and alertness for the tasks of daily life.

54. Managing stress and negative emotions in constructive ways.

55. Monitoring habits that affect health.

For more information about health-related skills, see Chapter 11.

Career management

56. Finding employment based on self-knowledge and accurate information about the work world.

57. Finding and learning from a mentor.

58. Taking the initiative with tasks and going beyond the minimum requirements of a job.

59. Updating skills continuously.

60. Working well with people from a variety of backgrounds.

For more information about career management skills, see Chapter 12.

JOURNAL ENTRY 3 *Discovery/Intention Statement*

Recognize the "five Cs" in yourself

Before you begin this Journal Entry, gather at least a hundred 3 × 5 cards and a pen or pencil. Or, start a new file in a word processing program or any software that allows you to create lists. Allow about one hour to do the suggested thinking and writing.

STEP 1 **List recent activities** Recall your activities during the past week or month. Write down as many of these activities as you can. (If you're using 3 × 5 cards, list each item on a separate card.) Include work-related activities, school activities, and hobbies. Spend 10 minutes on this step.

STEP 2 **List rewards and recognitions** Next, list any rewards you've received, or other recognition of your achievements, during the past year. Examples include scholarship awards, athletic awards, or recognitions for volunteer work. Allow 10 minutes for this step as well.

STEP 3 **List work-content skills** Now review the two lists you just created. Then take another 10 minutes to list any specialized areas of knowledge needed to do those activities, win those awards, and receive those recognitions.

These areas of knowledge indicate your *work-content skills*. For example, tutoring a French class requires a working knowledge of that language.

List all of your skills that fall into this category, labeling each one as "work-content."

STEP 4 **List transferable skills** Go over your list of activities one more time. Spend 10 minutes looking for examples of *transferable skills*—those that can be applied to a variety of situations. For instance, giving a speech or working as a salesperson in a computer store requires the ability to persuade people. Tuning a car means that you can attend to details and troubleshoot.

List all your skills that fall into this category, labeling each one as "transferable." Give special attention to the four Cs—skills that relate to creative thinking, critical thinking, communication, and collaboration.

STEP 5 **Describe your character** Your activities, rewards, and recognitions also reveal a deeper dimension of how you show up in the world—your character. Ask yourself: What are the qualities of a master student that I've demonstrated so far in my life? Create another list with your answers to this question.

STEP 6 **Review and plan** You now have a detailed picture of the five Cs in yourself. Review all the lists you created in the previous steps. See if you can add any new items that occur to you.

Save your lists in a place where you can easily find them again. Plan to update all of them at least once each year. Your lists will come in handy for writing your résumé, preparing for job interviews, and doing other career-planning tasks.

First Steps

Use this **Master Student Map** to ask yourself

WHY THIS CHAPTER MATTERS . . .

- Success starts with telling the truth about what is working—and what isn't—in our lives right now.

WHAT IS INCLUDED . . .

HOW I CAN USE THIS CHAPTER. . .

- Experience the power of telling the truth about my current skills.
- Discover my preferred learning styles.
- Choose learning strategies that promote my success.

WHAT IF . . .

- I could start to create new outcomes in my life by accepting the way I am right now?

JOURNAL ENTRY 5
Intention Statement

Create value from this chapter

Skim this chapter for three techniques that you'd like to use in school or in your personal life during the upcoming week. List each technique and a related page number here.

I intend to use . . .

_____

_____

_____

_____

_____

_____

_____

_____

_____

_____

_____

_____

_____

_____

_____

© Ruslan Ivantsov/Shutterstock.com

POWER process

Ideas are tools

There are many ideas in this book. When you first encounter them, don't believe any of them. Instead, think of the ideas as tools.

For example, you use a hammer for a purpose—to drive a nail. You don't try to figure out whether the hammer is "right." You just use it. If it works, you use it again. If it doesn't work, you get a different hammer.

People have plenty of room in their lives for different kinds of hammers, but they tend to limit their openness to different kinds of ideas. A new idea, at some level, is a threat to their very being—unlike a new hammer, which is simply a new hammer.

Most of us have a built-in desire to be right. Our ideas, we often think, represent ourselves.

Some ideas are worth dying for. But please note: This book does not contain any of those ideas. The ideas on these pages are strictly "hammers."

Imagine someone defending a hammer. Picture this person holding up a hammer and declaring, "I hold this hammer to be self-evident. Give me this hammer or give me death. Those other hammers are flawed. There are only two kinds of people in this world: people who believe in this hammer and people who don't."

That ridiculous picture makes a point. This book is not a manifesto. It's a toolbox, and tools are meant to be used.

If you read about a tool in this book that doesn't sound "right" or one that sounds a little goofy, remember that the ideas here are for using, not necessarily for believing. Suspend your judgment. Test the idea for yourself. If it works, use it. If it doesn't, don't use it.

Any tool—whether it's a hammer, a computer program, or a study technique based on your knowledge of learning styles—is designed to do a specific job. A master mechanic carries a variety of tools, because no single tool works for all jobs. If you throw a tool away because it doesn't work in one situation, you won't be able to pull it out later when it's just what you need. So if an idea doesn't work for you and you are satisfied that you gave it a fair chance, don't throw it away. File it away instead. The idea might come in handy soon.

And remember, this book is not about figuring out the "right" way. Even the "ideas are tools" approach is not "right."

It's a hammer . . . (or maybe a saw).

 You're One Click Away...
from accessing the Power Process Media online and finding out more about how "ideas are tools."

First Step: Truth is a *key to mastery*

The First Step technique is simple: Tell the truth about who you are and what you want. The First Step is one of the most valuable tools in this book. It magnifies the power of all the other techniques. It is a key to becoming a master student—and employee.

To succeed in school, tell the truth about what kind of student you are and what kind of student you want to become. Success starts with telling the truth about what *is* working—and what is *not* working—in our lives right now. When we acknowledge our strengths, we gain an accurate picture of what we can accomplish. When we admit that we have a problem, we are free to find a solution. Ignoring the truth, on the other hand, can lead to problems that stick around for decades.

FIRST STEPS ARE UNIVERSAL

An article about telling the truth might sound like pie-in-the-sky moralizing. However, there is nothing pie-in-the-sky or moralizing about a First Step. It is a practical, down-to-earth principle to use whenever we want to change our behavior.

When you see a doctor, the First Step is to tell the truth about your current symptoms. That way you can get an accurate diagnosis and effective treatment plan. This principle is universal. It works for just about any problem in any area of life.

First Steps are used by millions of people who want to turn their lives around. No technique in this book has been field-tested more often or more successfully—or under tougher circumstances.

For example, members of Alcoholics Anonymous start by telling the truth about their drinking. Their First Step is to admit that they are powerless over alcohol. That's when their lives start to change.

People dealing with a variety of other challenges—including troubled relationships with food, drugs, sex, and work—also start by telling the truth. They use First Steps to change their behavior, and they do it for a reason: First Steps work.

FIRST STEPS ARE CHALLENGING— AND REWARDING

Let's be truthful: It's not easy to tell the truth about ourselves. It's not fun to admit our weaknesses. We might end up admitting that we don't complete term papers on time or that coming up with the money to pay for tuition is a constant challenge.

There is another way to think about self-evaluations. If we could see them as opportunities to solve problems and take charge of our lives, we might welcome them.

It may seem natural to judge our own shortcomings and feel bad about them. Some people believe that such feelings are necessary to correct their errors. Others think that a healthy dose of shame can prevent the moral decay of our society.

Think again. Consider the opposite idea: We can gain skill without feeling rotten about the past. We can change the way things *are* without having to criticize the way things *have been*. We can learn to see shame or blame as excess baggage and set them aside.

If the whole idea of telling the truth about yourself puts a knot in your stomach, that's good. Notice the knot. It is your friend. It is

a reminder that First Steps call for courage and compassion. These are qualities of a master student.

FIRST STEPS FREE US TO CHANGE

Master students get the most value from a First Step by turning their perceived shortcomings into goals. "I don't exercise enough" turns into "I will walk briskly for 30 minutes at least three times per week."

Another quality of master students is that they refuse to let their First Steps turn into excuses. These students avoid using the phrase "I can't" and its endless variations.

The key is to state First Steps in a way that allows for new possibilities in the future. Use language in a way that reinforces your freedom to change. For example, "I can't succeed in math" is better stated like this: "During math courses, I tend to get confused early in the term and find it hard to ask questions. I could be more assertive in asking for help right away."

Telling the truth about what we don't want gives us more clarity about what we *do* want. By taking a First Step, we can free up all the energy that it takes to deny our problems and avoid change. We can redirect that energy and use it to take actions that align with our values.

FIRST STEPS INCLUDE STRENGTHS

For some of us, it's even harder to recognize our strengths than to recognize our weaknesses. Maybe we don't want to brag. Maybe we're attached to a poor self-image.

The reasons don't matter. The point is that using the First Step technique means telling the truth about our positive qualities, too.

Remember that weaknesses are often strengths taken to an extreme. The student who carefully revises her writing can make significant improvements in a term paper. If she revises too much and hands in the paper late, though, her grade might suffer. Any success strategy carried too far can backfire.

FIRST STEPS ARE SPECIFIC

Whether written or verbal, the ways that we express our First Steps are more powerful when they are specific. For example, if you want to improve your note-taking skills, you might write, "I am an awful note taker"; but it would be more effective to write, "I can't read 80 percent of the notes I took in Introduction to Psychology last week, and I have no idea what was important in that class."

The exercises and Journal Entries in this chapter are all about getting specific. They can help you tap resources you never knew you had. For example, do the Discovery Wheel to get a big-picture view of your personal effectiveness. And use the Learning Styles Inventory, along with the articles about multiple intelligences and the VAK system, to tell the truth about how you perceive and process information.

As you use these elements of this book you might feel surprised at what you discover. You might even disagree with the results of an exercise. That's fine. Just tell the truth about it. Use your disagreement as a tool for further discussion and self-discovery. ■

✓ CRITICAL THINKING EXERCISE 6

Taking the First Step

The purpose of this exercise is to give you a chance to discover and acknowledge your own strengths, as well as areas for improvement. For many students, this exercise is the most difficult one in the book. To make the exercise worthwhile, do it with courage.

Some people suggest that looking at areas for improvement means focusing on personal weaknesses. They view it as a negative approach that runs counter to positive thinking. Well, perhaps. Positive thinking is a great technique. So is telling the truth, especially when we see the whole picture—the negative aspects as well as the positive ones.

If you admit that you can't add or subtract and that's the truth, then you have taken a strong, positive First Step toward learning basic math. On the other hand, if you say that you are a terrible math student and that's not the truth, then you are programming yourself to accept unnecessary failure.

The point is to tell the truth. This exercise is similar to the Discovery Statements that appear throughout the chapters. The difference is that, in this case, for reasons of confidentiality, you won't write down your discoveries in the book.

You are likely to disclose some things about yourself that you wouldn't want others to read. You might even write down some truths that could get you into trouble. Do this exercise on separate sheets of paper; then hide or destroy them. Protect your privacy. To make this exercise work, follow these suggestions.

Be specific. It is not effective to write, "I can improve my communication skills." Of course you can. Instead, write down precisely what you can *do* to improve your communication skills—for example, "I can spend more time really listening while the other person is talking, instead of thinking about what I'm going to say next."

Be self-aware. Look beyond the classroom. What goes on outside school often has the greatest impact on your ability to be an effective student. Consider your strengths and weaknesses that you may think have nothing to do with school.

Be courageous. This exercise calls for an important master student quality—courage. It is a waste of time if this exercise is done half-heartedly. Be willing to take risks. You might open a door that reveals a part of yourself that you didn't want to admit was there. The power of this technique is that once you know what is there, you can do something about it.

Part 1

Time yourself, and for 10 minutes write as fast as you can, completing each of the following sentences at least 10 times with anything that comes to mind. If you get stuck, don't stop. Just write something—even if it seems crazy.

I never succeed when I . . .

I'm not very good at . . .

Something I'd like to change about myself is . . .

Part 2

When you have completed the first part of the exercise, review what you have written, crossing off things that don't make any sense. The sentences that remain suggest possible goals for becoming a master student.

Part 3

Here's the tough part. Time yourself, and for 10 minutes write as fast as you can, completing the following sentences with anything that comes to mind. As in Part 1, complete each sentence at least 10 times. Just keep writing, even if it sounds silly.

I always succeed when I . . .

I am very good at . . .

Something I like about myself is . . .

Part 4

Review what you have written, and circle the things that you can fully celebrate. This list is a good thing to keep for those times when you question your own value and worth.

 You're One Click Away...
from completing this exercise online under Exercises.

LEARNING STYLES
Discovering how you learn

Right now, you are investing substantial amounts of time, money, and energy in your education. What you get in return for this investment depends on how well you understand the process of learning and use it to your advantage.

If you don't understand learning, you might feel bored or confused in class. After getting a low grade, you might have no idea how to respond. Over time, frustration can mount to the point where you question the value of being in school.

Some students answer that question by dropping out of school. These students lose a chance to create the life they want, and society loses the contributions of educated workers.

You can prevent that outcome. Gain strategies for going beyond boredom and confusion. Discover new options for achieving goals, solving problems, listening more fully, speaking more persuasively, and resolving conflicts between people. Start by understanding the different ways that people create meaning from their experience and change their behavior. In other words, learn about *how* we learn.

WE LEARN BY PERCEIVING AND PROCESSING

When we learn well, says psychologist David Kolb, two things happen.[1] First, we *perceive*. That is, we notice events and "take in" new experiences.

Second, we *process*. We "deal with" experiences in a way that helps us make sense of them.

Some people especially prefer to perceive through *feeling* (also called *concrete experience*). They like to absorb information through their five senses. They learn by getting directly involved

in new experiences. When solving problems, they rely on intuition as much as intellect. These people typically function well in unstructured classes that allow them to take initiative.

Some people prefer to process by *watching* (also called *reflective observation*). They prefer to stand back, watch what is going on, and think about it. They consider several points of view as they attempt to make sense of things and generate many ideas about how something happens. They value patience, good judgment, and a thorough approach to learning.

Other people like to perceive by *thinking* (also called *abstract conceptualization*). They take in information best when they can think about it as a subject separate from themselves. They analyze, intellectualize, and create theories. Often these people take a scientific approach to problem solving and excel in traditional classrooms.

Other people like to process by *doing* (also called *active experimentation*). They prefer to jump in and start doing things immediately. These people do not mind taking risks as they attempt to make sense of things; this helps them learn. They are results oriented and look for practical ways to apply what they have learned.

PERCEIVING AND PROCESSING—AN EXAMPLE

Suppose that you get a new cell phone. It has more features than any phone you've used before. You have many options for learning how to use it. For example:

- Just get your hands on the phone right away, press some buttons, and see whether you can dial a number or send a text message.

- Recall experiences you've had with phones in the past and what you've learned by watching other people use their cell phones.

- Read the instruction manual and view help screens on the phone before you try to make a call.

- Ask a friend who owns the same type of phone to coach you as you experiment with making calls and sending messages.

These actions illustrate the different approaches to learning:

- Getting your hands on the phone right away and seeing whether you can make it work is an example of learning through *feeling* (or *concrete experience*).

- Recalling what you've experienced in the past is an example of learning through *watching* (or *reflective observation*).

- Reading the manual and help screens before you use the phone is an example of learning through *thinking* (or *abstract conceptualization*).

- Asking a friend to coach you through a "hands-on" activity with the phone is an example of learning through *doing* (or *active experimentation*).

In summary, your learning style is the unique way that you blend feeling, thinking, watching, and doing. You tend to use this approach in learning anything—from cell phones to English composition to calculus. Reading the next few pages and doing the recommended activities will help you explore your learning style in more detail. ■

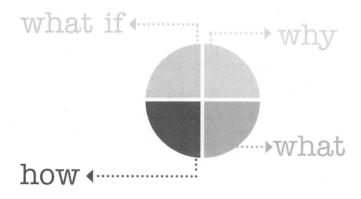

Prepare for the Learning Style Inventory (LSI)

As a "warm-up" for the Learning Style Inventory that follows, think about times when you felt successful at learning. Underline or highlight any of the following statements that describe those situations.

- I was in a structured setting, with a lot of directions about what to do.

- I was free to learn at my own pace and in my own way.

- I learned as part of a small group.

- I learned mainly by working alone in a quiet place.

- I learned in a place where there was a lot of activity going on.

- I formed pictures in my mind.

- I learned by *doing* something—moving around, touching something, or trying out a process for myself.

- I learned by talking to myself or explaining ideas to other people.

- I got the "big picture" before I tried to understand the details.

- I listened to a lecture and then thought about it after class.

- I read a book or article and then thought about it afterward.

- I used a variety of media—such as videos, films, audio recordings, or computers—to assist my learning.

- I was considering where to attend school and had to actually set foot on each campus before choosing.

- I was shopping for a car and paid more attention to how I felt about test-driving each one than to the sticker prices or mileage estimates.

- I was thinking about going to a movie and carefully read the reviews before choosing one.

Reviewing this list, do you see any patterns in the way you prefer to learn? If so, briefly describe them.

Directions for completing the Learning Style Inventory

To help you become more aware of learning styles, a psychologist named David Kolb developed the Learning Style Inventory (LSI). This inventory is included on the next page. Responding to the items in the LSI can help you discover a lot about the ways you learn. Following the LSI are suggestions for using your results to promote your success.

The LSI is not a test. There are no right or wrong answers. Your goal is simply to develop a profile of your current learning style. So, take the LSI quickly. You might find it useful to recall a recent time when you learned something new at school, home, or work. However, do not agonize over your responses.

Note that the LSI consists of 12 sentences, each with four different endings. You will read each sentence, and then write a "4" next to the ending that best describes the way you currently learn. Then you will continue ranking the other endings with a "3," "2," or "1," representing the ending that least describes you. This is a forced-choice inventory, so you must rank each ending. Do not leave any endings blank. Use each number only once for each question.

Following are more specific directions:

1. Before you write on page LSI–1, remove the sheet of paper following page LSI–2.

2. Read the instructions at the top of page LSI–1. When you understand example A, you are ready to begin.

3. While writing on page LSI–1, *press firmly* so that your answers will show up on page LSI–3.

Using your LEARNING STYLE PROFILE *to succeed*

DEVELOP ALL FOUR MODES OF LEARNING

Each mode of learning highlighted in the Learning Style Inventory represents a unique blend of concrete experience ("feeling"), reflective observation ("watching"), abstract conceptualization ("thinking"), and active experimentation ("doing"). You can explore new learning styles simply by adopting new habits related to each of these activities. Consider the following suggestions as places to start. Also remember that any idea about learning styles will make a difference in your life only when it leads to changes in your behavior.

- Conduct an informational interview with someone in your chosen career or "shadow" that person for a day on the job.
- Look for a part-time job, internship, or volunteer experience that complements what you do in class.
- Deepen your understanding of another culture and extend your foreign language skills by studying abroad.

To become more reflective:
- Keep a personal journal, and write about connections among your courses.

To gain concrete experiences:
- See a live demonstration or performance related to your course content.
- Engage your emotions by reading a novel or seeing a video related to your course.
- Interview an expert in the subject you're learning or a master practitioner of a skill you want to gain.
- Conduct role-plays, exercises, or games based on your courses.

- Form a study group to discuss and debate topics related to your courses.
- Set up a Web site, blog, e-mail listserv, or online chat room related to your major.
- Create analogies to make sense of concepts; for instance, see whether you can find similarities between career planning and putting together a puzzle.
- Visit your course instructor during office hours to ask questions.

- During social events with friends and relatives, briefly explain what your courses are about.

To develop abstract thinking:

- Take notes on your reading in outline form; consider using word-processing software with an outlining feature.
- Supplement assigned texts with other books, magazine and newspaper articles, and related Web sites.
- Attend lectures given by your current instructors and others who teach the same subjects.
- Take ideas presented in text or lectures and translate them into visual form—tables, charts, diagrams, and maps (see Chapter 6: Notes).
- Create visuals and use computer software to recreate them with more complex graphics and animation.

To become more active:

- Conduct laboratory experiments or field observations.
- Go to settings where theories are being applied or tested.
- Make predictions based on theories you learn, and then see whether events in your daily life confirm your predictions.
- Try out a new behavior described in a lecture or reading, and observe its consequences in your life.

LOOK FOR EXAMPLES OF THE MODES IN ACTION

To understand the modes of learning, notice when they occur in your daily life. You are a natural learner, and this means that the modes are often at work. You use them when you solve problems, make choices, and experiment with new ideas.

Suppose that your family asks about your career plans. You've just enrolled for your first semester of classes, and you think it's too early to think about careers. Yet you choose to brainstorm some career options anyway. If nothing else, it might be fun, and you'll have some answers for when people ask you what you're going to do after college. This is an example of Mode 1. You asked, "Why learn about career planning?" and came up with an answer.

During the next meeting of your psychology class, your instructor mentions the career planning center on campus. You visit the center's Web site and discover its list of services. While you're online, you also register for one of the center's workshops because you want more information about writing a career plan. This illustrates Mode 2: You asked, "What career planning options are available?" and discovered several answers.

In this workshop, you learn about the role that internships and extracurricular activities play in career planning. All of these are ways to test an early career choice and discover

whether it appeals to you. You enjoy being with children, so you choose to volunteer at a campus-based child care center. You want to discover how this service learning experience might help you choose a career. This is Mode 3: You asked, "How can I use what I learned in the workshop?" This led you to working with children.

Your experience at the center leads to a work-study assignment there. On the basis of this new experience, you choose to declare a major in early childhood education. This is an example of Mode 4: You asked, "What if this assignment points to a new direction for my future?" The answer led to a new commitment.

USE THE MODES WHILE CHOOSING COURSES

Remember your learning style profile when you're thinking about which classes to take and how to study for each class. Look for a fit between your preferred mode of learning and your course work.

If you prefer Mode 1, for example, then look for courses that sound interesting and seem worthwhile to you. If you prefer Mode 2, then consider classes that center on lectures, reading, and discussion. If you prefer Mode 3, then choose courses that include demonstrations, lab sessions, role-playing, and others ways to take action. And if you prefer Mode 4, then look for courses that could apply to many situations in your life—at work, at home, and in your relationships.

You won't always be able to match your courses to your learning styles. View those situations as opportunities to practice becoming a flexible learner. By developing your skills in all four modes, you can excel in many types of courses.

USE THE MODES TO EXPLORE YOUR MAJOR

If you enjoy learning in Mode 1, you probably value creativity and human relationships. When choosing a major, consider the arts, English, psychology, or political science.

If Mode 2 is your preference, then you enjoy gathering information and building theories. A major related to math or science might be ideal for you.

If Mode 3 is your favorite, then you like to diagnose problems, arrive at solutions, and use technology. A major related to health care, engineering, or economics is a logical choice for you.

And if your preference is Mode 4, you probably enjoy taking the initiative, implementing decisions, teaching, managing projects, and moving quickly from planning into action. Consider a major in business or education.

As you prepare to declare a major, remain flexible. Use your knowledge of learning styles to open up possibilities rather than restrict them. Remember that regardless of your mode, you can excel at any job or major; it just may mean developing new skills in other modes.

USE THE MODES OF LEARNING TO EXPLORE YOUR CAREER

Knowing about learning styles becomes especially useful when planning your career.

People who excel at Mode 1 are often skilled at tuning in to the feelings of clients and coworkers. These people can listen with an open mind, tolerate confusion, be sensitive to people's feelings, open up to problems that are difficult to define, and brainstorm a variety of solutions. If you like Mode 1, you may be drawn to a career in counseling, social services, the ministry, or another field that centers on human relationships. You might also enjoy a career in the performing arts.

People who prefer Mode 2 like to do research and work with ideas. They are skilled at gathering data, interpreting information, and summarizing—arriving at the big picture. They may excel at careers that center on science, math, technical communications, or planning. Mode 2 learners may also work as college teachers, lawyers, technical writers, or journalists.

People who like Mode 3 are drawn to solving problems, making decisions, and checking on progress toward goals. Careers in medicine, engineering, information technology, or another applied science are often ideal for them.

People who enjoy Mode 4 like to influence and lead others. These people are often described as "doers" and "risk takers." They like to take action and complete projects. Mode 4 learners often excel at managing, negotiating, selling, training, and teaching. They might also work for a government agency.

Keep in mind that there is no strict match between certain learning styles and certain careers. Learning is essential to success in all careers. Also, any career can attract people with a variety of learning styles. For instance, the health care field is large enough to include people who prefer Mode 3 and become family physicians—*and* people who prefer Mode 2 and become medical researchers.

> **Keep in mind that there is no strict match between certain learning styles and certain careers. Learning is essential to success in all careers.**

EXPECT TO ENCOUNTER DIFFERENT STYLES

As higher education and the workplace become more diverse and technology creates a global marketplace, you'll meet people who differ from you in profound ways. Your fellow students and coworkers will behave in ways that express a variety of preferences for perceiving information, processing ideas, and acting on what they learn. Consider these examples:

- A roommate who's continually moving while studying—reciting facts out loud, pacing, and gesturing—probably prefers concrete experience and learning by taking action.

- A coworker who talks continually on the phone about a project may prefer to learn by listening, talking, and forging key relationships.

- A supervisor who excels at abstract conceptualization may want to see detailed project plans and budgets submitted in writing well before a project swings into high gear.

- A study group member who always takes the initiative, manages the discussion, delegates any work involved, and follows up with everyone probably prefers active experimentation.

Differences in learning style can be a stumbling block—or an opportunity. When differences intersect, there is the potential for conflict as well as for creativity. Succeeding with peers often means seeing the classroom and workplace as a laboratory for learning from experience. Resolving conflict and learning from mistakes are all part of the learning cycle.

LOOK FOR SPECIFIC CLUES TO ANOTHER PERSON'S STYLE

You can learn a lot about other people's styles of learning simply by observing them during the work day. Look for clues such as these:

Approaches to a task that requires learning. Some people process new information and ideas by sitting quietly and reading or writing. When learning to use a piece of equipment, such as a new computer, they'll read the instruction manual first. Others will skip the manual, unpack all the boxes, and start setting up equipment. And others might ask a more experienced colleague to guide them in person, step by step.

Word choice. Some people like to process information visually. You might hear them say, "I'll look into that" or "Give me the big picture first." Others like to solve problems verbally: "Let's talk through this problem" or "I hear you!" In contrast, some people focus on body sensations ("This product feels great") or action ("Let's run with this idea and see what happens").

9

Body language. Notice how often coworkers or classmates make eye contact with you and how close they sit or stand next to you. Observe their gestures, as well as the volume and tone of their voice.

Content preferences. Notice what subjects coworkers or classmates openly discuss and which topics that they avoid. Some people talk freely about their feelings, their families, and even their personal finances. Others choose to remain silent on such topics and stick to work-related matters.

Process preferences. Look for patterns in the way that your coworkers and classmates meet goals. When attending meetings, for example, some of them might stick closely to the agenda and keep an eye on the clock. Other people might prefer to go with the flow, even if it means working an extra hour or scrapping the agenda.

ACCOMMODATE DIFFERING STYLES

Once you've discovered differences in styles, look for ways to accommodate them. As you collaborate on projects with other students or coworkers, keep the following suggestions in mind:

Remember that some people want to reflect on the big picture first. When introducing a project plan, you might say, "This process has four major steps." Before explaining the plan in detail, talk about the purpose of the project and the benefits of completing each step.

Allow time for active experimentation and concrete experience. Offer people a chance to try out a new product or process for themselves—to literally get the feel of it.

Allow for abstract conceptualization. When leading a study group or conducting a training session, provide handouts that include plenty of visuals and step-by-step instructions. Visual learners and people who like to think abstractly will appreciate it. Also schedule periods for questions and answers.

When planning a project, encourage people to answer key questions. Remember the four essential questions that guide learning. Answering *Why?* means defining the purpose and desired outcomes of the project. Answering *What?* means assigning major tasks, setting due dates for each task, and generating commitment to action. Answering *How?* means carrying out assigned tasks and meeting regularly to discuss things that are working well and ways to improve the project. And answering *What if?* means discussing what the team has learned from the project and ways to apply that learning to the whole class or larger organization.

When working on teams, look for ways that members can complement one another's strengths. If you're skilled at planning, find someone who excels at doing. Also seek people

who can reflect on and interpret the team's experience. Pooling different styles allows you to draw on everyone's strengths.

RESOLVE CONFLICT WITH RESPECT FOR STYLES

When people's styles clash in educational or work settings, you have several options. One is to throw up your hands and resign yourself to personality conflicts. Another option is to recognize differences, accept them, and respect them as complementary ways to meet common goals. Taking that perspective allows you to act constructively. You might do one of the following:

Resolve conflict within yourself. You might have mental pictures of classrooms and workplaces as places where people are all supposed to have the same style. Notice if you have those pictures and gently let them go. If you *expect* to find differences in styles, you can more easily respect those differences.

Introduce a conversation about learning styles. Attend a workshop on learning styles. Then bring such training directly to your classroom or office.

Let people take on tasks that fit their learning styles. People gravitate toward the kinds of tasks they've succeeded at in the past, and that's fine. Remember, though, that learning styles are both stable and dynamic. People can also broaden their styles by tackling new tasks to reinforce different modes of learning.

Rephrase complaints as requests. "This class is a waste of my time" can be recast as "Please tell me what I'll gain if I participate actively in class." "The instructor talks too fast" can become "What strategies can I use for taking notes when the instructor covers the material rapidly?"

ACCEPT CHANGE—AND OCCASIONAL DISCOMFORT

Seek out chances to develop new modes of learning. If your instructor asks you to form a group to complete an assignment, avoid joining a group where everyone shares your learning style. Work on project teams with people who learn differently than you. Get together with people who both complement and challenge you.

Also look for situations where you can safely practice new skills. If you enjoy reading, for example, look for ways to express what you learn by speaking, such as leading a study group on a textbook chapter.

Discomfort is a natural part of the learning process. Allow yourself to notice any struggle with a task or lack of interest in completing it. Remember that such feelings are temporary and that you are balancing your learning preferences. By choosing to move through discomfort, you consciously expand your ability to learn in new ways. ■

Claim your multiple INTELLIGENCES

People often think that being smart means the same thing as having a high IQ, and that having a high IQ automatically leads to success. However, psychologists are finding that IQ scores do not always foretell which students will do well in academic settings—or after they graduate.[2]

Howard Gardner of Harvard University believes that no single measure of intelligence can tell us how smart we are. Instead, Gardner defines intelligence in a flexible way as "the ability to solve problems, or to create products, that are valued within one or more cultural settings." He also identifies several types of intelligence, as described here.[3]

People using **verbal/linguistic intelligence** are adept at language skills and learn best by speaking, writing, reading, and listening. They are likely to enjoy activities such as telling stories and doing crossword puzzles.

People who use **mathematical/logical intelligence** are good with numbers, logic, problem solving, patterns, relationships, and categories. They are generally precise and methodical, and are likely to enjoy science.

When people learn visually and by organizing things spatially, they display **visual/spatial intelligence**. They think in images and pictures, and understand best by seeing the subject. They enjoy charts, graphs, maps, mazes, tables, illustrations, art, models, puzzles, and costumes.

People using **bodily/kinesthetic intelligence** prefer physical activity. They enjoy activities such as building things, woodworking, dancing, skiing, sewing, and crafts. They generally are coordinated and athletic, and they would rather participate in games than just watch.

Individuals using **musical/rhythmic intelligence** enjoy musical expression through songs, rhythms, and musical instruments. They are responsive to various kinds of sounds; remember melodies easily; and might enjoy drumming, humming, and whistling.

People using **intrapersonal intelligence** are exceptionally aware of their own feelings and values. They are generally reserved, self-motivated, and intuitive.

Outgoing people show evidence of **interpersonal intelligence.** They do well with cooperative learning and are sensitive to the feelings, intentions, and motivations of others. They often make good leaders.

People using **naturalist intelligence** love the outdoors and recognize details in plants, animals, rocks, clouds, and other natural formations. These people excel in observing fine distinctions among similar items.

Each of us has all of these intelligences to some degree. And each of us can learn to enhance them. Experiment with learning in ways that draw on a variety of intelligences—including those that might be less familiar. When we acknowledge all of our intelligences, we can constantly explore new ways of being smart. ■

✓ CRITICAL THINKING EXERCISE 8

Develop your multiple intelligences

Gardner's theory of multiple intelligences complements the discussion of different learning styles in this chapter. The main point is that there are many ways to gain knowledge and acquire new behaviors. You can use Gardner's concepts to explore a range of options for achieving success in school, work, and relationships.

The chart on the next page summarizes the content of "Claim your multiple intelligences" and suggests ways to apply the main ideas. Instead of merely glancing through this chart, get active. Place a check mark next to any of the "Possible characteristics" that describe you. Also check off the "Possible learning strategies" that you intend to use. Finally, underline or highlight any of the "Possible careers" that spark your interest.

Remember that the chart is *not* an exhaustive list or a formal inventory. Take what you find merely as points of departure. You can invent strategies of your own to cultivate different intelligences.

Type of intelligence	Possible characteristics	Possible learning strategies	Possible careers
Verbal/linguistic	❏ You enjoy writing letters, stories, and papers. ❏ You prefer to write directions rather than draw maps. ❏ You take excellent notes from textbooks and lectures. ❏ You enjoy reading, telling stories, and listening to them.	❏ Highlight, underline, and write notes in your textbooks. ❏ Recite new ideas in your own words. ❏ Rewrite and edit your class notes. ❏ Talk to other people often about what you're studying.	Librarian, lawyer, editor, journalist, English teacher, radio or television announcer
Mathematical/logical	❏ You enjoy solving puzzles. ❏ You prefer math or science class over English class. ❏ You want to know how and why things work. ❏ You make careful, step-by-step plans.	❏ Analyze tasks so you can order them in a sequence of steps. ❏ Group concepts into categories, and look for underlying patterns. ❏ Convert text into tables, charts, and graphs. ❏ Look for ways to quantify ideas—to express them in numerical terms.	Accountant, auditor, tax preparer, mathematician, computer programmer, actuary, economist, math or science teacher
Visual/spatial	❏ You draw pictures to give an example or clarify an explanation. ❏ You understand maps and illustrations more readily than text. ❏ You assemble things from illustrated instructions. ❏ You especially enjoy books that have a lot of illustrations.	❏ When taking notes, create concept maps, mind maps, and other visuals (see Chapter 6: Notes). ❏ Code your notes by using different colors to highlight main topics, major points, and key details. ❏ When your attention wanders, focus it by sketching or drawing. ❏ Before you try a new task, visualize yourself doing it well.	Architect, commercial artist, fine artist, graphic designer, photographer, interior decorator, engineer, cartographer
Bodily/kinesthetic	❏ You enjoy physical exercise. ❏ You tend not to sit still for long periods of time. ❏ You enjoy working with your hands. ❏ You use a lot of gestures when talking.	❏ Be active in ways that support concentration; for example, pace as you recite, read while standing up, and create flash cards. ❏ Carry materials with you, and practice studying in several different locations. ❏ Create hands-on activities related to key concepts; for example, create a game based on course content. ❏ Notice the sensations involved with learning something well.	Physical education teacher, athlete, athletic coach, physical therapist, chiropractor, massage therapist, yoga teacher, dancer, choreographer, actor

Type of intelligence	Possible characteristics	Possible learning strategies	Possible careers
Musical/rhythmic	❏ You often sing in the car or shower. ❏ You easily tap your foot to the beat of a song. ❏ You play a musical instrument. ❏ You feel most engaged and productive when music is playing.	❏ During a study break, play music or dance to restore energy. ❏ Put on background music that enhances your concentration while studying. ❏ Relate key concepts to songs you know. ❏ Write your own songs based on course content.	Professional musician, music teacher, music therapist, choral director, musical instrument sales representative, musical instrument maker, piano tuner
Intrapersonal	❏ You enjoy writing in a journal and being alone with your thoughts. ❏ You think a lot about what you want in the future. ❏ You prefer to work on individual projects over group projects. ❏ You take time to think things through before talking or taking action.	❏ Connect course content to your personal values and goals. ❏ Study a topic alone before attending a study group. ❏ Connect readings and lectures to a strong feeling or significant past experience. ❏ Keep a journal that relates your course work to events in your daily life.	Minister, priest, rabbi, professor of philosophy or religion, counseling psychologist, creator of a home-based or small business
Interpersonal	❏ You enjoy group work over working alone. ❏ You have plenty of friends and regularly spend time with them. ❏ You prefer talking and listening over reading or writing. ❏ You thrive in positions of leadership.	❏ Form and conduct study groups early in the term. ❏ Create flash cards, and use them to quiz study partners. ❏ Volunteer to give a speech or lead group presentations on course topics. ❏ Teach the topic you're studying to someone else.	Manager, school administrator, salesperson, teacher, counseling psychologist, arbitrator, police officer, nurse, travel agent, public relations specialist, creator of a midsize to large business
Naturalist	❏ As a child, you enjoyed collecting insects, leaves, or other natural objects. ❏ You enjoy being outdoors. ❏ You find that important insights occur during times you spend in nature. ❏ You read books and magazines on nature-related topics.	❏ During study breaks, take walks outside. ❏ Post pictures of outdoor scenes where you study, and play recordings of outdoor sounds while you read. ❏ Invite classmates to discuss course work while taking a hike or going on a camping trip. ❏ Focus on careers that hold the potential for working outdoors.	Environmental activist, park ranger, recreation supervisor, historian, museum curator, biologist, criminologist, mechanic, woodworker, construction worker, construction contractor or estimator

LEARNING BY SEEING, HEARING, AND MOVING: the VAK system

Another way to approach the topic of learning styles is to use a system that focuses on just three ways of perceiving through your senses:

- Seeing, or visual learning
- Hearing, or auditory learning
- Movement, or kinesthetic learning

To recall this system, remember the letters VAK, which stand for **visual**, **auditory**, and **kinesthetic**. The theory is that each of us prefers to learn through one of these senses. And we can enrich our learning with activities that draw on the other channels.

To reflect on your VAK preferences, answer the following questions. Each question has three possible answers. Circle the answer that best describes how you would respond in the stated situation. This is not a formal inventory—just a way to prompt some self-discovery.

When you have problems spelling a word, you prefer to:

1. Look it up in the dictionary.

2. Say the word out loud several times before you write it down.

3. Write out the word with several different spellings and then choose one.

You enjoy courses the most when you get to:

1. View slides, overhead displays, videos, and readings with plenty of charts, tables, and illustrations.

2. Ask questions, engage in small-group discussions, and listen to guest speakers.

3. Take field trips, participate in lab sessions, or apply the course content while working as a volunteer or intern.

When giving someone directions on how to drive to a destination, you prefer to:

1. Pull out a piece of paper and sketch a map.

2. Give verbal instructions.

3. Say, "I'm driving to a place near there, so just follow me."

When planning an extended vacation to a new destination, you prefer to:

1. Read colorful, illustrated brochures or articles about that place.

2. Talk directly to someone who's been there.

3. Spend a day or two at that destination on a work-related trip before taking a vacation there.

You've made a commitment to learn to play the guitar. The first thing you do is:

1. Go to a library or music store and find an instruction book with plenty of diagrams and chord charts.

2. Pull out your favorite CDs, listen closely to the guitar solos, and see if you can play along with them.

3. Buy or borrow a guitar, pluck the strings, and ask someone to show you how to play a few chords.

You've saved up enough money to lease a car. When choosing from among several new models, the most important factor in your decision is:

1. The car's appearance.

2. The information you get by talking to people who own the cars you're considering.

3. The overall impression you get by taking each car on a test drive.

You've just bought a new computer system. When setting up the system, the first thing you do is:

1. Skim through the printed instructions that come with the equipment.

2. Call someone with a similar system and ask her for directions.

3. Assemble the components as best as you can, see if everything works, and consult the instructions only as a last resort.

You get a scholarship to study abroad next semester, which starts in just three months. You will travel to a country where French is the most widely spoken language. To learn as much French as you can before you depart, you:

1. Buy a video-based language course that's recorded on a DVD or downloaded from the Internet.

2. Set up tutoring sessions with a friend who's fluent in French.

3. Sign up for a short immersion course in an environment in which you speak only French, starting with the first class.

Now take a few minutes to reflect on the meaning of your responses. All of the answers numbered "1" are examples of visual learning. The "2's" refer to auditory learning, and the "3's" illustrate kinesthetic learning. Finding a consistent pattern in your answers indicates that you prefer learning through one sense channel more than the others. Or you might find that your preferences are fairly balanced.

Listed here are suggestions for learning through each sense channel. Experiment with these examples, and create more techniques of your own. Use the suggestions to build on your current preferences and develop new options for learning.

TO ENHANCE VISUAL LEARNING:

- Preview reading assignments by looking for elements that are highlighted visually—bold headlines, charts, graphs, illustrations, and photographs.

- When taking notes in class, leave plenty of room to add your own charts, diagrams, tables, and other visuals later.

- Whenever an instructor writes information on a blackboard or overhead display, copy it exactly in your notes.

- Transfer your handwritten notes to your computer. Use word-processing software that allows you to format your notes in lists, add headings in different fonts, and create visuals in color.

- Before you begin an exam, quickly sketch a diagram on scratch paper. Use this diagram to summarize the key formulas or facts you want to remember.

- During tests, see if you can visualize pages from your handwritten notes or images from your computer-based notes.

TO ENHANCE AUDITORY LEARNING:

- Reinforce memory of your notes and readings by talking about them. When studying, stop often to recite key points and examples in your own words.

- After reciting several summaries of key points and examples, record your favorite version or write it out.

- Read difficult passages in your textbooks slowly and out loud.

- Join study groups, and create short presentations about course topics.
- Visit your instructors during office hours to ask questions.

TO ENHANCE KINESTHETIC LEARNING:

- Look for ways to translate course content into three-dimensional models that you can build. While studying biology, for example, create a model of a human cell, using different colors of clay.

- Supplement lectures with trips to museums, field observations, lab sessions, tutorials, and other hands-on activities.
- Recite key concepts from your courses while you walk or exercise.
- Intentionally set up situations in which you can learn by trial and error.
- Create a practice test, and write out the answers in the room where you will actually take the exam.

Master Employees
IN ACTION

You're One Click Away...
from a video about Master Students in Action.

"*The skills I learned in college are initiative and being proactive. Similar to making the effort to attend office hours to speak with a professor about a project, I have been proactive in reaching out to people within my division to learn more about their job responsibilities. Through doing so, I have been able to gain insights as to areas I may want to learn more about as well as further my knowledge about how our jobs are connected.*"

—Kristen Oats
Financial Analyst

© iStockphoto.com/Jose Antonio Santiso Fernández

masterstudentprofile

Fabian Pfortmüller

(1983–) Cofounder of Holstee, a company that aims to *"create the greatest social impact while simultaneously creating the smallest environmental impact."*

Most mission statements contain words like *value* and *service* but often fail to explain what the founders truly care about, much less inspire anyone else to care. Holstee's mission statement is an exception. The Brooklyn, New York–based company, which sells eco-friendly clothing and accessories, rose from obscurity last year after its statement, dubbed the Holstee Manifesto, went viral. The document has been viewed online more than 50 million times and translated into 12 languages. ...

Inc. reporter Issie Lapowsky recently spoke with [Holstee cofounder] Pfortmüller about the impact a strong mission statement can have on a company.

Q: How did you come up with your mission statement?

A: We wrote it a few months after we started Holstee, in 2009. We were talking about how every entrepreneur, including us, wants to build a lifestyle for himself. But even though you're your own boss, sometimes a start-up becomes something you can't control. You build your business, but at the end of the day, you might not even want to work there. So we wanted to define what success means to us in nonmonetary terms. We also knew that down the road, it would help to have a reminder of why we started Holstee. Dave and Mike quit their jobs in the middle of the recession to start the company. The manifesto was a reminder that we took all these risks for a reason, to live a lifestyle we loved.

Q: How did it get so big?

A: Two bloggers picked it up. That just kicked off a chain reaction. We saw it all over Tumblr and Twitter. People started making it their Facebook photo. We were so surprised at how people responded to it. I think society is just hungry for genuine values.

Q: Whose idea was it to turn the manifesto into merchandise?

A: Actually, customers started asking for it. At first, we were hesitant about putting it on a poster. It was really personal to us, and putting anything on a big poster or T-shirt can cheapen it. But we got so many requests that one of our freelancers convinced us to try it. We got amazing feedback. We sold about 11,000 posters last year. They accounted for roughly 50 percent of our revenue in November.

Q: How has the popularity of the posters influenced your brand?

A: Usually people make a product first, then build a brand around it. In our case, it happened the other way around. That has helped us build trust with customers. People see the manifesto and automatically understand what we stand for. Then again, we're not a manifesto company, whatever that would be. The success of the posters helped us bootstrap, but at the end of the day, we're about products with a unique story that are designed with a conscience.

Fabian Pfortmüller ... is willing to take risks.
YOU ... can take appropriate risks by defining what success means to you.

Source: Issie Lapowski, "A Powerful (Mission) Statement," Inc. Magazine, January 24, 2012. Copyright 2012 by MANSUETO VENTURES LLC. Reproduced with permission of MANSUETO VENTURES LLC via Copyright Clearance Center.

Read the Holstee Manifesto online at http://shop.holstee.com /pages/about.

You're One Click Away...
from learning more about Fabian Pfortmüller online at the Master Student Profiles. You can also visit the Master Student Hall of Fame to learn more about other master students.

FIVE Cs
FOR YOUR CAREER

In the workplace, performance reviews often end with a personal development plan that includes specific ways to improve an employee's performance. After reading and using this book, you can think of these plans in a new way: They are opportunities to take a First Step about how you're doing at work.

Link your personal development plan to your character strengths. Standard advice from many self-development experts is to focus your plan on identifying and changing your greatest personal weaknesses. Think critically about this advice for three reasons:

- Tackling your weaknesses can feel threatening and lead to procrastination.
- A major weakness may be hard to change before your next performance review.
- Eliminating weaknesses might affect your life outside work and have little or no impact on your career.

Of course, it's fine to take a First Step about things you'd like to change. Another option is to focus your plan on listing and developing your strengths. This is a chance to think about character in a way that creates new possibilities for your future.

Think creatively and critically about your plan. Think about any of your recent accomplishments at work. Describe them in writing, including specific details about what you did and the results of your actions.

Next, set a goal to build on one of these accomplishments. This calls for creative thinking. Say that you made a suggestion to change the workflow in your department, and this change allowed your team to finish a project well before the scheduled due date. Consider setting a goal to make this a permanent change in your department's procedures. You could also set a goal to find other time-saving procedures.

You can always set a goal that targets one of your weaknesses. Just stay positive. Instead of focusing on a current behavior that you want to stop, for example, describe a new behavior that you want to start. Change "I will stop taking unclear notes at meetings" to "I will review my meeting notes to clarify the major agreements we made and next actions to take."

In any case, focus your development plan on goals that you can actually achieve in the near future, leading to clear benefits at work. Translate your goal into concrete behaviors. Ask yourself:

What exactly will I do differently based on my goal? Answering such questions involves critical thinking.

You can monitor your progress toward any goal, no matter how ambitious. To monitor listening skills, for example, you could count the number of times each day that you interrupt other people.

Remember that the point of monitoring your behavior is not to become a cold-blooded measurement machine. Rather, the idea is to make a change that really makes a difference over the long term. Behaviors that we measure carefully and consistently are likely to change.

As you monitor your behavior, remember the essence of a First Step: suspend all self-judgment. Just record the facts. If you deviate from your plan, just look for the next chance to practice your new behavior.

Use your knowledge of learning styles to communicate and collaborate with your boss. You probably feel more comfortable with a person when you feel that you have something in common. That feeling is called rapport. Whenever you establish rapport with someone in the workplace, you enter into a collaborative relationship.

When meeting with your boss for a performance review, for example, look for clues to that person's learning style. Then see if you can establish rapport by matching his or her style in a small, significant way.

For example, mirror your boss's word choice. She might like to process information visually. Clues to this preference are words such as, "I'll believe that when I see it" and "Give me an overview of your proposal." If she has a preference for verbal learning, she might say, "Let's talk through this" or "I'm hearing good things about you." And if she has kinesthetic preferences, she might signal those by referring to physical sensations ("I feel good about that idea") or action ("Walk me through your presentation before you give it").

Kinesthetic preferences are also expressed in posture, facial expressions, and other forms on nonverbal communication. Notice whether your boss is sitting with arms and legs crossed or open. If you can mirror that posture in a natural way, then do so.

As you look for ways to establish rapport, be subtle. The goal is not to manipulate. It's to communicate effectively and find common ground for collaboration.

Now, make a personal commitment to developing the five Cs. Take another look at the Discovery Wheel in this chapter—especially the sections labeled Character, Creative and Critical Thinking, Communicating, and Collaborating. Take a snapshot of your current skills in these areas after reading and doing this chapter.

DISCOVERY

My scores on the "Five C" sections of the Discovery Wheel were:	As of today, I would give myself the following scores in these areas:	At the end of this course, I would like my scores in these areas to be:
Character _____	Character _____	Character _____
Creative & Critical Thinking _____	Creative & Critical Thinking _____	Creative & Critical Thinking _____
Communicating _____	Communicating _____	Communicating _____
Collaborating _____	Collaborating _____	Collaborating _____

Next, skim this chapter and look for a technique that you want to explore in depth. Choose one that would enhance your self-rating in at least one of the five Cs. For example, you could choose a technique for enhancing visual learning presented in "Learning by seeing, hearing and moving: The VAK system." Practicing this technique could help you become more skilled at communicating and collaborating with people who favor visual learning.

I discovered that my preferred technique is . . .

_____

_____

_____

_____

In light of the five Cs, I can use this technique to become more . . .

_____

_____

_____

_____

INTENTION
To use this technique, I intend to . . .

_____

_____

_____

_____

NEXT ACTION
The specific action I will take is . . .

_____

_____

_____

_____

1. The "Power Process: Ideas are tools" states that if you want to use an idea, you must believe in it. True or false? Explain your answer.

_276_ _False, ~~but~~ due to the fact that when you first encounter ideas, you must think of them as tools + use them, practice them before you make a choice_

2. The First Step technique refers only to telling the truth about your areas for improvement. True or false? Explain your answer.

_277_ _True, so one can become an expert at what needs to be improved._

False

3. The ~~four~~ modes of learning are associated with certain questions. Give the appropriate question for each mode.

_285_ _why, how, what what if_

4. List the types of intelligence defined by Howard Gardner.

_275_ _~~Learning Style Inventory~~, ~~the VAIS system~~_
_+285_ _Verbal, mathematical/logical, visual bodily, musical, interpersonal and naturalist intrapersonal_

5. Describe two learning strategies related to one type of intelligence that you listed.

290-9 Interpersonal •form + conduct study groups early in term •create flash cards + use them to quiz group

6. The word kinesthetic refers to

_290_ (a) Moving

(b) Hearing

(c) Seeing

(d) Listening

7. Give an example of turning a First Step into a goal.

_278_ _Be specific and write down goal + what you can do to improve._

8. According to the text, the process of change starts with making negative judgments about our personal shortcomings. True or false? Explain your answer.

9. List three strategies for gaining concrete experiences when you learn something.

_283_ _①Percieve through feelings ③using five senses ②getting hands on and seeing if it works_

10. Clues to another person's learning style include

(a) approaches to a task that requires learning.

(b) word choice.

(c) body language.

(d) all of the above.

Time & Money

10

Use this **Master Student Map** to ask yourself

WHY THIS CHAPTER MATTERS . . .

- Procrastination, lack of planning, and money problems can undermine your success.

WHAT IS INCLUDED . . .

HOW I CAN USE THIS CHAPTER . . .

- Discover the details about how I currently manage time and money.
- Set time and money goals that make a difference in the quality of my life.
- Eliminate procrastination.

WHAT IF . . .

- I could meet my goals with time and money to spare?

© Ruslan Ivantsov/Shutterstock.com

JOURNAL ENTRY 7
Intention Statement

Create value from this chapter

Take a few minutes to skim this chapter. Find at least three techniques that you intend to use. List them below, along with their associated page numbers.

Strategy	Page number
_____	_____
_____	_____
_____	_____
_____	_____
_____	_____
_____	_____
_____	_____
_____	_____
_____	_____
_____	_____
_____	_____
_____	_____
_____	_____
_____	_____
_____	_____
_____	_____
_____	_____
_____	_____

POWER process
Be here now

Being right here, right now is such a simple idea. It seems obvious. Where else can you be but where you are? When else can you be there but when you are there?

The answer is that you can be somewhere else at any time—in your head. It's common for our thoughts to distract us from where we've chosen to be. When we let this happen, we lose the benefits of focusing our attention on what's important to us in the present moment.

To "be here now" means to do what you're doing when you're doing it. It means to be where you are when you're there. Students consistently report that focusing attention on the here and now is one of the most powerful tools in this book.

We all have a voice in our head that hardly ever shuts up. If you don't believe it, conduct this experiment: Close your eyes for 10 seconds, and pay attention to what is going on in your head. Please do this right now.

Notice something? Perhaps a voice in your head was saying, "Forget it. I'm in a hurry." Another might have said, "I wonder when 10 seconds is up?" Another could have been saying, "What little voice? I don't hear any little voice."

That's the voice.

This voice can take you anywhere at any time—especially when you are studying. When the voice takes you away, you might appear to be studying, but your brain is somewhere else.

All of us have experienced this voice, as well as the absence of it. When our inner voices are silent, time no longer seems to exist. We forget worries, aches, pains, reasons, excuses, and justifications. We fully experience the here and now. Life is magic.

Do not expect to be rid of the voice entirely. That is neither possible nor desirable. Inner voices serve a purpose. They enable us to analyze, predict, classify, and understand events out there in the "real" world. The trick is to consciously choose when to be with your inner voice and when to let it go.

Instead of trying to force a stray thought out of your head, simply notice it. Accept it. Tell yourself, "There's that thought again." Then gently return your attention to the task at hand. That thought, or another, will come back. Your mind will drift. Simply notice again where your thoughts take you, and gently bring yourself back to the here and now.

Also remember that planning supports this Power Process. Goals are tools that we create to guide our action in the present. Time management techniques—calendars, lists, and all the rest—have only one purpose. They reveal what's most important for you to focus on right *now*.

The idea behind this Power Process is simple. When you listen to a lecture, listen to a lecture. When you read this book, read this book. And when you choose to daydream, daydream. Do what you're doing when you're doing it. Be where you are when you're there.

Be here now . . . and now . . . and now.

iKO/Shutterstock.com

You're One Click Away...
from accessing Power Process Media online and finding out more about how to "be here now."

You've got the time—
and the money

The words *time management* may call forth images of restriction and control. You might visualize a prune-faced Scrooge hunched over your shoulder, stopwatch in hand, telling you what to do every minute. Bad news.

Good news: You do have enough time for the things you want to do. All it takes is thinking about the possibilities and making conscious choices.

. . . .

> **Time is an equal opportunity resource. All of us, regardless of gender, race, creed, or national origin, have exactly the same number of hours in a week. No matter how famous we are, no matter how rich or poor, we get 168 hours to spend each week—no more, no less.**

. . . .

Time is also an unusual commodity. It cannot be saved. You can't stockpile time like wood for the stove or food for the winter. It can't be seen, heard, touched, tasted, or smelled. You can't sense time directly. Even scientists and philosophers find it hard to describe. Because time is so elusive, it is easy to ignore. That doesn't bother time at all. Time is perfectly content to remain hidden until you are nearly out of it. And when you are out of it, you are out of it.

Time is a nonrenewable resource. If you're out of wood, you can chop some more. If you're out of money, you can earn a little extra. If you're out of love, there is still hope. If you're out of health, it can often be restored. But when you're out of time, that's it. When this minute is gone, it's gone.

Sometimes it seems that your friends control your time; your boss controls your time; your teachers or your parents or your kids or somebody else controls your time. Maybe that is not true, though.

Approach time as if you were in control. When you say you don't have enough time, you might really be saying that you are not spending the time you *do* have in the way that you want. This chapter is about ways to solve that problem.

The same idea applies to money. When you say you don't have enough money, the real issue might be that you are not spending the money you *do* have in the way that you want.

Most money problems result from spending more than is available. It's that simple, even though we often do everything we can to make the problem much more complicated. The solution also is simple: Don't spend more than you have. If you are spending more than you have, then increase your income, decrease your spending, or do both.

Again, you are in control of what you spend. This idea has never won a Nobel Prize in Economics, but you won't go broke applying it.

Everything written about time and money management can be reduced to three main ideas:

1. **Know exactly *what* you want.** State your wants as clear, specific goals. And put them in writing.

2. **Know *how* to get what you want.** Take action to meet your goals, including financial goals. Determine what you'll do *today* to get what you want in the future. Put those actions in writing as well.

3. **Take action to *get* what you want.** When our lives lack this quality, we spend most of our time responding to interruptions, last-minute projects, and emergencies. Life feels like a scramble to just survive. We're so busy achieving someone else's goals that we forget about getting what *we* want.

When schedules get tight, we often drop important activities such as exercising and fixing nutritious meals. We postpone them for that elusive day when we'll finally "have the time" or "have the money."

Don't wait for that time to come. *Make* the time. Use the suggestions and exercises in this chapter to empower yourself.

The most useful strategies for managing time and money are not new. They apply to people at *any* stage of their lives. These strategies are all based on the cycle of discovery, intention, and action that you're already practicing in this book. Throw in the ability to add and subtract, and you have everything you need to manage your time and your money. Spend these valuable resources in ways that align with your values. ■

CRITICAL THINKING EXERCISE 9

The Time Monitor

The purpose of this exercise is to transform time into a knowable and predictable resource. To do this, monitor your time in 15-minute intervals, 24 hours a day, for 7 days. Record how much time you spend sleeping, eating, studying, attending lectures, traveling to and from class, working, watching television, listening to music, taking care of the kids, running errands—everything.

If this sounds crazy, hang on for a minute. This exercise is not about keeping track of the rest of your life in 15-minute intervals. It is an opportunity to become conscious of how you spend your time—your life. Use the Time Monitor only for as long as it helps you do that.

When you know exactly how you spend your time, you can make choices with open eyes. You can plan to spend more time on the things that are most important to you and less time on the unimportant. Monitoring your time puts you in control of your life.

To do this exercise, complete the following steps:

1. **Look at Figure 10.2, a sample Time Monitor, on page 303.** On Monday, the student in this sample got up at 6:45 A.M., showered, and got dressed. He finished this activity and began breakfast at 7:15. He put this new activity in at the time he began, and drew a line just above it. He ate from 7:15 to 7:45. It took him 15 minutes to walk to class (7:45 to 8:00), and he attended classes from 8:00 to 11:00.

   You will list your activities in the same way. When you begin an activity, write it down next to the time you begin. Round off to the nearest 15 minutes. If, for example, you begin eating at 8:06, enter your starting time as 8:00.

2. **Fill out *your* Time Monitor.** Now it's your turn. Make copies of the blank Time Monitor (Figure 10.3 on page 304), or plan to do this exercise online. With your instructor, choose a day to begin monitoring your time. On that day, start filling out your Time Monitor. Keep it with you all day and use it for one full week. Take a few moments every couple of hours to record what you've done. Or, enter a note each time that you change activities.

3. **After you've monitored your time for one week, group your activities together into categories.** List them in the "Category" column in Figure 10.4 on page 306. This chart already includes the categories "sleep," "class," "study," and "meals." Think of other categories to add. "Grooming" might include showering, putting on makeup, brushing teeth, and getting dressed. "Travel" could include walking, driving, taking the bus, and riding your bike. Other categories might be "exercise," "entertainment," "work," "television," "domestic," and "children." Write in the categories that work for you.

4. **List your *estimated* hours for each category of activity.** Guess how many hours you *think* you spent on each category of activity. List these hours in the "Estimated" column in Figure 10.4.

5. **List your *actual* hours for each category of activity.** Now, add up the figures from your Time Monitor. List these hours in the "Actual" column in Figure 10.4. Make sure that the grand total of all categories is 168 hours.

6. **Reflect on the results of this exercise.** Compare the "Estimated" and "Actual" columns. Take a few minutes and let these numbers sink in. Notice your reactions. You might feel disappointed or even angry about where your time goes. Use those feelings as motivation to make different choices. Complete the following sentences:

   I was surprised at the amount of time I spent on . . .

   _____

   I want to spend more time on . . .

   _____

   I want to spend less time on . . .

   _____

7. **Repeat this exercise.** Do this exercise as many times as you want. The benefit is developing a constant awareness of your activities. With that awareness, you can make informed choices about how to spend the time of your life.

 You're One Click Away...
from doing this exercise online under Exercises.

MONDAY _9_ / _12_	
	Get up
	Shower
7:00	
7:15	Breakfast
7:30	
7:45	Walk to class
8:00	Econ 1
8:15	
8:30	
8:45	
9:00	
9:15	
9:30	
9:45	
10:00	Bio 1
10:15	
10:30	
10:45	
11:00	
11:15	Study
11:30	
11:45	
12:00	
12:15	Lunch
12:30	
12:45	
1:00	
1:15	Eng. Lit
1:30	
1:45	
2:00	
2:15	Coffeehouse
2:30	
2:45	
3:00	
3:15	
3:30	
3:45	
4:00	
4:15	Study
4:30	
4:45	
5:00	
5:15	Dinner
5:30	
5:45	
6:00	
6:15	
6:30	Babysit
6:45	
7:00	

TUESDAY _9_ / _13_	
	Sleep
7:00	
7:15	
7:30	
7:45	Shower
8:00	Dress
8:15	Eat
8:30	
8:45	
9:00	Art
9:15	Apprec.
9:30	Project
9:45	
10:00	
10:15	
10:30	
10:45	
11:00	Data
11:15	process
11:30	
11:45	
12:00	
12:15	
12:30	
12:45	
1:00	
1:15	Lunch
1:30	
1:45	
2:00	Work
2:15	on book
2:30	report
2:45	
3:00	Art
3:15	Apprec.
3:30	
3:45	
4:00	
4:15	
4:30	
4:45	
5:00	Dinner
5:15	
5:30	
5:45	
6:00	Letter to
6:15	Uncle Jim
6:30	
6:45	
7:00	

10

Figure 10.2 Sample Time Monitor

MONDAY __/__/__	TUESDAY __/__/__	WEDNESDAY __/__/__	THURSDAY __/__/__
7:00	7:00	7:00	7:00
7:15	7:15	7:15	7:15
7:30	7:30	7:30	7:30
7:45	7:45	7:45	7:45
8:00	8:00	8:00	8:00
8:15	8:15	8:15	8:15
8:30	8:30	8:30	8:30
8:45	8:45	8:45	8:45
9:00	9:00	9:00	9:00
9:15	9:15	9:15	9:15
9:30	9:30	9:30	9:30
9:45	9:45	9:45	9:45
10:00	10:00	10:00	10:00
10:15	10:15	10:15	10:15
10:30	10:30	10:30	10:30
10:45	10:45	10:45	10:45
11:00	11:00	11:00	11:00
11:15	11:15	11:15	11:15
11:30	11:30	11:30	11:30
11:45	11:45	11:45	11:45
12:00	12:00	12:00	12:00
12:15	12:15	12:15	12:15
12:30	12:30	12:30	12:30
12:45	12:45	12:45	12:45
1:00	1:00	1:00	1:00
1:15	1:15	1:15	1:15
1:30	1:30	1:30	1:30
1:45	1:45	1:45	1:45
2:00	2:00	2:00	2:00
2:15	2:15	2:15	2:15
2:30	2:30	2:30	2:30
2:45	2:45	2:45	2:45
3:00	3:00	3:00	3:00
3:15	3:15	3:15	3:15
3:30	3:30	3:30	3:30
3:45	3:45	3:45	3:45
4:00	4:00	4:00	4:00
4:15	4:15	4:15	4:15
4:30	4:30	4:30	4:30
4:45	4:45	4:45	4:45
5:00	5:00	5:00	5:00
5:15	5:15	5:15	5:15
5:30	5:30	5:30	5:30
5:45	5:45	5:45	5:45
6:00	6:00	6:00	6:00
6:15	6:15	6:15	6:15
6:30	6:30	6:30	6:30
6:45	6:45	6:45	6:45
7:00	7:00	7:00	7:00
7:15	7:15	7:15	7:15
7:30	7:30	7:30	7:30
7:45	7:45	7:45	7:45
8:00	8:00	8:00	8:00
8:15	8:15	8:15	8:15
8:30	8:30	8:30	8:30
8:45	8:45	8:45	8:45
9:00	9:00	9:00	9:00
9:15	9:15	9:15	9:15
9:30	9:30	9:30	9:30
9:45	9:45	9:45	9:45
10:00	10:00	10:00	10:00
10:15	10:15	10:15	10:15
10:30	10:30	10:30	10:30
10:45	10:45	10:45	10:45
11:00	11:00	11:00	11:00
11:15	11:15	11:15	11:15
11:30	11:30	11:30	11:30
11:45	11:45	11:45	11:45
12:00	12:00	12:00	12:00

Figure 10.3 Your Time Monitor

FRIDAY ___ / ___ / ___ /	SATURDAY ___ / ___ / ___ /	SUNDAY ___ / ___ / ___ /
7:00	7:00	7:00
7:15	7:15	7:15
7:30	7:30	7:30
7:45	7:45	7:45
8:00	8:00	8:00
8:15	8:15	8:15
8:30	8:30	8:30
8:45	8:45	8:45
9:00	9:00	9:00
9:15	9:15	9:15
9:30	9:30	9:30
9:45	9:45	9:45
10:00	10:00	10:00
10:15	10:15	10:15
10:30	10:30	10:30
10:45	10:45	10:45
11:00	11:00	11:00
11:15	11:15	11:15
11:30	11:30	11:30
11:45	11:45	11:45
12:00	12:00	12:00
12:15	12:15	12:15
12:30	12:30	12:30
12:45	12:45	12:45
1:00	1:00	1:00
1:15	1:15	1:15
1:30	1:30	1:30
1:45	1:45	1:45
2:00	2:00	2:00
2:15	2:15	2:15
2:30	2:30	2:30
2:45	2:45	2:45
3:00	3:00	3:00
3:15	3:15	3:15
3:30	3:30	3:30
3:45	3:45	3:45
4:00	4:00	4:00
4:15	4:15	4:15
4:30	4:30	4:30
4:45	4:45	4:45
5:00	5:00	5:00
5:15	5:15	5:15
5:30	5:30	5:30
5:45	5:45	5:45
6:00	6:00	6:00
6:15	6:15	6:15
6:30	6:30	6:30
6:45	6:45	6:45
7:00	7:00	7:00
7:15	7:15	7:15
7:30	7:30	7:30
7:45	7:45	7:45
8:00	8:00	8:00
8:15	8:15	8:15
8:30	8:30	8:30
8:45	8:45	8:45
9:00	9:00	9:00
9:15	9:15	9:15
9:30	9:30	9:30
9:45	9:45	9:45
10:00	10:00	10:00
10:15	10:15	10:15
10:30	10:30	10:30
10:45	10:45	10:45
11:00	11:00	11:00
11:15	11:15	11:15
11:30	11:30	11:30
11:45	11:45	11:45
12:00	12:00	12:00

WEEK OF ___ / ___ / ___ /		
Category	Estimated Hours	Actual Hours
Sleep		
Class		
Study		
Meals		

Figure 10.4 Your Estimated and Actual Hours

SETTING *and* ACHIEVING *goals*

Many people have no goals, or have only vague, idealized notions of what they want. These notions float among the clouds in their heads. They are wonderful, fuzzy, safe thoughts such as "I want to be a good person," "I want to be financially secure," or "I want to be happy."

Generalized outcomes have great potential as achievable goals. When we keep these goals in a nonspecific form, however, we may become confused about ways to actually achieve them.

Make your goal as real as a finely tuned engine. There is nothing vague or fuzzy about engines. You can see them, feel them, and hear them. You can take them apart and inspect the moving parts. Goals can be every bit as real and useful. If you really want to meet a goal, then take it apart. Inspect the moving parts—the physical actions that you will take to make the goal happen and fine-tune your life.

There are many useful methods for setting goals. You're about to learn one of them. This method is based on writing goals that relate to several time frames and areas of your life. Experiment, and modify as you see fit.

Write down your goals. Writing down your goals greatly increases your chances of meeting them. Writing exposes undefined terms, unrealistic time frames, and other symptoms of fuzzy thinking. If you've been completing Intention Statements as explained in the Introduction to this book, then you've already had experience writing goals. Both goals and Intention Statements address changes you want to make in your behavior, your values, your circumstances—or all of these.

To keep track of your goals, write each one on a separate 3 × 5 card, or type them all into a file on your computer. Update this file as your goals change, and back it up when you back up your other files. Consider storing this file on a flash drive so you can access it any time you are at a computer.

Write specific goals. State your goals in writing as observable actions or measurable results. Think in detail about how things will be different once your goals are attained. List the changes in what you'll see, feel, touch, taste, hear, be, do, or have.

Suppose that one of your goals is to become a better student by studying harder. You're headed in a powerful direction; now translate that goal into a concrete action, such as "I will study 2 hours for every hour I'm in class." Specific goals make clear what actions are needed or what results are expected.

Vague goal	Specific goal
Get a good education.	Graduate with B.S. degree in engineering, with honors, by 2012.
Get good grades.	Earn a 3.5 grade point average next semester.
Enhance my spiritual life.	Meditate for 15 minutes daily.
Improve my appearance.	Lose 6 pounds during the next 6 months
Get control of my money.	Transfer $100 to my savings account each month.

When stated specifically, a goal might look different to you. If you examine it closely, a goal you once thought you wanted might not be something you want after all. Or you might discover that you want to choose a new path to achieve a goal that you are sure you want.

Write goals in several time frames. To get a comprehensive vision of your future, write down the following:

- *Long-term goals.* Long-term goals represent major targets in your life. These goals can take 5 to 20 years to achieve. In some cases, they will take a lifetime. They can include goals in education, careers, personal relationships, travel, financial security—whatever is important to you. Consider the answers to the following questions as you create your long-term goals: What do you want to accomplish in your life? Do you want your life to make a statement? If so, what is that statement?

- *Midterm goals.* Midterm goals are objectives you can accomplish in 1 to 5 years. They include goals such as completing a course of education, paying off a car loan, or achieving a specific career level. These goals usually support your long-term goals.

- *Short-term goals.* Short-term goals are the ones you can accomplish in a year or less. These goals are specific achievements, such as completing a particular course, hiking the Appalachian Trail, or organizing a family reunion. A short-term financial goal would probably include a dollar amount. Whatever your short-term goals are, they require action now or in the near future.

Write goals in several areas of life. People who set goals in only one area of life—such as their career—may find that their personal growth becomes one-sided. They might experience success at work while neglecting their health or relationships with family members and friends.

To avoid this outcome, set goals in a variety of categories. Consider what you want to experience in these areas and add goals in other areas as they occur to you:

- Education
- Career
- Financial life
- Family life or relationships
- Social life
- Spiritual life
- Level of health

Reflect on your goals. Each week, take a few minutes to think about your goals. You can perform the following spot checks:

- *Check in with your feelings.* Think about how the process of setting your goals felt. Consider the satisfaction you'll gain in attaining your objectives. If you don't feel a significant emotional connection with a written goal, consider letting it go or filing it away to review later.
- *Check for alignment.* Look for connections among your goals. Do your short-term goals align with your midterm goals? Will your midterm goals help you achieve your long-term goals? Look for a fit between all of your goals and your purpose for taking part in higher education, as well as your overall purpose in life.
- *Check for obstacles.* All kinds of things can come between you and your goals, such as constraints on time and money. Anticipate obstacles, and start looking now for workable solutions.

Move into action immediately. To increase your odds of success, take immediate action. Decrease the gap between stating a goal and starting to achieve it. If you slip and forget about the goal, you can get back on track at any time by *doing* something about it. Here's a way to link goal setting to time management. Decide on a list of small, achievable steps you can take right away to accomplish each of your short-term goals. Write these small steps down on a daily to-do list. If you want to accomplish some of these steps by a certain date, enter them in a calendar that you consult daily. Then, over the coming weeks, review your to-do list and calendar. Take note of your progress and celebrate your successes.

One of the most effective actions you can take is to share your goals with people who will assist you to achieve them. Tap into the the power of a supportive community.

Reward yourself with care. When you meet your goal on time, reward yourself. Remember that there are two types of rewards. The first type includes rewards that follow naturally from achieving a goal. For example, your reward for earning a degree might be getting the job you've always wanted.

The second type of reward is something that you design. After turning in a paper, you might reward yourself with a nap or an afternoon in the park. A reward like this works best when you're willing to withhold it. If you plan to take a nap on Sunday afternoon, whether you've finished your chemistry assignment or not, then the nap is not an effective reward.

Another way to reward yourself after you achieve a goal is to just sit quietly and savor the feeling. One reason why success breeds success is that it feels good.

Get back to benefits. Achieving a long-term goal, such as graduating from school, poses a special challenge. You might go through periods when you lose enthusiasm. The payoff in the future seems so distant. And the work in the present seems so hard.

See whether you can close that gap in time. Take the future rewards of your goals and make them as vivid as possible in the present. Post visible reminders of the benefits you'll gain. If you want to graduate, then post photographs of people wearing caps and gowns at a ceremony. If you want to stop smoking, then post a list of the benefits that you'll gain from quitting.

Some presentations about goal setting make the whole process seem like a dry, dusty exercise in self-discipline. Don't believe it. In the end, setting and achieving goals is about having the most fun over the long run. It's about getting what you want in the future and enjoying every step along the way. ■

✔ CRITICAL THINKING EXERCISE 10

Create a lifeline

On a large sheet of paper, draw a horizontal line. This line will represent your lifetime. Now add key events in your life to this line, in chronological order. Examples are birth, first day at school, graduation from high school, and enrollment in higher education.

Now extend the lifeline into the future. Write down key events you would like to see occur 1 year, 5 years, and 10 or more years from now. Choose events that align with your core values. Work quickly in the spirit of a brainstorm, bearing in mind that this plan is not a final one.

Afterward, take a few minutes to review your lifeline. Select one key event for the future, and list any actions

you could take in the next month to bring yourself closer to that goal. Do the same with the other key events on your lifeline. You now have the rudiments of a comprehensive plan for your life.

Finally, extend your lifeline another 50 years beyond the year when you would reach age 100. Describe in detail what changes in the world you'd like to see as a result of the goals you attained in your lifetime.

 You're One Click Away...
from doing this exercise online under Exercises.

✓ CRITICAL THINKING EXERCISE 11

Get real with your goals

One way to make goals effective is to examine them up close. That's what this exercise is about. Using a process of brainstorming and evaluation, you can break a long-term goal into smaller segments until you have taken it completely apart. When you analyze a goal to this level of detail, you're well on the way to meeting it.

For this exercise, you will use a pen, extra paper, and a watch with a second hand. (A digital watch with a built-in stopwatch feature is even better.) Timing is an important part of the brainstorming process, so follow the stated time limits. This entire exercise takes about an hour.

Part 1: Long-term goals

Brainstorm. Begin with an 8-minute brainstorm. Use a separate sheet of paper for this part of the exercise. For 8 minutes, write down everything you think you want in your life. Write as fast as you can, and write whatever comes into your head. Leave no thought out. Don't worry about accuracy. The object of a brainstorm is to generate as many ideas as possible.

Evaluate. After you have finished brainstorming, spend the next 6 minutes looking over your list. Analyze what you wrote. Read the list out loud. If something is missing, add it. Look for common themes or relationships among your goals. Then select three long-term goals that are important to you—goals that will take many years to achieve. Write these goals below in the space provided.

_____

_____

_____

Before you continue, take a minute to reflect on the process you've used so far. What criteria did you use to select your top three goals?

Part 2: Midterm goals

Brainstorm. Read out loud the three long-term goals you selected in Part 1. Choose one of them. Then brainstorm a list of goals you might achieve in the next 1 to 5 years that would lead to the accomplishment of that one long-term goal. These are midterm goals. Spend 8 minutes on this brainstorm. Go for quantity.

Evaluate. Analyze your brainstorm of midterm goals. Then select three that you determine to be important in meeting the long-term goal you picked. Allow yourself 6 minutes for this part of the exercise. Write your selections below in the space provided.

_____

_____

_____

Why do you see these three goals as more important than the other midterm goals you generated? On a separate sheet of paper, write about your reasons for selecting these three goals.

Part 3: Short-term goals

Brainstorm. Review your list of midterm goals and select one. In another 8-minute brainstorm, generate a list of short-term goals—those you can accomplish in a year or less that will lead to the attainment of that midterm goal. Write down everything that comes to mind. Do not evaluate or judge these ideas yet. For now, the more ideas you write down, the better.

Evaluate. Analyze your list of short-term goals. The most effective brainstorms are conducted by suspending judgment, so you might find some bizarre ideas on your list. That's fine. Now is the time to cross them out. Next, evaluate your remaining short-term goals, and select three that you are willing and able to accomplish. Allow yourself 6 minutes for this part of the exercise. Then write your selections below in the space provided.

_____

_____

_____

The more you practice, the more effective you can be at choosing goals that have meaning for you. You can repeat this exercise, employing the other long-term goals you generated or creating new ones.

 You're One Click Away...
from completing this exercise online under Exercises.

One of the most effective ways to stay on track and actually get things done is to use a daily to-do list. Although the Time Monitor gives you a general picture of the week, your daily to-do list itemizes specific tasks you want to complete within the next 24 hours.

© Deborah Jaffe/The Image Bank/Getty

The ABC
daily to-do list

One advantage of keeping a daily to-do list is that you don't have to remember what to do next. It's on the list. A typical day in the life of a student is full of separate, often unrelated tasks—reading, attending lectures, reviewing notes, working at a job, writing papers, researching special projects, running errands. It's easy to forget an important task on a busy day. When that task is written down, you don't have to rely on your memory.

The following steps present one method for creating and using to-do lists. This method involves ranking each item on your list according to three levels of importance—A, B, or C. Experiment with these steps, modify them as you see fit, and invent new techniques that work for you.

STEP 1 BRAINSTORM TASKS

To get started, list all of the tasks you want to get done tomorrow. Each task will become an item on a to-do list. Don't worry about putting the entries in order or scheduling them yet. Just list everything you want to accomplish on a sheet of paper or planning calendar, or in a special notebook. You can also use 3 × 5 cards, writing one task on each card. Cards work well because you

can slip them into your pocket or rearrange them, and you never have to copy to-do items from one list to another.

STEP 2 ESTIMATE TIME

For each task you wrote down in Step 1, estimate how long it will take you to complete it. This can be tricky. If you allow too little time, you end up feeling rushed. If you allow too much time, you become less productive. For now, give it your best guess. If you are unsure, overestimate rather than underestimate how long it will take for each task. Overestimating has two benefits: (1) It avoids a schedule that is too tight, missed deadlines, and the resulting feelings of frustration and failure; and (2) it allows time for the unexpected things that come up every day—the spontaneous to-dos. Now pull out your calendar or Time Monitor. You've probably scheduled some hours for activities such as classes or work. This leaves the unscheduled hours for tackling your to-do lists.

Add up the time needed to complete all your to-do items. Also add up the number of unscheduled hours in your day. Then compare the two totals. The power of this step is that you can spot overload in advance. If you have 8 hours' worth of to-do items but only 4 unscheduled hours, that's a potential problem. To solve it, proceed to Step 3.

Step 1: Brainstorm tasks
Step 2: Estimate time
Step 3: Rate each task by priority
Step 4: Cross off tasks
Step 5: Evaluate
Bonus Step: Tinker

STEP 3 RATE EACH TASK BY PRIORITY

To prevent overscheduling, decide which to-do items are the most important, given the time you have available. One suggestion for making this decision comes from the book *How to Get Control of Your Time and Your Life,* by Alan Lakein: Simply label each task A, B, or C.[1]

The A's on your list are those things that are the most critical. They include assignments that are coming due or jobs that need to be done immediately. Also included are activities that lead directly to your short-term goals.

The B's on your list are important, but less so than the A's. B's might someday become A's. For the present, these tasks are not as urgent as A's. They can be postponed, if necessary, for another day.

The C's do not require immediate attention. C priorities include activities such as "shop for a new blender" and "research genealogy on the Internet." C's are often small, easy jobs with no set time line. They too can be postponed.

Once you've labeled the items on your to-do list, schedule time for all of the A's. The B's and C's can be done randomly during the day when you are in between tasks and are not yet ready to start the next A. Even if you only get only one or two of your A's done, you'll still be moving toward your goals.

STEP 4 CROSS OFF TASKS

Keep your to-do list with you at all times. Cross off activities when you finish them, and add new ones when you think of them. If you're using 3 × 5 cards, you can toss away or recycle the cards with completed items. Crossing off tasks and releasing cards can be fun—a visible reward for your diligence. This step fosters a sense of accomplishment.

When using the ABC priority method, you might experience an ailment common to students: C fever. Symptoms include the uncontrollable urge to drop that A task and begin crossing C's off your to-do list. If your history paper is due tomorrow, you might feel compelled to vacuum the rug, call your third cousin in Tulsa, and make a trip to the store for shoelaces. The reason C fever

is so common is that A tasks are usually more difficult or time-consuming to achieve, with a higher risk of failure.

If you notice symptoms of C fever, ask yourself, "Does this job really need to be done now? Do I really need to alphabetize my DVD collection, or might I better use this time to study for tomorrow's data-processing exam?" Use your to-do list to keep yourself on task, working on your A's. But don't panic or berate yourself when you realize that in the last 6 hours, you have completed eleven C's and not a single A. Just calmly return to the A's.

STEP 5 EVALUATE

At the end of the day, evaluate your performance. Look for A priorities you didn't complete. Look for items that repeatedly turn up as B's or C's on your list and never seem to get done. Consider changing them to A's or dropping them altogether. Similarly, you might consider changing an A that didn't get done to a B or C priority.

Be willing to admit mistakes. You might at first rank some items as A's only to realize later that they are actually C's. And some of the C's that lurk at the bottom of your list day after day might really be A's. When you keep a daily to-do list, you can adjust these priorities *before* they become problems.

When you're done evaluating, start on tomorrow's to-do list. That way you can wake up and start getting things done right away.

BONUS STEP TINKER

When it comes to to-do lists, one size does not fit all. Feel free to experiment. Tweak the format of your list so that it works for you.

For example, the ABC system is not the only way to rank items on your to-do list. Some people prefer the 80-20 system. This method is based on the idea that 80 percent of the value of any to-do list comes from only 20 percent of the tasks on that list. So on a to-do list of 10 items, find the 2 that will contribute most to your life today. Complete those tasks without fail.

Another option is to rank items as "yes," "no," or "maybe." Do all of the tasks marked "yes." Delete those marked "no." And put all of the "maybes" on the shelf for later. You can come back to the "maybes" at a future point and rank them as "yes" or "no."

You might find that grouping items by categories such as "errands" and "calls" works best. Be creative.

In any case, use your to-do list in close connection with your calendar. On your calendar, note appointments, classes, and other events that take place on a specific date, a specific time, or both. Use your to-do list for items that you can complete between scheduled events. Keeping a separate to-do list means that you don't have to clutter up your calendar with all those reminders.

In addition, consider planning a whole week or even 2 weeks in advance. Planning in this way can make it easier to put activities in context and see how your daily goals relate to your long-term goals. Weekly planning can also free you from feeling that you have to polish off your whole to-do list in 1 day. Instead, you can spread tasks out over the whole week.

In any case, make starting your own to-do list an A priority. ∎

You're One Click Away...
from finding more strategies online for daily planning.

BREAK IT DOWN, GET IT DONE
Using a long-term planner

With a long-term planner, you can eliminate a lot of unpleasant surprises. Long-term planning allows you to avoid scheduling conflicts—the kind that obligate you to be in two places at the same time 3 weeks from now. You can also anticipate busy periods, such as finals week, and start preparing for them now. Good-bye, all-night cram sessions. Hello, serenity.

Find a long-term planner, or make your own. Many office supply stores carry academic planners in paper form that cover an entire school year. Computer software for time management offers the same features. You can also be creative and make your own long-term planner. A big roll of newsprint pinned to a bulletin board or taped to a wall will do nicely. You can also search the Internet for a computer application or smartphone app that's designed for planning.

Enter scheduled dates that extend into the future. Use your long-term planner to list commitments that extend beyond the current month. Enter test dates, lab sessions, days that classes will be canceled, and other events that will take place over this term and next term.

Create a master assignment list. Find the syllabus for each course you're currently taking. Then, in your long-term planner, enter the due dates for all of the assignments in all of your courses. This step can be a powerful reality check.

The purpose of this technique is to not to make you feel overwhelmed with all the things you have to do. Rather, its aim is to help you take a First Step toward recognizing the demands on your time. Armed with the truth about how you use your time, you can make more accurate plans.

Include nonacademic events. In addition to tracking academic commitments, you can use your long-term planner to mark significant events in your life outside school. Include birthdays, doctors' appointments, concert dates, credit card payment due dates, and car maintenance schedules.

Planning a day, a week, or a month ahead is a powerful practice. Using a long-term planner—one that displays an entire quarter, semester, or year at a glance—can yield even more benefits.

Use your long-term planner to divide and conquer. For some people, academic life is a series of last-minute crises punctuated by periods of exhaustion. You can avoid that fate. The trick is to break down big assignments and projects into smaller assignments and subprojects, each with their own due date.

When planning to write a paper, for instance, enter the final due date in your long-term planner. Then set individual due dates for each milestone in the writing process—creating an outline, completing your research, finishing a first draft, editing the draft, and preparing the final copy. By meeting these interim due dates, you make steady progress on the assignment throughout the term. That sure beats trying to crank out all those pages at the last minute. ■

You're One Click Away...
from finding printable copies of this long-term planner online.

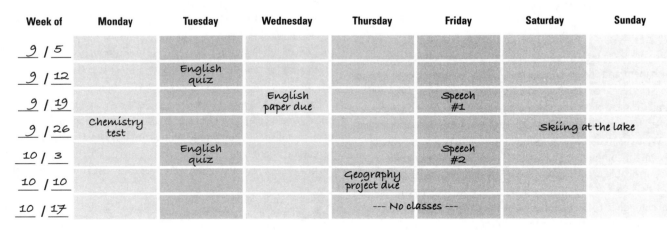

Week of	Monday	Tuesday	Wednesday	Thursday	Friday	Saturday	Sunday
9 / 5							
9 / 12		English quiz					
9 / 19			English paper due		Speech #1		
9 / 26	Chemistry test					Skiing at the lake	
10 / 3		English quiz			Speech #2		
10 / 10				Geography project due			
10 / 17				--- No classes ---			

LONG-TERM PLANNER ___ / ___ / ___ to ___ / ___ / ___

Week of	Monday	Tuesday	Wednesday	Thursday	Friday	Saturday	Sunday
___ / ___							
___ / ___							
___ / ___							
___ / ___							
___ / ___							
___ / ___							
___ / ___							
___ / ___							
___ / ___							
___ / ___							
___ / ___							
___ / ___							
___ / ___							
___ / ___							
___ / ___							
___ / ___							
___ / ___							
___ / ___							
___ / ___							
___ / ___							
___ / ___							
___ / ___							
___ / ___							
___ / ___							
___ / ___							
___ / ___							
___ / ___							
___ / ___							
___ / ___							
___ / ___							

10

LONG-TERM PLANNER ___ / ___ / ___ to ___ / ___ / ___

Week of	Monday	Tuesday	Wednesday	Thursday	Friday	Saturday	Sunday
___ / ___							
___ / ___							
___ / ___							
___ / ___							
___ / ___							
___ / ___							
___ / ___							
___ / ___							
___ / ___							
___ / ___							
___ / ___							
___ / ___							
___ / ___							
___ / ___							
___ / ___							
___ / ___							
___ / ___							
___ / ___							
___ / ___							
___ / ___							
___ / ___							
___ / ___							
___ / ___							
___ / ___							
___ / ___							
___ / ___							
___ / ___							
___ / ___							
___ / ___							
___ / ___							
___ / ___							

STOP
Procrastination
Now

Consider a bold idea: The way to stop procrastinating is to stop procrastinating. Giving up procrastination is actually a simple choice. People just make it complicated.

Sound crazy? Well, test this idea for yourself.

Think of something that you've been putting off. Choose a small, specific task—one that you can complete in 5 minutes or less. Then do that task today.

Tomorrow, choose another task and do it. Repeat this strategy each day for 1 week. Notice what happens to your habit of procrastination.

If the above suggestion just doesn't work for you, then experiment with any strategy from the 7-day antiprocrastination plan on page 90.

DISCOVER THE COSTS. Find out whether procrastination keeps you from getting what you want. Clearly seeing the side effects of procrastination can help you kick the habit.

DISCOVER YOUR PROCRASTINATION STYLE. Psychologist Linda Sapadin identifies different styles of procrastination.[2] For example, *dreamers* have big goals that they seldom translate into specific plans. *Worriers* focus on the worst-case scenario and are likely to talk more about problems than about solutions. *Defiers* resist new tasks or promise to do them and then don't follow through. *Overdoers* create extra work for themselves

by refusing to delegate tasks and neglecting to set priorities. And *perfectionists* put off tasks for fear of making a mistake.

Awareness of your procrastination style is a key to changing your behavior. If you exhibit the characteristics of an overdoer, for example, then say no to new projects. Also ask for help in completing your current projects.

To discover your procrastination style, observe your behavior. Avoid judgments. Just be a scientist: Record the facts. Write Discovery Statements about specific ways you procrastinate. Follow up with Intention Statements about what to do differently.

TRICK YOURSELF INTO GETTING STARTED. If you have a 50-page chapter to read, then grab the book and say to yourself, "I'm not really going to read this chapter right now. I'm just going to flip through the pages and scan the headings for 10 minutes." Tricks like these can get you started on a task you've been dreading.

LET FEELINGS FOLLOW ACTION. If you put off exercising until you feel energetic, you might wait for months. Instead, get moving now. Then watch your feelings change. After 5 minutes of brisk walking, you might be in the mood for a 20-minute run. This principle—action generates motivation—can apply to any task that you've put on the back burner.

CHOOSE TO WORK UNDER PRESSURE. Sometimes people thrive under pressure. As one writer puts it, "I don't do my *best* work under deadline. I do my *only* work under deadline." Used selectively, this strategy might also work for you.

Put yourself in control. If you choose to work with a due date staring you right in the face, then schedule a big block of time during the preceding week. Until then, enjoy!

THINK AHEAD. Use the long-term planner on page 87 to list due dates for assignments in all your courses. Using these tools, you can anticipate heavy demands on your time and take action to prevent last-minute crunches. Make *From Master Student to Master Employee* your home base—the first place to turn in taking control of your schedule.

CREATE GOALS THAT DRAW YOU FORWARD. A goal that grabs you by the heartstrings is an inspiration to act now. If you're procrastinating, then set some goals that excite you. Then you might wake up one day and discover that procrastination is part of your past. ■

 You're One Click Away... *from finding more strategies online for ending procrastination.*

THE 7-DAY
antiprocrastination plan

Listed here are seven strategies you can use to reduce or eliminate many sources of procrastination. The suggestions are tied to the days of the week to help you remember them. Use this list to remind yourself that each day of your life presents an opportunity to stop the cycle of procrastination.

MONDAY Make it Meaningful. What is important about the task you've been putting off? List all the benefits of completing that task. Look at it in relation to your short-, mid-, or long-term goals. Be specific about the rewards for getting it done, including how you will feel when the task is completed. To remember this strategy, keep in mind that it starts with the letter *M*, as in the word *Monday*.

TUESDAY Take it Apart. Break big jobs into a series of small ones you can do in 15 minutes or less. If a long reading assignment intimidates you, divide it into two- or three-page sections. Make a list of the sections, and cross them off as you complete them so you can see your progress. Even the biggest projects can be broken down into a series of small tasks. This strategy starts with the letter *T*, so mentally tie it to *Tuesday*.

WEDNESDAY Write an Intention Statement. If you can't get started on a term paper, you might write, "I intend to write a list of at least 10 possible topics by 9:00 p.m. I will reward myself with an hour of guilt-free recreational reading." Write your intention on a 3 × 5 card. Carry it with you or post it in your study area, where you can see it often. In your memory, file the first word in this strategy—*write*—with *Wednesday*.

THURSDAY Tell Everyone. Publicly announce your intention to get a task done. Tell a friend that you intend to learn 10 irregular French verbs by Saturday. Tell your spouse, roommate, parents, and children. Include anyone who will ask whether you've completed the assignment or who will suggest ways to get it done. Make the world your support group. Associate *tell* with *Thursday*.

FRIDAY Find a Reward. Construct rewards to yourself carefully. Be willing to withhold them if you do not complete the task. Don't pick a movie as a reward for studying biology if you plan to go to the movie anyway. And when you legitimately reap your reward, notice how it feels. Remember that *Friday* is a fine day to *find* a reward. (Of course, you can find a reward on any day of the week. Rhyming *Friday* with *fine* day is just a memory trick.)

SATURDAY Settle it Now. Do it now. The minute you notice yourself procrastinating, plunge into the task. Imagine yourself at a cold mountain lake, poised to dive. Gradual immersion would be slow torture. It's often less painful to leap. Then be sure to savor the feeling of having the task behind you. Link *settle* with *Saturday*.

SUNDAY Say No. When you keep pushing a task into a low-priority category, reexamine your purpose for doing that task at all. If you realize that you really don't intend to do something, quit telling yourself that you will. That's procrastinating. Just say no. Then you're not procrastinating. You don't have to carry around the baggage of an undone task. *Sunday*—the last day of this 7-day plan—is a great day to finally let go and just *say* no.

25 WAYS
TO GET
THE MOST
OF OUT OF
now

Ferenc Szelepcsenyi/Shutterstock.com

The following techniques are about getting the most from study time. They're listed in four categories:

- When to study

- Where to study

- Getting focused when you study

- Questions that keep you focused

Don't feel pressured to use all of the techniques or to tackle them in order. As you read, note the suggestions you think will be helpful. Pick one technique to use now. When it becomes a habit, come back to this article and select another one. Repeat this cycle, and enjoy the results as they unfold in your life.

WHEN TO STUDY

Study difficult (or boring) subjects first. If your chemistry problems put you to sleep, get to them first, while you are fresh. We tend to give top priority to what we enjoy studying, yet the courses that we find most difficult often require the most creative energy. Save your favorite subjects for later. If you find yourself avoiding a particular subject, get up an hour earlier to study it before breakfast. With that chore out of the way, the rest of the day can be a breeze.

Continually being late with course assignments indicates a trouble area. Further action is required. Clarify your intentions about the course by writing down your feelings in a journal, talking with an instructor, or asking for help from a friend or counselor. Consistently avoiding study tasks can also be a signal to reexamine your major or course program.

Be aware of your best time of day. Many people learn best in daylight hours. If this is true for you, schedule study time for your most difficult subjects or most difficult people before nightfall.

Unless you grew up on a farm, the idea of being conscious at 5:00 A.M. might seem ridiculous. Yet many successful businesspeople begin the day at 5:00 A.M. or earlier. Athletes and yoga practitioners use the early morning too. Some writers complete their best work before 9:00 A.M.

Others experience the same benefits by staying up late. They flourish after midnight. If you aren't convinced, then experiment. When you're in a time crunch, get up early or stay up late. You might even see a sunrise.

Use waiting time. Five minutes waiting for a subway, 20 minutes waiting for the dentist, 10 minutes in between classes—waiting time adds up fast. Have short study tasks ready to do during these periods, and keep your study materials handy. For example, carry 3 × 5 cards with facts, formulas, or definitions and pull them out anywhere. A mobile phone with an audio recording app can help you use commuting time to your advantage. Make a recording of yourself reading your notes. Play back the recording as you drive, or listen through headphones as you ride on the bus or subway.

Study 2 hours for every hour you're in class. Students in higher education are regularly advised to allow 2 hours of study time for every hour spent in class. If you are taking 15 credit hours, then plan to spend 30 hours a week studying. That adds up to 45 hours each week for school—more than a full-time job. The benefits of thinking in these terms will be apparent at exam time.

This guideline is just that—a guideline, not an absolute rule. Consider what's best for you. If you do the Time Monitor exercise in this chapter, note how many hours you actually spend studying for each hour of class. Then ask how your schedule is working. You might want to allow more study time for some subjects.

Keep in mind that the "2 hours for 1" rule doesn't distinguish between focused time and unfocused time. In one 4-hour block of study time, it's possible to use up 2 of those hours with phone calls, breaks, daydreaming, and doodling. With study time, quality counts as much as quantity.

Avoid marathon study sessions. With so many hours ahead of you, the temptation is to tell yourself, "Well, it's going to be a long day. No sense rushing into it. Better sharpen about a dozen of these pencils and change the light bulbs." Three 3-hour sessions are usually more productive than one 9-hour session.

If you must study in a large block of time, work on several subjects. Avoid studying similar topics one after the other.

Whenever you study, stop and rest for a few minutes every hour. Give your brain a chance to take a break. Simply moving to a new location might be enough to maintain your focus. When taking breaks fails to restore your energy, it's time to close the books and do something else for a while.

Monitor how much time you spend online. To get an accurate picture of your involvement in social networking and other online activities, use the Time Monitor process in this chapter. Then make conscious choices about how much time you want to spend on these activities. Staying connected is fine. Staying on constant alert for a new text, Twitter stream, or Facebook update distracts you from achieving your goals.

WHERE TO STUDY

Use a regular study area. Your body and your mind know where you are. Using the same place to study, day after day, helps train your responses. When you arrive at that particular place, you can focus your attention more quickly.

Study where you'll be alert. In bed, your body gets a signal. For most students, that signal is more likely to be "Time to sleep!" than "Time to study!" Just as you train your body to be alert at your desk, you also train it to slow down near your bed. For that reason, don't study where you sleep.

Easy chairs and sofas are also dangerous places to study. Learning requires energy. Give your body a message that energy is

needed. Put yourself in a situation that supports this message. For example, some schools offer empty classrooms as places to study. If you want to avoid distractions, look for a room where friends are not likely to find you.

Use a library. Libraries are designed for learning. The lighting is perfect. The noise level is low. A wealth of material is available. Entering a library is a signal to focus the mind and get to work. Many students can get more done in a shorter time frame at the library than anywhere else. Experiment for yourself.

GETTING FOCUSED WHEN YOU STUDY

Pay attention to your attention. Breaks in concentration are often caused by internal interruptions. Your own thoughts jump in to divert you from your studies. When this happens, notice these thoughts and let them go. Perhaps the thought of getting something else done is distracting you. One option is to handle that other task now and study later. Or you can write yourself a note about it or schedule a specific time to do it.

Agree with living mates about study time. This agreement includes roommates, spouses, and children. Make the rules about study time clear, and be sure to follow them yourself. Explicit agreements—even written contracts—work well. One student always wears a colorful hat when he wants to study. When his wife and children see the hat, they respect his wish to be left alone.

Get off the phone. The phone is the ultimate interrupter. People who wouldn't think of distracting you in person might call or text you at the worst times because they can't see that you are studying. You don't have to be a victim of your cell phone. If a simple "I can't talk; I'm studying" doesn't work, use dead silence. It's a conversation killer. Or short-circuit the whole problem: Turn off your phone or silence it.

Learn to say no. Saying no is a time-saver and a valuable life skill for everyone. Some people feel it is rude to refuse a request. But you can say no effectively and courteously. Others want you to succeed as a student. When you tell them that you can't do what they ask because you are busy educating yourself, most people will understand.

Hang a "do not disturb" sign on your door. Many hotels will give you a free sign, for the advertising. Or you can create a sign yourself. They work. Using signs can relieve you of making a decision about cutting off each interruption—a time-saver in itself.

Get ready the night before. Completing a few simple tasks just before you go to bed can help you get in gear the next day. If you need to make some phone calls first thing in the morning, look up those numbers, write them on 3 × 5 cards, and set them near the phone. If you need to drive to a new location, make a note of the address and put it next to your car keys. If you plan to spend the next

SETTING LIMITS ON screen time

Access to the Internet and wireless communication offers easy ways to procrastinate. We call it "surfing," "texting," "IMing,"—and sometimes "researching" or "working." In his book *Crazy Busy: Overstretched, Overbooked, and About to Snap*, Edward Hallowell coined a word to describe these activities when they're done too often—*screensucking*.

Digital devices create value. With a computer you can stream music, watch videos, listen to podcasts, scan newspapers, read books, check e-mail, and send instant messages. With a smartphone you consume online content while staying available to key people when it counts. And any of these activities can become a constant source of distraction.

Discover how much time you spend online. People who update their Twitter stream or Facebook page every hour may be sending an unintended message—that they have no life offline.

To get an accurate picture of your involvement in social networking and other online activity, use the Time Monitor exercise included earlier in this chapter. Then make conscious choices about how much time you want to spend online and on the phone. Don't let social networking distract you from meeting personal and academic goals.

Go offline to send the message that other people matter. It's hard to pay attention to the person who is right in front of you when you're hammering out text messages or updating your Twitter stream. You can also tell when someone else is doing these things and only half-listening to you. How engaged in your conversation do you think that person is?

An alternative is to close up your devices and "be here now." When you're eating, stop answering the phone. Notice how the food tastes. When you're with a friend, close up your laptop. Hear every word he says. Rediscover where life actually takes place—in the present moment.

Developing emotional intelligence requires being with people and away from a computer or cell phone. People who break up with a partner through text messaging are not developing that intelligence. True friends know when to go offline and head across campus to resolve a conflict. They know when to go back home and support a family member in crisis. When it counts, your presence is your greatest present.

---

afternoon writing a paper, get your materials together: dictionary, notes, outline, paper, pencil, flash drive, laptop—whatever you need. Pack your lunch or put gas in the car. Organize the baby's diaper bag and your briefcase or backpack.

Call ahead. We often think of talking on the telephone as a prime time-waster. Used wisely, though, the telephone can actually help manage time. Before you go shopping, call the store to see whether it carries the items you're looking for. A few seconds on the phone or computer can save hours in wasted trips and wrong turns.

Avoid noise distractions. To promote concentration, avoid studying in front of the television, and turn off the radio. Many students insist that they study better with background noise, and it might be true. Some students report good results with carefully selected and controlled music. For many others, silence is the best form of music to study by.

At times noise levels might be out of your control. A neighbor or roommate might decide to find out how far she can turn up her music before the walls crumble. Meanwhile, your ability to concentrate on the principles of sociology goes down the drain. To avoid this scenario, schedule study sessions during periods when your living environment is usually quiet. If you live in a residence

hall, ask whether study rooms are available. Or go somewhere else where it's quiet, such as the library. Some students have even found refuge in quiet coffee shops, self-service laundries, and places of worship.

Manage interruptions. Notice how others misuse your time. Be aware of repeat offenders. Ask yourself whether there are certain friends or relatives who consistently interrupt your study time.

If avoiding the interrupter is impractical, send a clear message. Sometimes others don't realize that they are breaking your concentration. You can give them a gentle, yet firm, reminder: "What you're saying is important. Can we schedule a time to talk about it when I can give you my full attention?" If this strategy doesn't work, there are other ways to make your message more effective. For more ideas, see Chapter 9: Communicating.

See whether you can "firewall" yourself for selected study periods each week. Find a place where you can count on being alone and work without interruption.

Sometimes interruptions still happen, though. Create a system for dealing with them. One option is to take an index card and write a quick note about what you're doing the moment an interruption occurs. As soon as possible, return to the card and pick up the task where you left off.

QUESTIONS THAT
KEEP YOU FOCUSED

Ask: "What is one task I can accomplish toward achieving my goal?" This technique is helpful when you face a big, imposing job. Pick out one small accomplishment, preferably one you can complete in about 5 minutes; then do it. The satisfaction of getting one thing done can spur you on to get one more thing done. Meanwhile, the job gets smaller.

Ask: "Am I being too hard on myself?" If you are feeling frustrated with a reading assignment, your attention wanders repeatedly, or you've fallen behind on math problems that are due tomorrow, take a minute to listen to the messages you are giving yourself. Are you scolding yourself too harshly? Lighten up. Allow yourself to feel a little foolish, and then get on with the task at hand. Don't add to the problem by berating yourself.

Worrying about the future is another way people beat themselves up: "How will I ever get all this done?" "What if every paper I'm assigned turns out to be this hard?" "If I can't do the simple calculations now, how will I ever pass the final?" Instead of promoting learning, such questions fuel anxiety and waste valuable time.

Labeling and generalizing weaknesses are other ways people are hard on themselves. Being objective and specific in the messages you send yourself will help eliminate this form of self-punishment and will likely generate new possibilities. An alternative to saying "I'm terrible in algebra" is to say, "I don't understand factoring equations." This rewording suggests a plan to improve.

You might be able to lighten the load by discovering how your learning styles affect your behavior. For example, you may have a bias toward concrete experience rather than abstract thinking. If so, after setting a goal, you might want to move directly into action.

In large part, the ability to learn through concrete experience is a valuable trait. After all, action is necessary to achieve goals. At the same time, you might find it helpful to allow extra time to plan. Careful planning can help you avoid unnecessary activity. Instead of using a planner that shows a day at a time, experiment with a calendar that displays a week or month at a glance. The expanded format can help you look further into the future and stay on track as you set out to meet long-term goals.

Ask: "Is this a piano?" Carpenters who construct rough frames for buildings have a saying they use when they bend a nail or accidentally hack a chunk out of a two-by-four: "Well, this ain't no piano." It means that perfection is not necessary. Ask yourself whether what you are doing needs to be perfect. Perhaps you don't have to apply the same standards of grammar to lecture notes that you would apply to a term paper. If you can complete a job 95 percent perfectly in 2 hours and 100 percent perfectly in 4 hours, ask yourself whether the additional 5 percent improvement is worth doubling the amount of time you spend.

Sometimes, though, it *is* a piano. A tiny miscalculation can ruin an entire lab experiment. A misstep in solving a complex math problem can negate hours of work. Computers are notorious for turning little errors into nightmares. Accept lower standards only when appropriate.

A related suggestion is to weed out low-priority tasks. The to-do list for a large project can include dozens of items, not all of which are equally important. Some can be done later, while others can be skipped altogether, if time is short.

Apply this idea when you study. In a long reading assignment, look for pages you can skim or skip. When it's appropriate, read chapter summaries or article abstracts. As you review your notes, look for material that might not be covered on a test, and decide whether you want to study it.

Ask: "Would I pay myself for what I'm doing right now?" If you were employed as a student, would you be earning your wages? Ask yourself this question when you notice that you've taken your third snack break in 30 minutes. Then remember that you are, in fact, employed as a student. You are investing in your own productivity and are paying a big price for the privilege of being a student. Doing a mediocre job now might result in fewer opportunities in the future.

Ask: "Can I do just one more thing?" Ask yourself this question at the end of a long day. Almost always you will have enough energy to do just one more short task. The overall increase in your productivity might surprise you.

Ask: "Can I delegate this?" Instead of slogging through complicated tasks alone, you can draw on the talents and energy of other people. Busy executives know the value of delegating tasks to coworkers. Without delegation, many projects would flounder or die.

You can apply the same principle in your life. Instead of doing all the housework or cooking by yourself, for example, you can assign some of the tasks to family members or roommates. Rather than making a trip to the library to look up a simple fact, you can call and ask a library assistant to research it for you. Instead of driving across town to deliver a package, you can hire a delivery service to do so. All of these tactics can free up extra hours for studying.

It's not practical to delegate certain study tasks, such as writing term papers or completing reading assignments. However, you can still draw on the ideas of others in completing such tasks. For instance, form a writing group to edit and critique papers, brainstorm topics or titles, and develop lists of sources.

If you're absent from a class, find a classmate to summarize the lecture, discussion, and any upcoming assignments. Presidents depend on briefings. You can use the same technique.

Ask: "How did I just waste time?" Notice when time passes and you haven't accomplished what you had planned to do. Take a minute to review your actions and note the specific ways you wasted time. We tend to operate by habit, wasting time in the same ways over and over again. When you are aware of things you do that drain your time, you are more likely to catch yourself in the act next time. Observing one small quirk might save you hours. But keep this in mind: Asking you to notice how you waste time is not intended to make you feel guilty. The point is to increase your skill by getting specific information about how you use time.

Ask: "Could I find the time if I really wanted to?" The way people speak often rules out the option of finding more time. An alternative is to speak about time with more possibility.

The next time you're tempted to say, "I just don't have time," pause for a minute. Question the truth of this statement. Could you find 4 more hours this week for studying? Suppose that someone offered to pay you $10, 000 to find those 4 hours. Suppose too that you will get paid only if you don't lose sleep, call in sick for work, or sacrifice anything important to you. Could you find the time if vast sums of money were involved?

Remember that when it comes to school, vast sums of money *are* involved.

Ask: "Am I willing to promise it?" This time-management idea might be the most powerful of all: If you want to find time for a task, promise yourself—and others—that you'll get it done. Unleash one of the key qualities of master students and take responsibility for producing an outcome.

To make this technique work, do more than say that you'll try to keep a promise or that you'll give it your best shot. Take an oath, as you would in court. Give it your word.

One way to accomplish big things in life is to make big promises. There's little reward in promising what's safe or predictable. No athlete promises to place seventh in the Olympic games. Chances are that if you're not making big promises, you're not stretching yourself.

The point of making a promise is not to chain yourself to a rigid schedule or impossible expectations. You can promise to reach goals without unbearable stress. You can keep schedules flexible and carry out your plans with ease, joy, and satisfaction.

At times, though, you might go too far. Some promises may be truly beyond you, and you might break them. However, failing to keep a promise is just that—failing to keep a promise. A broken promise is not the end of the world.

Promises can work magic. When your word is on the line, it's possible to discover reserves of time and energy you didn't know existed. Promises can push you to exceed your expectations. ▪

 You're One Click Away...
from discovering even more ways online to get the most out of now.

10

....

Master Employees
IN ACTION

 You're One Click Away...
from a video about Master Students in Action.

"*In my college classes I would get syllabi from professors that laid out the whole year. Assignments were never mentioned again and it was up to me to do them on time. At work, I have a whole series of tasks to complete on my own from week to week. And I now know how/when to do those things without being asked.*"

—Karlis Bryan,
Assistant Media Buyer

....

Make choices about
MULTITASKING

When we get busy, we get tempted to do several things at the same time. It seems like such a natural solution: Watch TV *and* read a textbook. Talk on the phone *and* outline a paper. Write an e-mail *and* listen to a lecture. These are examples of multitasking.

There's a problem with this strategy: Multitasking is much harder than it looks.

Despite the awe-inspiring complexity of the human brain, research reveals that we are basically wired to do one thing at a time.[3] One study found that people who interrupted work to check e-mail or surf the Internet took up to 25 minutes to get back to their original task.[4] In addition, people who use cell phones while driving have more accidents than anyone except drunk drivers.[5]

The solution is an old-fashioned one: Whenever possible, take life one task at a time. Develop a key quality of master students—focused attention. Start by reviewing and using the "Power Process: Be here now." Then add the following strategies to your toolbox.

UNPLUG FROM TECHNOLOGY

To reduce the temptation of multitasking, turn off distracting devices. Shut off your TV and cell phone. Disconnect from the Internet unless it's required for your planned task. Later, you can take a break to make calls, send texts, check e-mail, and browse the Web.

CAPTURE FAST-BREAKING IDEAS WITH MINIMAL INTERRUPTION

Your brain is an expert nagger. After you choose to focus on one task, it might issue urgent reminders about 10 more things you need to do. Keep 3 × 5 cards or paper and a pen handy to write down those reminders. You can take a break later and add them to your to-do list. Your mind can quiet down once it knows that a task has been captured in writing.

MONITOR THE MOMENT-TO-MOMENT SHIFTS IN YOUR ATTENTION

Whenever you're studying and notice that you're distracted by thoughts of doing something else, make a tally mark on a sheet of paper. Simply being aware of your tendency to multitask can help you reclaim your attention.

HANDLE INTERRUPTIONS WITH CARE

Some breaking events are so urgent that they call for your immediate attention. When this happens, note what you were doing when you were interrupted. For example, write down the number of the page you were reading, or the name of the computer file you were creating. When you return to the task, your notes can help you get up to speed again.

MULTITASK BY CONSCIOUS CHOICE

If multitasking seems inevitable, then do it with skill. Pair one activity that requires concentration with another activity that you can do almost automatically. For example, studying for your psychology exam while downloading music is a way to reduce the disadvantages of multitasking. Pretending to listen to your children while watching TV is not.

ALIGN YOUR ACTIVITIES WITH YOUR PASSIONS

Our attention naturally wanders when we find a task to be trivial, pointless, or irritating. At those times, switching attention to another activity becomes a way to reduce discomfort.

Handling routine tasks is a necessary part of daily life. But if you find that your attention frequently wanders throughout the day, ask yourself: Am I really doing what I want to do? Do my work and my classes connect to my interests?

If the answer is no, then the path beyond multitasking might call for a change in your academic and career plans. Determine what you want most in life. Then use the techniques in this chapter to set goals that inspire you. Whenever an activity aligns with your passion, the temptation to multitask loses power. ■

The Money Monitor/Money Plan

Many of us find it easy to lose track of money. It likes to escape when no one is looking. And usually, no one is looking. That's why the simple act of noticing the details about money can be so useful—even if this is the only idea from the chapter that you ever apply.

Use this exercise as a chance to discover how money flows into and out of your life. The goal is to record all the money you receive and spend over the course of 1 month. This sounds like a big task, but it's simpler than you might think. Besides, there's a big payoff for this action. With increased awareness of income and expenses, you can make choices about money that will change your life. Here's how to begin.

STEP 1 **Tear out the Money Monitor/Money Plan form on page 100.** Make photocopies of this form to use each month. The form helps you do two things. One is to get a big picture of the money that flows in and out of your life. The other is to plan specific and immediate changes in how you earn and spend money.

STEP 2 **Keep track of your income and expenses.** Use your creativity to figure out how you want to carry out this step. The goal is to create a record of exactly how much you earn and spend each month. Use any method that works for you. And keep it simple. Following are some options:

- **Carry 3 × 5 cards in your pocket, purse, backpack, or briefcase.** Every time you buy something or get paid, record a few details on a card. List the date. Add a description of what you bought or what you got paid. Note whether the item is a source of income (money coming in) or an expense (money going out). Be sure to use a separate card for each item. This makes it easier to sort your cards into categories at the end of the month and fill out your Money Monitor/Money Plan.

- **Save all receipts and file them.** This method does not require you to carry any 3 × 5 cards. But it does require that you faithfully hang on to every receipt and record of payment. Every time you buy something, ask for a

receipt. Then stick it in your wallet, purse, or pocket. When you get home, make notes about the purchase on the receipt. Then file the receipts in a folder labeled with the current month and year (for example, January 2011). Every time you get a paycheck during that month, save the stub and add it to the folder. If you do not get a receipt or record of payment, whip out a 3 × 5 card and create one of your own. Detailed receipts will help you later on when you file taxes, categorize expenses (such as food and entertainment), and check your purchases against credit card statements.

- **Use personal finance software.** Learn to use Quicken or a similar product that allows you to record income and expenses on your computer and to sort them into categories.

- **Use online banking services.** If you have a checking account that offers online services, take advantage of the records that the bank is already keeping for you. Every time you write a check, use a debit card, or make a deposit, the transaction will show up online. You can use a computer to log in to your account and view these transactions at any time. If you're unclear about how to use online banking, go in to your bank and ask for help.

- **Experiment with several of the above options.** Settle into one that feels most comfortable to you. Or create a method of your own. Anything will work, as long as you end each month with an *exact and accurate* record of your income and expenses.

STEP 3 **On the last day of the month, fill out your Money Monitor/Money Plan.** Pull out a blank Money Monitor/Money Plan. Label it with the current month and year. Fill out this form using the records of your income and expenses for the month.

Notice that the far left column of the Money Monitor/Money Plan includes categories of income and expenses. (You can use the blank rows for categories of income and expenses that are not already included.) Write your total for each category in the middle column.

For example, if you spent $300 at the grocery store this month, write that amount in the middle column next to *Groceries*. If you work a part-time job and received two paychecks for the month, write the total in the middle column next to *Employment*. See the sample Money Monitor/Money Plan on page 99 for more examples.

Remember to split expenses when necessary. For example, you might write one check each month to pay the balance due on your credit card. The purchases listed on your credit card bill might fall into several categories. Total up your expenses in each category, and list them separately.

Suppose that you used your credit card to buy music online, purchase a sweater, pay for three restaurant meals, and buy two tanks of gas for your car. Write the online music expense next to *Entertainment*. Write the amount you paid for the sweater next to *Clothes*. Write the total you spent at the restaurants next to *Eating Out*. Finally, write the total for your gas stops next to *Gas*.

Now look at the column on the far right of the Money Monitor/Money Plan. This column is where the magic happens. Review each category of income and expense. If you plan to reduce your spending in a certain category during the next month, write a minus sign (−) in the far right column. If you plan a spending increase in any category next month, write a plus sign (+) in the far right column. If you think that a category of income or expense will remain the same next month, leave the column blank.

Look again at the sample Money Monitor/Money Plan on page 99. This student plans to reduce her spending for clothes, eating out, and entertainment (which for her includes movies and DVD rentals). She plans to increase the total she spends on groceries. She figures that even so, she'll save money by cooking more food at home and eating out less.

STEP 4 **After you've filled out your first Money Monitor/ Money Plan, take a moment to congratulate yourself.** You have actively collected and analyzed the data needed to take charge of your financial life. No matter how the numbers add up, you are now in conscious control of your money. Repeat this exercise every month. It will keep you on a steady path to financial freedom.

You're One Click Away...
from doing this exercise online at your College Success CourseMate.

No budgeting required

Notice one more thing about the Money Monitor/Money Plan: It does not require you to create a budget. Budgets—like diets—often fail. Many people cringe at the mere mention of the word *budget*. To them it is associated with scarcity, drudgery, and guilt. The idea of creating a budget conjures up images of a penny-pinching Ebenezer Scrooge shaking a bony, wrinkled finger at them and screaming, "You spent too much, you loser!"

That's not the idea behind the Money Monitor/Money Plan. In fact, there is no budget worksheet for you to complete each month. And no one is pointing a finger at you. Instead of budgeting, you simply write a plus sign or a minus sign next to each expense or income category that you *freely choose* to increase or decrease next month. There's no extra paperwork, no shame, and no blame.

Sample Money Monitor/Money Plan

Income	This Month	Next Month
Employment	500	
Grants	100	
Interest from Savings		
Loans	300	
Scholarships	100	
Total Income	1000	

Expenses	This Month	Next Month
Books and Supplies		
Car Maintenance		
Car Payment		
Clothes		–
Deposits into Savings Account		
Eating Out	50	–
Entertainment	50	–
Gas	100	
Groceries	300	+
Insurance (Car, Life, Health, Home)		
Laundry	20	
Phone	55	
Rent/Mortgage Payment	400	
Tuition and Fees		
Utilities	50	
Total Expenses	1025	–

10

Money Monitor/Money Plan
Month_____ Year_____

Income	This Month	Next Month
Employment		
Grants		
Interest from Savings		
Loans		
Scholarships		
Total Income		

Expenses	This Month	Next Month
Books and Supplies		
Car Maintenance		
Car Payment		
Clothes		
Deposits into Savings Account		
Eating Out		
Entertainment		
Gas		
Groceries		
Insurance (Car, Life, Health, Home)		
Laundry		
Phone		
Rent/Mortgage Payment		
Tuition and Fees		
Utilities		
Total Expenses		

Money Monitor/Money Plan
Month_____ Year_____

Income	This Month	Next Month
Employment		
Grants		
Interest from Savings		
Loans		
Scholarships		
Total Income		

Expenses	This Month	Next Month
Books and Supplies		
Car Maintenance		
Car Payment		
Clothes		
Deposits into Savings Account		
Eating Out		
Entertainment		
Gas		
Groceries		
Insurance (Car, Life, Health, Home)		
Laundry		
Phone		
Rent/Mortgage Payment		
Tuition and Fees		
Utilities		
Total Expenses		

10

EARN MORE MONEY

For many people, finding a way to increase income is the most appealing way to fix a money problem. This approach is reasonable, but it has a potential problem: When their income increases, many people continue to spend more than they make. This means that money problems persist even at higher incomes. To avoid this problem, manage your expenses no matter how much money you make.

If you do succeed at controlling your expenses over the long term, then increasing your income is definitely a way to build wealth.

Focus on your education. Your most important assets are not your bank accounts, your car, or your house, but your skills. That's why your education is so important. Right now, you're developing knowledge, experience, and abilities that you can use to create income for the rest of your life.

Once you graduate and land a job in your chosen field, continue your education. Look for ways to gain additional skills or certifications that lead to higher earnings and more fulfilling work assignments.

Work while you're in school. If you work while you're in school, you earn more than money. You gain experience, establish references, interact with a variety of people, and make contact with people who might hire you in the future. Also, regular income in any amount can make a difference in your monthly cash flow.

Many students work full-time or part-time jobs. Work and school don't have to conflict, especially if you plan carefully and ask for your employer's support.

See if you can find a job related to your chosen career. Even an entry-level job in your field can provide valuable experience. Once you've been in such a job for a while, explore the possibilities for getting a promotion.

Treat people well. No matter where you work, you are meeting people. Build positive relationships. Do this with people at any level of an organization—from the CEO to the people who empty the trash. Treat them all as equals. Look for common ground and make friendly conversation. And if you ever feel someone at work has taken advantage of you, take steps to protect yourself while letting go of the desire to get revenge.

Treating people well offers two benefits. First, you create a more pleasant work environment. Second, someone that you treat with kindness today might be in a position to recommend you for a promotion or a higher-paying job in the future. Kindness pays off in many ways.

Use "downtime" to your advantage. Some jobs involve workloads that come in cycles. During certain times of the year—when a new product is launched, for example—people work longer

> If your employer offers training and development programs, take advantage of them. Use downtime to contribute to your employer and yourself.

hours. At other points in the year, they experience downtimes—days when they have much less to do.

If your work slows down, look for something useful to do. Instead of sharpening pencils or surfing the Internet, do a task that's important but not urgent. If your employer offers training and development programs, take advantage of them. Use downtime to contribute to your employer and yourself.

Do your best at every job. Once you get a job, make it your intention to excel as an employee. A positive work experience can pay off for years by leading to other jobs, recommendations, and contacts.

This means doing every task with full attention and care—even the "menial" jobs. Straightening up shelves or updating a mailing list are opportunities to shine as an employee.

Every job involves tasks that are less than glamorous. Think beyond what you're *doing* to who you're *being*. Any task allows you to align your actions with a commitment to quality and other core values.

Take the long view. To maximize your earning power, keep honing your job-hunting and career-planning skills. You can find a wealth of ideas on these topics in Chapter 12: Career Management.

Finally, keep things in perspective. If your current job is lucrative and rewarding, great. If not, remember that almost any job can support you in becoming a master student and a master employee. ■

You're One Click Away...
from discovering more ways online to increase your income.

SPEND LESS MONEY

Controlling your expenses is something you can do right away, and it's usually easier than increasing your income. Start with the following ideas.

Look at big-ticket items. When you look for places to cut expenses, start with the items that cost the most. Choices about where to live, for example, can save you thousands of dollars. Sometimes a place a little farther from campus, or a smaller house or apartment, will be much less expensive.

Use "Critical Thinking Exercise 12: The Money Monitor/Money Plan" on page 97 to discover the main drains on your finances. Then focus on one or two areas where you can reduce spending.

Do comparison shopping. Prices vary dramatically. Shop around, wait for off-season sales, and use coupons. Check out secondhand stores, thrift stores, and garage sales. Before plunking down the full retail price for a new item, consider whether you could buy it used.

Be aware of quality. The cheapest product is not always the least expensive over the long run. Sometimes, a slightly more expensive item is the best buy because it will last longer. Remember, there is no correlation between the value of something and the amount of money spent to advertise it.

Save money on eating and drinking. This single suggestion could significantly lower your expenses. Instead of hitting a restaurant or bar, head to the grocery store. Fresh fruits, fresh vegetables, and whole grains are not only better for you than processed food—they also cost less.

Cooking for yourself doesn't need to take much time. Do a little menu planning. Create a list of your five favorite home-cooked meals. Learn how to prepare them. Then keep ingredients for these meals always on hand. To reduce grocery bills, buy these ingredients in bulk.

Lower your phone bills. If you use a cell phone, pull out a copy of your latest bill. Review how many minutes you used last month. Perhaps you could get by with a less expensive phone, fewer minutes, fewer text messages, and a cheaper plan.

Go "green." To conserve energy and save money on utility bills, turn out the lights when you leave a room. Keep windows and doors closed in winter. In summer, keep windows open early in the day to invite lots of cool air into your living space. Then close up the apartment or house to keep it cool during the hotter hours of the day. Leave air-conditioning set at 72 degrees or above. In cool weather, dress warmly and keep the house at 68 degrees or less. In hot weather, take shorter, cooler showers.

Postpone purchases. If you plan to buy something, leave your credit card at home when you first go shopping. Look at all the possibilities. Then go home and make your decision when you don't feel pressured. When you are ready to buy, wait a week, even if the salesperson pressures you. What seems like a necessity today may not even cross your mind the day after tomorrow.

Use the envelope system. After reviewing your monthly income and expenses, put a certain amount of cash each week in an envelope labeled *Entertainment/Eating Out*. When the envelope is empty, stop spending money on these items for the rest of the week. If you use online banking, see if you can create separate accounts for various spending categories. Then deposit a fixed amount of money into each of those accounts. This is an electronic version of the envelope system.

Use the money you save to prepare for emergencies and reduce debt. If you apply strategies such as those listed here, you might see your savings account swell nicely. Congratulate yourself. Then choose what to do with the extra money. To protect yourself during tough times, create an emergency fund. Then reduce your debt by paying more than the minimum on credit card bills and loan payments (see "Take Charge of Your Credit" on page 107.) ∎

> Remember, there is no correlation between the value of something and the amount of money spent to advertise it.

You're One Click Away...
from discovering more cost-cutting strategies online.

Managing money during tough times

A short-term crisis in the overall economy can reduce your income and increase your expenses. So can the decision to go back to school. The biggest factor in your long-term financial well-being, though, is your daily behavior. Habits that help you survive during tough times will also help you prosper after you graduate and when the economy rebounds. Taking informed action is a way to cut through financial confusion and move beyond fear.

Start by doing "Critical Thinking Exercise 12: Money Monitor/Money Plan" on page 97, if you have not yet completed it. This exercise will give you the details about what you're spending and earning right now. With that knowledge, you can choose your next strategy from among the following.

TAKE A FIRST STEP

If the economy tanks, we can benefit by telling the truth about it. We can also tell the truth about ourselves. It's one thing to condemn the dishonesty of mortgage bankers and hedge fund managers. It's another thing to have an unpaid balance on a credit card or wipe out a savings accounts and still believe that we are in charge of our money. The first step to changing such behaviors is simply to admit that they don't work.

SPEND LESS AND SAVE MORE

The less you spend, the more money you'll have on hand. Use that money to pay your monthly bills, pay off your credit cards, and create an emergency fund to use in case you lose your job or a source of financial aid. See "Spend less money" on page 103 for ideas.

Author Suze Orman recommends three actions to show that you can reduce spending at any time: (1) Do not spend money for 1 day, (2) do not use your credit card for 1 week, and (3) do not eat out for 1 month. Success with any of these strategies can open up your mind to other possibilities for spending less and saving more.[6]

MAKE SURE THAT YOUR SAVINGS ARE PROTECTED

The Federal Deposit Insurance Corporation (FDIC) backs individual saving accounts. The National Credit Union Administration (NCUA) offers similar protection for credit union members. If your savings are protected by these programs, every penny you deposit is safe. Check your statements to find out, or go online to www.myfdicinsurance.gov.

PAY OFF YOUR CREDIT CARDS

If you have more than one credit card with an outstanding balance, then find out which one has the highest interest rate. Put as much money as you can toward paying off that balance while making the minimum payment on the other cards. Repeat this process until all unpaid balances are erased.

INVEST ONLY AFTER SAVING

The stock market is only for money that you can afford to lose. Before you speculate, first save enough money to live on for at least 6 months in case you're unemployed. Then consider what you'll need over the next 5 years to finish your schooling and handle other major expenses. Save for these expenses before taking any risks with your money.

DO STELLAR WORK AT YOUR CURRENT JOB

The threat of layoffs increases during a recession. However, companies will hesitate to shed their star employees. If you're working right now, then think about ways to become indispensable. Gain skills and experience that will make you more valuable to your employer.

No matter what job you have, be as productive as possible. Look for ways to boost sales, increase quality, or accomplish tasks in less time. Ask yourself every day how you can create extra value by solving a problem, reducing costs, improving service, or attracting new clients or customers.

THINK ABOUT YOUR NEXT JOB

Create a career plan that describes the next job you want, the skills that you'll develop to get it, and the next steps you'll take to gain those skills. Stay informed about the latest developments in your field. Find people who are already working in this area, and contact them for information interviews.

You might want to start an active job hunt now, even if you have a job. Find time to build your network, go to job-related conferences, and stay on top of current job openings in your field. For related ideas, see Chapter 12: Career Management.

RESEARCH UNEMPLOYMENT BENEFITS

Unemployment benefits have limits and may not replace your lost wages. However, they can cushion the blow of losing a job while you put other strategies in place. To learn about the benefits offered in your state, go online to www.servicelocator.org. Click "Unemployment Benefits." Then enter your state.

GET HEALTH INSURANCE

A sudden illness or lengthy hospital stay can drain your savings. Health insurance can pick up all or most of the costs instead. If possible, get health insurance through your school or employer. Another option is private health insurance. This can be cheaper than extending an employer's policy if you lose your job. To find coverage, go online to the Web site of the National Association of Health Underwriters (www.nahu.org) and www.ehealthinsurance.com.

GET HELP THAT YOU CAN TRUST

Avoid debt consolidators that offer schemes to wipe out your debt. What they don't tell you is that their fees are high, and that using them can lower your credit rating. Turn instead to the National Foundation for Credit Counseling (www.nfcc.org). Find a credit counselor that is accredited by this organization. Work with someone who is open about fees and willing to work with all your creditors. Don't pay any fees up front, before you actually get help.

PUT YOUR PLAN IN WRITING

List the specific ways that you will reduce spending and increase income. If you have a family, consider posting this list for everyone to see. The act of putting your plan in writing can help you feel in control of your money. Review your plan regularly to make sure that it's working and that everyone who's affected is on board.

COPE WITH STRESS IN POSITIVE WAYS

When times get tough, some people are tempted to reduce stress with unhealthy behaviors like smoking, drinking, and overeating. Find better ways to cope. Exercise, meditation, and a sound sleep can do wonders. For specific suggestions, see Chapter 11: Health.

Social support is one of the best stress busters. If you're unemployed or worried about money, connect with family members and friends often. Turn healthy habits such as exercising and preparing healthy meals into social affairs.

CHOOSE YOUR MONEY CONVERSATIONS

When the economy tanks, the news is filled with gloomy reports and dire predictions. Remember that reports are constantly competing for your attention. Sometimes they use gloom-and-doom headlines to boost their ratings.

Keep financial news in perspective. Recessions can be painful. And they eventually end. The mortgage credit crisis in recent years was due to speculation, not to a lack of innovation. Our economy will continue to reward people who create valuable new products and services.

To manage stress, limit how much attention you pay to fear-based articles and programs. You can do this even while staying informed about news. Avoid conversations that focus on problems. Instead, talk about ways to take charge of your money and open up job prospects. Even when the economy takes a nosedive, there is always at least one more thing you can do to manage stress and get on a firmer financial footing.

Talk about what gives your life meaning beyond spending money. Eating at home instead of going out can bring your family closer together and save you money weekly, monthly, and annually. Avoiding loud bars and making time for quiet conversation can deepen your friendships. Finding free sources of entertainment can lead you to unexpected sources of pleasure. Letting go of an expensive vacation can allow you to pay down your debts and find time for a fun hobby. Keeping your old car for another year might allow you to invest in extra skills training.

When tough times happen, use them as a chance to embrace the truth about your money life rather than resist it. Live from conscious choice rather than unconscious habit. Learning to live within your means is a skill that can bring financial peace of mind for the rest of your life. ■

 You're One Click Away...
*from finding more ways online to
thrive during tough times.*

Education is worth it—
and you can pay for it

Education is one of the few things you can buy that will last a lifetime. It can't rust, corrode, break down, or wear out. It can't be stolen, repossessed, or destroyed. Once you have a degree, no one can take it away. That makes your education a safer investment than real estate, gold, oil, diamonds, or stocks.

Higher levels of education are associated with the following:[7]

- Greater likelihood of being employed
- Greater likelihood of having health insurance
- Higher income
- Higher job satisfaction
- Higher tax revenues for governments, which fund libraries, schools, parks, and other public goods
- Lower dependence on income support services, such as food stamps
- Higher involvement in volunteer activities

In short, education is a good deal for you and for society. It's worth investing in it periodically to update your skills, reach your goals, and get more of what you want in life.

Millions of dollars are waiting for people who take part in higher education. The funds flow to students who know how to find them. There are many ways to pay for school. The kind of help you get depends on your financial need. In general, *financial need* equals the cost of your schooling minus what you can reasonably be expected to pay. A financial aid package includes three major types of assistance:

- Money you do not pay back (grants and scholarships)
- Money you *do* pay back (loans)
- Work-study programs

Many students who get financial aid receive a package that includes all of the above elements.

To find out more, visit your school's financial aid office on a regular basis. Also go online. Start with Student Aid on the Web at http://studentaid.ed.gov. ∎

You're One Click Away...
from discovering more ways online to pay for school.

✔ CRITICAL THINKING EXERCISE 13

Education by the hour

Determine exactly what it costs you to go to school. Fill in the blanks, using totals for one term. **Note:** Include only the costs that relate directly to going to school. For example, under "Transportation," list only the amount that you pay for gas to drive back and forth to school—not the total amount you spend on gas in a term.

Tuition	$_____
Books	$_____
Fees	$_____
Transportation	$_____
Clothing	$_____
Food	$_____
Housing	$_____
Entertainment	$_____
Other expenses (such as insurance, medical costs, and child care)	$_____
Subtotal	$_____
Salary you could earn per term if you weren't in school	$_____
Total (A)	$_____

Now figure out how many classes you attend in one term. This is the number of your scheduled class periods per week multiplied by the number of weeks in your school term. Put that figure below:

Total (B) $_____

Divide the **Total (B)** into the
Total (A), and put that amount here: $_____

This is what it costs you to go to one class one time.

On a separate sheet of paper, describe your responses to discovering this figure. Also list anything you will do differently as a result of knowing the hourly cost of your education.

You're One Click Away...
from completing this exercise online under Exercises.

Take charge of *your credit*

A good credit rating will serve you for a lifetime. With this asset, you'll be able to borrow money any time you need it. A poor credit rating, however, can keep you from getting a car or a house in the future. You might also have to pay higher insurance rates, and you could even be turned down for a job.

To take charge of your credit, borrow money only when truly necessary. If you do borrow, make all of your payments, and make them on time. This is especially important for managing credit cards and student loans.

USE CREDIT CARDS WITH CAUTION

A credit card is compact and convenient. That piece of plastic seems to promise peace of mind. Low on cash this month? Just whip out your credit card, slide it across the counter, and relax. Your worries are over—that is, until you get the bill.

Credit cards do offer potential benefits, of course. Having one means that you don't have to carry around a checkbook or large amounts of cash, and they're pretty handy in emergencies. Used unwisely, however, credit cards can create a debt that takes decades to repay. Use the following strategies to take control of your credit cards.

Pay off the balance each month. An unpaid credit card balance is a sure sign that you are spending more money than you have. To avoid this outcome, keep track of how much you spend with credit cards each month. Pay off the card balance each month, on time, and avoid finance or late charges.

If you do accumulate a large credit card balance, go to your bank and ask about ways to get a loan with a lower interest rate. Use this loan to pay off your credit cards. Then promise yourself never to accumulate credit card debt again.

Scrutinize credit card offers. Finding a card with a lower interest rate can make a dramatic difference. However, look carefully at credit card offers. Low rates might be temporary. After a few months, they could double or even triple. Also look for annual fees, late fees, and other charges buried in the fine print.

Be especially wary of credit card offers made to students. Remember that the companies who willingly dispense cards on campus are not there to offer an educational service. They are in business to make money by charging you interest.

Avoid cash advances. Due to their high interest rates and fees, credit cards are not a great source of spare cash. Even when you get a cash advance on a card from an ATM, it's still borrowed money. As an alternative, get a debit card tied to a checking account, and use that card when you need cash on the go.

Check statements against your records. File your credit card receipts each month. When you get the bill for each card, check it against your receipts for accuracy. Mistakes in billing are rare, but they can happen. In addition, checking your statement reveals the interest rate and fees that are being applied to your account.

Credit card companies can change the terms of your agreement with little or no warning. Check bills carefully for any changes in late fees, service charges, and credit limits. When you get letters about changes in your credit card policies, read them carefully. Cancel cards from companies that routinely raise fees.

Use just one credit card. To simplify your financial life and take charge of your credit, consider using only one card. Choose one with no annual fee and the lowest interest rate. Consider the bottom line, and be selective. If you do have more than one credit card, pay off the one with the highest interest rate first. Then consider canceling that card.

Get a copy of your credit report. A credit report is a record of your payment history and other credit-related items. You are entitled to get a free copy each year. Go to your bank and ask someone there how to do this. You can also request a copy of your credit report online at https://www.annualcreditreport.com. This site was created by three nationwide consumer credit–reporting companies—Equifax, Experian, and TransUnion. Check your report carefully for errors or accounts that you did not open. Do this now, before you're in financial trouble.

Protect your credit score. Whenever you apply for a loan, the first thing a lender will do is check your credit score. The higher your score, the more money you can borrow at lower interest rates. To protect your credit score:

- Pay all your bills on time.

- Hold on to credit cards that you've had for a while.

- Avoid applying for new credit cards.

- Pay off your credit card balance every month—especially for the cards that you've had the longest.

- If you can't pay off the entire balance, then pay as much as you can above the minimum monthly payment.

- Never charge more than your limit.

- Avoid using a credit card as a source of cash.

- Avoid any actions that could lead a credit card company to reduce your credit limit.

MANAGE STUDENT LOANS

A college degree is one of the best investments you can make. But you don't have to go broke to get that education. You can make that investment with the lowest debt possible.

Choose schools with costs in mind. If you decide to transfer to another school, you can save thousands of dollars the moment you sign your application for admission. In addition to choosing schools on the basis of reputation, consider how much they cost and the financial aid packages that they offer.

> A college degree is one of the best investments you can make. But you don't have to go broke to get that education. You can make that investment with the lowest debt possible.

Avoid debt when possible. The surest way to manage debt is to avoid it altogether. If you do take out loans, borrow only the amount that you cannot get from other sources—scholarships, grants, employment, gifts from relatives, and personal savings. Predict what your income will be when the first loan payments are due and whether you'll make enough money to manage continuing payments.

Also set a target date for graduation, and stick to it. The fewer years you go to school, the lower your debt.

Shop carefully for loans. Go the financial aid office and ask if you can get a Stafford loan. These are fixed-rate, low-interest loans from the federal government. If you qualify for a subsidized Stafford loan, the government pays the interest due while you're in school. Unsubsidized Stafford loans do not offer this benefit, but they are still one of the cheapest student loans you can get. Remember that *anyone* can apply for a Stafford loan.

If your parents are helping to pay for your education, they can apply for a PLUS loan. There is no income limit, and parents can borrow up to the total cost of their children's education. With these loans, your parents—not you—are the borrowers. A new option allows borrowers to defer repayment until after they graduate. For more information on the loans that are available to you, visit www.studentaid.ed.gov.

If at all possible, avoid loans from privately owned companies. These companies often charge higher interest rates and impose terms that are less favorable to students.

While you're shopping around, ask about options for repaying your loans. Lenders might allow you to extend the payments over a longer period, or adjust the amount of your monthly payment based on your income.

Some lenders will forgive part of a student loan if you agree to take a certain type of job for a few years—for example, teaching in a public school in a low-income neighborhood, or working as a nurse in a rural community.

Repay your loans. If you take out student loans, find out exactly when the first payment is due on each of them. Make all your payments, and make them on time.

Also ask your financial aid office about whether you can consolidate your loans. This means that you lump them all together and owe just one payment every month. Loan consolidation makes it easier to stay on top of your payments and protect your credit score. ■

You're One Click Away...
from finding more strategies online for credit mastery.

masterstudentprofile

Richard Anderson

(1955–) CEO of Delta Airlines

Q: What was the most important leadership lesson you learned?

A: I've learned to be patient and not lose my temper. And the reason that's important is everything you do is an example, and people look at everything you do and take a signal from everything you do. And when you lose your temper, it really squelches debate and sends the wrong signal about how you want your organization to run. . . .

Q: Are there other things that you've learned to do more of, or less?

A: You've got to be thankful to the people who get the work done, and you've got to be thankful to your customers. So, I find myself, more and more, writing hand-written notes to people. I must write a half a dozen a day.

Q. Looking back over your career, even to the early years, do you recall an insight that set you on a different trajectory?

A: Yes, and it was actually at my first job while I went to night law school at South Texas College of Law. And I had a good full-time job as the administrative assistant to the D.A. And what you understood was you really needed to be a problem-solver, not a problem-creator. You know, don't bring a Rubik's cube to the table, unless you have an idea on how you're going to try to get an answer. And always try to be a leader that comes up with the creative answers to the hard problems.

Q: And what about advice on your career?

A: If you just focus on getting your job done and being a good colleague and a team player in an organization, and not focused about being overly ambitious and wanting pay raises and promotions and the like, and just doing your job and being a part of a team, the rest of it all takes care of itself.

Q: Did somebody give you that advice, or was that something that you came to understand yourself?

A: My mother and father died from cancer when I was 20, and so I was working full time, and I was pretty fortunate to be around a lot of good people that had that kind of culture and approach to things. It was just by osmosis that I came to those kinds of conclusions. . . .

Q: And is there any change in the kind of qualities you're looking for [in job candidates] compared with 5, 10 years ago?

A: I think this communication point is getting more and more important. People really have to be able to handle the written and spoken word. And when I say written word, I don't mean PowerPoints. I don't think PowerPoints help people think as clearly as they should because you don't have to put a complete thought in place. You can just put a phrase with a bullet in front of it. And it doesn't have a subject, a verb and an object, so you aren't expressing complete thoughts. . . .

Q: What about time management?

A: Only touch paper once. No. 2, always have your homework done. No. 3, return your calls very promptly. No. 4, stick to your schedule. I keep my watch about 10 minutes ahead. It's important to run on time, particularly at an airline. And use your time wisely. And then, once a month, take the rest of the calendar year, or the next six months and re-review how you are using your time and reprioritize what you're doing.

RICHARD ANDERSON ... is responsible.

YOU ... can see time and money as areas for practicing responsibility.

Source: "Richard Anderson, CEO of Delta Airlines" adapted from Adam Bryant, "He Wants Subjects, Verbs, and Objects," *New York Times*, April 26, 2009. Copyright © 2009 The New York Times. All rights reserved. Reproduced by permission and protected by the Copyright Laws of the United States. The printing, copying, redistribution, or retransmission of this Content without express written permission is prohibited.

You're One Click Away...
from learning more about Richard Anderson online at the Master Student Profiles. You can also visit the Master Student Hall of Fame to learn about other master students.

FIVE Cs
FOR YOUR CAREER

CHARACTER • CRITICAL THINKING • CREATIVE THINKING • COLLABORATION • COMMUNICATION

Jobs involve managing time, money, or both. This chapter is rich with strategies that you can take to work. Consider the following examples.

See time and money management as elements of your character. When you're looking for work, be on time for job interviews. When you're employed, be punctual, and work with full energy until you leave. Also find ways to help your employer, customers, or clients to increase their revenue, decrease their expenses, or both. Behaviors such as these show people that you value their time and their money.

Think creatively to "show me the money." See if you can use *From Master Student to Master Employee* to create a financial gain that is many times more than the cost of the book. Scan the entire text and look for suggestions that could help you save money or increase income in significant ways. For example, use suggestions in "Tap the hidden job market" in Chapter 12 to find your next job more quickly—and start earning money sooner. Get a higher-paying job with strategies from the article "Use job interviews to 'hire' an employer" in Chapter 12. Use suggestions from this chapter to reduce your monthly expenses and fatten up your savings account.

Practice creative thinking by expanding this list. Focus on strategies that will work for you.

Think critically to create balance in your life. If you're used to planning one day or one week in advance, then try your hand at planning *two weeks ahead*. This allows enough time for you to spot potential "crunches" in your schedules at work and at home. If you discover that you're pressed for time, you can take action to prevent burnout. Following are the major steps in two-week planning.

List upcoming tasks. Write down all the significant tasks you want to complete in the next 14 days. List each task on a separate 3 × 5 card, or create your list with a computer.

Estimate the time you need for these tasks. Take the tasks you listed in the previous step and estimate the number of hours needed to complete each one. When in doubt, take your first estimate and double it. Add up all your estimates to get a total number of hours.

Sort tasks into categories and choose how much time you want to spend on each category. Common categories are work, school, and family. Figure out the number of hours you want to spend on each category. If you're employed full-time, for instance, you might want to limit yourself to 80 hours at work (40 hours per week for the next two weeks).

Assign task priorities. Rate each task based on your commitment to completing it. Tasks that you're absolutely committed to getting done in the next two weeks get an "A" priority. Tasks that you could get done but are less urgent or important get a "C" priority. *Note:* This is a twist on the ABC priority system recommended in this chapter. See if using just two levels of priority rather than three helps you to get a clearer sense of your commitments.

Schedule "A" priority tasks. Now take your calendar and block out an appropriate number of hours for "A" priority tasks. Schedule specific dates and times.

Add up the number of hours for all your "A" priority tasks. This step could be revealing. For example, you might discover that you need 100 hours to complete work tasks over the next two weeks—even though you only want to work 80 hours. If something like this happens, use the "three D's" to reduce your "A" priority tasks: Downgrade some of them to C-priority; delay some tasks to the following two-week period; delegate tasks to someone else.

Collaborate through effective delegating. The last bullet in the above list is key to success at work. Skilled collaborators are master delegators.

To delegate effectively, get permission from your coworkers to do so. Also think about their individual learning styles. Find common ground between the tasks that *you* want to delegate and the tasks that *they* want to complete.

When delegating tasks to members of a project team, set a clear due date for each task. Also keep a list of tasks that you've delegated, when they're due, and who's handling each task. Check this list at least once each week.

Communicate about time and money in more powerful ways. Comments about time and money often reinforce a view of the world that doesn't leave much room for learning and mastery. Consider statements such as *I've love to pursue that possibility, but there's never enough time* and *I always have more "month" left over at the end of my money.* These suggest that we are victims of forces beyond our control.

In response, you can open up conversations about time and money that create real possibilities for change. For example, talk about what you learned by doing the Time Monitor and Money Monitor exercises in this chapter. Also share any successes you experienced in freeing up more hours per week, increasing income, or reducing expenses. Your speaking can open up new options for other people and make a lasting contribution to their lives.

Now, make a personal commitment to developing the five Cs. Take another look at the Discovery Wheel in Chapter 2—especially the sections labeled Character, Creative and Critical Thinking, Communicating, and Collaborating. Take a snapshot of your current skills in these areas after reading and doing this chapter.

DISCOVERY

My scores on the "Five C" sections of the Discovery Wheel were:	As of today, I would give myself the following scores in these areas:	At the end of this course, I would like my scores in these areas to be:
Character _____	Character _____	Character _____
Creative & Critical Thinking _____	Creative & Critical Thinking _____	Creative & Critical Thinking _____
Communicating _____	Communicating _____	Communicating _____
Collaborating _____	Collaborating _____	Collaborating _____

Next, skim this chapter and look for a time or money management technique that you want to explore in depth. Choose one that would enhance your self-rating in at least one of the five Cs.

I discovered that my preferred technique is . . .

_____

_____

_____

_____

In light of the five Cs, I can use this technique to become more . . .

_____

_____

_____

_____

INTENTION
To use this technique, I intend to . . .

_____

_____

_____

_____

NEXT ACTION
The specific action I will take is . . .

_____

_____

_____

_____

10 QUIZ

1. The "Power Process: Be here now" rules out planning. True or false? Explain your answer.

p300 false, True because it emphasizes on how goals are tools we create to guide our actions in the present & near future.

2. According to the text, everything written about time and money management can be reduced to three main ideas. What are they?

p301
(1) Know exactly what you want
(2) Know how to get what you want
(3) Take action to get what you want

3. Rewrite the statement "I want to study harder" so that it becomes a specific goal.

I want to study harder so that it becomes a specific goal!

4. Define C fever as it applies to the ABC priority method.

311. Uncontrollable urge to drop that A task and begin to cross off C's on to do list.

5. You can rank your to-do list items with the ABC system. Explain an alternative to this system.

310 you rank each item on your list according to 3 levels of importance (A, B, C).

6. According to the text, overcoming procrastination is a complex process that can take months or even years. True or false? Explain your answer.

315 False, because people make it complicated when it is simple.

7. Describe a strategy for increasing your income.

328 work while you're in school, spend less keep more.

8. List three ways to decrease your expenses.

329
Do comparison shopping
save money on eating and drinking
Be aware of quality

9. According to the text, the biggest factor in your long-term financial well-being is

330
(a) the state of the overall economy.
(b) the interest rates on your credit cards.
(c) the federal deficit.
(d) your daily behavior.
(e) none of the above.

10. What are three ways that you can avoid getting into financial trouble when you use credit cards?

333 pay off the balances each month   use one credit card.
get a copy of credit report

Notes

Use this **Master Student Map**
to ask yourself

WHY THIS CHAPTER MATTERS . . .

- Note taking helps you remember course content and influences how well you do on tests.

WHAT IS INCLUDED . . .

HOW I CAN USE THIS CHAPTER . . .

- Experiment with several formats for note taking.
- Create a note-taking format that works well for me.
- Take effective notes in special situations—such as while reading and when instructors talk quickly.

WHAT IF . . .

- I could take notes that remain informative and useful for weeks, months, or even years to come?

© Ruslan Ivantsov/Shutterstock.com

JOURNAL ENTRY 11
Intention Statement

Get what you want from this chapter

Recall a recent incident in which you had difficulty taking notes. Perhaps you were listening to an instructor who talked fast, or you got confused and stopped taking notes altogether. Then preview this chapter to find at least three strategies that you can use right away to help you take better notes.

Strategy	Page number
_____	_____
_____	_____
_____	_____
_____	_____
_____	_____
_____	_____
_____	_____
_____	_____
_____	_____
_____	_____
_____	_____
_____	_____
_____	_____
_____	_____
_____	_____
_____	_____
_____	_____
_____	_____

I create it all

This article describes a powerful tool for times of trouble. In a crisis, "I create it all" can lead the way to solutions. The main point of this Power Process is to treat experiences, events, and circumstances in your life *as if* you created them.

"I create it all" is one of the most unusual and bizarre suggestions in this book. It certainly is not a belief. Use it when it works. Don't when it doesn't.

Keeping that in mind, consider how powerful this Power Process can be. It is really about the difference between two distinct positions in life: being a victim or being responsible.

A victim of circumstances is controlled by outside forces. We've all felt like victims at one time or another. Sometimes we felt helpless.

In contrast, we can take responsibility. Responsibility is "response-ability"—the ability to choose a *response* to any event. You can choose your *response* to any event, even when the event itself is beyond your control.

Many students approach grades from the position of being victims. When the student who sees the world this way gets an "F," she reacts something like this:

"Another 'F'! That teacher couldn't teach her way out of a wet paper bag. She can't teach English for anything. There's no way to take notes in that class. And that textbook—what a bore!"

The problem with this viewpoint is that in looking for excuses, the student is robbing herself of the power to get any grade other than an "F." She's giving all of her power to a bad teacher and a boring textbook.

There is another way, called *taking responsibility*. You can recognize that you choose your grades by choosing your actions. Then you are the source, rather than the result, of the grades you get. The student who got an "F" could react like this:

"Another 'F'! Oh, shoot! Well, hmmm . . . What did I do to create it?"

Now, that's power. By asking, "How did I contribute to this outcome?" you are no longer the victim. This student might continue by saying, "Well, let's see. I didn't review my notes after class. That might have done it." Or "I went out with my friends the night before the test. Well, that probably helped me fulfill some of the requirements for getting an 'F.'"

The point is this: When the "F" is the result of your friends, the book, or the teacher, you probably can't do anything about it. However, if you *chose* the "F," you can choose a different grade next time. You are in charge.

You're One Click Away...
from accessing Power Process Media online and finding out more about how to "create it all."

The **Note-Taking** Process FLOWS

One way to understand note taking is to realize that taking notes is just one part of the process. Effective note taking consists of three parts: observing, recording, and reviewing. First, you **observe** an "event." This can be a statement by an instructor, a lab experiment, a slide show of an artist's works, or a chapter of required reading.

Then you **record** your observations of that event. That is, you "take notes."

Finally, you **review** what you have recorded. You memorize, reflect, apply, and rehearse what you're learning. This step lifts ideas off the page and turns them into a working part of your mind.

Each part of the note-taking process is essential, and each depends on the other. Your observations determine what you record. What you record determines what you review. And the quality of your review can determine how effective your next observations will be. If you review your notes on the Sino-Japanese War of 1894, for example, the next day's lecture on the Boxer Rebellion of 1900 will make more sense.

Legible and speedy handwriting is also useful in taking notes. Knowledge of outlining is handy too. A nifty pen, a new notebook, and a laptop computer are all great note-taking devices.

And they're all worthless—unless you participate as an energetic observer *in* class and regularly review your notes *after* class. If you take those two steps, you can turn even the most disorganized chicken scratches into a powerful tool.

This is a well-researched aspect of student success in higher education. Study after study points to the benefits of taking notes. The value is added in two ways. First, you create a set of materials that refreshes your memory and helps you prepare for tests. Second, taking notes prompts you to listen effectively during class. You translate new ideas into your own words and images. You impose a personal and meaningful structure on what you see, read, and hear. You move from passive observer to active participant.[1] It's not that you take notes so that you can learn from them later. Instead, you learn *while* taking notes.

Computer technology takes traditional note taking to a whole new level. You can capture key notes with word-processing, outlining, database, and publishing software. Your notes become living documents that you can search, bookmark, tag, and archive like other digital files.

Sometimes note taking looks like a passive affair, especially in large lecture classes. One person at the front of the room does most of the talking. Everyone else is seated and silent, taking notes. The lecturer seems to be doing all of the work.

11

Don't be deceived.

Look more closely. You'll see some students taking notes in a way that radiates energy. They're awake and alert, poised on the edge of their seats. They're writing—a physical activity that expresses mental engagement. These students listen for levels of ideas and information, make choices about what to record, and compile materials to review.

In higher education, you might spend hundreds of hours taking notes. Making them more effective is a direct investment in your success.

Think of your notes as a textbook that *you* create—one that's more current and more in tune with your learning preferences than any textbook you could buy. ■

OBSERVE

The note-taking process flows

OBSERVE

Sherlock Holmes, a fictional master detective and student of the obvious, could track down a villain by observing the fold of his scarf and the mud on his shoes. In real life, a doctor can save a life by observing a mole—one a patient has always had—that undergoes a rapid change.

An accountant can save a client thousands of dollars by observing the details of a spreadsheet. A student can save hours of study time by observing that she gets twice as much done at a particular time of day.

Keen observers see facts and relationships. They know ways to focus their attention on the details and then tap their creative energy to discover patterns. To sharpen your classroom observation skills, experiment with the following techniques, and continue to use those that you find most valuable. Many of these strategies can be adapted to the notes you take while reading.

SET THE STAGE

Complete outside assignments. Nothing is more discouraging (or boring) than sitting through a lecture about the relationship of Le Chatelier's principle to the principle of kinetics if you've never heard of Henri Louis Le Chatelier or kinetics. The more familiar you are with a subject, the more easily you can absorb important information during class lectures. Instructors usually assume that students complete assignments, and they construct their lectures accordingly.

Bring the right materials. A good pen does not make you a good observer, but the lack of a pen or notebook can be distracting enough to take the fine edge off your concentration. Make sure you have a pen, pencil, notebook, or any other materials you need. Bring your textbook to class, especially if the lectures relate closely to the text.

If you are consistently unprepared for a class, that might be a message about your intentions concerning the course. Find out if it is. The next time you're in a frantic scramble to borrow pen and paper 37 seconds before the class begins, notice the cost. Use the borrowed pen and paper to write a Discovery Statement about your lack of preparation. Consider whether you intend to be successful in the course.

Sit front and center. Students who get as close as possible to the front and center of the classroom often do better on tests for several reasons. The closer you sit to the lecturer, the harder it is to fall asleep. The closer you sit to the front, the fewer interesting or distracting classmates are situated between you and the instructor. Material on the board is easier to read from up front. Also, the instructor can see you more easily when you have a question.

Instructors are usually not trained to perform. Some can project their energy to a large audience, but some cannot. A professor who sounds boring from the back of the room might sound more interesting up close.

Sitting up front enables you to become a constructive force in the classroom. By returning the positive energy that an engaged teacher gives out, you can reinforce the teacher's enthusiasm and enhance your experience of the class.

In addition, sound waves from the human voice begin to degrade at a distance of 8 to 12 feet. If you sit more than 15 feet from the speaker, your ability to hear and take effective notes might be compromised. Get close to the source of the sound. Get close to the energy.

Sitting close to the front is a way to commit yourself to getting what you want out of school. One reason students gravitate to the back of the classroom is that they think the instructor is less likely to call on them. Sitting in back can signal a lack of commitment. When you sit up front, you are declaring your willingness to take a risk and participate.

Conduct a short preclass review. Arrive early, and then put your brain in gear by reviewing your notes from the previous class. Scan your reading assignment. Look at the sections you have underlined or highlighted. Review assigned problems and exercises. Note questions you intend to ask.

Clarify your intentions. Take a 3 × 5 card to class with you. On that card, write a short Intention Statement about what you plan to get from the class. Describe your intended level of participation or the quality of attention you will bring to the subject. Be specific. If you found your previous class notes to be inadequate, write down what you intend to do to make your notes from this class session more useful.

"BE HERE NOW" IN CLASS

Accept your wandering mind. The techniques in Chapter 3's "Process: Be here now" can be especially useful when your head soars into the clouds. Don't fight daydreaming. When you notice your mind wandering during class, look at it as an opportunity to refocus your attention. If thermodynamics is losing out to beach parties, let go of the beach.

Notice your writing. When you discover yourself slipping into a fantasyland, feel the weight of your pen in your hand. Notice how your notes look. Paying attention to the act of writing can bring you back to the here and now.

You also can use writing in a more direct way to clear your mind of distracting thoughts. Pause for a few seconds, and write those thoughts down. If you're distracted by thoughts of errands you need to run after class, list them on a 3 × 5 card and stick it in your pocket. Or simply put a symbol, such as an arrow or asterisk, in your notes to mark the places where your mind started to wander. Once your distractions are out of your mind and safely stored on paper, you can gently return your attention to taking notes.

Be with the instructor. In your mind, put yourself right up front with the instructor. Imagine that you and the instructor are the only ones in the room and that the lecture is a personal conversation between the two of you. Pay attention to the instructor's body language and facial expressions. Look the instructor in the eye.

Remember that the power of this suggestion is immediately reduced by digital distractions—Web surfing, e-mail checking, or text messaging. Taking notes is a way to stay focused. The physical act of taking notes signals your mind to stay in the same room as the instructor.

Notice your environment. When you become aware of yourself daydreaming, bring yourself back to class by paying attention to the temperature in the room, the feel of your chair, or the quality of light coming through the window. Run your hand along the surface of your desk. Listen to the chalk on the blackboard or the sound of the teacher's voice. Be in that environment. Once your attention is back in the room, you can focus on what's happening in class.

Postpone debate. When you hear something you disagree with, note your disagreement and let it go. Don't allow your internal dialogue to drown out subsequent material. If your disagreement is persistent and strong, make note of it and then move on. Internal debate can prevent you from absorbing new

What to do when you miss a class

For most courses, you'll benefit by attending every class session. This allows you to observe and actively participate. If you miss a class, then catch up as quickly as possible. Find additional ways to observe class content.

Clarify policies on missed classes.
On the first day of classes, find out about your instructors' policies on absences. See whether you will be allowed to make up assignments, quizzes, and tests. Also inquire about doing extra-credit assignments.

Contact a classmate.
Early in the semester, identify a student in each class who seems responsible and dependable. Exchange e-mail addresses and phone numbers. If you know you won't be in class, contact this student ahead of time. When you notice that your classmate is absent, pick up extra copies of handouts, make assignments lists, and offer copies of your notes.

Contact your instructor.
If you miss a class, e-mail or call your instructor, or put a note in his mailbox. Ask whether he has another section of the same course that you can attend so you won't miss the lecture information. Also ask about getting handouts you might need before the next class meeting.

Consider technology.
If there is a Web site for your class, check it for assignments and the availability of handouts you missed. Free online services such as NoteMesh allow students to share notes with one another. These services use wiki software, which allows you to create and edit Web pages using any browser. Before using such tools, however, check with instructors for their policies on note sharing.

11

information. It's okay to absorb information you don't agree with. Just absorb it with the mental tag "My instructor says . . . , and I don't agree with it."

Let go of judgments about lecture styles. Human beings are judgment machines. We evaluate everything, especially other people. If another person's eyebrows are too close together (or too far apart), if she walks a certain way or speaks with an unusual accent, we instantly make up a story about her. We do this so quickly that the process is usually not a conscious one.

Don't let your attitude about an instructor's lecture style, habits, or appearance get in the way of your education. You can decrease the power of your judgments if you pay attention to them and let them go.

You can even let go of judgments about rambling, unorganized lectures. Turn them to your advantage. Take the initiative and organize the material yourself. While taking notes, separate the key points from the examples and supporting evidence. Note the places where you got confused, and make a list of questions to ask.

Participate in class activities. Ask questions. Volunteer for demonstrations. Join in class discussions. Be willing to take a risk or look foolish, if that's what it takes for you to learn. Chances are, the question you think is dumb is also on the minds of several of your classmates.

Relate the class to your goals. If you have trouble staying awake in a particular class, write at the top of your notes how that class relates to a specific goal. Identify the reward or payoff for reaching that goal.

Think critically about what you hear. This suggestion might seem contrary to the previously mentioned technique "postpone debate." It's not. You might choose not to think critically about the instructor's ideas during the lecture. That's fine. Do it later, as you review and edit your notes. This is the time to list questions or write down your agreements and disagreements.

WATCH FOR CLUES

Be alert to repetition. When an instructor repeats a phrase or an idea, make a note of it. Repetition is a signal that the instructor thinks the information is important.

Listen for introductory, concluding, and transition words and phrases. Introductory, concluding, and transition words and phrases include phrases such as *the following three factors, in conclusion, the most important consideration, in addition to,* and *on the other hand.* These phrases and others signal relationships, definitions, new subjects, conclusions, cause and effect, and examples. They reveal the structure of the lecture. You can use these phrases to organize your notes.

Watch the board or PowerPoint presentation. If an instructor takes the time to write something down on the board or show a PowerPoint presentation, consider the material to be important.

Copy all diagrams and drawings, equations, names, places, dates, statistics, and definitions.

Watch the instructor's eyes. If an instructor glances at her notes and then makes a point, it is probably a signal that the information is especially important. Anything she reads from her notes is a potential test question.

Highlight the obvious clues. Instructors often hint strongly or tell students point-blank that certain information is likely to appear on an exam. Make stars or other special marks in your notes next to this information. Instructors are not trying to hide what's important.

Notice the instructor's interest level. If the instructor is excited about a topic, it is more likely to appear on an exam. Pay attention when she seems more animated than usual. ■

You're One Click Away...
from finding more strategies for observing online.

JOURNAL ENTRY 12
Discovery/Intention Statement

Create more value from lectures

Think back on the last few lectures you have attended. How do you currently observe (listen to) lectures? What specific behaviors do you have as you sit and listen? Do you listen more closely in some classes than others? Briefly describe your responses in the space below.

I discovered that I . . .

_____

_____

_____

Now write an Intention Statement about any changes you want to make in the way you respond to lectures.

I intend to . . .

_____

_____

_____

_____

RECORD

The note-taking process flows

RECORD

The format and structure of your notes are more important than how fast you write or how elegant your handwriting is. The following techniques can improve the effectiveness of your notes.

GENERAL TECHNIQUES FOR NOTE TAKING

Use key words. An easy way to sort the extraneous material from the important points is to take notes using key words. Key words or phrases contain the essence of communication. They include these:

- Concepts, technical terms, names, and numbers

- Linking words, including words that describe action, relationship, and degree (for example, *most, least,* and *faster*)

Key words evoke images and associations with other words and ideas. They trigger your memory. That characteristic makes them powerful review tools. One key word can initiate the recall of a whole cluster of ideas. A few key words can form a chain from which you can reconstruct an entire lecture.

To see how key words work, take yourself to an imaginary classroom. You are now in the middle of an anatomy lecture. Picture what the room looks like, what it feels like, how it smells. You hear the instructor say:

Okay, what happens when we look directly over our heads and see a piano falling out of the sky? How do we take that signal and translate it into the action of getting out of the way? The first thing that happens is that a stimulus is generated in the neurons—receptor neurons—of the eye. Light reflected from the piano reaches our eyes. In other words, we see the piano.

The receptor neurons in the eye transmit that sensory signal—the sight of the piano—to the body's nervous system. That's all they can do—pass on information. So we've got a sensory signal coming into the nervous system. But the neurons that initiate movement in our legs are effector neurons. The information from the sensory neurons must be transmitted to effector neurons, or we will get squashed by the piano. There must be some kind of interconnection between receptor and effector neurons. What happens between the two? What is the connection?

Key words you might note in this example include *stimulus, generated, receptor neurons, transmit, sensory signals, nervous*

Woman in white: © John Molloy/Getty Images/Frame: Shutterstock/ Digital Camera: © iStockphoto.com/tezzstock

system, effector neurons, and *connection.* You can reduce the instructor's 163 words to these 12 key words. With a few transitional words, your notes might look like this:

> Stimulus (piano) generated in receptor neurons (eye)
>
> Sensory signals transmitted by nervous system to effector neurons (legs)
>
> What connects receptor to effector?

Note the last key word of the lecture: *connection.* This word is part of the instructor's question and leads to the next point in the lecture. Be on the lookout for questions like this. They can help you organize your notes and are often clues for test questions.

Use pictures and diagrams. Make relationships visual. Copy all diagrams from the board, and invent your own. A drawing of a piano falling on someone who is looking up, for example, might be used to demonstrate the relationship of receptor neurons to effector neurons. Label the eyes "receptor" and the feet "effector." This picture implies that the sight of the piano must be translated into a motor response. By connecting the explanation of the process with the unusual picture of the piano falling, you can link the elements of the process together.

Write notes in paragraphs. When it is difficult to follow the organization of a lecture or put information into outline form, create a series of informal paragraphs. These paragraphs should contain few complete sentences. Reserve complete sentences for precise definitions, direct quotations, and important points that the instructor emphasizes by repetition or other signals—such as the phrase "This is an important point."

Copy material from the board or a PowerPoint presentation. Record key formulas, diagrams, and problems that the teacher presents on the board or in a PowerPoint presentation. Copy dates, numbers, names, places, and other facts. You can even use your own signal or code to flag important material.

Use a three-ring binder. Three-ring binders have several advantages over other kinds of notebooks. First, pages can be removed and spread out when you review. This way, you can get the whole picture of a lecture. Second, the three-ring-binder format allows you to insert handouts right into your notes. Third, you can insert your own out-of-class notes in the correct order.

Use only one side of a piece of paper. When you use one side of a page, you can review and organize all your notes by spreading them out side by side. Most students find the benefit well worth the cost of the paper. Perhaps you're concerned about the environmental impact of consuming more paper. If so, you can use the blank side of old notes and use recycled paper.

Use 3 · 5 cards. As an alternative to using notebook paper, use 3 × 5 cards to take lecture notes. Copy each new concept onto a separate 3 × 5 card.

Keep your own thoughts separate. For the most part, avoid making editorial comments in your lecture notes. The danger is that when you return to your notes, you might mistake your own ideas for those of the instructor. If you want to make a comment, clearly label it as your own.

Use an "I'm lost" signal. No matter how attentive and alert you are, you might get lost and confused in a lecture. If it is inappropriate to ask a question, record in your notes that you were lost. Invent your own signal—for example, a circled question mark. When you write down your code for "I'm lost," leave space for the explanation or clarification that you will get later. The space will also be a signal that you missed something. Later, you can speak to your instructor or ask to see a fellow student's notes.

Label, number, and date all notes. Develop the habit of labeling and dating your notes at the beginning of each class. Number the page too. Sometimes the sequence of material in a lecture is important. Write your name and phone number in each notebook in case you lose it.

Use standard abbreviations. Be consistent with your abbreviations. If you make up your own abbreviations or symbols, write a key explaining them in your notes. Avoid vague abbreviations. When you use an abbreviation such as *comm.* for *committee,* you run the risk of not being able to remember whether you meant *committee, commission, common,* or *commit.* One way to abbreviate is to leave out vowels. For example, *talk* becomes *tlk, said* becomes *sd, American* becomes *Amrcn.*

Leave blank space. Notes tightly crammed into every corner of the page are hard to read and difficult to use for review. Give your eyes a break by leaving plenty of space.

Later, when you review, you can use the blank spaces in your notes to clarify points, write questions, or add other material.

Take notes in different colors. You can use colors as highly visible organizers. For example, you can signal important points with red. Or use one color of ink for notes about the text and another color for lecture notes.

Use graphic signals. The following ideas can be used with any note-taking format:

- Use brackets, parentheses, circles, and squares to group information that belongs together.

- Use stars, arrows, and underlining to indicate important points. Flag the most important points with double stars, double arrows, or double underlines.

- Use arrows and connecting lines to link related groups.

- Use equal signs and greater-than and less-than signs to indicate compared quantities.

To avoid creating confusion with graphic symbols, use them carefully and consistently. Write a "dictionary" of your symbols in the front of your notebooks; an example is shown here.

I I, ( ), ⬭, ▢ = info
that belongs together

*, ↘, = = important

**, ↘↘, ≡, !!! = extra important

> = greater than   < = less than
= = equal to

⟶ = leads to, becomes
Ex: school ⟶ job ⟶ money

? = huh?, lost

?? = big trouble, clear up
immediately

Use recorders effectively. Some students record lectures with audio or digital recorders, but there are persuasive arguments against doing so. When you record a lecture, there is a strong temptation to daydream. After all, you can always listen to the lecture again later on. Unfortunately, if you let the recorder do all of the work, you are skipping a valuable part of the learning process.

There are other potential problems as well. Listening to recorded lectures can take a lot of time—more time than reviewing written notes. Recorders can't answer the questions you didn't ask in class. Also, recording devices malfunction. In fact, the unscientific Hypothesis of Recording Glitches states that the tendency of recorders to malfunction is directly proportional to the importance of the material. With those warnings in mind, you can use a recorder effectively if you choose. For example, you can use recordings as backups to written notes. (Check with your instructor first. Some prefer not to be recorded.) Turn the recorder on; then take notes as if it weren't there. Recordings can be especially useful if an instructor speaks fast.

THE CORNELL METHOD

A note-taking system that has worked for students around the world is the *Cornell method*.[2] Originally developed by Walter Pauk at Cornell University during the 1950s, this approach continues to be taught across the United States and in other countries as well.

The cornerstone of this method is what Pauk calls the *cue column*—a wide margin on the left-hand side of the paper. The cue column is the key to the Cornell method's many benefits. Here's how to use it.

Format your paper. On each sheet of your notepaper, draw a vertical line, top to bottom, about 2 inches from the left edge of

the paper. This line creates the cue column—the space to the left of the line. You can also find Web sites that allow you to print out pages in this format. Just do an Internet search using the key words *cornell method pdf*.

Take notes, leaving the cue column blank. As you read an assignment or listen to a lecture, take notes on the right-hand side of the paper. Fill up this column with sentences, paragraphs, outlines, charts, or drawings. Do not write in the cue column. You'll use this space later, as you do the next steps.

Condense your notes in the cue column. Think of the notes you took on the right-hand side of the paper as a set of answers. In the cue column, list potential test questions that correspond to your notes. Write one question for each major term or point.

As an alternative to questions, you can list key words from your notes. Yet another option is to pretend that your notes are a series of articles on different topics. In the cue column, write a newspaper-style headline for each "article." In any case, be brief. If you cram the cue column full of words, you defeat its purpose—to reduce the number and length of your notes.

Write a summary. Pauk recommends that you reduce your notes even more by writing a brief summary at the bottom of each page. This step offers you another way to engage actively with the material.

11

Cue column	Notes
What are the 3 phases of Muscle Reading?	Phase 1: Before you read Phase 2: While you read Phase 3: After you read
What are the steps in phase 1?	1. Preview 2. Outline 3. Question
What are the steps in phase 2?	4. Focus 5. Flag answers
What are the steps in phase 3?	6. Recite 7. Review 8. Review again
What is an acronym for Muscle Reading?	Pry = preview Out = outline Questions = question Focus Flag Answers Recite Review Review again
Summary	
Muscle Reading includes 3 phases: before, during, and after reading. Each phase includes specific steps. Use the acronym to recall all the steps.	

Use the cue column to recite. Cover the right-hand side of your notes with a blank sheet of paper. Leave only the cue column showing. Then look at each item you wrote in the cue column and talk about it. If you wrote questions, answer each question. If you wrote key words, define each word and talk about why it's important. If you wrote headlines in the cue column, explain what each one means and offer supporting details. After reciting, uncover your notes and look for any important points you missed.

MIND MAPPING

Mind mapping, a system developed by Tony Buzan,[3] can be used in conjunction with the Cornell method to take notes. In some circumstances, you might want to use mind maps exclusively.

To understand mind maps, first review the features of traditional note taking. Outlines (explained in the next section) divide major topics into minor topics, which in turn are subdivided further. They organize information in a sequential, linear way.

The traditional outline reflects only a limited range of brain function—a point that is often made in discussions about "left-brain" and "right-brain" activities. People often use the term *right brain* when referring to creative, pattern-making, visual, intuitive brain activity. They use the term *left brain* when talking about orderly, logical, step-by-step characteristics of thought. Writing teacher Gabrielle Rico uses another metaphor. She refers to the left-brain mode as our "sign mind" (concerned with words) and the right-brain mode as our "design mind" (concerned with visuals).[4] A mind map uses both kinds of brain functions. Mind maps can contain lists and sequences and show relationships. They can also provide a picture of a subject. They work on both verbal and nonverbal levels.

One benefit of mind maps is that they quickly, vividly, and accurately show the relationships between ideas. Also, mind mapping helps you think from general to specific. By choosing a main topic, you focus first on the big picture, then zero in on subordinate details. And by using only key words, you can condense a large subject into a small area on a mind map. You can review more quickly by looking at the key words on a mind map than by reading notes word for word.

Give yourself plenty of room. To create a mind map, use blank paper that measures at least 11 by 17 inches. If that's not available, turn regular notebook paper on its side so that you can take notes in a horizontal (instead of vertical) format. If you use a computer in class to take notes, consider software that allows you to create digital mind maps that can include graphics, photos, and URL links.

Determine the main concept of the lecture, article, or chapter. As you listen to a lecture or read, figure out the main concept. Write it in the center of the paper and circle it, underline it, or highlight it with color. You can also write the concept in large letters. Record concepts related to the main concept on lines that radiate outward from the center. An alternative is to circle or box in these concepts.

Use key words only. Whenever possible, reduce each concept to a single word per line or circle or box in your mind map. Although this reduction might seem awkward at first, it prompts you to summarize and to condense ideas to their essence. That means fewer words for you to write now and fewer to review when it's time to prepare for tests. (Using shorthand symbols and abbreviations can help.) Key words are usually nouns and verbs that communicate the bulk of the speaker's ideas. Choose words that are rich in associations and that can help you recreate the lecture.

Create links. A single mind map doesn't have to include all of the ideas in a lecture, book, or article. Instead, you can link mind maps. For example, draw a mind map that sums up the five key points in a chapter, and then make a separate, more detailed mind map for each of those key points. Within each mind map, include references to the other mind maps. This technique helps explain and reinforce the relationships among many ideas. Some students pin several mind maps next to one another on a bulletin board or tape them to a wall. This allows for a dramatic—and effective—look at the big picture.

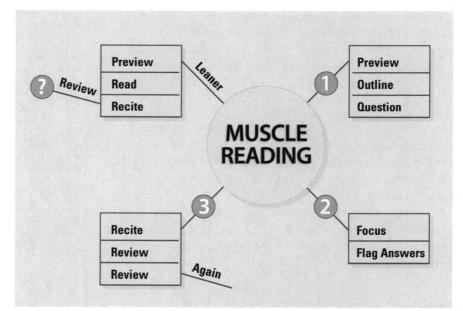

OUTLINING

A traditional outline shows the relationships among major points and supporting ideas. One benefit of taking notes in the outline format is that doing so can totally occupy your attention. You are recording ideas and also organizing them. This process can be an advantage if the material has been presented in a disorganized way. By playing with variations, you can discover the power of outlining to reveal relationships among ideas. Technically, each word, phrase, or sentence that appears in an outline is called a *heading*. Headings are arranged in different levels:

- In the first, or top, level of headings, note the major topics presented in a lecture or reading assignment.

- In the second level of headings, record the key points that relate to each topic in the first-level headings.

- In the third level of headings, record specific facts and details that support or explain each of your second-level headings. Each additional level of subordinate heading supports the ideas in the previous level of heading.

Roman numerals offer one way to illustrate the difference between levels of headings. See the following examples.

First-level heading

Second-level heading   I. Muscle Reading includes 3 phases.
    A. Phase 1: Before you read
        1. Preview   **Third-level heading**
        2. Outline
        3. Question
    B. Phase 2: While you read
        4. Focus
        5. Flag answers
    C. Phase 3: After you read
        6. Recite
        7. Review
        8. Review again

COMBINING FORMATS

Feel free to use different note-taking systems for different subjects and to combine formats. Do what works for you.

Distinguish levels with indentations only:

Muscle Reading includes 3 phases
    Phase 1: Before you read
        Preview

Distinguish levels with bullets and dashes:

MUSCLE READING INCLUDES 3 PHASES
  • Phase 1: Before you read
    – Preview

Distinguish headings by size:

MUSCLE READING INCLUDES 3 PHASES
Phase 1: Before you read
Preview

For example, combine mind maps along with the Cornell method. You can modify the Cornell format by dividing your notepaper in half. Reserve one half for mind maps and the other for linear information such as lists, graphs, and outlines, as well as equations, long explanations, and word-for-word definitions. You can incorporate a mind map into your paragraph-style notes whenever you feel one is appropriate. Minds maps are also useful for summarizing notes taken in the Cornell format.

John Sperry, a teacher at Utah Valley State College, developed a note-taking system that can include all of the formats discussed in this article:

- Fill up a three-ring binder with fresh paper. Open your notebook so that you see two blank pages—one on the left and one on the right. Plan to take notes across this entire two-page spread.

- During class or while reading, write your notes only on the left-hand page. Place a large dash next to each main topic or point. If your instructor skips a step or switches topics unexpectedly, just keep writing.

- Later, use the right-hand page to review and elaborate on the notes that you took earlier. This page is for anything you want. For example, add visuals such as mind maps. Write review questions, headlines, possible test questions, summaries, outlines, mnemonics, or analogies that link new concepts to your current knowledge.

- To keep ideas in sequence, place appropriate numbers on top of the dashes in your notes on the left-hand page. Even if concepts are presented out of order during class, they'll still be numbered correctly in your notes. ■

You're One Click Away...
from seeing more examples of notes in various formats online.

REVIEW

The note-taking process flows

© ballyscanlon/Getty Images

Think of reviewing as an integral part of note taking rather than an added task. To make new information useful, encode it in a way that connects it to your long-term memory. The key is reviewing.

Review within 24 hours. In Chapter 5, when you read the suggestion to review what you've read within 24 hours, you were asked to sound the trumpet. If you have one, get it out and sound it again. This note-taking technique might be the most powerful one you can use. It might save you hours of review time later in the term.

Many students are surprised that they can remember the content of a lecture in the minutes and hours after class. They are even more surprised by how well they can read the sloppiest of notes at that time. Unfortunately, short-term memory deteriorates quickly. The good news is that if you review your notes soon enough, you can move that information from short-term to long-term memory. And you can do it in just a few minutes—often 10 minutes or less.

The sooner you review your notes, the better, especially if the content is difficult. In fact, you can start reviewing during class. When your instructor pauses to set up the overhead display or erase the board, scan your notes. Dot the *i*'s, cross the *t*'s, and write out unclear abbreviations. Another way to use this technique is to get to your next class as quickly as you can. Then use the 4 or 5 minutes before the lecture begins to review the notes you just took in the previous class. If you do not get to your notes immediately after class, you can still benefit by reviewing them later in the day. A review right before you go to sleep can also be valuable.

Think of the day's unreviewed notes as leaky faucets, constantly dripping and losing precious information until you shut them off with a quick review. Remember, it's possible to forget most of the material within 24 hours—unless you review.

Edit your notes. During your first review, fix words that are illegible. Write out abbreviated words that might be unclear to you later. Make sure you can read everything. If you can't read something or don't understand something you *can* read, mark it, and make a note to ask your instructor or another student about it. Check to see that your notes are labeled with the date and class and that the pages are numbered.

Fill in key words in the left-hand column. This task is important if you are to get the full benefit of using the Cornell method. Using the key word principles described earlier in this chapter, go through your notes and write key words or phrases in the left-hand column. These key words will speed up the review process later. As you read your notes, focus on extracting important concepts.

Use your key words as cues to recite. Cover your notes with a blank sheet of paper so that you can see only the key words in the left-hand margin. Take each key word in order, and recite as much as you can about the point. Then uncover your notes and look for any important points you missed.

Conduct short weekly review periods. Once a week, review all of your notes again. These review sessions don't need to take a lot of time. Even a 20-minute weekly review period is valuable. Some students find that a weekend review—say, on Sunday afternoon— helps them stay in continuous touch with the material. Scheduling regular review sessions on your calendar helps develop the habit.

As you review, step back to see the larger picture. In addition to reciting or repeating the material to yourself, ask questions about it: Does this relate to my goals? How does this compare to information I already know, in this field or another? Will I be tested on this material? What will I do with this material? How can I associate it with something that deeply interests me?

Consider typing your notes. Some students type up their handwritten notes on the computer. The argument for doing so is threefold. First, typed notes are easier to read. Second, they take up less space. Third, the process of typing them forces you to review the material.

Another alternative is to bypass handwriting altogether and take notes in class on a laptop. This solution has a potential drawback, though: Computer errors can wipe out your notes files. If you like using this method of taking notes, save your files frequently, and back up your work onto a jump drive, external hard drive, or online backup service.

Create summaries. Mind mapping is an excellent way to summarize large sections of your course notes or reading assignments. Create one map that shows all the main topics you want to remember. Then create another map about each main topic. After drawing your maps, look at your original notes, and fill in anything you missed. This system is fun and quick.✗

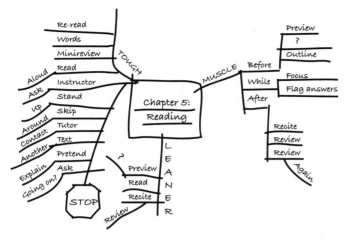

While you're reviewing, evaluate your notes. Review sessions are excellent times to look beyond the *content* of your notes and reflect on your note-taking *process*. Remember these common goals of taking notes in the first place:

* *Reduce* course content to its essentials.
* *Organize* the content.
* Demonstrate that you *understand* the content.

If your notes consistently fall short on one of these points, then review this chapter for a strategy that can help.

Hermann Ebbinghaus, a psychologist, discovered that most forgetting occurs during the first 9 hours after we learn new information—especially during the first hour. Use the strategies in this chapter to prevent forgetting and reverse this "Ebbinghaus curve." ■

Another option is to create a "cheat sheet." There's only one guideline: Fit all your review notes on a single sheet of paper. Use any note-taking format that you want—mind map, outline, Cornell method, or a combination of all of them. The beauty of this technique is that it forces you to pick out main ideas and key details. There's not enough room for anything else!

If you're feeling adventurous, create your cheat sheet on a single index card. Start with the larger sizes (5 × 7 or 4 × 6) and then work down to a 3 × 5 card.

Some instructors might let you use a summary sheet during an exam. But even if you can't use it, you'll benefit from creating one while you study for the test. Summarizing is a powerful way to review.

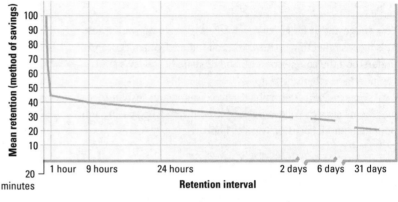

 You're One Click Away...
from finding more strategies for reviewing online.

JOURNAL ENTRY 13 *Discovery Statement*

Reflect on your review habits

Respond to the following statements by checking "Always," "Often," "Sometimes," "Seldom," or "Never" after each.

1. I review my notes immediately after class.

   _____ Always _____ Often _____ Sometimes _____ Seldom _____ Never

2. I conduct weekly reviews of my notes.

   _____ Always _____ Often _____ Sometimes _____ Seldom _____ Never

3. I make summary sheets of my notes.

   _____ Always _____ Often _____ Sometimes _____ Seldom _____ Never

4. I edit my notes within 24 hours.

   _____ Always _____ Often _____ Sometimes _____ Seldom _____ Never

5. Before class, I conduct a brief review of the notes I took in the previous class.

   _____ Always _____ Often _____ Sometimes _____ Seldom _____ Never

Create more VALUE from your NOTES

Effective notes are living documents—words and images that gain clarity as your understanding of a subject deepens. Notes that are not used continuously throughout a term can quickly become inaccurate—or even useless. Instead, you can create notes that are clear enough for you to understand and useful enough to consult for weeks, months, or years to come.

Observing, recording, and reviewing will give you a great start. In addition, experiment with the following strategies.

EDIT TO REDUCE, ORGANIZE, AND UNDERSTAND

One suggested strategy for reviewing is to evaluate your notes. This means reflecting on how well you reduced, organized, and understood the course content. The table below reviews strategies for meeting each of these goals.

As you evaluate, remember to avoid vague and absolute judgments such as *I'm a lousy note taker*. Instead, be specific and nonjudgmental. Focus on ways to improve.

RECREATE YOUR NOTES IN A NEW FORMAT

The goal of *taking* notes in the first place is to condense a lecture or discussion to its essence, leaving you with a compact set of ideas and information to study. A goal of *revising* your notes is to reflect on the subject matter and bring your insights into clear focus.

Sometimes it helps to get a different perspective on the material. You can do that by recreating your notes in a new format. If you took notes in Cornell format, convert sections to outline format. If your original notes are outlined, then convert sections to mind maps or concept maps. Use all these formats at different points in your notes for a course, or invent new formats of your own.

The benefit of playing with all these formats is that they engage your mind in different ways. Taking notes in Cornell format can help you get a handle on details—key terms and facts. Outlines force you to pay attention to the way that material is structured. And maps are visual devices that help you see connections between many topics at once. Each format yields a different cross section of the subject matter. And each format deepens your understanding.

EXPAND ON YOUR NOTES WITH A PERSONAL JOURNAL

Here is a chance for you to stretch out mentally. Use your personal journal to put class notes in a larger perspective. Reflect on the significance of your courses. Mine your own experiences for examples of the ideas you're learning about. Speculate about how you might apply what you're learning in class.

Goal	Strategies
Reduce course content to its essentials.	• Use meaningful abbreviations. • Use key words. • Focus on major topics, terms, and points; record only key details.
Clarify the organization of course content.	• Use concept maps, mind maps, and other visual devices to highlight key ideas and their relationships. • Use outlines with headings that clearly distinguish between different levels of ideas. • Create graphic cues to aid review: underline or capitalize key words and phrases; indent key passages or record them in a different color; use simple lists and numbered lists.
Reveal understanding of the course content.	• When possible, use your own words rather than the lecturer's. • Take notes in several different formats. • Use key words, but avoid condensing material so much that it becomes impossible to decode. • Record essential points in complete sentences.

A simple way to start a journal and gradually expand its content is to make lists. Experiment with many kinds of lists. For example:

- List new words and their definitions.
- List the top five ideas that you want to remember from your classes or assigned readings.
- List the five most influential people in your life and what they taught you.
- List the three most important things you want to teach your children.
- List your favorite quotations, including notable things that you and your friends say.

Also imagine that you're sitting face to face with the author of your textbook or a historical figure that you're studying. Write what you would say to this person. Argue. Debate. Note questions you want to ask this person; later, pose these questions in class. In each case, you will build your skills at creative and critical thinking. ■

Turn POWERPOINTS into POWERFUL NOTES

PowerPoint presentations are common. They can also be lethal for students who want to master course content or those who simply want to stay awake.

Some students stop taking notes during a PowerPoint presentation. This choice can be hazardous to your academic health for three major reasons:

- *PowerPoint presentations don't include everything.* Instructors and other speakers use PowerPoint to organize their presentations. Topics covered in the slides make up an outline of what your instructor considers important. Slides are created to flag the main points and signal transitions between points. However, speakers usually add examples and explanations that don't appear on the slides. In addition, slides will not include any material from class discussion, including any answers that the instructor gives in response to questions.

- *You stop learning.* Taking notes forces you to capture ideas and information in your own words. Also, the act of writing things down helps you remember the material. If you stop writing and let your attention drift, you can quickly get lost.

- *You end up with major gaps in your notes.* When it's time to review your notes, you'll find that material from PowerPoint presentations is missing. This can be a major pain at exam time.

To create value from PowerPoint presentations, take notes on them. Continue to observe, record, and review. See PowerPoint as a way to *guide* rather than to *replace* your own note taking. Even the slickest, smartest presentation is no substitute for your own thinking.

Experiment with the following suggestions. They include ideas about what to do before, during, and after a PowerPoint presentation.

BEFORE THE PRESENTATION

Sometimes instructors make PowerPoint slides available before a lecture. If you have computer access, download these files. Scan the slides, just as you would preview a reading assignment.

Consider printing out the slides and bringing them along to class. (If you own a copy of PowerPoint, then choose the "handouts" option when printing. This will save paper and ink.) You can take notes directly on the pages that you print out as in the figure below. Be sure to add the slide numbers if they are missing.

If you use a laptop computer for taking notes during class, then you might not want to bother with printing. Just open up the PowerPoint file and type your notes in the window that appears at the bottom of each slide. After class, you can print out the slides in note view. This will show the original slides plus any text that you added.

DURING THE PRESENTATION

In many cases, PowerPoint slides are presented visually by the instructor *only during class*. The slides are not provided as handouts, and they are not available online for students to print out.

This makes it even more important to take effective notes in class. Capture the main points and key details as you normally would. Use your preferred note-taking strategies.

Be selective in what you write down. Determine what kind of material is on each slide. Stay alert for new topics, main points, and important details. Taking too many notes makes it hard to keep up with a speaker and separate main points from minor details.

In any case, go *beyond* the slides. Record valuable questions and answers that come up during a discussion, even if they are not a planned part of the presentation.

AFTER THE PRESENTATION

If you printed out slides before class and took notes on those pages, then find a way to integrate them with the rest of your notes. For example, add references in your notebook to specific slides. Or create summary notes that include the major topics and points from readings, class meetings, and PowerPoint presentations.

Printouts of slides can provide review tools. Use them as cues to recite. Cover up your notes so that only the main image or words on each slide are visible. See whether you can remember what else appears on the slide, along with the key points from any notes you added.

Also consider "editing" the presentation. If you have the PowerPoint file on your computer, make another copy of it. Open up this copy, and see whether you can condense the presentation. Cut slides that don't include anything you want to remember. Also rearrange slides so that the order makes more sense to you. Remember that you can open up the original file later if you want to see exactly what your instructor presented. ■

11-

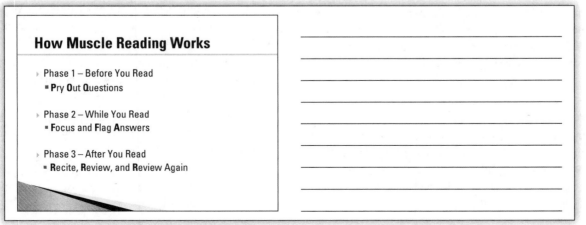

How Muscle Reading Works

- Phase 1 – Before You Read
  - **P**ry **O**ut **Q**uestions

- Phase 2 – While You Read
  - **F**ocus and **F**lag **A**nswers

- Phase 3 – After You Read
  - **R**ecite, **R**eview, and **R**eview Again

When your instructor talks QUICKLY

Take more time to prepare for class. Familiarity with a subject increases your ability to pick up on key points. If an instructor lectures quickly or is difficult to understand, conduct a thorough preview of the material to be covered.

Be willing to make choices. Focus your attention on key points. Instead of trying to write everything down, choose what you think is important. Occasionally, you will make a less than perfect choice or even neglect an important point. Worse things could happen. Stay with the lecture, write down key words, and revise your notes immediately after class.

Exchange photocopies of notes with classmates. Your fellow students might write down something you missed. At the same time, your notes might help them. Exchanging photocopies can fill in the gaps.

Leave large empty spaces in your notes. Leave plenty of room for filling in information you missed. Use a symbol that signals you've missed something, so you can remember to come back to it.

See the instructor after class. Take your class notes with you, and show the instructor what you missed.

Use an audio recorder. Recording a lecture gives you a chance to hear it again whenever you choose. Some audio recording software allows you to vary the speed of the recording. With this feature, you can perform magic and actually slow down the instructor's speech.

Before class, take notes on your reading assignment. You can take detailed notes on the text before class. Leave plenty of blank space. Take these notes with you to class, and simply add your lecture notes to them.

Go to the lecture again. Many classes are taught in multiple sections. That gives you the chance to hear a lecture at least twice—once in your regular class and again in another section of the class.

Learn shorthand. Some note-taking systems, known as shorthand, are specifically designed for getting ideas down fast. Books and courses are available to help you learn these systems. You can also devise your own shorthand method by inventing one- or two-letter symbols for common words and phrases.

Ask questions—even if you're totally lost. Many instructors allow a question session. This is the time to ask about the points you missed.

At times you might feel so lost that you can't even formulate a question. That's okay. One option is to report this fact to the instructor. He can often guide you to a clear question. Another option is to ask a related question. Doing so might lead you to the question you really wanted to ask.

Ask the instructor to slow down. This solution is the most obvious. If asking the instructor to slow down doesn't work, ask her to repeat what you missed. ■

✓ CRITICAL THINKING EXERCISE 17

Taking notes under pressure

With note taking, as with other skills, the more you practice, the better you become. You can use TV programs and videos to practice listening for key words, writing quickly, focusing your attention, and reviewing. Programs that feature speeches and panel discussions work well for this purpose. So do documentary films.

The next time you watch such a program, use pen and paper to jot down key words and information. If you fall behind, relax. Just leave a space in your notes and return your attention to the program. If a program includes commercial breaks, use them to review and revise your notes.

At the end of the program, spend 5 minutes reviewing all of your notes. Create a mind map based on your notes. Then sum up the main points of the program for a friend.

This exercise will help you develop an ear for key words. Because you can't ask questions or request that speakers slow down, you train yourself to stay totally in the moment.

Don't be discouraged if you miss a lot the first time around. Do this exercise several times, and observe how your mind works.

Another option is to record a program and then take notes. You can stop the recording at any point to review what you've written.

Ask a classmate to do this exercise with you. Compare your notes and look for any points that either of you missed.

Taking notes
WHILE READING

Taking notes while reading requires the same skills that apply to taking class notes: observing, recording, and reviewing. Use these skills to take notes for review and for research.

REVIEW NOTES

Review notes will look like the notes you take in class. Take review notes when you want more detailed notes than writing in the margin of your text allows. You might want to single out a particularly difficult section of a text and make separate notes. Or make summaries of overlapping lecture and text material. Because you can't underline or make notes in library books, these sources will require separate notes, too. To take more effective review notes, use the following suggestions.

Set priorities. Single out a particularly difficult section of a text and make separate notes. Or make summaries of overlapping lecture and text material.

Use a variety of formats. Translate text into Cornell notes, mind maps, or outlines. Combine these formats to create your own. Translate diagrams, charts, and other visual elements into words. Then reverse the process by translating straight text into visual elements.

However, don't let the creation of formats get in your way. Even a simple list of key points and examples can become a powerful review tool. Another option is to close your book and just start writing. Write quickly about what you intend to remember from the text, and don't worry about following any format.

Condense a passage to key quotes. Authors embed their essential ideas in key sentences. As you read, continually ask yourself, "What's the point?" Then see whether you can point to a specific sentence on the page to answer your question. Look especially at headings, subheadings, and topic sentences of paragraphs. Write these key sentences word for word in your notes, and put them within quotation marks. Copy as few sentences as you can and still retain the core meaning of the passage.

Condense by paraphrasing. Pretend that you have to summarize a chapter, article, or book on a postcard. Limit yourself to a single paragraph—or a single sentence—and use your own words. This is a great way to test your understanding of the material.

Take a cue from the table of contents. Look at the table of contents in your book. Write each major heading on a piece of paper, or key those headings into a word-processing file on your computer. Include page numbers. Next, see whether you can improve on the table of contents. Substitute your own headings for those that appear in the book. Turn single words or phrases into complete sentences, and use words that are meaningful to you.

Adapt to special cases. The style of your notes can vary according to the nature of the reading material. If you are assigned a short story or poem, for example, then read the entire work once without taking any notes. On your first reading, simply enjoy the piece. When you finish, write down your immediate impressions. Then go over the piece again. Make brief notes on characters, images, symbols, settings, plot, point of view, or other aspects of the work.

Note key concepts in math and science. When you read mathematical, scientific, or other technical materials, copy important formulas or equations. Recreate important diagrams, and draw your own visual representations of concepts. Also write down data that might appear on an exam.

RESEARCH NOTES

Take research notes when preparing to write a paper or deliver a speech. One traditional method of research is to take notes on index cards. You write *one* idea, fact, or quotation per card, along with a note about the source (where you found it). The advantage of limiting each card to one item is that you can easily arrange cards according to the sequence of ideas in your outline. If you change your outline, no problem. Just resort your cards.

Taking notes on a computer offers the same flexibility as index cards. Just include one idea, fact, or quotation per paragraph along with the source. Think of each paragraph as a separate "card." When you're ready to create the first draft of your paper or presentation, just move paragraphs around so that they fit your outline.

11

Include your sources. No matter whether you use cards or a computer, be sure to *include a source for each note that you take*.

Say, for example, that you find a useful quotation from a book. You want to include that quotation in your paper. Copy the quotation word for word onto a card, or key the quotation into a computer file. Along with the quotation, note the book's author, title, date and place of publication, and publisher. You'll need such information later when you create a formal list of your sources—a bibliography, or a list of endnotes or footnotes.

For guidelines on what information to record about each type of source, see the sidebar to this article as a place to start. Your instructors might have different preferences, so ask them for guidance as well.

Note this information about
YOUR SOURCES

Following are checklists of the information to record about various types of sources. Whenever possible, print out or make photocopies of each source. For books, include a copy of the title page and copyright page, both of which are found in the front matter. For magazines and scholarly journals, copy the table of contents.

For each *book* you consult, record the following:

- Author
- Editor (if listed)
- Translator (if listed)
- Edition number (if listed)
- Full title, including the subtitle
- Name and location of the publisher
- Copyright date
- Page numbers for passages that you quote, summarize, or paraphrase

For each *article* you consult, record the following:

- Author
- Editor (if listed)
- Translator (if listed)
- Full title, including the subtitle
- Name of the periodical
- Volume number
- Issue number
- Issue date
- Page numbers for passages that you quote, summarize, or paraphrase

For each *computer-based source* you consult (CD-ROMs and Internet documents), record the following:

- Author
- Editor (if listed)
- Translator (if listed)
- Full title of the page or article, including the subtitle
- Name of the organization that posted the site or published the CD-ROM
- Dates when the page or other document was published and revised
- Date when you accessed the source
- URL for Web pages (the uniform resource locator, or Web site address, which often starts with http://)
- Version number (for CD-ROMs)
- Volume, issue number, and date for online journals

Note: Computer-based sources may not list all the above information. For Web pages, at a minimum record the date you accessed the source and the URL.

For each *interview* you conduct, record the following:

- Name of the person you interviewed
- Professional title of the person you interviewed
- Contact information for the person you interviewed—mailing address, phone number, e-mail address
- Date of the interview

Avoid plagiarism. When people take material from a source and fail to acknowledge that source, they are committing plagiarism. Even when plagiarism is accidental, the consequences can be harsh. For essential information on this topic, see "Academic integrity: Avoid plagiarism" on page 41.

Many cases of plagiarism occur during the process of taking research notes. To prevent this problem, remember that a major goal of taking research notes is to *clearly separate your own words and images from words and images created by someone else*. To meet this goal, develop the following habits:

- If you take a direct quote from one of your sources, then enclose those words in quotation marks and note information about that source.

- If you take an image (photo, illustration, chart, or diagram) from one of your sources, then note information about that source.

- If you summarize or paraphrase *a specific passage* from one of your sources, then use your own words and note information about that source.

> The bottom line: Always present your own work— not materials that have been created or revised by someone else. If you're ever in doubt about what to do, then take the safest course: Cite a source. Give credit where credit is due.

- If your notes include any idea that is closely identified with a particular person, then note information about the source.

- When you include one of your own ideas in your notes, then simply note the source as "me."

If you're taking notes on a computer and using Internet sources, be especially careful to avoid plagiarism. When you copy text or images from a Web site, separate those notes from your own ideas. Use a different font for copied material, or enclose it in quotation marks.

You do *not* need to note a source for these:

- Facts that are considered common knowledge ("The history of the twentieth century includes two world wars").

- Facts that can be easily verified ("The United States Constitution includes a group of amendments known as the Bill of Rights").

- Your own opinion ("Hip-hop artists are the most important poets of our age").

The bottom line: Always present your own work—not materials that have been created or revised by someone else. If you're ever in doubt about what to do, then take the safest course: Cite a source. Give credit where credit is due.

Reflect on your notes. Schedule time to review all the information and ideas that your research has produced. By allowing time for rereading and reflecting on all the notes you've taken, you create the conditions for genuine understanding.

Start by summarizing major points of view on your topic. Note points of agreement and disagreement among your sources.

Also see whether you can find direct answers to the questions that you had when you started researching. These answers could become headings in your paper.

Look for connections in your material, including ideas, facts, and examples that occur in several sources. Also look for connections between your research and your life—ideas that you can verify based on personal experience. ■

You're One Click Away...
from finding examples of effective research and review notes online.

Get to the BONES of your BOOK with CONCEPT MAPS

Concept mapping, pioneered by Joseph Novak and D. Bob Gowin, is a tool to make major ideas in a book leap off the page.[5] In creating a concept map, you reduce an author's message to its essence—its bare bones. Concept maps can also be used to display the organization of lectures and discussions.

Concepts and links are the building blocks of knowledge. A *concept* is a name for a group of related things or ideas. *Links* are words or phrases that describe the relationship between concepts. Consider the following paragraph:

Muscle Reading consists of three phases. Phase 1 includes tasks to complete before reading. Phase 2 tasks take place during reading. Finally, Phase 3 includes tasks to complete after reading.

In this paragraph, examples of concepts are Muscle Reading, reading, phases, tasks, Phase 1, Phase 2, and Phase 3. Links include consists of, includes, before, during, and after.

To create a concept map, list concepts and then arrange them in a meaningful order from general to specific. Then fill in the links between concepts, forming meaningful statements.

Concept mapping promotes critical thinking. It alerts you to missing concepts or faulty links between concepts. In addition, concept mapping mirrors the way that your brain learns—that is, by linking new concepts to concepts that you already know.

To create a concept map, use the following steps:

1. **List the key concepts in the text.** Aim to express each concept in three words or less. Most concept words are nouns, including terms and proper names. At this point, you can list the concepts in any order.

2. **Rank the concepts so that they flow from general to specific.** On a large sheet of paper, write the main concept at the top of the page. Place the most specific concepts near the bottom. Arrange the rest of the concepts in appropriate positions throughout the middle of the page. Circle each concept.

3. **Draw lines that connect the concepts.** On these connecting lines, add words that describe the relationship between the concepts. Again, limit yourself to the fewest words needed to make an accurate link—three words or less. Linking words are often verbs, verb phrases, or prepositions.

4. **Finally, review your map.** Look for any concepts that are repeated in several places on the map. You can avoid these repetitions by adding more links between concepts. ■

You're One Click Away...
from seeing more examples of concept maps online.

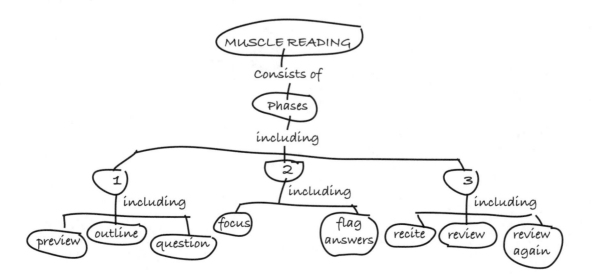

Taking *effective notes* for *online coursework*

If you are taking an online course, or a course that is heavily supported by online materials, then get ready for new challenges to note taking. You can use a variety of strategies to succeed.

Do a trial run with technology. Verify your access to course Web sites, including online tutorials, PowerPoint presentations, readings, quizzes, tests, assignments, bulletin boards, and chat rooms. Ask your instructors for Web site addresses, e-mail addresses, and passwords. Work out any bugs when you start the course and well before that first assignment is due.

If you're planning to use a computer lab on campus, find one that meets course requirements. Remember that on-campus computer labs may not allow you to install all the software needed to access Web sites for your courses or textbooks.

Develop a contingency plan. Murphy's Law of Computer Crashes states that technology tends to break down at the moment of greatest inconvenience. You might not believe this piece of folklore, but it's still wise to prepare for it:

- Find a "technology buddy" in each of your classes—someone who can contact the instructor if you lose Internet access or experience other computer problems.
- Every day, make backup copies of files created for your courses.
- Keep extra printer supplies—paper and toner or ink cartridges—on hand at all times. Don't run out of necessary supplies on the day a paper is due.

Get actively involved with the course. Your online course will include a page that lists homework assignments and test dates. That's only the beginning. Look for ways to engage with the material by submitting questions, completing assignments, and interacting with the instructor and other students.

Take notes on course material. You can print out anything that appears on a computer screen. This includes online course materials—articles, books, manuscripts, e-mail messages, chat room sessions, and more.

The potential problem is that you might skip the note-taking process altogether. ("I can just print out everything!") You would then miss the chance to internalize a new idea by restating it in your own words—a principal benefit of note taking. Result: Material passes from computer to printer without ever intersecting with your brain.

To prevent this problem, take notes in Cornell, mind map, concept map, or outline format. Write Discovery and Intention Statements to capture key insights from the materials and next actions to take. Also talk about what you're learning. Recite key points out loud, and discuss what you find online with other students.

© iStockphoto.com/RichVintage

Of course, it's fine to print out online material. If you do, treat your printouts like mini-textbooks. Apply the steps of Muscle Reading as explained in Chapter 5.

Another potential problem with online courses is the physical absence of the teacher. In a classroom, you get lots of visual and verbal clues to what kinds of questions will appear on a test. Those clues are often missing from an online course, which means that they could be missing from your notes. Ask your online instructor about what material she considers to be most important.

Set up folders and files for easy reference. Create a separate folder for each class on your computer's hard drive. Give each folder a meaningful name, such as *biology—spring2009*. Place all files related to a course in the appropriate folder. Doing this can save you from one of the main technology-related time wasters: searching for lost files.

Also name individual files with care. Avoid changing extensions that identify different types of files, such as .ppt for PowerPoint presentations or .pdf for files in the Adobe Reader portable document format. Changing extensions might lead to problems when you're looking for files later or sharing them with other users.

Take responsibility. If you register for an online course with no class meetings, you might miss the motivating presence of an instructor and classmates. Instead, manufacture your own motivation. Be clear about what you'll gain by doing well in the course. Relate course content to your major and career goals. Don't wait to be contacted by your classmates and instructor. Initiate that contact on your own.

11

Ask for help. If you feel confused about anything you're learning online, ask for help right away. This is especially important when you don't see the instructor face-to-face in class. Some students simply drop online courses rather than seek help. E-mail or call the instructor before you make that choice. If the instructor is on campus, you might be able to arrange for a meeting during office hours.

Manage time and tasks carefully. Courses that take place mostly or totally online can become invisible in your weekly academic schedule. This reinforces the temptation to put off dealing with these courses until late in the term.

Avoid this mistake! Consider the real possibility that an online course can take *more* time than a traditional, face-to-face lecture class. Online courses tend to embrace lots of activities—sending and receiving e-mails, joining discussion forums, commenting on blog posts, and more. New content might appear every day. One key to keeping up with the course is frequent contact and careful time management:

- Early in the term, create a detailed schedule for online courses. In your calendar, list a due date for each assignment. Break big assignments into smaller steps, and schedule a due date for each step.

- Schedule times in your calendar to complete online course work. Give these scheduled sessions the same priority as regular classroom meetings. At these times, check for online announcements relating to assignments, tests, and other course events. Check for course-related e-mails daily.

- If the class includes discussion forums, check those daily as well. Look for new posts and add your replies. The point of these tools is to create a lively conversation that starts early and continues throughout the term.

- -

Consider the real possibility that an online course can take *more* time than a traditional, face-to-face lecture class. Online courses tend to embrace lots of activities—sending and receiving e-mails, joining discussion forums, commenting on blog posts, and more.

- -

- When you receive an online assignment, e-mail any questions immediately. If you want to meet with an instructor in person, request an appointment several days in advance.

- Give online instructors plenty of time to respond. They are not always online. Many online instructors have traditional courses to teach, along with administration and research duties.

- Download or print out online course materials as soon as they're posted on the class Web site. These materials might not be available later in the term.

- If possible, submit online assignments early. Staying ahead of the game will help you avoid an all-nighter at the computer during finals week.

Find tools that help with online courses. BlackBoard and other portals for online courses offer tools to help you access the content. See whether there are any created specifically for your class.

These tools might include "apps"—software programs designed to run on smart phones, iPods, iPads, and similar devices. Most apps have specific, limited features. They're designed to just do one or two things well. Look for apps that allow you to manage to-do lists, maintain a calendar, create flash cards, take notes, make voice recordings, read ebooks, and listen to audio books.

Many apps are free. Others cost just a few dollars or come in trial versions that you can use for free.

Focus your attention. Some students are used to visiting Web sites while watching television, listening to loud music, or using instant messaging software. When applied to online learning, these habits can reduce your learning and endanger your grades. To succeed with technology, turn off the television, quit online chat sessions, and turn down the music. Whenever you go online, stay in charge of your attention.

Ask for feedback. To get the most from online learning, request feedback from your instructor via e-mail. When appropriate, also ask for conferences by phone or in person.

Sharing files offers another source of feedback. For example, Microsoft Word has a Track Changes feature that allows other people to insert comments into your documents and make suggested revisions. These edits are highlighted on the screen. Use such tools to get feedback on your writing from instructors and peers.

Note: Be sure to check with your instructors to see how they want students enrolled in their online courses to address and label their e-mails. Many teachers ask their online students to use a standard format for the subject area so they can quickly recognize e-mails from them.

Contact other students. Make personal contact with at least one other student in each of your classes—especially classes that involve lots of online course work. Create study groups to share notes, quiz each other, critique papers, and do other cooperative learning tasks. This kind of support can help you succeed as an online learner. ▪

masterstudentprofile

Faye Wattleton

(1943–) President of the Planned Parenthood Federation of America from 1978 until 1992. She is currently the founder and president of the Center for the Advancement of Women.

I don't ever recall not wanting to be a nurse, or not saying I wanted to be a nurse. This was, in part, certainly my mother's influence. She wanted me to be a missionary nurse. It wasn't sufficient just to be a nurse, I had to commit to a religious cause as well. Missionary nurses work in church hospitals, in Africa and all over the world. I suspect this was suggested to me before I even understood the power of suggestion, and I always grew up saying I was going to be a nurse. I earned two degrees in nursing, but never practiced as a nurse. In the broadest sense of the word, you can say I have nursed all the time, but not in the technical sense. After undergraduate school, I taught nursing for two years. Then I went to graduate school at Columbia University and earned my master's degree. Following that I moved to Dayton, Ohio, to work in a public health department. There, I was asked to join the board of the local Planned Parenthood. Two years later, I became executive director of the local chapter. Then, seven years later, I became the national president of the organization.

I'm sure the suggestion to become a nurse was colored by the limitation on women's options in those years. Women were nurses, social workers, or teachers. I don't ever remember being explicitly told, "Oh, you can't be that because you're a girl." It just was. . . . It was never conveyed to me there were any limitations on what I could do and what my work could be, although I'm sure the idea that I be a nurse, as opposed to a doctor or something else, was due to the limitations on the role of women at that time.

Even though we lived in a working class community, there wasn't as much integration, so blacks of all economic levels lived in the black community. My father was a laborer, and my mother was a seamstress, but I went to nursing school with our doctor's son. The doctor's family lived a few blocks from us. This was before the Civil Rights movement, and before blacks moved into white or integrated neighborhoods. That experience also played a very important role in my sense of who I am ethnically, as well as what the possibilities were for me. We lived next door to professionals, as well as the housepainter who had the most beautiful house on the block because he painted and decorated it beautifully.

I try to find the best people I can in various specialties so I can learn from them. I want people who are better than me in their specialties, maybe not better than me in running the whole shebang, but better than me in the communications field or legal field. Stitching everything together to make it work as a [piece of] machinery is, for me, the challenge and the excitement.

I try very hard to listen. If there is conflict, I want to hear what the other side says. . . . As long as I feel there is mutual respect, it does not hurt me to listen to someone with whom I am really in conflict, to hear what they are saying even if I disagree. If it's a conflict I really want to resolve, I try to find ways we can come to mutual points of agreement. One thing I always believe is if you talk long enough you can almost always reach a resolution. Just the process of talking has a de-fanging influence. I have great faith in human beings finding ways to relate if they have enough contact with each other.

FAYE WATTLETON ... is willing to participate.

YOU ... can participate by listening with respect, even to people who disagree with you.

Excerpt from Lucinda Watson, *How They Achieved: Stories of Personal Achievement and Business Success,* © 2001, pp. 208–212, John Wiley & Sons. Reproduced with permission of John Wiley & Sons, Inc.

You're One Click Away...
from learning more about Faye Wattleton online at the Master Student Profiles. You can also visit the Master Student Hall of Fame to learn about other master students.

FIVE Cs
FOR YOUR CAREER

CHARACTER • CRITICAL THINKING • CREATIVE THINKING • COLLABORATION • COMMUNICATION

Taking notes at work allows you to apply many of the transferable skills covered in this book—including the five Cs. Remember that the ability to take clear and concise notes is one way to make yourself valuable to an employer. It might even help you get promoted.

Connect note taking to character through the qualities of a Master Student. The way that you take notes at school and work says a lot about who you are. For example, sitting front and center in class tells your instructor that you're engaged and willing to participate. Rewriting your notes into a different format demonstrates that you can organize and sort, and that you're willing to change. Making the effort to listen fully when you disagree with an instructor or coworker shows that you are willing to suspend judgment.

Taking notes calls for split-second decisions about what's important to remember. In addition, you monitor your emotional responses and stay physically active through the act of writing. Effective note taking engages your mind, emotions, and body all at once.

Think creatively by experimenting with formats. During meetings, experiment with Cornell format notes, mind mapping, outlining, concept mapping, or some combination of these. Feel free to add boldface headings, charts, tables, graphs, and other visuals that make the main ideas stand out.

Think critically about your notes. Before meetings, complete background reading on the topics to be discussed, including minutes from relevant meetings in the past. Doing this sets the stage for taking better notes in upcoming meetings. It's easier to make sense of what people say when you already know something about the meeting topics.

When taking notes during fast-paced meetings and conference calls, use suggestions from the article "When your instructor talks *quickly*" in this chapter. Focus on the main points and major details. Immediately after the call or meeting, review and edit your notes.

After meetings, review the notes you took. Edit and rewrite your notes for clarity and accuracy. If you took handwritten notes, consider entering them into a computer file.

If you're taking notes to distribute to coworkers, they will appreciate it if you get to the point and keep paragraphs short.

Use notes to promote collaboration. Take meeting notes in a way that helps your team members move projects to completion. Focus on the following topics:

Attendance. In many organizations, people expect meeting notes to include a list of attendees. For large meetings, see if you can get an advance list of the people who are expected to attend. Bring this to the meeting and check off peoples' names as they enter the room. Along with your list of attendees, include the name of your department, the date, the time, and the name of the person who led the meeting.

Agenda. Think of the agenda as a road map—a way to keep the discussion on track. Skilled planners often put an agenda in writing and distribute it in advance of a meeting. Use this agenda while you take notes.

Agreements. The purpose of most meetings is to reach an agreement about something—a policy, project, or plan. Focus on capturing the details about each agreement.

Actions. During meetings, people often commit to take some type of action in the future. Record each follow-up action and who agreed to do it.

Follow-up action is often a make-or-break point for project teams. One mark of exceptional teams is that people make agreements about what they will do—and then keep those agreements.

You can set a powerful example. Ask whether any of the points you included in your notes call for follow-up action on your part. Highlight such items in your notes. Then add them to your calendar or to-do list and follow through.

Take notes for clear communication. Your employer may have specific guidelines for taking meeting notes. Ask your supervisor about this. Note that in some cases—such as minutes taken during a board of directors meeting—notes may function as legal documents reviewed by the IRS or another independent auditor.

Now, make a personal commitment to developing the five Cs. Take another look at the Discovery Wheel in Chapter 2—especially the sections labeled Character, Creative and Critical Thinking, Communicating, and Collaborating. Take a snapshot of your current skills in these four areas after reading and doing this chapter.

DISCOVERY

My scores on the "Five C" sections of the Discovery Wheel were:	As of today, I would give myself the following scores in these areas:	At the end of this course, I would like my scores in these areas to be:
Character _____	Character _____	Character _____
Creative & Critical Thinking _____	Creative & Critical Thinking _____	Creative & Critical Thinking _____
Communicating _____	Communicating _____	Communicating _____
Collaborating _____	Collaborating _____	Collaborating _____

Next, choose your favorite note-taking technique and consider how it could enhance your skill at least one of the five Cs.

I discovered that my favorite technique for taking notes is . . .

_____

_____

_____

_____

I can use this technique to become a more effective thinker, communicator, or collaborator by . . .

_____

_____

_____

_____

INTENTION
To use this technique, I intend to . . .

_____

_____

_____

_____

NEXT ACTION
The specific action I will take is . . .

_____

_____

_____

_____

11

11 QUIZ

Name _____

Date _____

1. Define the word *responsibility* as it is used in the "Power Process: I create it all."

340 The ability to choose a response to any event.

2. What are the three major parts of effective note taking as explained in this chapter? Summarize each step in one sentence.

341 Observe an event, than record the observations of the event and lastly review what was recorded.

3. According to the text, neat handwriting and a knowledge of outlining are the only requirements for effective notes. True or false? Explain your answer.

341 False, legible handwriting, a new notebook, laptop are all good for taking notes.

4. What are some advantages of sitting in the front and center of the classroom?

340 Enables the student to become a constructive force in the classroom.

5. Describe a way to apply the "Power Process: Be here now" to the job of taking notes in class.

X

6. Instructors sometimes give clues that the material they are presenting is important. List at least three of these clues.

344 Be alert of repetition, listen for introductory, concluding and transition words/phrases and watch the board or Powerpoint presentations.

7. Postponing judgment while taking notes means that you have to agree with everything that the instructor says. True or false? Explain your answer.

— False, it means that after the instructer is done talking, you will go back and analyze the notes.

8. Describe the two main types of key words. Then write down at least five key words from this chapter.

X

9. Graphic signals include which of the following?

(a) Brackets and parentheses

(b) Stars and arrows

(c) Underlining and connecting lines

(d) Equal signs and greater-than and less-than signs

(e) All of the above

10. Describe at least three strategies for reviewing notes.

— Typing notes, edit notes, and create summaries.

364 Chapter 11 • Notes

Tests

Use this **Master Student Map**
to ask yourself

WHY THIS CHAPTER MATTERS . . .

- Adopting a few simple techniques can make a major difference in how you feel about tests—and how you perform on them.

WHAT IS INCLUDED . . .

HOW I CAN USE THIS CHAPTER . . .

- Predict test questions and use my study time more effectively.
- Harness the power of cooperative learning by studying with other people.
- Gain strategies for raising my scores on tests.
- Separate my self-image from my test scores.

WHAT IF . . .

- I could let go of anxiety about tests—or anything else?

JOURNAL ENTRY 14
Intention Statement

Use this chapter to transform your experience with tests

Think about how you want your experience of test taking to change. For example, you might want to walk into every test feeling well rested and thoroughly prepared. Next, preview this chapter to find at least three strategies to accomplish your goal. List those strategies below, and note the page numbers where you can find out more about each one.

Strategy	Page number
_____	_____
_____	_____
_____	_____
_____	_____
_____	_____
_____	_____
_____	_____
_____	_____
_____	_____
_____	_____

© Ruslan Ivantsov/Shutterstock.com

POWER process

DETACH

This Power Process helps you release the powerful, natural student within you. It is especially useful whenever negative emotions are getting in your way.

Attachments are addictions. When we are attached to something, we think we cannot live without it, just as a drug addict feels he cannot live without drugs. We believe our well-being depends on maintaining our attachments.

We can be attached to just about anything: beliefs, emotions, people, roles, objects. The list is endless.

One person, for example, might be so attached to his car that he takes an accident as a personal attack. Pity the poor unfortunate who backs into this person's car. He might as well have backed into the owner himself.

Another person might be attached to her job. Her identity and sense of well-being depend on it. She could become depressed if she got fired.

When we are attached and things don't go our way, we can feel angry, sad, afraid, or confused.

Suppose you are attached to getting an "A" on your physics test. You feel as though your success in life depends on getting that "A." As the clock ticks away, you work harder on the test, getting more stuck. That voice in your head gets louder: "I must get an 'A.' I MUST get an 'A.' I MUST GET AN 'A!'"

Now is a time to detach. See whether you can just *observe* what's going on, letting go of all your judgments. When you just observe, you reach a quiet state above and beyond your usual thoughts. This is a place where you can be aware of being aware. It's a tranquil spot, apart from your emotions. From here, you can see yourself objectively, as if you were watching someone else.

That place of detachment might sound far away and hard to reach. You can get there in three ways.

First, pay attention to your thoughts and physical sensations. If you are confused and feeling stuck, tell yourself, "Here I am, confused and stuck." If your palms are sweaty and your stomach is one big knot, admit it.

Second, practice relaxation. Start by simply noticing your breathing. Then breathe more slowly and more deeply. See whether you can breathe the relaxing feeling into your whole body.

Third, practice seeing current events from a broader perspective. In your mind, zoom out to a bigger picture. Ask yourself how much today's test score will matter to you in one week, one month, one year, or one decade from today. You can apply this technique to any challenge in life.

Caution: Giving up an *attachment* to being an "A" student does not mean giving up *being* an "A" student. Giving up an attachment to a job doesn't mean giving up the job. When you detach, you get to keep your values and goals. However, you know that you will be okay even if you fail to achieve a goal.

Remember that you are more than your goals. You are more than your thoughts and feelings. These things come and go. Meanwhile, the part of you that can *just observe* is always there and always safe, no matter what happens.

Behind your attachments is a master student. Release that mastery. Detach.

You're One Click Away...
from accessing Power Process Media online and finding out more about how to "detach."

DISARM TESTS

On the surface, tests don't look dangerous. Maybe that's why we sometimes treat them as if they were land mines. Suppose a stranger walked up to you on the street and asked, "Does a finite abelian P-group have a basis?" Would you break out in a cold sweat? Would your muscles tense up? Would your breathing become shallow?

Probably not. Even if you had never heard of a finite abelian P-group, you probably would remain coolly detached. However, if you find the same question on a test and you have never heard of a finite abelian P-group, your hands might get clammy.

Grades (A to F) are what we use to give power to tests. And there are lots of misconceptions about what grades are. Grades are not a measure of intelligence or creativity. They are not an indication of our ability to contribute to society. Grades are simply a measure of how well we do on tests.

Some people think that a test score measures what a student has accomplished in a course. This idea is false. A test score is a measure of what a student scored on a test. If you are anxious about a test and blank out, the grade cannot measure what you've learned. The reverse is also true: If you are good at taking tests and you are a lucky guesser, the score won't be an accurate reflection of what you know.

Grades are not a measure of self-worth. Yet we tend to give test scores the power to determine how we feel about ourselves. Common thoughts include "If I fail a test, I am a failure" or "If I do badly on a test, I am a bad person." The truth is that if you do badly on a test, you are a person who did badly on a test. That's all.

If you experience test anxiety, then you might find this line of reasoning hard to swallow. Test anxiety is a common problem among students. And it can surface in many ways, masquerading as a variety of emotions. Here are some examples:

- *Anger:* "The teacher never wanted me to pass this stupid course anyway."
- *Blame:* "If only the class were not so boring."
- *Fear:* "I'll never have enough time to study."

Believing in any of these statements leaves us powerless. We become victims of things that we don't control—the teacher, the textbook, or the wording of the test questions.

Another option is to ask: What can *I* do to experience my next test differently? How can I prepare more effectively? How can I manage stress before, during, and after the test? When you answer such questions, you take back your power.

Carrying around misconceptions about tests and grades can put undue pressure on your performance. It's like balancing on a railroad track. Many people can walk along the rail and stay balanced for long periods. Yet the task seems entirely different if the rail is placed between two buildings, 52 stories up.

It is easier to do well on exams if you don't put too much pressure on yourself. Don't give the test some magical power over your own worth as a human being. Academic tests are not a matter of life and death. Scoring low on important tests—standardized tests or medical school exams, bar exams, CPA exams—usually means only a delay.

Whether the chance of doing poorly is real or exaggerated, worrying about it can become paralyzing. The way to deal with tests is to keep them in perspective. Keep the railroad track on the ground. ■

"F" is for feedback

When some students get an "F" on an assignment, they interpret that letter as a message: "You are a failure." That interpretation is not accurate. Getting an "F" means only that you failed a test—not that you failed your life.

From now on, imagine that the letter "F" when used as a grade represents another word: *feedback.* An "F" is an indication that you didn't understand the material well enough. It's a message to do something differently before the next test or assignment. If you interpret "F" as *failure,* you don't get to change anything. But if you interpret "F" as *feedback,* you can change your thinking and behavior in ways that promote your success. You can choose a new learning strategy, or let go of an excuse about not having the time to study.

Getting prompt and meaningful feedback on your performance is a powerful strategy for learning *anything.* Tests are not the only source of feedback. Make a habit of asking for feedback from your instructors, advisors, classmates, coworkers, friends, family members, and anyone else who knows you. Just determine what you want to improve and ask, "How am I doing?"

JOURNAL ENTRY 15
Discovery Statement

Explore your feelings about tests

Complete the following sentences:

As exam time gets closer, one thing I notice that I do is . . .

_____
_____
_____

When it comes to taking tests, I have trouble . . .

_____
_____
_____

The night before a test, I usually feel . . .

_____
_____
_____

The morning of a test, I usually feel . . .

_____
_____
_____

During a test, I usually feel . . .

_____
_____
_____

After a test, I usually feel . . .

_____
_____
_____

When I learn a test score, I usually feel . . .

_____
_____
_____

You're One Click Away...
from accessing and completing this Journal Entry online under Success Tools in From Master Student to Master Employee's *College Success CourseMate.*

JOURNAL ENTRY 16
Discovery/Intention Statement

Notice your excuses and let them go

Do a timed, 4-minute brainstorm of all the reasons, rationalizations, justifications, and excuses you have used to avoid studying. Be creative. Write your list of excuses in the space below. Use additional paper as needed.

Review your list. Then write a Discovery Statement about patterns that you see in your excuses.

I discovered that I . . .

Next, review your list, pick the excuse that you use the most, and circle it. In the space below, write an Intention Statement about what you will do to begin eliminating your favorite excuse. Make this Intention Statement one that you can keep, with a time line and a reward.

I intend to . . .

_____
_____
_____
_____
_____
_____
_____
_____
_____
_____
_____
_____
_____
_____
_____
_____
_____
_____

WHAT TO DO
BEFORE THE TEST

Do daily reviews. Daily reviews include short preclass and postclass reviews of lecture notes. Also conduct brief daily reviews with textbooks: Before reading a new assignment, scan your notes and the sections you underlined or highlighted in the previous assignment. In addition, use the time you spend waiting for the bus or doing the laundry to conduct short reviews.

Concentrate daily reviews on two kinds of material. One is material you have just learned, either in class or in your reading. Second is material that involves simple memorization—equations, formulas, dates, definitions.

Begin to review on the first day of class. Most instructors outline the whole course at that time. You can even start reviewing within seconds after learning. During a lull in class, go over the notes you just took. Immediately after class, review your notes again.

Do weekly reviews. Review each subject at least once a week, allowing about 1 hour per subject. Include reviews of assigned reading and lecture notes. Look over any mind map summaries or flash cards you have created. Also practice working on sample problems.

Do major reviews. Major reviews are usually most helpful when conducted the week before finals or other critical exams. They help you integrate concepts and deepen your understanding of material presented throughout the term. These are longer review periods—2 to 5 hours at a stretch, with sufficient breaks. Remember that the effectiveness of your review begins to drop after an hour or so unless you give yourself a short rest.

After a certain point, short breaks every hour might not be enough to refresh you. That's when it's time to quit. Learn your limits by being conscious of the quality of your concentration.

During long sessions, study the most difficult subjects when you are the most alert: at the beginning of the session.

Schedule reviews. Schedule specific times in your calendar for reviews. Start reviewing key topics at least 5 days before you'll be tested on them. This allows plenty of time to find the answers to questions and close any gaps in your understanding.

Create study checklists. You can use study checklists the way a pilot uses a preflight checklist. Pilots go through a standard routine before they take off. They physically mark off each item: test flaps, check magnetos, check fuel tanks, adjust instruments, check rudder. A written list helps them to be sure they don't miss anything. Once they are in the air, it's too late. Taking an exam is like flying a plane. Once the test begins, it's too late to memorize that one equation you forgot to include in your review.

Make a checklist for each subject. List reading assignments by chapters or page numbers. List dates of lecture notes. Write down various types of problems you will need to solve. Write down other skills to master. Include major ideas, definitions, theories, formulas, and equations. For math and science tests, choose some problems and do them over again as a way to review for the test.

A. BACALL

© Aaron Bacall

"'How To Do Well In School Without Studying' is over there in the fiction section."

12

Remember that a study checklist is not a review sheet; it is a to-do list. Checklists contain the briefest possible description of each item to study.

Instead of a checklist, you may want to use a test prep plan. This written plan goes beyond a study checklist to include the following:

- The date and time of each test, along with the name of the course and instructor.
- The type of items—such as essay or multiple choice—that are likely to appear on each test.
- Specific dates and times that you intend to study for each test (which you then enter on your calendar).
- Specific strategies that you intend to use while studying for each test.

Create mind map summary sheets. There are several ways to make a mind map as you study for tests. Start by creating a map totally from memory. You might be surprised by how much you already know. After you have gone as far as you can using recall alone, go over your notes and text, and fill in the rest of the map. Another option is to go through your notes and write down key words as you pick them out. Then, without looking at your notes, create a mind map of everything you can recall about each key word. Finally, go back to your notes, and fill in material you left out.

Create flash cards. Flash cards are like portable test questions. On one side of some 3×5 cards, write questions. On the other side, write the answers. It's that simple. Always carry a pack of flash cards with you, and review them whenever you have a minute to spare. Use flash cards for formulas, definitions, theories, key words from your notes, axioms, dates, foreign language phrases, hypotheses, and sample problems. Create flash cards regularly as the term progresses. Buy an inexpensive card file to keep your flash cards arranged by subject.

Monitor your reviews. Each day that you prepare for a test, assess what you have learned and what you still want to learn. See how many items you've covered from your study checklist. Look at the tables of contents in your textbooks, and mark an X next to the sections that you've summarized. This helps you gauge the thoroughness of your reviews and alerts you to areas that still need attention.

Take a practice test. Write up your own questions based on course material—a good activity for study groups. Take your practice test several times before the actual exam. You might type this "test" so that it looks like the real thing. If possible, take your practice test in the same room where you will take the actual test.

Also meet with your instructor to go over your practice test. Ask whether your questions focus on appropriate topics and represent the kind of items you can expect to see. The instructor might decline to give you any of this information. More often, though, instructors will answer some or all of your questions about an upcoming test.

Get copies of old exams. Copies of previous exams for the class might be available from the instructor, the instructor's department, the library, or the counseling office. Old tests can help you plan a review strategy. One caution: If you rely on old tests exclusively, you might gloss over material the instructor has added since the last test. Also, check your school's policy about making past tests available to students. Some schools might not allow it. ■

 You're One Click Away...
from seeing examples of mind map summary sheets and other review tools online.

How to cram (even though you "shouldn't")

Know the limitations of cramming, and be aware of its costs. Cramming won't work if you've neglected all of the reading assignments or if you've skipped most of the lectures and daydreamed through the rest. The more courses you have to cram for, the less effective cramming will be. Also, cramming is not the same as learning: You won't remember what you cram.

If you are going to cram, however, then avoid telling yourself that you *should* have studied earlier, you *should* have read the assignments, or you *should* have been more conscientious. All those *shoulds* get you nowhere. Instead, write an Intention Statement about how you will change your study habits. Give yourself permission to be the fallible human being you are. Then make the best of the situation.

Make choices Pick out a *few* of the most important elements of the course and learn them backward, forward, and upside down. For example, devote most of your attention to the topic sentences, tables, and charts in a long reading assignment.

Make a plan After you've chosen what elements you want to study, determine how much time to spend on each one.

Recite and recite again The key to cramming is repetition. Go over your material again and again.

Ways to PREDICT TEST QUESTIONS

Predicting test questions can do more than get you a better grade. It can also keep you focused on the purpose of a course and help you design your learning strategies. Making predictions can be fun too—especially when they turn out to be accurate.

Ask about the nature of the test. Eliminate as much guesswork as possible. Ask your instructor to describe upcoming tests. Do this early in the term so you can be alert for possible test questions throughout the course. Here are some questions to ask:

- What course material will the test cover—readings, lectures, lab sessions, or a combination?
- Will the test be cumulative, or will it cover just the most recent material you've studied?
- Will the test focus on facts and details or major themes and relationships?
- Will the test call on you to solve problems or apply concepts?
- Will you have choices about which questions to answer?
- What types of questions will be on the test—true/false, multiple choice, short answer, essay?

Note: In order to study appropriately for essay tests, find out how much detail the instructor wants in your answers. Ask how much time you'll be allowed for the test and about the length of essay answers (number of pages, blue books, or word limit). Having that information before you begin studying will help you gauge your depth for learning the material.

Put yourself in your instructor's shoes. If you were teaching the course, what kinds of questions would you put on an exam? You can also brainstorm test questions with other students—a great activity for study groups.

Look for possible test questions in your notes and readings. Have a separate section in your notebook labeled "Test questions." Add several questions to this section after every lecture and assignment. You can also create your own code or graphic signal—such as a "*T!*" in a circle—to flag possible test questions in your notes. Use the same symbol to flag review questions and problems in your textbooks that could appear on a test.

Remember that textbook authors have many ways of pointing you to potential test items. Look for clues in chapter overviews and summaries, headings, lists of key words, and review questions. Some textbooks have related Web sites where you can take practice tests.

Look for clues to possible questions during class. During lectures, you can predict test questions by observing what an instructor says and how he says it. Instructors often give clues. They might repeat important points several times, write them on the board, or return to them in later classes.

Gestures can indicate critical points. For example, your instructor might pause, look at notes, or read passages word for word.

Notice whether your teacher has any strong points of view on certain issues. Questions on those issues are likely to appear on a test. Also pay attention to questions the instructor poses to students, and note questions that other students ask.

When material from reading assignments is covered extensively in class, it is likely to be on a test. For science courses and other courses involving problem solving, work on sample problems using different variables.

Save all quizzes, papers, lab sheets, and graded materials of any kind. Quiz questions have a way of reappearing, in slightly altered form, on final exams. If copies of previous exams and other graded materials are available, use them to predict test questions.

Apply your predictions. To get the most value from your predictions, use them to guide your review sessions.

Remember the obvious. Be on the lookout for these words: *This material will be on the test.* ■

What to do **during the test**

Prepare yourself for the test by arriving early. Being early often leaves time to do a relaxation exercise. While you're waiting for the test to begin and talking with classmates, avoid asking the question "How much did you study for the test?" This question might fuel anxious thoughts that you didn't study enough.

AS YOU BEGIN

Ask the teacher or test administrator if you can use scratch paper during the test. (If you use a separate sheet of paper without permission, you might appear to be cheating.) If you *do* get permission, use this paper to jot down memory aids, formulas, equations, definitions, facts, or other material you know you'll need and might forget. An alternative is to make quick notes in the margins of the test sheet.

Pay attention to verbal directions given as a test is distributed. Then scan the whole test immediately. Evaluate the importance of each section. Notice how many points each part of the test is worth; then estimate how much time you'll need for each section, using its point value as your guide. For example, don't budget 20 percent of your time for a section that is worth only 10 percent of the points.

Read the directions slowly. Then reread them. It can be agonizing to discover that you lost points on a test merely because you failed to follow the directions. When the directions are confusing, ask to have them clarified.

Now you are ready to begin the test. If necessary, allow yourself a minute or two of "panic" time. Notice any tension you feel, and apply one of the techniques explained in the article "Let Go of Test Anxiety" later in this chapter.

Answer the easiest, shortest questions first. This gives you the experience of success. It also stimulates associations and prepares you for more difficult questions. Pace yourself, and watch the time. If you can't think of an answer, move on. Follow your time plan.

If you are unable to determine the answer to a test question, keep an eye out throughout the test for context clues that may remind you of the correct answer or provide you with evidence to eliminate wrong answers.

MULTIPLE-CHOICE QUESTIONS

- **Answer each question in your head first.** Do this step before you look at the possible answers. If you come up with an answer that you're confident is right, look for that answer in the list of choices.

- **Read all possible answers before selecting one.** Sometimes two answers will be similar and only one will be correct.

- **Test each possible answer.** Remember that multiple-choice questions consist of two parts: the stem (an incomplete statement or question at the beginning) and a list of possible answers. Each answer, when combined with the stem, makes a complete statement or question-and-answer pair that is either true or false. When you combine the stem with each possible answer, you are turning each multiple-choice question into a small series of true/false questions. Choose the answer that makes a true statement.

- **Eliminate incorrect answers.** Cross off the answers that are clearly not correct. The answer you cannot eliminate is probably the best choice.

TRUE/FALSE QUESTIONS

- **Read the entire question.** Separate the statement into its grammatical parts—individual clauses and phrases—and then test each part. If any part is false, the entire statement is false.

- **Look for qualifiers.** Qualifiers include words such as *all, most, sometimes,* or *rarely.* Absolute qualifiers such as *always* or *never* generally indicate a false statement.

- **Find the devil in the details.** Double-check each number, fact, and date in a true/false statement. Look for numbers that have been transposed or facts that have been slightly altered. These are signals of a false statement.

- **Watch for negatives.** Look for words such as *not* and *cannot.* Read the sentence without these words and see whether you come up with a true/false statement. Then reinsert the negative words and see whether the statement makes more sense. Watch especially for sentences with two negative words. As in math operations, two negatives cancel each other out: *We cannot say that Chekhov never succeeded at short story writing* means the same as *Chekhov succeeded at short story writing.*

COMPUTER-GRADED TESTS

- Make sure that the answer you mark corresponds to the question you are answering.

- Check the test booklet against the answer sheet whenever you switch sections and whenever you come to the top of a column.

- Watch for stray marks on the answer sheet; they can look like answers.

- If you change an answer, be sure to erase the wrong answer thoroughly, removing all pencil marks completely.

OPEN-BOOK TEST

- Carefully organize your notes, readings, and any other materials you plan to consult when writing answers.

- Write down any formulas you will need on a separate sheet of paper.

- Bookmark the table of contents and index in each of your textbooks. Place sticky notes and stick-on tabs or paper clips on other important pages of books (pages with tables, for instance).

- Create an informal table of contents or index for the notes you took in class.

- Predict which material will be covered on the test, and highlight relevant sections in your readings and notes.

SHORT-ANSWER/FILL-IN-THE-BLANK TESTS

- Concentrate on key words and facts. Be brief.

- Overlearning material can really pay off. When you know a subject backward and forward, you can answer this type of question almost as fast as you can write.

MATCHING TESTS

- Begin by reading through each column, starting with the one with fewer items. Check the number of items in each column to see whether they're equal. If they're not, look for an item in one column that you can match with two or more items in the other column.

- Look for any items with similar wording, and make special note of the differences between these items.

- Match words that are similar grammatically. For example, match verbs with verbs and nouns with nouns.

- When matching individual words with phrases, first read a phrase. Then look for the word that logically completes the phrase.

- Cross out items in each column when you are through with them.

ESSAY QUESTIONS

Managing your time is crucial in answering essay questions. Note how many questions you have to answer, and monitor your progress during the test period. Writing shorter answers and completing all of the questions on an essay test will probably yield a better score than leaving some questions blank.

Find out what an essay question is asking—precisely. If a question asks you to *compare* the ideas of Sigmund Freud and Karl Marx, no matter how eloquently you *explain* them, you are on a one-way trip to No Credit City.

Before you write, make a quick outline. An outline can help speed up the writing of your detailed answer; you're less likely to leave out important facts; and if you don't have time to finish your answer, your outline could win you some points. To use test time efficiently, keep your outline brief. Focus on key words to use in your answer.

Introduce your answer by getting to the point. General statements such as "There are many interesting facets to this difficult question" can cause irritation to teachers grading dozens of tests.

One way to get to the point is to begin your answer with part of the question. Suppose the question is "Discuss how increasing the city police budget might or might not contribute to a decrease in street crime." Your first sentence might be this: "An increase in police expenditures will not have a significant effect on street crime for the following reasons." Your position is clear. You are on your way to an answer.

Then expand your answer with supporting ideas and facts. Start out with the most solid points. Be brief and avoid filler sentences.

Write legibly. Grading essay questions is in large part a subjective process. Sloppy, difficult-to-read handwriting might actually lower your grade.

Write on one side of the paper only. If you write on both sides of the paper, writing may show through and obscure the words on the other side. If necessary, use the blank side to add points you missed. Leave a generous left-hand margin and plenty of space between your answers, in case you want to add points that you missed later on.

Finally, if you have time, review your answers for grammar and spelling errors, clarity, and legibility. ▪

Words to watch for in

ESSAY QUESTIONS

The following words are commonly found in essay test questions. They give you precise directions about what to include in your answer. Get to know these words well. When you see them on a test, underline them. Also look for them in your notes. Locating such key words can help you predict test questions.

Analyze: Break into separate parts and discuss, examine, or interpret each part. Then give your opinion.

Compare: Examine two or more items. Identify similarities and differences.

Contrast: Show differences. Set in opposition.

Criticize: Make judgments about accuracy, quality, or both. Evaluate comparative worth. Criticism often involves analysis.

Define: Explain the exact meaning—usually, a meaning specific to the course or subject. Definitions are usually short.

Describe: Give a detailed account. Make a picture with words. List characteristics, qualities, and parts.

Diagram: Create a drawing, chart, or other visual element. Label and explain key parts.

Discuss: Consider and debate or argue the pros and cons of an issue. Write about any conflict. Compare and contrast.

Enumerate: List the main parts or features in a meaningful order and briefly describe each one.

Evaluate: Make judgments about accuracy, quality, or both (similar to *criticize*).

Explain: Make an idea clear. Show logically how a concept is developed. Give the reasons for an event.

Illustrate: Clarify an idea by giving examples of it. Illustration often involves comparison and contrast. Read the test directions to see whether the question calls for actually drawing a diagram as well.

Interpret: Explain the meaning of a new idea or event by showing how it relates to more familiar ideas or events. Interpretation can involve evaluation.

List: Write a series of concise statements (similar to *enumerate*).

Outline: List the main topics, points, features, or events and briefly describe each one. (This does not necessarily mean creating a traditional outline with Roman numerals, numbers, and letters.)

Prove: Support with facts, examples, and quotations from credible sources (especially those presented in class or in the text).

Relate: Show the connections between ideas or events. Provide a larger context for seeing the big picture.

State: Explain precisely and clearly.

Summarize: Give a brief, condensed account. Include main ideas and conclusions. Avoid supporting details, or include only significant details.

Trace: Show the order of events or the progress of a subject or event.

Notice how these words differ. For example, *compare* asks you to do something different from *contrast*. Likewise, *criticize* and *explain* call for different responses.

If any of these terms are still unclear to you, look them up in an unabridged dictionary.

During a test, you might be allowed to ask for an explanation of a key word. Check with instructors for policies.

 You're One Click Away...
from reviewing these key words and other helpful vocabulary terms by using online flash cards.

The test isn't over *UNTIL* . . .

Many students believe that a test is over as soon as they turn in the answer sheet. Consider another point of view: You're not done with a test until you know the answer to any question that you missed—and why you missed it.

This point of view offers major benefits. Tests in many courses are cumulative. In other words, the content included on the first test is assumed to be working knowledge for the second test, midterm, or final exam. When you discover what questions you missed and understand the reasons for lost points, you learn something—and you greatly increase your odds of achieving better scores later in the course.

To get the most value from any test, take control of what you do at two critical points: the time immediately following the test and the time when the test is returned to you.

Immediately following the test. After finishing a test, your first thought might be to nap, snack, or go out with friends to celebrate. Restrain those impulses for a short while so that you can reflect on the test. The time you invest now carries the potential to raise your grades in the future.

To begin with, sit down in a quiet place. Take a few minutes to write some Discovery Statements related to your experience of taking the test. Describe how you felt about taking the test, how effective your review strategies were, and whether you accurately predicted the questions that appeared on the test.

Follow up with an Intention Statement or two. State what, if anything, you will do differently to prepare for the next test. The more specific you are, the better.

When the test is returned. When a returned test includes a teacher's comments, view this document as a treasure trove of intellectual gold.

First, make sure that the point totals add up correctly, and double-check for any other errors in grading. Even the best teachers make an occasional mistake.

Next, look at the test items that you missed. Ask these questions:

- On what material did the teacher base test questions—readings, lectures, discussions, or other class activities?
- What types of questions appeared in the test—objective (such as matching items, true/false questions, or multiple choice), short answer, or essay?
- What types of questions did you miss?
- Can you learn anything from the instructor's comments that will help you prepare for the next test?
- What strategies did you use to prepare for this test? What would you do differently to prepare for your next test?

Also see whether you can correct any answers that lost points. To do this, carefully analyze the source of your errors, and find a solution. Consult the chart below for help. ■

Source of test error	Possible solutions
Study errors—studying material that was not included on the test, or spending too little time on material that did appear on the test	• Ask your teacher about specific topics that will be included on a test. • Practice predicting test questions. • Form a study group with class members to create mock tests.
Careless errors, such as skipping or misreading directions	• Read and follow directions more carefully—especially when tests are divided into several sections with different directions. • Set aside time during the next test to proofread your answers.
Concept errors—mistakes made when you do not understand the underlying principles needed to answer a question or solve a problem	• Look for patterns in the questions you missed. • Make sure that you complete all assigned readings, attend all lectures, and show up for laboratory sessions. • Ask your teacher for help with specific questions.
Application errors—mistakes made when you understand underlying principles but fail to apply them correctly	• Rewrite your answers correctly. • When studying, spend more time on solving sample problems. • Predict application questions that will appear on future tests, and practice answering them.
Test mechanics errors—missing more questions in certain parts of the test than others, changing correct answers to incorrect ones at the last minute, leaving items blank, miscopying answers from scratch paper to the answer sheet	• Set time limits for taking each section of a test, and stick to them. • Proofread your test answers carefully. • Look for patterns in the kind of answers you change at the last minute. • Change answers only if you can state a clear and compelling reason to do so.

12

© Comstock/Masterfile

Let go of
TEST ANXIETY

A little tension before a test is fine. That tingly, butterflies-in-the-stomach feeling you get from extra adrenaline can sharpen your awareness and keep you alert. You can enjoy the benefits of a little tension while you stay confident and relaxed.

Sometimes, however, tension is persistent and extreme. If it interferes with your daily life and consistently prevents you from doing your best in school, then it might be test anxiety. Anxiety has three elements: mental, physical, and emotional. The mental element includes your thoughts, including predictions of failure. The physical component includes physical sensations such as shallow breathing and muscle tension. The emotional element occurs when thoughts and physical sensations combine. The following techniques can help you deal with these elements of stress in *any* situation, from test anxiety to stage fright.

Yell "Stop!" If you notice that your mind is consumed with worries and fears—that your thoughts are spinning out of control—mentally yell "Stop!" If you're in a situation that allows it, yell it out loud. This action can allow you to redirect your thoughts. Once you've broken the cycle of worry or panic, you can use any of the following techniques.

Describe your thoughts in writing. Certain thoughts tend to increase test anxiety. One way to defuse them is to simply acknowledge them. To get the full benefit of this technique, take the time to make a list. Write down what you think and feel about an upcoming test. Capture everything that's on your mind, and don't stop to edit. One study indicates that this technique can relieve anxiety and potentially raise your test score.[1]

Dispute your thoughts. You can take the above technique one step further. Do some critical thinking. Remember that anxiety-creating thoughts about tests often boil down to this statement: *Getting a low grade on a test is a disaster*. Do the math, however: A four-year degree often involves taking about 32 courses (eight courses per year over four years for a full-time student). This means that your final grade on any one course amounts to about only 3 percent of your total grade point

average. This is *not* an excuse to avoid studying. It is simply a reason to keep tests in perspective.

Praise yourself. Many of us take the first opportunity to belittle ourselves: "Way to go, dummy! You don't even know the answer to the first question on the test." We wouldn't dream of treating a friend this way, yet we do it to ourselves. An alternative is to give yourself some encouragement. Treat yourself as if you were your own best friend. Prepare carefully for each test. Then remind yourself, "I am ready. I can do a great job on this test."

Consider the worst. Rather than trying to put a stop to your worrying, consider the very worst thing that could happen. Take your fear to the limit of absurdity. Imagine the catastrophic problems that might occur if you were to fail the test. You might say to yourself, "Well, if I fail this test, I might fail the course, lose my financial aid, and get kicked out of school. Then I won't be able to get a job, so the bank will repossess my car, and I'll start drinking." Keep going until you see the absurdity of your predictions. After you stop chuckling, you can backtrack to discover a reasonable level of concern.

Breathe. You can calm physical sensations within your body by focusing your attention on your breathing. Concentrate on the air going in and out of your lungs. Experience it as it passes through your nose and mouth. If you notice that you are taking short, shallow breaths, begin to take longer and deeper breaths.

Scan your body. Simple awareness is an effective response to unpleasant physical sensations. Discover this for yourself by bringing awareness to each area of your body.

To begin, sit comfortably and close your eyes. Focus your attention on the muscles in your feet, and notice if they are relaxed. Tell the muscles in your feet that they can relax.

Move up to your ankles and repeat the procedure. Next go to your calves and thighs and buttocks, telling each group of muscles to relax.

Do the same for your lower back, diaphragm, chest, upper back, neck, shoulders, jaw, face, upper arms, lower arms, fingers, and scalp.

As you become aware of physical sensations, open up to them. If you let them arise without resistance, they will eventually pass away.

Use guided imagery. Relax completely and take a quick fantasy trip. Close your eyes, free your body of tension, and imagine yourself in a beautiful, peaceful, natural setting. Create as much of the scene as you can. Be specific. Use all of your senses.

For example, you might imagine yourself at a beach. Hear the surf rolling in and the seagulls calling to each other. Feel the sun on your face and the hot sand between your toes. Smell the sea breeze. Taste the salty mist from the surf. Notice the ships on the horizon and the rolling sand dunes. Use all of your senses to create a vivid imaginary trip.

Find a place that works for you, and practice getting there. When you become proficient, you can return to it quickly for trips that might last only a few seconds.

With practice, you can use this technique even while you are taking a test.

Exercise aerobically. This is one technique that won't work in the classroom or while you're taking a test. Yet it is an excellent way to reduce body tension. Exercise regularly during the days that you review for a test. See what effect this has on your ability to focus and relax during the test.

Do some kind of exercise that will get your heart beating at twice your normal rate and keep it beating at that rate for 15 or 20 minutes. Aerobic exercises include rapid walking, jogging, swimming, bicycling, basketball, and anything else that elevates your heart rate and keeps it elevated.

Practice defusing. To *defuse* means to step back from something and see it as separate from ourselves. When we defuse from an emotion, we no longer identify with it. We no longer say "*I am afraid*" or "*I am sad.*" We say something like "There's fear again" or "I feel sadness right now." Using language such as this offers a way to step back from our internal experiences and keep them in perspective.

Before a test, you might find it especially useful to defuse from your thoughts. Borrow some techniques from Acceptance and Commitment Therapy, used by a growing number of therapists.[2] Take an anxiety-producing thought—such as *I always screw up on tests*—and do any of the following:

1. Repeat it over and over again out loud until it becomes just a meaningless series of sounds.

2. Repeat the thought while using the voice of a cartoon character such as Mickey Mouse or Homer Simpson.

3. Rephrase the thought so that you can sing it to the tune of a nursery rhyme or the song "Happy Birthday."

4. Preface the statement with "I'm having the thought that. . . . (*I'm having the thought that I always screw up on tests.*)

5. Talk back to your mind by saying, "That's an interesting thought, mind; thanks a lot for sharing." Or simply, "Thanks, mind."

· ·

To *defuse* means to step back from something and see it as separate from ourselves. When we defuse from an emotion, we no longer identify with it.

· ·

Make contact with the present moment. If you feel anxious, see if you can focus your attention on a specific sight, sound, or other sensation that's happening in the present moment. Examine the details of a painting. Study the branches on a tree. Observe the face of your watch right down to the tiny scratches in the glass. During an exam, take a few seconds to listen to the sounds of squeaking chairs, the scratching of pencils, the muted coughs. Touch the surface of your desk and notice the texture.

Focus all of your attention on one point—anything other than the flow of thoughts through your head. This is an example of using the "Power Process: Be here now." ∎

Have some **FUN!**

Contrary to popular belief, finals week does not have to be a drag. In fact, if you have used techniques in this chapter, exam week can be fun. You will have done most of your studying long before finals arrive.

When you are well prepared for tests, you can even use fun as a technique to enhance your performance. The day before a final, go for a run or play a game of basketball. Take in a movie or a concert. A relaxed brain is a more effective brain. If you have studied for a test, your mind will continue to prepare itself even while you're at the movies. Get plenty of rest too. There's no need to cram until 3:00 A.M. when you have reviewed material throughout the term.

✔ CRITICAL THINKING EXERCISE 18

Twenty things I like to do

One way to relieve tension is to mentally yell "Stop!" and substitute a pleasant daydream for the stressful thoughts and emotions you are experiencing.

To create a supply of pleasant images to recall during times of stress, conduct an 8-minute brainstorm about things you like to do. Your goal is to generate at least twenty ideas. Time yourself, and write as fast as you can in the space below.

When you have completed your list, study it. Pick out two activities that seem especially pleasant, and elaborate on them by creating a mind map in the space below. Write down all of the memories you have about that activity.

You can use these images to calm yourself in stressful situations.

Getting ready for math tests

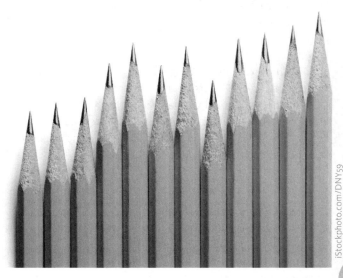

Many students who could succeed in math shy away from the subject. Some had negative experiences in past courses. Others believe that math is only for gifted students.

At some level, however, math is open to all students. There's more to this subject than memorizing formulas and manipulating numbers. Imagination, creativity, and problem-solving skills are important too.

Consider a three-part program for math success. Begin with strategies for overcoming math anxiety. Next, boost your study skills. Finally, let your knowledge shine during tests.

OVERCOME MATH ANXIETY

Many schools offer courses in overcoming math anxiety. Ask your advisor about resources on your campus. Also experiment with the following suggestions.

Connect math to life. Think of the benefits of mastering math courses. You'll have more options for choosing a major and a career. Math skills can also put you at ease in everyday situations—calculating the tip for a waiter, balancing your checkbook, working with a spreadsheet on a computer. If you follow baseball statistics, cook, do construction work, or snap pictures with a camera, you'll use math. And speaking the language of math can help you feel at home in a world driven by technology.

Pause occasionally to get an overview of the branch of math that you're studying. What's it all about? What basic problems is it designed to solve? How do people apply this knowledge in daily life? For example, many architects, engineers, and space scientists use calculus daily.

Take a First Step. Math is cumulative. Concepts build upon each other in a certain order. If you struggled with algebra, you may have trouble with trigonometry or calculus.

To ensure that you have an adequate base of knowledge, tell the truth about your current level of knowledge and skill. Before you register for a math course, locate assigned texts for the prerequisite courses. If the material in those books seems new or

difficult for you, see the instructor. Ask for suggestions on ways to prepare for the course.

Notice your pictures about math. Sometimes what keeps people from succeeding at math is their mental picture of mathematicians. They see a man dressed in a baggy plaid shirt and brown wingtip shoes. He's got a calculator on his belt and six pencils jammed in his shirt pocket.

These pictures are far from realistic. Succeeding in math won't turn you into a nerd. Actually, you'll be able to enjoy school more, and your friends will still like you.

Mental pictures about math can be funny, but they can have serious effects. If math is seen as a field for white males, then women and people of color are likely to get excluded. Promoting math success for all students helps to overcome racism and sexism.

Change your conversation about math. When students fear math, they often say negative things to themselves about their abilities in this subject. Many times this self-talk includes statements such as *I'll never be fast enough at solving math problems* or *I'm good with words, so I can't be good with numbers.*

Get such statements out in the open, and apply some emergency critical thinking. You'll find two self-defeating assumptions lurking there: *Everybody else is better at math and science than I am* and *Since I don't understand a math concept right now, I'll never understand it.* Both of these statements are illogical.

Replace negative beliefs with logical, realistic statements that affirm your ability to succeed in math: *Any confusion I feel now can be resolved. I learn math without comparing myself to others.* And *I ask whatever questions are needed to aid my understanding.*

Choose your response to stress. Math anxiety is seldom just "in your head." It can also register as sweaty palms, shallow breathing, tightness in the chest, or a mild headache. Instead of trying to ignore these sensations, just notice them without judgment. Over time, simple awareness decreases their power.

In addition, use stress management techniques. "Let Go of Test Anxiety" on page 196 offers a bundle of them.

No matter what you do, remember to breathe. You can relax in any moment just by making your breath slower and deeper. Practice doing this while you study math. It will come in handy at test time.

BOOST STUDY SKILLS FOR MATH

Choose teachers with care. Whenever possible, find a math teacher whose approach to math matches your learning style. Talk with several teachers until you find one you enjoy.

Another option is to ask around. Maybe your academic advisor can recommend math teachers. Also ask classmates to name their favorite math teachers—and to explain the reasons for their choices.

In some cases, only one teacher will be offering the math course you need. The suggestions that follow can be used to learn from a teacher regardless of her teaching style.

Take math courses back to back. Approach math in the same way that you learn a foreign language. If you take a year off in between Spanish I and Spanish II, you won't gain much fluency. To master a language, you take courses back to back. It works the same way with math, which is a language in itself.

Avoid short courses. Courses that you take during summer school or another shortened term are condensed. You might find yourself doing far more reading and homework each week than you do in longer courses. If you enjoy math, the extra intensity can provide a stimulus to learn. But if math is not your favorite subject, give yourself extra time. Enroll in courses spread out over more calendar days.

Form a study group. During the first week of each math course, organize a study group. Ask each member to bring five problems to group meetings, along with solutions. Also exchange contact information so that you can stay in touch via e-mail, phone, and text messaging.

Make your text top priority. Math courses are often text driven. Budget for math textbooks and buy them as early as possible. Class activities usually closely follow the book. This fact underscores the importance of completing your reading assignments. Master one concept before going on to the next, and stay current with your reading. Be willing to read slowly and reread sections as needed.

Do homework consistently. Students who succeed in math do their homework daily—from beginning to end, and from the easy problems all the way through the hard problems. If you do homework consistently, you're not likely to be surprised on a test.

When doing homework, use a common process to solve similar problems. There's comfort in rituals, and using familiar steps can help to reduce math anxiety.

Take notes that promote success in math. Though math courses are often text-driven, you might find that the content and organization of your notes makes a big difference as well. Take notes during every class and organize them by date. Also number the pages of your notes. Create a table of contents or index for them so that you can locate key concepts quickly.

In addition, make separate notes to integrate material from class meetings and reading assignments. Paul Nolting, author of the *Math Study Skills Workbook*, suggests that you create a large table with three columns: Key Words/Rules, Examples, and Explanation.[3] Updating this table weekly is a way to review for tests, uncover questions, and monitor your understanding.

Participate in class. Success in math depends on your active involvement. Attend class regularly. Complete homework assignments *when they're due*—not just before the test. If you're confused, get help right away from an instructor, tutor, or study group. Instructors' office hours, free on-campus tutoring, and classmates are just a few of the resources available to you. Also support class participation with time for homework. Make daily contact with math.

1: Prepare

- Read each problem two or three times, slowly and out loud whenever possible.
- Consider creating a chart with three columns labeled *What I already know, What I want to find out,* and *What connects the two.* The third column is the place to record a formula that can help you solve the problem.
- Determine which arithmetic operations (addition, subtraction, multiplication, division) or formulas you will use to solve the problem.
- See if you can estimate the answer before you compute it.

2: Compute

- Reduce the number of unknowns as much as you can. Consider creating a separate equation to solve each unknown.
- When solving equations, carry out the algebra as far as you can before plugging in the actual numbers.
- Cancel and combine. For example, if the same term appears in both dividend and divisor, they will cancel each other out.
- Remember that it's OK to make several attempts at solving the problem before you find an answer.

3: Check

- Plug your answer back into the original equation or problem and see if it works out correctly.
- Ask yourself if your answer seems likely when compared with your estimate. For example, if you're asked to apply a discount to an item, that item should cost less in your solution.
- Perform opposite operations. If a problem involves multiplication, check your work by division; add, then subtract; factor, then multiply; find the square root, then the square; differentiate, then integrate.
- Keep units of measurement clear. Say that you're calculating the velocity of an object. If you're measuring distance in meters and time in seconds, the final velocity should be in meters per second.

12

Math tests often involve lists of problems to solve. Ask your instructor about what type of tests to expect. Then prepare for the tests using strategies from this chapter.

Ask questions fearlessly. It's a cliché, and it's true: In math, there are no dumb questions. Ask whatever questions will aid your understanding. Keep a running list of them, and bring the list to class.

Read actively. To get the most out of your math texts, read with paper and pencil in hand. Work out examples. Copy diagrams, formulas, and equations. Use chapter summaries and introductory outlines to organize your learning. From time to time, stop, close your book, and mentally reconstruct the steps in solving a problem. Before you memorize a formula, understand the basic concepts behind it.

USE TESTS TO SHOW WHAT YOU KNOW

Practice problem solving. To get ready for math tests, work *lots* of problems. Find out whether practice problems or previous tests are on file in the library, in the math department, or with your math teacher.

Isolate the types of problems that you find the most difficult. Practice them more often. Be sure to get help with these kinds of problems *before* exhaustion or frustration sets in.

To prepare for tests, practice working problems fast. Time yourself. This activity is a great one for math study groups.

Approach problem solving with a three-step process, as shown in the chart on this page. During each step, apply an appropriate strategy.

Practice test taking. In addition to solving problems, create practice tests:

- Print out a set of problems, and set a timer for the same length of time as your testing period.
- Whenever possible, work on these problems in the same room where you will take the actual test.
- Use only the kinds of supporting materials—such as scratch paper or lists of formulas—that will be allowed during the test.
- As you work problems, use deep breathing or another technique to enter a more relaxed state.

To get the most value from practice tests, use them to supplement—not replace—your daily homework.

Ask appropriate questions. If you don't understand a test item, ask for clarification. The worst that can happen is that an instructor or proctor will politely decline to answer your question.

Write legibly. Put yourself in the instructor's place. Imagine the prospect of grading stacks of illegible answer sheets. Make your answers easy to read. If you show your work, underline key sections and circle your answer.

Do your best. There are no secrets involved in getting ready for math tests. Master some stress management techniques, do your homework, get answers to your questions, and work sample problems. If you've done those things, you're ready for the test and deserve to do well. If you haven't done all those things, just do the best you can.

Remember that your personal best can vary from test to test, and even from day to day. Even if you don't answer all test questions correctly, you can demonstrate what you *do* know right now.

During the test, notice when solutions come easily. Savor the times when you feel relaxed and confident. If you ever feel math anxiety in the future, these are the times to remember.[4] ■

Notable failures

As you experiment with memory techniques, you may try a few that fail at crucial moments—such as during a test. Just remember that many people before you have failed miserably before succeeding brilliantly. Consider a few examples.

In his first professional race, cyclist **Lance Armstrong** finished last.

The first time **Jerry Seinfeld** walked onstage at a comedy club as a professional comic, he looked out at the audience and froze.

When **Lucille Ball** began studying to be an actress in 1927, she was told by the head instructor of the John Murray Anderson Drama School, "Try any other profession."

In high school, actor and comic **Robin Williams** was voted "Least Likely to Succeed."

Walt Disney was fired by a newspaper editor because "he lacked imagination and had no good ideas."

R. H. Macy failed seven times before his store in New York City caught on.

Emily Dickinson had only seven poems published in her lifetime.

Decca Records turned down a recording contract with the **Beatles** with an unprophetic evaluation: "We don't like their sound. Groups of guitars are on their way out."

In 1954, Jimmy Denny, manager of the Grand Ole Opry, fired **Elvis Presley** after one performance.

Babe Ruth is famous for his past home run record, but for decades he also held the record for strikeouts. **Mark McGwire** broke that record.

After **Carl Lewis** won the gold medal for the long jump in the 1996 Olympic Games, he was asked to what he attributed his longevity, having competed for almost 20 years. He said, "Remembering that you have both wins and losses along the way. I don't take either one too seriously."

"I've missed more than 9,000 shots in my career," **Michael Jordan** said. "I've lost almost 300 games. Twenty-six times I've been trusted to take the game winning shot . . . and missed. I've failed over and over and over again in my life. That is why I succeed."

Adapted from "But They Did Not Give Up," Division of Educational Studies, Emory University, accessed January 20, 2011, from www.des.emory.edu/mfp/OnFailingG.html.

You're One Click Away...
from finding more notable failures online.

masterstudentprofile

Al Gore

(1948–) Former vice president of the United States. Gore refocused his career on climate change, won a Nobel Peace Prize, and—in his film *An Inconvenient Truth*—invented a new type of documentary.

One hundred and nineteen years ago, a wealthy inventor read his own obituary, mistakenly published years before his death. Wrongly believing the inventor had just died, a newspaper printed a harsh judgment of his life's work, unfairly labeling him "The Merchant of Death" because of his invention—dynamite. Shaken by this condemnation, the inventor made a fateful choice to serve the cause of peace.

Seven years later, Alfred Nobel created this prize and the others that bear his name.

Seven years ago tomorrow, I read my own political obituary in a judgment that seemed to me harsh and mistaken—if not premature. But that unwelcome verdict also brought a precious if painful gift: an opportunity to search for fresh new ways to serve my purpose.

Unexpectedly, that quest has brought me here. Even though I fear my words cannot match this moment, I pray what I am feeling in my heart will be communicated clearly enough that those who hear me will say, "We must act." . . .

In the last few months, it has been harder and harder to misinterpret the signs that our world is spinning out of kilter. Major cities in North and South America, Asia, and Australia are nearly out of water due to massive droughts and melting glaciers. Desperate farmers are losing their livelihoods. Peoples in the frozen Arctic and on low-lying Pacific islands are planning evacuations of places they have long called home. Unprecedented wildfires have forced a half million people from their homes in one country and caused a national emergency that almost brought down the government in another. Climate refugees have migrated into areas already inhabited by people with different cultures, religions, and traditions, increasing the potential for conflict. Stronger storms in the Pacific and Atlantic have threatened whole cities. Millions have been displaced by massive flooding in South Asia, Mexico, and 18 countries in Africa. As temperature extremes have increased, tens of thousands have lost their lives. We are recklessly burning and clearing our forests and driving more and more species into extinction.

There is an African proverb that says, "If you want to go quickly, go alone. If you want to go far, go together." We need to go far, quickly. . . .

Fifteen years ago, I made that case at the "Earth Summit" in Rio de Janeiro. Ten years ago, I presented it in Kyoto. This week, I will urge the delegates in Bali to adopt a bold mandate for a treaty that establishes a universal global cap on emissions and uses the market in emissions trading to efficiently allocate resources to the most effective opportunities for speedy reductions.

This treaty should be ratified and brought into effect everywhere in the world by the beginning of 2010— 2 years sooner than presently contemplated. The pace of our response must be accelerated to match the accelerating pace of the crisis itself. . . .

Make no mistake, the next generation will ask us one of two questions. Either they will ask: "What were you thinking; why didn't you act?"

Or they will ask instead: "How did you find the moral courage to rise and successfully resolve a crisis that so many said was impossible to solve?"

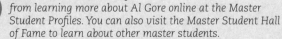

AL GORE ... is optimistic.
YOU ... can be more optimistic by focusing on your goals.

Al Gore Nobel Lecture, Oslo, 10 December 2007. Copyright © The Nobel Foundation 2007. Reproduced by permission.

You're One Click Away...
from learning more about Al Gore online at the Master Student Profiles. You can also visit the Master Student Hall of Fame to learn about other master students.

12

FIVE Cs
FOR YOUR CAREER

Like tests, performance reviews are evaluations. Think of them as the workplace equivalent of the First Step exercise in Chapter 9. Treat these reviews as opportunities to discover your strengths—and to take your experience of the five Cs to a new level.

Connect performance reviews to character. Some employees look forward to annual performance reviews about as much as getting a root canal. To develop the qualities of a Master Student, experiment with a different attitude. When handled with skill, performance reviews are tools for re-creating your experience of work and enjoying more long-term success.

Performance reviews will probably take place in a meeting with your direct supervisor at work. Meetings follow various formats, and many organizations have their own systems for rating performance. Yet the basic idea in any case is for you to walk away with answers to three questions: What am I doing well? What could I do better? And, how can I develop the skills to do better? Answering these questions demonstrates a professional work ethic and gets to the heart of character development.

Think creatively to prepare for the review. As the date of your performance review approaches, imagine the kind of questions your supervisor will ask. For example:

- What was your biggest accomplishment since your last performance review?
- In light of your stated goals, how did you feel about your performance?
- What prevented you from performing well or meeting any of your goals?
- What can you do to overcome those obstacles?
- What can coworkers and managers do to help you overcome those obstacles?

Put your answers to such questions in writing, and revise them to clarify your thinking.

Think critically to set goals. Your organization may schedule performance reviews only once or twice per year. Another option is to see effective performance review as a continuous process.

For optimum results, begin this process on your first day at work. When you start a new job, meet with your direct supervisor to define exactly what "effective performance" means for you.

Here's where your skills at goal setting—a form of critical thinking—can be a lifesaver (see Chapter 10). Translate your definition of effective performance into goals that you can achieve. State them in specific, measurable terms. When the goal is achieved:

- What will you *have* that you don't have now?
- What will you *do* differently?
- How will you *be* different?

Whenever possible, set a specific date to meet each goal. Then put your goals in writing and share them with your supervisor. Also ask if you can submit self-reviews of your performance in preparation for the formal review.

Communicate to keep the tone positive. Sometimes performance reviews are stiff and formal. Supervisor and employees go through the motions, and both are relieved when the meeting is over.

Here is your chance to take the conversation to a deeper level.

During your performance review, refer to your list of goals and note which ones you met. Take time to celebrate your accomplishments and set new goals.

If you missed a goal, talk about how that happened. Instead of focusing on failure or placing blame, take a problem-solving approach. If you made a mistake, talk about what you learned from the experience and what you intend to do differently in the future. Revise the goal and create a new plan for achieving it.

Remember that communication is the creating of shared understanding. Take the assumptions and guesswork out of performance reviews by getting everyone's expectations out on the table, and in writing.

Turn performance reviews into opportunities to collaborate. Effective performance reviews include time for you to *give* feedback as well as receive it. Discuss what you like about your job and what you would like to change. Meeting your goals might call for changes in your job description or extra resources—new equipment, training, coaching, or more. Ask for these.

Instead of complaining about working conditions during your review, make suggestions. "My office is way too noisy for me to be productive" is a complaint. "Let's set up a quiet room in our building where people can go to do work that requires long periods of concentration" is a suggestion. Suggestions are easier to hear than complaints and naturally lend themselves to follow-up action. That action is often taken by a team of people who collaborate to make a change in the workplace.

Now make a personal commitment to develop the five Cs. Take another look at the Discovery Wheel in Chapter 9—especially the sections labeled Character, Creative and Critical Thinking, Communicating, and Collaborating. Take a snapshot of your current skills in these areas after reading and doing this chapter.

DISCOVERY

My scores on the "Five C" sections of the Discovery Wheel were:	As of today, I would give myself the following scores in these areas:	At the end of this course, I would like my scores in these areas to be:
Character _____	Character _____	Character _____
Creative & Critical Thinking _____	Creative & Critical Thinking _____	Creative & Critical Thinking _____
Communicating _____	Communicating _____	Communicating _____
Collaborating _____	Collaborating _____	Collaborating _____

Next, choose your favorite test-taking technique and consider how it could enhance your skill in at least one of the five Cs.

I discovered that my favorite technique for taking tests is . . .

_____

_____

_____

_____

This technique will help me further develop at least one of the five Cs because . . .

_____

_____

_____

_____

INTENTION
To use this technique, I intend to . . .

_____

_____

_____

_____

NEXT ACTION
The specific action I will take is . . .

_____

_____

_____

_____

Name Michelle Ramos

Date _____

366 1. Describe how using the "Power Process: Detach" differs from giving up.

It differs from giving up because we have to observe whats going on and let go of our judgements.

367 2. According to the text, test scores measure your accomplishments in a course. True or false? Explain your answer.

False because it is a measure of what a student scored on a test.

369 3. Briefly explain the difference between a *daily review* and a *major review*.

A daily review is are short preclass + postclass reviews of lecture notes. major reviews are conducted a week before finals.

369 4. Define the term *study checklist*, and give three examples of what to include on such checklists.

A checklist written list that has stuff one has to do and check off as the day goes by. Include reading assignments by pages + chapters, dates of lecture, and major ideas or definitions.

✗ 5. According to the text, you are not finished with a test until you know the answer to any question you missed—and why you missed it. True or false? Explain your answer.

6372 6. When answering multiple-choice questions, the recommended strategy is to read all of the possible answers before answering the question in your head. True or false? Explain your answer.

True because sometimes two answers may be similar.

372 7. The presence of absolute qualifiers, such as *always* or *never*, generally indicates a false statement. True or false? Explain your answer.

True because these words lead to the false statement

✗ 8. Describe three techniques for dealing with test anxiety.

✗ 9. The text offers a three-step process for solving math problems. Name these steps, and list a strategy related to each one.

373 10. Suggestions for taking essay tests include the following:

(a) Find out what an essay question is asking—precisely.

(b) Make a quick outline before you write.

(c) Introduce your answer by getting to the point.

(d) Write legibly.

(e) All of the above

Creative & Critical Thinking

Use this **Master Student Map** to ask yourself

WHY THIS CHAPTER MATTERS . . .

- The ability to think creatively and critically helps you succeed in any course and opens up new career possibilities.

WHAT IS INCLUDED . . .

HOW I CAN USE THIS CHAPTER. . .

- Solve problems creatively.
- Make decisions with more confidence.
- Protect myself from stereotypes, misleading claims, and manipulative advertising.
- Boost my skills in speaking, listening, reading, and writing.

WHAT IF . . .

- I could meet any challenge with a fresh perspective that creates new possibilities for my life?

JOURNAL ENTRY 17
Intention Statement

Choose to create value from this chapter

Remember a time in your life when you felt unable to choose among several different solutions to a problem or struggled with making a decision. Then scan this chapter to find useful suggestions for creative thinking, critical thinking, decision making, and problem solving. Below, note at least three techniques that you definitely intend to use.

Strategy	Page number
_____	_____
_____	_____
_____	_____
_____	_____
_____	_____
_____	_____
_____	_____
_____	_____
_____	_____
_____	_____
_____	_____
_____	_____
_____	_____
_____	_____
_____	_____
_____	_____

© Ruslan Ivantsov/Shutterstock.com

POWER process

Find a bigger problem

It is impossible to live a life that's free of problems. Besides, problems serve a purpose. They provide opportunities to participate in life. Problems stimulate us and pull us forward.

Seen from this perspective, our goal becomes not to eliminate problems, but to find problems that are worthy of us. Worthy problems are those that challenge us to think, consider our values, and define our goals. Solving the biggest problems offers the greatest potential benefits for others and ourselves. Engaging with big problems changes us for the better. Bigger problems give more meaning to our lives.

Problems expand to fill whatever space is available. Suppose that your only problem for today is to write a thank-you letter to a job interview. You could spend the entire day thinking about what you're going to say, writing the letter, finding a stamp, going to the post office—and then thinking about all of the things you forgot to say.

Now suppose that you get a phone call with an urgent message: A close friend has been admitted to the hospital and wants you to come right away. It's amazing how quickly and easily that letter can get finished when there's a bigger problem on your plate.

True, the smaller problems that enter our lives still need to be solved. The goal is simply to solve them in less time and with less energy.

Bigger problems are easy to find—world hunger, child abuse, environmental pollution, terrorism, human rights violations, drug abuse, street crime, energy shortages, poverty, and wars. These problems await your attention and involvement.

Tackling a bigger problem does not have to be depressing. In fact, it can be energizing—a reason for getting up in the morning. A huge project can channel your passion and purpose.

When we take on a bigger problem, we play full out. We do justice to our potentials. We start to love what we do and do what we love. We're awake, alert, and engaged. Playing full out means living our lives as if our lives depended on it.

Perhaps a little voice in your mind is saying, "That's crazy. I can't do anything about global problems." In the spirit of critical thinking, put that idea to the test. Get involved in solving a bigger problem. Then notice the difference that you *can* make. And just as important, notice how your other problems dwindle—or even vanish.

You're One Click Away...
from accessing Power Process Media online and finding out more about how to "find bigger problems."

Jan Martin Will/Shutterstock.com

THINKING: Moving from "aha!" to follow-through

This chapter offers you a chance to practice two types of thinking: creative thinking and critical thinking. Both are essential to your success in school and in the workplace. One path to having good ideas is to have *lots* of ideas. Open up alternatives. Consider many options. Define problems in different ways. Keep asking new questions and looking for fresh answers. These are elements of creative thinking.

Next, pick and choose from among the ideas you create. Combine them. Refine them. Look for ways to take a new concept and turn it into a persuasive paper, a stunning presentation, a useful service, or a product that's ready to sell and ship. This is where critical thinking comes into play.

Creative thinking is the process of generating ideas to look at issues in new and different ways. Critical thinking is when we narrow down our choice by picking and choosing from among these ideas to come up with new and exciting ways to think and do things.

Use creative thinking to cultivate "aha!" Central to creative thinking is something called the "aha!" experience. Nineteenth-century poet Emily Dickinson described *aha!* this way: "If I feel physically as if the top of my head were taken off, I know that is poetry." Aha! is the burst of creative energy heralded by the arrival of a new, original idea. It is the sudden emergence of an unfamiliar pattern, a previously undetected relationship, or an unusual combination of familiar elements. It is an exhilarating experience.

Aha! does not always result in a timeless poem or a Nobel Prize. It can be inspired by anything from playing a new riff on a guitar to figuring out why your car's fuel pump doesn't work. A nurse might notice a patient's symptom that everyone else missed. That's an aha! An accountant might discover a tax break for a client. That's an aha! A teacher might devise a way to reach a difficult student. Aha!

Use critical thinking to follow through. The flip side of aha! is following through. Thinking is both fun and work. It is both effortless and uncomfortable. It's the result of luck and persistence. It involves spontaneity and step-by-step procedures, planning and action, convergent and creative thinking.

Employers want people who can find aha! and do something with it to develop new products and services. This calls for the abilities to spot assumptions, weigh evidence, separate fact from opinion, organize thoughts, and avoid errors in logic. All these skills involve demanding work. Just as often, they can be energizing and fun.

Use critical thinking to make wise choices. Society depends on persuasion. Advertisers want us to spend money on their products. Political candidates want us to "buy" their stands on the issues. Teachers want us to agree that their classes are vital to our success. Parents want us to accept their values. Authors want us to read their books. Broadcasters want us to spend our time in front of the radio or television, consuming their programs and not those of the competition. The business of persuasion has an impact on all of us.

A typical American sees thousands of television commercials each year—and TV is just one medium of communication. Add to that the writers and speakers who enter our lives through radio shows, magazines, books, billboards, brochures, Internet sites, and fund-raising appeals—all with a product, service, cause, or opinion for us to embrace.

This flood of appeals leaves us with hundreds of choices about what to buy, where to go, and who to be. It's easy to lose our heads in the crosscurrent of competing ideas—unless we develop skills in critical thinking. When we think critically, we can make choices with open eyes.

> This flood of appeals leaves us with hundreds of choices about what to buy, where to go, and who to be. It's easy to lose our heads in the crosscurrent of competing ideas—unless we develop skills in critical thinking.

13

It has been said that human beings are rational creatures. Yet no one is born an effective thinker. Critical thinking is a learned skill. This is one reason that you study so many subjects in higher education—math, science, history, psychology, literature, and more. A broad base of courses helps you develop as a thinker. You see how people with different viewpoints arrive at conclusions, make decisions, and solve problems. This gives you a foundation for dealing with complex challenges in your career, your relationships, and your community.

Use critical thinking to avoid deception. One of the reasons that critical thinking is so challenging—and so rewarding—is that we have a remarkable capacity to fool ourselves. Some of our ill-formed thoughts and half-truths have a source that hits a little close to home. That source is ourselves.

For example, consider someone who stakes her identity on the fact that she is a valued employee. During a recession, she gets laid off. On her last day at work, she learns that her refusal to take part in on-the-job training sessions was the major reason that the company let her go. This brute fact contradicts her belief in her value. Her response: "I didn't need that training. I already knew that stuff anyway. Nobody at that company could teach me anything."

A skilled critical thinker would go beyond such self-justifying statements and ask questions instead: "What training sessions did I miss? Could I have learned something from them? Were there any signs that I was about to be laid off, and did I overlook them? What can I do to prevent this from happening again?"

Master students are willing to admit the truth when they discover that their thinking is fuzzy, lazy, based on a false assumption, or dishonest. These students value facts. When a solid fact contradicts a cherished belief, they are willing to change the belief.

More uses of creative and critical thinking. Clear thinking promotes your success inside and outside the classroom. Any time that you are faced with a choice about what to believe or what to do, your thinking skills come in to play. Consider the following applications.

- *Thinking informs reading, writing, speaking, and listening.* These elements are the basis of communication—a process that occupies most of our waking hours.

- *Thinking promotes social change.* The institutions in any society—courts, governments, schools, businesses, nonprofit groups—are the products of cultural customs and trends. All social movements—from the American Revolution to the Civil Rights movement—come about through the work of engaged individuals who actively participated in their communities and questioned what was going on around them. As creative and critical thinkers, we strive to understand and influence the institutions in our society.

- *Thinking uncovers bias and prejudice.* Working through our preconceived notions is a first step toward communicating with people of other races, ethnic backgrounds, and cultures.

- *Thinking reveals long-term consequences.* Crises occur when our thinking fails to keep pace with reality. An example is the world's ecological crisis, which arose when people polluted the earth, air, and water without considering the long-term consequences. Imagine how different our world would be if our leaders had thought like the first female chief of the Cherokees. Asked about the best advice her elders had given her, she replied, "Look forward. Turn what has been done into a better path. If you are a leader, think about the impact of your decision on seven generations into the future."

Master the cycle of creative and critical thinking. The key is to make conscious choices about what kind of thinking to do in any given moment. Generally speaking, creative thinking is more appropriate in the early stages of planning and problem solving. Feel free to dwell in this domain for a while. If you narrow down your options too soon, you run the risk of missing an exciting solution or of neglecting a novel viewpoint.

Remember that creative thinking and critical thinking take place in a continuous cycle. After you've used critical thinking to narrow down your options, you can return to creative thinking at any time to generate new ones.

Use the suggestions in this chapter to claim the thinking powers that are your birthright. The creative thinker and the critical thinker are qualities of the master student who lives inside you. ■

> Master students are willing to admit the truth when they discover that their thinking is fuzzy, lazy, based on a false assumption, or dishonest. These students value facts. When a solid fact contradicts a cherished belief, they are willing to change the belief.

WAYS TO CREATE IDEAS

Anyone can think creatively. Use the following techniques to generate ideas about anything—whether you're studying math problems, remodeling a house, or writing a best seller.

Conduct a brainstorm. Brainstorming is a technique for creating plans, finding solutions, and discovering new ideas. When you are stuck on a problem, brainstorming can break the logjam. For example, if you run out of money 2 days before payday every week, you can brainstorm ways to make your money last longer. You can brainstorm ways to pay for your education. You can brainstorm ways to find a job.

The overall purpose of brainstorming is to generate as many solutions as possible. Sometimes the craziest, most outlandish ideas, while unworkable in themselves, can lead to new ways to solve problems. Use the following steps to try out the brainstorming process:

• *Focus on a single problem or issue.* State your focus as a question. Open-ended questions that start with the words *what, how, who, where,* and *when* often make effective focusing questions. For example, What is my ideal career? What is my ideal major? How can I raise the quality of relationships? What is the single most important change I can make in my life right now?

• *Relax.* Creativity is enhanced by a state of relaxed alertness. If you are tense or anxious, use relaxation techniques such as those described in "Let Go of Text Anxiety" in Chapter 12.

• *Set a quota or goal for the number of solutions you want to generate.* Goals give your subconscious mind something to aim for.

• *Set a time limit.* Use a clock to time it to the minute. Digital sports watches with built-in stopwatches work well. Experiment with various lengths of time. Both short and long brainstorms can be powerful.

• *Allow all answers.* Brainstorming is based on attitudes of permissiveness and patience. Accept every idea. At this stage, there are no wrong answers. If it pops into your head, put it

Sitting woman: Floresco Productions/Getty Images; Word bubbles: maigi/Shutterstock.com

down on paper. Quantity, not quality, is the goal. Avoid making judgments and evaluations during the brainstorming session. If you get stuck, think of an outlandish idea, and write it down. One crazy idea can unleash a flood of other, more workable solutions.

• *Brainstorm with others.* Group brainstorming is a powerful technique. Group brainstorms take on lives of their own. Assign one member of the group to write down solutions. Feed off the ideas of others, and remember to avoid evaluating or judging anyone's ideas during the brainstorm.

After your brainstorming session, evaluate the results. Toss out any truly nutty ideas, but not before you give them a chance.

Focus and let go. Focusing and letting go are alternating parts of the same process. Intense focus taps the resources of your conscious mind. Letting go gives your subconscious mind time to work. When you focus for intense periods and then let go for a while, the conscious and subconscious parts of your brain work in harmony.

Focusing attention means being in the here and now. To focus your attention on a project, notice when you pay attention and when your mind starts to wander. And involve all of your senses. For example, if you are having difficulty writing a paper at a computer, practice focusing by listening to the sounds as you type. Notice the feel of the keys as you strike them. When you know the sights, sounds, and sensations you associate with being truly in focus, you'll be able to repeat the experience and return to your paper more easily.

Be willing to recognize conflict, tension, and discomfort in yourself. Notice them and fully accept them rather than fight against them. Look for the specific thoughts and body sensations that make up the discomfort. Allow them to come fully into your awareness, and then let them pass.

You might not be focused all of the time. Periods of inspiration might last only seconds. Be gentle with yourself when you notice that your concentration has lapsed. In fact, that might be a time to let go. *Letting go* means not forcing yourself to be creative. Practice focusing for short periods at first, and then give yourself a break. Play a board game. Go outside and look for shapes in the clouds. Switch to a new location. Take a nap when you are tired. Thomas Edison, the inventor, took frequent naps. Then the lightbulb clicked on.

Cultivate creative serendipity. The word *serendipity* was coined by the English author Horace Walpole from the title of an ancient Persian fairy tale, "The Three Princes of Serendip." The princes had a knack for making lucky discoveries. Serendipity is that knack, and it involves more than luck. It is the ability to see something valuable that you weren't looking for.

History is full of people who make serendipitous discoveries. Country doctor Edward Jenner noticed "by accident" that milkmaids seldom got smallpox. The result was his discovery that mild cases of cowpox immunized them. Penicillin was also discovered "by accident." Scottish scientist Alexander Fleming was growing bacteria in a laboratory petri dish. A spore of *Penicillium notatum,* a kind of mold, blew in the window and landed in the dish, killing the bacteria. Fleming isolated the active ingredient. A few years later, during World War II, it saved thousands of lives. Had Fleming not been alert to the possibility, the discovery might never have been made.

Keep your eyes open. You might find a solution to an accounting problem in a Saturday morning cartoon. You might discover a topic for your term paper at the corner convenience store. Multiply your contacts with the world. Resolve to meet new people. Join a study or discussion group. Read. Go to plays, concerts, art shows, lectures, and movies. Watch television programs you normally wouldn't watch.

Also expect discoveries. One secret for success is being prepared to recognize "luck" when you see it.

Keep idea files. We all have ideas. People who treat their ideas with care are often labeled "creative." They not only recognize ideas but also record them and follow up on them.

One way to keep track of ideas is to write them down on 3 × 5 cards. Invent your own categories, and number the cards so you can cross-reference them. For example, if you have an idea about making a new kind of bookshelf, you might file a card under "Remodeling." A second card might also be filed under "Marketable Ideas." On the first card, you can write down your ideas, and on the second, you can write, "See card #321—Remodeling."

Include in your files powerful quotations, random insights, notes on your reading, and useful ideas that you encounter in class. Collect jokes too.

Keep a journal. Journals don't have to be exclusively about your own thoughts and feelings. You can record observations about the world around you, conversations with friends, important or offbeat ideas—anything.

To fuel your creativity, read voraciously, including newspapers, magazines, blogs, and other Web sites. Explore beyond mainstream journalism. Hundreds of low-circulation specialty magazines and online news journals cover almost any subject you can imagine. Keep letter-size file folders of important documents. Bookmark Web sites in your browser. Use an online service such as Evernote, Delicious, or Pinboard to save articles that you want to read and refer to later. Create idea files on your computer.

Safeguard your ideas, even if you're pressed for time. Jotting down four or five words is enough to capture the essence of an idea. You can write down one quotation in a minute or two. And if you carry 3 × 5 cards in a pocket or purse, you can record ideas while standing in line or sitting in a waiting room.

Review your files regularly. Some amusing thought that came to you in November might be the perfect solution to a problem in March.

Collect and play with data. Look from all sides at the data you collect. Switch your attention from one aspect to another. Examine each fact, and avoid getting stuck on one particular part of a problem. Turn a problem upside down by picking a solution first and then working backward. Ask other people to look at the data. Solicit opinions.

Living with the problem invites a solution. Write down data, possible solutions, or a formulation of the problem on 3 × 5 cards, and carry them with you. Look at them before you go to bed at night. Review them when you are waiting for the bus. Make them part of your life, and think about them frequently.

Look for the obvious solutions or the obvious "truths" about the problem—then toss them out. Ask yourself, "Well, I know *x* is true, but if *x* were *not* true, what would happen?" Or ask the reverse: "If that *were* true, what would follow next?"

Put unrelated facts next to each other and invent a relationship between them, even if it seems absurd at first. In *The Act of Creation,* novelist Arthur Koestler says that finding a context in which to combine opposites is the essence of creativity.[1]

Make imaginary pictures with the data. Condense it. Categorize it. Put it in chronological order. Put it in alphabetical order. Put it in random order. Order it from most to least complex. Reverse all of those orders. Look for opposites.

It has been said that there are no new ideas—only new ways to combine old ideas. Creativity is the ability to discover those new combinations.

Create while you sleep. A part of our mind works as we sleep. You've experienced this fact directly if you've ever fallen asleep with a problem on your mind and awakened the next morning with a solution. For some of us, the solution appears in a dream or just before we fall asleep or wake up.

You can experiment with this process. Ask yourself a question as you fall asleep. Keep pencil and paper or a recorder near your bed. The moment you wake up, begin writing or speaking, and see whether an answer to your question emerges.

Many of us have awakened from a dream with a great idea, only to fall asleep again and lose it forever. To capture your ideas, keep a notebook by your bed at all times. Put the notebook where you can find it easily.

There is a story about how Benjamin Franklin used this suggestion. Late in the evenings, as he was becoming drowsy, he would sit in his rocking chair with a rock in his right hand and a metal bucket on the floor beneath the rock. The moment he fell asleep, the rock would fall from his grip into the bottom of the bucket, making a loud noise that awakened him. Having placed a pen and paper nearby, he immediately wrote down what he was thinking. Experience taught him that his thoughts at these moments were often insightful and creative.

Promote creative thinking in groups. Sometimes creative thinking dies in committee. People are afraid to disagree with a forceful leader and instead keep their mouths shut. Or a longstanding group ignores new members with new ideas. The result can be "group think," where no one questions the prevailing opinion. To stimulate creative thinking in groups, try these strategies:

- *Put your opinion on hold.* If you're leading a meeting, ask other people to speak up first. Then look for the potential value in *any* idea. Avoid nonverbal language that signals a negative reaction, such as frowning or rolling your eyes.

- *Rotate group leadership.* Ask group members to take turns. This strategy can work well in groups where people have a wide range of opinions.

- *Divide larger groups into several teams.* People might be more willing to share their ideas in a smaller group.

- *Assign a devil's advocate.* Give one person free permission to poke holes in any proposal.

- *Invite a guest expert.* A fresh perspective from someone outside the group can spark an aha!

- *Set up a suggestion box.* Let people submit ideas anonymously, in writing.

Refine ideas and follow through. Many of us ignore the part of the creative process that involves refining ideas and following through. How many great moneymaking schemes have we had that we never pursued? How many good ideas have we had for short stories that we never wrote? How many times have we said to ourselves, "You know, what they ought to do is attach two handles to one of those things, paint it orange, and sell it to police departments. They'd make a fortune." And we never realize that we are "they."

Genius resides in the follow-through—the application of perspiration to inspiration. One powerful tool you can use to follow through is the Discovery and Intention Journal Entry system. First write down your idea in a Discovery Statement, and then write what you intend to do about it in an Intention Statement. You also can explore the writing techniques discussed in Chapter 9: Communicating as a guide for refining your ideas.

Another way to refine an idea is to simplify it. And if that doesn't work, mess it up. Make it more complex.

Finally, keep a separate file in your ideas folder for your own inspirations. Return to it regularly to see whether there is anything you can use. Today's defunct term paper idea could be next year's "A" in speech class.

Trust the process. Learn to trust the creative process—even when no answers are in sight. We are often reluctant to look at problems if no immediate solution is at hand. Trust that a solution will show up. Frustration and a feeling of being stuck are often signals that a solution is imminent.

Sometimes solutions break through in a giant AHA! More often they come in a series of little aha!s. Be aware of what your aha!s look, feel, and sound like. This understanding sets the stage for even more flights of creative thinking. ■

You're One Click Away...
from finding more strategies online for creative thinking.

CREATE on your feet

A popular trend in executive offices is the stand-up desk—a raised working surface at which you stand rather than sit.

Standing has advantages over sitting for long periods. You can stay more alert and creative when you're on your feet. One theory is that our problem-solving ability improves when we stand, due to increased heart rate and blood flow to the brain.

Standing can ease lower-back pain too. Sitting for too long aggravates the spine and its supporting muscles.

Photo courtesy of David Ellis

Standing while working is a technique with tradition. If you search the Web for stand-up desks, you'll find models based on desks used by Thomas Jefferson, Winston Churchill, and writer Virginia Woolf. Consider setting your desk up on blocks or putting a box on top of your desk so that you can stand while writing, preparing speeches, or studying. Discover how long you can stand comfortably while working, and whether this approach works for you.

Creative thinking at WORK

What does creative thinking have to do with working? Everything.

Every product you've ever bought started out as an idea in someone's head. Before it was manufactured, assembled, or sold, it was created. The same is true of any service that you can purchase—from pet sitting to digital publishing.

Creative thinking at work can change lives and create fortunes. Daniel Ek created Spotify because he wanted to create a legal music service that's more convenient than piracy. Marco Arment created an Internet-based tool called Instapaper because he wanted to "clip" articles that he found online and save them to read later. And William Kamkwamba used scrap materials to create a windmill that still powers his family's home in Malawi.[2]

Creative thinking at work is not accidental. Instead, it's carefully cultivated and sustained through dozens of simple daily choices. Get started with the following strategies.

Set aside a physical space for creative thinking. Step into any office and notice whether it's designed for creative thinking. If people hide behind desks and close their office doors, there's probably not much room for free-wheeling conversation and collaboration. If you see open workspaces and large, bright meeting rooms, then you're probably in an organization that values innovation.

Most people don't get the luxury—or the permission—to tear down cubicles and completely redesign their work spaces. Fortunately, you don't have to do that. Other options are to:

- Open shades and windows to allow more light and fresh air into an office.
- Scrounge up some high stools—which encourage alertness and an upright posture—for people to sit on during meetings.
- Ask your coworkers to stand up during meetings, which encourages people to get to the point and adjourn earlier.
- Use floor lamps to flood a room with warm light.
- Play music while people are filing into a room and waiting for a meeting to start.
- Set up meeting space so that people sit in a circle, which promotes informal conversation.

Set aside solitary time for creative thinking. A calendar that's filled with work and social activities doesn't always allow time for thinking that's free of interruptions. If you want to think creatively, then schedule time for it.

See if you can set aside one hour per week for this purpose. To free your mind from its usual patterns, get away from your work environment during a break or lunch time. Power down your phone and other digital devices for a little while, and grab a pen and some paper instead. Then walk to a library, coffee shop, or safe public space where you can be alone.

Next, sit in silence for a little while and practice the "Power Process: Be here now." Shift into a more receptive state of mind by simply noticing what you hear, see, and feel.

After a few moments, turn your attention to a single question, and let it roll around in your mind for a while. For example:

- What is my biggest current challenge at work?
- What would allow me to do my job with more fun and favorable outcomes?
- What is working well in my job, and how can I get to experience more of it?
- What frustrations do my coworkers, customers, or clients experience on a daily basis, and what would make life easier for them?

Jot down any answers that occur to you, and save them for your next creative thinking session.

Set aside group time for creative thinking. Use the questions from the Master Student Map at the beginning of each chapter in this book to fuel creative thinking with coworkers. You can adapt those questions to any project that your team is assigned to complete. For example:

- *Why are we doing this project?* Will it increase revenues, decrease costs, or improve services to our customers or clients? If this project aligns with none of those goals, then why bother?
- *What will we do to meet our goal?* What's the very next action that must occur in order for this project to move forward? Who will take that action? When?
- *How will we know whether our project succeeds?* What visible or measurable outcomes would occur? What would people say or do differently? What new products or services would result?
- *What if we did nothing?* Would the problem we're trying to solve go away on its own? Would it be better handled by another group of people with different skills? Could we free up time and energy for another project that's more urgent or important?

Questions such as these might make people uncomfortable. That's okay. Hang out with them until they take you to the next level of creative thinking at work. ■

Becoming a CRITICAL THINKER

Thinking is a path to intellectual adventure. Although there are dozens of possible approaches to thinking well, the process boils down to asking and answering questions.

Steve Cole/Getty Images

One quality of a master student is the ability to ask questions that lead to deeper learning. Your mind is an obedient servant. It will deliver answers at the same level as your questions. Becoming a critical thinker means being flexible and asking a wide range of questions.

GETTING READY FOR CRITICAL THINKING

A psychologist named Benjamin Bloom named six levels of thinking. (He called them *educational objectives*, or goals for learning).[3] Each level of thinking calls for asking and answering different kinds of questions.

LEVEL 1: Remembering. At this level of thinking, the key question is *Can I recall the key terms, facts, or events?* To prompt level 1 thinking, an instructor might ask you to do the following:

- List the nine steps of Muscle Reading.
- State the primary features of a mind map.
- Name the master student profiled in Chapter 11 of this book.

To study for a test with level 1 questions, you could create flash cards to review ideas from your readings and class notes. You could also read a book with a set of questions in mind and underline the answers to those questions in the text. Or, you could memorize a list of definitions so that you can recite them exactly. These are just a few examples.

Although remembering is important, this is a relatively low level of learning. No critical or creative thinking is involved. You simply recognize or recall something that you've observed in the past.

LEVEL 2: Understanding. At this level, the main question is *Can I explain this idea in my own words?* Often this means giving examples of an idea based on your own experience.

Suppose that your instructor asks you to do the following:

- Explain the main point of the "Power Process: I create it all."
- Summarize the steps involved in creating a concept map.
- Compare mind mapping with concept mapping, stating how they're alike and how they differ.

Other key words in level 2 questions are *discuss, estimate,* and *restate.* All of these are cues to go one step beyond remembering and to show that you truly *comprehend* an idea.

13

LEVEL 3: Applying. Learning at level 3 means asking: *Can I use this idea to produce a desired result?* That result might include completing a task, meeting a goal, making a decision, or solving a problem.

Some examples of level 3 thinking are listed here:

- Write an affirmation about succeeding in school, based on the guidelines in this text.
- Write an effective goal statement.
- Choose a mnemonic to remember the names of the Great Lakes.

Some key words in level 3 questions include *apply, solve, construct, plan, predict,* and *produce.*

LEVEL 4: Analyzing. Questions at this level boil down to this: *Can I divide this idea into parts or steps?* For example, you could do the following:

- Divide the steps of Muscle Reading into three major phases.
- Take a list of key events in the Vietnam War and arrange them in chronological order.
- Organize the 20 memory techniques from Chapter 4 into different categories.

Other key words in level 4 questions are *classify, separate, distinguish,* and *outline.*

LEVEL 5: Evaluating. Learning at level 5 means asking, *Can I rate the truth, usefulness, or quality of this idea—and give reasons for my rating?* This is the level of thinking you would use to do the following:

- Judge the effectiveness of an Intention Statement.
- Recommend a method for taking lecture notes when an instructor talks fast.
- Rank the Power Processes in order of importance to you—from most useful to least useful.

Level 5 involves genuine critical thinking. At this level you agree with an idea, disagree with it, or suspend judgment until you get more information. In addition, you give reasons for your opinion and offer supporting evidence.

Some key words in level 5 questions are *critique, defend,* and *comment.*

LEVEL 6: Creating. To think at this level, ask, *Can I invent something new based on this idea?* For instance, you might do the following:

- Invent your own format for taking lecture notes.
- Prepare a list of topics that you would cover if you were teaching a student success course.

- Imagine that you now have enough money to retire and then write goals you would like to accomplish with your extra time.
- Create a Power Point presentation based on ideas found in this chapter. Put the material in your own words, and use visual elements to enhance the points.

Creative thinking often involves analyzing an idea into parts and then combining those parts in a new way. Another source of creativity is taking several ideas and finding an unexpected connection among them. In either case, you are thinking at a very high level. You are going beyond agreement and disagreement to offer something unique—an original contribution of your own.

Questions for creative thinking often start with words such as *adapt, change, collaborate, compose, construct, create, design,* and *develop.* You might also notice phrases such as *What changes would you make . . . ? How could you improve . . . ? Can you think of another way to . . . ? What would happen if . . . ?*

GAINING SKILL AS A CRITICAL THINKER

Critical and creative thinking are exciting. The potential rewards are many, and the stakes are high. Your major decisions in life—from choosing a major to choosing a spouse—depend on your skills at critical and creative thinking.

All levels of thinking are useful. Notice that the lower levels of thinking (1 to 3) give you fewer options than the highest

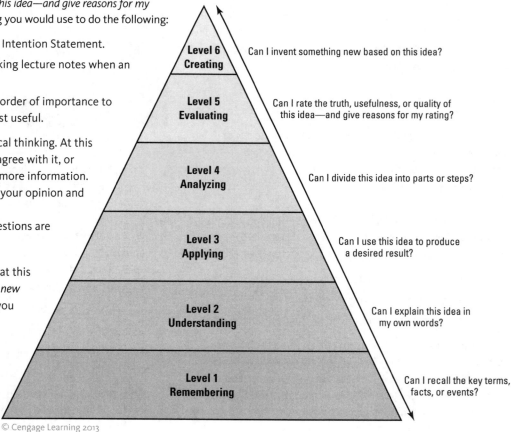

Level 6 Creating — Can I invent something new based on this idea?

Level 5 Evaluating — Can I rate the truth, usefulness, or quality of this idea—and give reasons for my rating?

Level 4 Analyzing — Can I divide this idea into parts or steps?

Level 3 Applying — Can I use this idea to produce a desired result?

Level 2 Understanding — Can I explain this idea in my own words?

Level 1 Remembering — Can I recall the key terms, facts, or events?

© Cengage Learning 2013

levels (4 to 6). Lower levels of thinking are sometimes about finding the "right" answer to a question. At levels 4, 5, and 6, you might discover several valid answers or create several workable solutions.

Also notice that the levels build on each other. Before you agree or disagree with an idea, make sure that you *remember* it accurately and truly *understand* it. Your understanding will go deeper if you can *apply* and *analyze* the idea as well. Master students stay aware of their current level of thinking. They can also move to other levels with a clear intention.

Remember that the highest levels of thinking call for the highest investments of time and energy. Also, moving from a lower level of thinking to a higher level often requires courage, along with an ability to tolerate discomfort. Give yourself permission to experiment, practice, and learn from mistakes.

The suggestions here will help you to deepen your skills at critical thinking. To learn more about creative thinking, see "Thinking: Moving from "aha!" to follow through" on page 209 and "Ways to create ideas" on page 211.

Find various points of view on any issue. Imagine George Bush, Cesar Chavez, and Barack Obama assembled in one room to debate the most desirable way to reshape our government. Picture Madonna, Oprah Winfrey, and Mark Zuckerberg leading a workshop on how to plan your career. When seeking out alternative points of view, let scenes like these unfold in your mind.

Dozens of viewpoints exist on every important issue—reducing crime, ending world hunger, preventing war, educating our children, and countless other concerns. In fact, few problems have any single, permanent solution. Each generation produces its own answers to critical questions, based on current conditions. Our search for answers is a conversation that spans centuries. On each question, many voices are waiting to be heard.

You can take advantage of this diversity by seeking out alternative views with an open mind. When talking to another person, be willing to walk away with a new point of view—even if it's the one you brought to the table, supported with new evidence.

Examining different points of view is an exercise in analysis, which you can do with the suggestions that follow.

Define terms. Imagine two people arguing about whether an employer should limit health care benefits to members of a family. To one person, the word *family* means a mother, father, and children; to the other person, the word *family* applies to any individuals who live together in a long-term, supportive relationship. Chances are the debate will go nowhere until these two people realize that they're defining the same word in different ways.

Conflicts of opinion can often be resolved—or at least clarified—when we define our key terms up front. This is especially true with abstract, emotion-laden terms such as *freedom, peace,*

progress, or *justice.* Blood has been shed over the meaning of those words. Define terms with care.

Look for assertions. Speakers and writers present their key terms in a larger context called an *assertion.* An assertion is a complete sentence that directly answers a key question. For example, consider this sentence from the article "Master student qualities" in the Introduction to this book: "Mastery means attaining a level of skill that goes beyond technique." This sentence is an assertion that answers an important question: How do we recognize mastery?

Look for at least three viewpoints. When asking questions, let go of the temptation to settle for just a single answer. Once you have come up with an answer, say to yourself, "Yes, that is one answer. Now what's another?" Using this approach can sustain honest inquiry, fuel creativity, and lead to conceptual breakthroughs. Be prepared: The world is complicated, and critical thinking is a complex business. Some of your answers might contradict others. Resist the temptation to have all of your ideas in a neat, orderly bundle.

Practice tolerance. One path to critical thinking is tolerance for a wide range of opinions. Taking a position on important issues is natural. When we stop having an opinion on things, we've probably stopped breathing.

Problems occur when we become so attached to our current viewpoints that we refuse to consider alternatives. Likewise, it can be disastrous when we blindly follow everything any person or group believes without questioning its validity. Many ideas that are widely accepted in Western cultures—for example, civil

> Each generation produces its own answers to critical questions, based on current conditions. Our search for answers is a conversation that spans centuries. On each question, many voices are waiting to be heard.

13

liberties for people of color and the right of women to vote—were once considered dangerous. Viewpoints that seem outlandish today might become widely accepted a century, a decade, or even a year from now. Remembering this idea can help us practice tolerance for differing beliefs and, in doing so, make room for new ideas that might alter our lives.

Look for logic and evidence. Uncritical thinkers shield themselves from new information and ideas. As an alternative, you can follow the example of scientists, who constantly search for evidence that contradicts their theories. The following suggestions can help you do so.

The aim of using logic is to make statements that are clear, consistent, and coherent. As you examine a speaker's or writer's assertions, you might find errors in logic—assertions that contradict each other or assumptions that are unfounded.

Also assess the evidence used to support points of view. Evidence comes in several forms, including facts, expert testimony, and examples. To think critically about evidence, ask questions such as these:

- Are all or most of the relevant facts presented?
- Are the facts consistent with one another?
- Are facts presented accurately—or in a misleading way?
- Are opinions mistakenly being presented as facts?
- Are enough examples included to make a solid case for the viewpoint?
- Do the examples truly support the viewpoint?
- Are the examples typical? That is, could the author or speaker support the assertion with other examples that are similar?
- Is the expert credible—truly knowledgeable about the topic?
- Does this evidence affirm or contradict something that I already know?

Consider the source. Look again at that article on the problems of manufacturing cars powered by natural gas. It might have been written by an executive from an oil company. Check out the expert who disputes the connection between smoking and lung cancer. That "expert" might be the president of a tobacco company.

This is not to say that we should dismiss the ideas of people who have a vested interest in stating their opinions. Rather, we should take their self-interest into account as we consider their ideas.

Understand before criticizing. Polished debaters are good at summing up their opponents' viewpoints—often better than the people who support those viewpoints themselves. Likewise, critical thinkers take the time to understand a statement of opinion before agreeing or disagreeing with it.

Effective understanding calls for listening without judgment. Enter another person's world by expressing her viewpoint in your own words. If you're conversing with that person, keep revising your summary until she agrees that you've stated her position accurately. If you're reading an article, write a short summary of it. Then scan the article again, checking to see whether your synopsis is on target.

Watch for hot spots. Many people have mental "hot spots"—topics that provoke strong opinions and feelings. Examples are abortion, homosexuality, gun control, and the death penalty.

To become more skilled at examining various points of view, notice your own particular hot spots. Make a clear intention to accept your feelings about these topics and to continue using critical thinking techniques in relation to them.

One way to cool down our hot spots is to remember that we can change or even give up our current opinions without giving up ourselves. That's a key message behind the "Power Processes: Ideas are tools" and "Detach." These articles remind us that human beings are much more than the sum of their current opinions.

Be willing to be uncertain. Some of the most profound thinkers have practiced the art of thinking by using a magic sentence: "I'm not sure yet."

Those are words that many people do not like to hear. Our society rewards quick answers and quotable sound bites. We're under considerable pressure to utter the truth in 10 seconds or less.

In such a society, it is courageous and unusual to take the time to pause, to look, to examine, to be thoughtful, to consider many points of view—and to be unsure. When a society adopts half-truths in a blind rush for certainty, a willingness to embrace uncertainty can move us forward.

Write about it. Thoughts can move at blinding speed. Writing slows down that process. Gaps in logic that slip by us in thought or speech are often exposed when we commit the same ideas to paper. Writing down our thoughts allows us to compare, contrast, and combine points of view more clearly—and therefore to think more thoroughly.

Notice your changing perspectives. Researcher William Perry found that students in higher education move through stages of intellectual development.[4] In earlier stages, students tend to think there is only one correct viewpoint on each issue, and they look to their instructors to reveal that truth. Later, students acknowledge a variety of opinions on issues and construct their own viewpoints.

Remember that the process of becoming a critical thinker will take you through a variety of stages. Give yourself time, and celebrate your growing mastery. ■

WAYS TO FOOL YOURSELF:
common mistakes IN LOGIC

Rich Reid/National Geographic/Getty Images

Logic is a branch of philosophy that seeks to distinguish between effective and ineffective reasoning. Students of logic look for valid steps in an *argument,* or a series of statements. The opening statements of the argument are the premises, and the final statement is the conclusion.

Effective reasoning is not just an idle pastime for unemployed philosophers. Learning to think logically offers many benefits: When you think logically, you take your reading, writing, speaking, and listening skills to a higher level. You avoid costly mistakes in decision making. You can join discussions and debates with more confidence, cast your election votes with a clear head, and become a better-informed citizen. People have even improved their mental health by learning to dispute illogical beliefs.[5]

Over the last 2,500 years, specialists have listed some classic land mines in the field of logic—common mistakes in thinking that are called *fallacies.* The study of fallacies could fill a yearlong course. Following are 15 examples to get you started. Knowing about them before you string together a bunch of assertions can help you avoid getting fooled.

1 Jumping to conclusions. Jumping to conclusions is the only exercise that some lazy thinkers get. This fallacy involves drawing conclusions without sufficient evidence. Take the bank officer who hears about a student's failing to pay back an education loan. After that, the officer turns down all loan applications from students. This person has formed a rigid opinion on the basis of hearsay. Jumping to conclusions—also called *hasty generalization*—is at work here.

Following are more examples of this fallacy:

- *When I went to Mexico for spring break, I felt sick the whole time. Mexican food makes people sick.*

- *Google's mission is to "organize the world's information." Their employees must be on a real power trip.*

- *During a recession, more people go to the movies. People just want to sit in the dark and forget about their money problems.*

Each item in the above list includes two statements, and the second statement does not necessarily follow from the first. More evidence is needed to make any possible connection.

2 Attacking the person. The mistake of attacking the person is common at election time. An example is the candidate who claims that her opponent has failed to attend church regularly during the campaign. People who indulge in personal attacks are attempting an intellectual sleight of hand to divert our attention away from the truly relevant issues.

3 Appealing to authority. A professional athlete endorses a brand of breakfast cereal. A famous musician features a soft drink company's product in a rock video. The promotional brochure for an advertising agency lists all of the large companies that have used its services.

In each case, the people involved are trying to win your confidence—and your dollars—by citing authorities. The underlying assumption is usually this: *Famous people and organizations buy our product. Therefore, you should buy it too.* Or: *You should accept this idea merely because someone who's well-known says it's true.*

13

Appealing to authority is usually a substitute for producing real evidence. It invites sloppy thinking. When our only evidence for a viewpoint is an appeal to authority, it's time to think more thoroughly.

4 Pointing to a false cause. The fact that one event follows another does not necessarily mean that the two events have a cause-and-effect relationship. All we can actually say is that the events might be correlated. For example, as children's vocabularies improve, they can get more cavities. This does not mean that cavities are the result of an improved vocabulary. Instead, the increase in cavities is due to other factors, such as physical maturation and changes in diet or personal care.

Suppose that you see this newspaper headline: "Student tries to commit suicide after failing to pass bar exam." Seeing this headline, you might conclude that the student's failure to pass the exam lead to a depression that caused his suicide attempt. However, this is simply an assumption that can be stated in the following way: *When two events occur closely together in time, the first event is the cause of the second event.* Perhaps the student's depression was in fact caused by another traumatic event not mentioned in the headline, such as breaking up with a longtime girlfriend.

5 Thinking in all-or-nothing terms. Consider these statements: *Doctors are greedy. You can't trust politicians. Students these days are in school just to get high-paying jobs; they lack idealism. Homeless people don't want to work.*

These opinions imply the word *all.* They gloss over individual differences, claiming that all members of a group are exactly alike. They also ignore key facts—for instance, that some doctors volunteer their time at free medical clinics and that many homeless people are children who are too young to work.

All-or-nothing thinking is one of the most common errors in logic. To avoid this fallacy, watch out for words such as *all, everyone, no one, none, always,* and *never.* Statements that include these words often make sweeping claims that require a lot of evidence. See whether words such as *usually, some, many, few,* and *sometimes* lead to more accurate statements. Sometimes the words are implied. For example, the implication in the claim "Doctors are greedy" is that *all* doctors are greedy.

6 Basing arguments on emotion. The politician who ends every campaign speech with flag waving and slides of his mother eating apple pie is staking his future on appeals to emotion. So is the candidate who paints a grim scenario of the disaster and ruination that will transpire unless she is elected. Get past the fluff and histrionics to see whether you can uncover any worthwhile ideas.

7 Using a faulty analogy. An *analogy* states a similarity between two things or events. Some arguments rest on analogies that hide significant differences. On June 25, 1987, the Associated Press reported an example: U.S. representative Tom DeLay opposed a bill to ban chlordane, a pesticide that causes cancer in laboratory animals. Supporting this bill, he argued, would be like banning cars because they kill people. DeLay's analogy was faulty. Banning

automobiles would have a far greater impact on society than banning a single pesticide, especially if safer pesticides are available.

8 Creating a straw man. The name of this fallacy comes from the scarecrows traditionally placed in gardens to ward off birds. A scarecrow works because it looks like a man. Likewise, a person can attack ideas that *sound like* his opponent's ideas but are actually absurd. For example, some legislators attacked the Equal Rights Amendment by describing it as a measure to abolish separate bathrooms for men and women. In fact, supporters of this amendment proposed no such thing.

9 Begging the question. Speakers and writers beg the question when their colorful language glosses over an idea that is unclear or unproven. Consider this statement: *Support the American tradition of individual liberty and oppose mandatory seat belt laws!* Anyone who makes such a statement "begs" (fails to answer) a key question: Are laws that require drivers to use seat belts actually a violation of individual liberty?

10 Confusing fact and opinion. Facts are statements verified by direct observation or compelling evidence that creates widespread agreement. In recent years, some politicians argued for tax cuts on the grounds that the American economy needed to create more jobs. However, it's not a fact that tax cuts automatically create more jobs. This statement is almost impossible to verify by direct observation, and there's actually evidence against it.

11 Creating a red herring. When hunters want to throw a dog off a trail, they can drag a smoked red herring (or some other food with a strong odor) over the ground in the opposite direction. This distracts the dog, who is fooled into following a false trail. Likewise, people can send our thinking on false trails by raising irrelevant issues. Case in point: In 2006, some people who opposed a presidential campaign by U.S. Senator Barack Obama emphasized his middle name: Hussein. This was an irrelevant attempt to link the senator to Saddam Hussein, the dictator and former ruler of Iraq.

12 Appealing to tradition. Arguments based on an appeal to tradition take a classic form: *Our current beliefs and behaviors have a long history; therefore, they are correct.* This argument has been used to justify the divine right of kings, feudalism, witch burnings, slavery, child labor, and a host of other traditions that are now rejected in most parts of the world. Appeals to tradition ignore the fact that unsound ideas can survive for centuries before human beings realize that they are being fooled.

13 Appealing to "the people." Consider this statement: *Millions of people use Wikipedia as their main source of factual information. Wikipedia must be the best reference work in the world.* This is a perfect example of the *ad populum* fallacy. (In Latin, that phrase means "to the people.") The essential error is assuming that popularity, quality, and accuracy are the same.

Appealing to "the people" taps into our universal desire to be liked and to associate with a group of people who agree with us.

No wonder this fallacy is also called "jumping on the bandwagon." Following are more examples:

- *Internet Explorer is the most widely used Web browser. It must be the best one.*
- *Dan Brown's books, including* The Da Vinci Code, *did not sell as well as the Harry Potter books by J. K. Rowling. I guess we know who's the better writer.*
- *Same-sex marriages must be immoral. Most Americans think so.*

You can refute such statements by offering a single example: Many Americans once believed that slavery was moral and that people of color should not be allowed to vote. That did not make either belief right.

14 **Distracting from the real issue.** The fallacy of distracting from the real issue occurs when a speaker or writer makes an irrelevant statement and then draws a conclusion based on that statement. For example: *The most recent recession was caused by people who borrowed too much money and bankers who loaned too much money. Therefore, you should never borrow money to go to school.* This argument ignores the fact that a primary source of the recession was loans to finance housing—not loans to finance education. Two separate topics are mentioned, and statements about one do not necessarily apply to the other.

15 **Sliding a slippery slope.** The fallacy of sliding a slippery slope implies that if one undesired event occurs, then other, far more serious events will follow: *If we restrict our right to own guns, then all of our rights will soon be taken away. If people keep downloading music for free, pretty soon they'll demand to get everything online for free. I notice that more independent bookstores are closing; it's just a matter of time before people stop reading.*

When people slide a slippery slope, they assume that different types of events have a single cause. They also assume that a particular cause will operate indefinitely. In reality, the world is far more complex. Grand predictions about the future often prove to be wrong.

Finding fallacies before they become a fatal flaw (bonus suggestions). Human beings have a long history of fooling themselves. This article presents just a partial list of logical fallacies. You can prevent them and many more by following a few suggestions:

- When outlining a paper or speech, create a two-column chart. In one column, make a list of your main points. In the other column, summarize the evidence for each point. If you have no evidence for a point, a logical fallacy may be lurking in the wings.

- Go back to some of your recent writing—assigned papers, essay tests, journal entries, and anything else you can find. Look for examples of logical fallacies. Note any patterns, such as repetition of one particular fallacy. Write an Intention Statement about avoiding this fallacy.

- Be careful when making claims about people who disagree with you. One attitude of a critical thinker is treating everyone with fairness and respect. ■

 You're One Click Away...
from practicing hunting for fallacies online.

Master Employees
IN ACTION

 You're One Click Away...
from a video about Master Students in Action.

"*I am lucky to work for a company that actively encourages creativity. Although we are expected to fulfill all the responsibilities of our position, there is also time set aside during which we can pursue more free-thinking activities. I stay motivated by remembering that there is an outlet for my creativity and always come back to the more mundane tasks with a renewed energy.*"

—Kate Chiu,
Associate Director of Communications

© Vadim Ponomarenko/Shutterstock

THINKING CRITICALLY about information on the *INTERNET*

Sources of information on the Internet range from the reputable (such as the Library of Congress) to the flamboyant (such as the *National Enquirer*). People are free to post *anything* on the Internet, including outdated facts as well as intentional misinformation.

Newspaper, magazine, and book publishers often employ fact checkers, editors, and lawyers to screen out errors and scrutinize questionable material before publication. Authors of Web pages and other Internet sources might not have these resources or choose to use them.

Taking a few simple precautions when you surf the Internet can keep you from crashing onto the rocky shore of misinformation.

Distinguish between *ideas* and *information*. To think more powerfully about what you find on the Internet, remember the difference between information and ideas. For example, consider the following sentence: *Nelson Mandela became president of South Africa in 1994.* That statement provides information about South Africa. In contrast, the following sentence states an idea: *Nelson Mandela's presidency means that apartheid has no future in South Africa.*

Information refers to facts that can be verified by independent observers. *Ideas* are interpretations or opinions based on facts. These include statements of opinion and value judgments. Several people with the same information might adopt different ideas based on that information.

People who speak of the Internet as the "information superhighway" often forget to make the distinction between information and ideas. Don't assume that an idea is more current,

reasonable, or accurate just because you find it on the Internet. Apply your critical thinking skills to all published material—print and online.

Look for overall quality. Examine the features of a Web site in general. Notice the effectiveness of the text and visuals as a whole. Also note how well the site is organized and whether you can navigate the site's features with ease. Look for the date that crucial information was posted, and determine how often the site is updated.

Next, get an overview of the site's content. Examine several of the site's pages, and look for consistency of facts, quality of information, and competency with grammar and spelling. Are the links within the site easy to navigate?

Also evaluate the site's links to related Web pages. Look for links to pages of reputable organizations. Click on a few of those links. If they lead you to dead ends, it might indicate that the site you're evaluating is not updated often—a clue that it's not a reliable source for late-breaking information.

Look at the source. Find a clear description of the person or organization responsible for the Web site. Many sites include this information in an "About" link.

The domain in the uniform resource locator (URL) for a Web site gives you clues about sources of information and possible bias. For example, distinguish among information from a for-profit commercial enterprise (URL ending in .com); a nonprofit organization (.org); a government agency (.gov); and a school, college, or university (.edu).

If the site asks you to subscribe or become a member, then find out what it does with the personal information that you provide. Look for a way to contact the site's publisher with questions and comments.

Look for documentation. When you encounter an assertion on a Web page or some other Internet resource, note the types and quality of the evidence offered. Look for credible examples, quotations from authorities in the field, documented statistics, or summaries of scientific studies.

Remember that wikis (peer-edited sites) such as Wikipedia do not employ editors to screen out errors or scrutinize questionable material before publication. Do not rely on these sites when researching a paper or presentation. Also, be cautious about citing blogs, which often are not reviewed for accuracy. Such sources may, however, provide you with key words and concepts that help lead you to scholarly research on your topic.

Set an example. In the midst of the Internet's chaotic growth, you can light a path of rationality. Whether you're sending a short e-mail message or building a massive Web site, bring your own critical thinking skills into play. Every word and image that you send down the wires to the Web can display the hallmarks of critical thinking— sound logic, credible evidence, and respect for your audience. ∎

> People who speak of the Internet as the "information superhighway" often forget to make the distinction between information and ideas. Don't assume that an idea is more current, reasonable, or accurate just because you find it on the Internet.

OVERCOME STEREOTYPES
with critical thinking

Consider assertions such as these: "College students like to drink heavily," "People who speak English as a second language are hard to understand," and "Americans who criticize the president are unpatriotic."

These assertions are examples of stereotyping—generalizing about a group of people based on the behavior of isolated group members. The word *stereotype* originally referred to a method used by printers to produce duplicate pages of text. This usage still rings true. When we stereotype, we gloss over individual differences and assume that every member of a group is a "duplicate." These assumptions are learned, and they can be changed.

Stereotypes infiltrate every dimension of human individuality. People are stereotyped on the basis of their race, ethnic group, religion, political affiliation, geographic location, birthplace, accent, job, economic status, age, gender, sexual orientation, IQ, height, hair color, or hobbies.

Stereotypes have many possible sources: fear of the unknown, uncritical thinking, and negative encounters between individual members of different groups. Whatever their cause, stereotypes abound.

In themselves, generalizations are neither good nor bad. In fact, they are essential. Mentally sorting people, events, and objects into groups allows us to make sense of the world. But when we consciously or unconsciously make generalizations that rigidly divide the people of the world into "us" versus "them," we create stereotypes and put on the blinders of prejudice.

You can take several steps to free yourself from stereotypes.

Look for errors in thinking. Some of the most common errors in thinking are the following:

- *Selective perception.* Stereotypes can literally change the way we see the world. If we assume that homeless people are lazy, for instance, we tend to notice only the examples that support our opinion. Stories about homeless people who are too young or too ill to work will probably escape our attention.

- *Self-fulfilling prophecy.* When we interact with people based on stereotypes, we set them up in ways that confirm our thinking. For example, when people of color were denied access to higher education based on stereotypes about their intelligence, they were deprived of opportunities to demonstrate their intellectual gifts.

- *Self-justification.* Stereotypes can allow people to assume the role of victim and to avoid taking responsibility for their own lives. An unemployed white male might believe that affirmative action programs are making it impossible for him to get a job—even as he overlooks his own lack of experience or qualifications.

Create categories in a more flexible way. Stereotyping has been described as a case of "hardening of the categories." Avoid

> The word *stereotype* originally referred to a method used by printers to produce duplicate pages of text. This usage still rings true. When we stereotype, we gloss over individual differences and assume that every member of a group is a "duplicate."

this problem by making your categories broader. Instead of seeing people based on their skin color, you could look at them on the basis of their heredity. (People of all races share most of the same genes.) Or you could make your categories narrower. Instead of talking about "religious extremists," look for subgroups among the people who adopt a certain religion. Distinguish between groups that advocate violence and those that shun it.

Test your generalizations about people through action. You can test your generalizations by actually meeting people of other cultures. It's easy to believe almost anything about certain groups of people as long as we never deal directly with individuals. Inaccurate pictures tend to die when people from different cultures study together, work together, and live together. Consider joining a school or community organization that will put you in contact with people of other cultures. Your rewards will include a more global perspective and an ability to thrive in a multicultural world.

Be willing to see your own stereotypes. The "Power Process: Notice your pictures and let them go" can help you see your own stereotypes. One belief about yourself that you can shed is *I have no pictures about people from other cultures.* Even people with the best of intentions can harbor subtle biases. Admitting this possibility allows you to look inward even more deeply for stereotypes.

Every time we notice an inaccurate picture buried in our mind and let it go, we take a personal step toward embracing diversity. ■

13

You're One Click Away...
from finding more examples online of stereotypes and critical responses to them.

✓ CRITICAL THINKING EXERCISE 19

Take your thinking to another level

Recall an idea or suggestion from the chapter that you'd like to explore in more detail. Summarize it, and include the page number where it appears:

_____

_____

_____

_____

You've just done some thinking at **Level 1: Remembering**—Now, take your thinking about this idea or suggestion to **one** of the higher levels:

Level 2: Understanding—Explain this idea in your own words and give examples from your own experience.

Level 3: Applying—Use the idea to produce a desired result.

Level 4: Analyzing—Divide this idea into parts or steps.

Level 5: Evaluating—Rate the truth, usefulness or quality of the idea—and give reasons for your rating.

Level 6: Creating—Invent something new based on the idea.

Demonstrate your higher-level thinking by writing a brief paragraph in the space below. If you want to show your thinking in another way, then check with your instructor. In either case, clearly state your intended level of thinking (For example, "To *apply* this idea, I would . . . .")

_____

_____

_____

_____

_____

Asking questions—
learning through inquiry

Thinking is born of questions. Questions wake us up. Questions alert us to hidden assumptions. Questions promote curiosity and create new distinctions. Questions open up options that otherwise go unexplored. Besides, teachers love questions.

There's a saying: "Tell me, and I forget; show me, and I remember; involve me, and I understand." Asking questions is a way to stay involved. One of the main reasons you are in school is to ask questions—a process called *inquiry-based learning*. This process takes you beyond memorizing facts and passing tests. Asking questions turns you into a lifelong learner.

One of the main reasons you are in school is to ask questions. This kind of learning goes beyond memorizing facts and passing tests. Educated people do more than answer questions. They also *ask* questions. They continually search for better questions, including questions that have never been asked before.

Questions have practical power. Asking for directions can shave hours off a trip. Asking a librarian for help can save hours of research time. Asking how to address an instructor, whether by first name or formal title, can change your relationship with that person. Asking your academic advisor a question can alter your entire education. Asking people about their career plans can alter *your* career plans.

Asking questions is also a way to improve relationships with friends and coworkers. When you ask a question, you offer a huge gift to people—an opportunity for them to speak their brilliance and for you to listen to their answers.

George Bernard Shaw, the playwright, knew the power of questions. "Some men see things as they are, and say, Why?" he wrote. "I dream of things that never were, and say, Why not?"

Students often say, "I don't know what to ask." If you have ever been at a loss for questions, here are some ways to discover them. Apply these strategies to any subject you study in school or to any area of your life that you choose to examine.

Ask questions that create possibilities. In Japan, there is a method called *Naikan* that is sometimes used in treating alcoholism. This program is based on asking three questions: "What have I received from others? What have I given to others? And what troubles and difficulties have I caused others?"[8] Taking the time to answer these questions in detail, and with rigorous honesty, can turn someone's life around.

Asking questions is also a way to help people release rigid, unrealistic beliefs: "Everyone should be kind to me." "If I make a mistake, it's terrible." "Children should always do what I say." In her book *Loving What Is*, Byron Katie recommends that you ask four questions about such beliefs: Is it true? Can you absolutely know that it's true? How do you react when you believe that thought? And, who would you be *without* that thought?[9]

At any moment you can ask a question that opens up a new possibility for someone. Suppose a friend walks up to you and says, "People just never listen to me."

You listen carefully. Then you say, "Let me make sure I understand. Who, specifically, doesn't listen to you? And how do you know they're not listening?"

Another friend comes up to you and says, "I just lost my job to someone who has less experience. That should never happen."

"Wow, that's hard," you say. "I'm sorry you lost your job. Who can help you find another job?"

Then a relative seeks your advice. "My mother-in-law makes me mad," she says.

"You're having a hard time with this person," you say. "What does she say and do when you feel mad at her? And are there times when you *don't* get mad at her?"

These kinds of questions—asked with compassion and a sense of timing—can help people move from complaining about problems to solving them.

13

Ask questions for critical thinking. In their classic *How to Read a Book*, Mortimer Adler and Charles Van Doren list four different questions to sum up the whole task of thinking critically about any body of ideas:[10]

What is this piece of writing about as a whole? To answer this question, state the main topic in one sentence. Then list the related subtopics.

What is being said in detail, and how? List the main terms, assertions, and arguments. Also state what problems the writer or speaker is trying to solve.

Is it true? Examine the logic and evidence behind the ideas. Look for missing information, faulty information, and errors in reasoning. Also determine which problems were solved and which remain unsolved.

What of it? After answering the first three questions, prepare to change your thinking or behavior as a result of encountering new ideas.

Discover your own questions. Students sometimes say, "I don't know what questions to ask." Consider the following ways to create questions about any subject you want to study, or about any area of your life that you want to change.

Let your pen start moving. Sometimes you can access a deeper level of knowledge by taking out your pen, putting it on a piece of paper, and writing down questions—even before you know what to write. Don't think. Just watch the pen move across the paper. Notice what appears. The results might be surprising.

Ask about what's missing. Another way to invent useful questions is to notice what's missing from your life and then ask how to supply it. For example, if you want to take better notes, you can write, "What's missing is skill in note taking. How can I gain more skill in taking notes?" If you always feel rushed, you can write, "What's missing is time. How do I create enough time in my day to actually do the things that I say I want to do?"

Pretend to be someone else. Another way to invent questions is first to think of someone you greatly respect. Then pretend you're that person. Ask the questions you think she would ask.

Begin a general question; then brainstorm endings. By starting with a general question and then brainstorming a long list of endings, you can invent a question that you've never asked before. For example:

- What can I do when . . . an instructor calls on me in class and I have no idea what to say? When a teacher doesn't show up for class on time? When I feel overwhelmed with assignments?

- How can I . . . take the kind of courses that I want? Expand my career options? Become much more effective as a student, starting today?

- When do I . . . decide on a major? Transfer to another school? Meet with an instructor to discuss an upcoming term paper?

- What else do I want to know about . . . my academic plan? My career plan? My options for job hunting? My friends? My relatives? My spouse?

- Who can I ask about . . . my career options? My major? My love life? My values and purpose in life?

Ask questions to promote social change. If your friends are laughing at racist jokes, you have a right to ask why. If you're legally registered to vote and denied access to a voting booth, you have a right to ask for an explanation. Asking questions can advance justice.

Ask what else you want to know. Many times you can quickly generate questions by simply asking yourself, "What else do I want to know?" Ask this question immediately after you read a paragraph in a book or listen to someone speak.

Start from the assumption that you are brilliant. Then ask questions to unlock your brilliance. ■

15 questions to try on for size

1. What is the most important problem in my life to solve right now?
2. What am I willing to do to solve this problem?
3. How can I benefit from solving this problem?
4. Who can I ask for help?
5. What are the facts in this situation?
6. What are my options in this situation?
7. What can I learn from this situation?
8. What do I want?
9. What am I willing to do to get what I want?
10. What will be the consequences of my decision in one week? One month? One year?
11. What is the most important thing for me to accomplish today?
12. What's the best possible use of my time right now?
13. What am I grateful for?
14. Who loves me?
15. Whom do I love?

Gaining skill at DECISION MAKING

© Mike Baldwin / Cornered

© Mike Baldwin

We make decisions all the time, whether we realize it or not. Even avoiding decisions is a form of decision making. The student who puts off studying for a test until the last minute might really be saying, "I've decided this course is not important" or "I've decided not to give this course much time." In order to escape such a fate, decide right now to experiment with the following suggestions.

Recognize decisions. Decisions are more than wishes or desires. There's a world of difference between "I wish I could be a better student" and "I will take more powerful notes, read with greater retention, and review my class notes daily." Decisions are specific and lead to focused action. When we decide, we narrow down. We give up actions that are inconsistent with our decision. Deciding to eat fruit for dessert instead of ice cream rules out the next trip to the ice cream store.

Establish priorities. Some decisions are trivial. No matter what the outcome, your life is not affected much. Other decisions can shape your circumstances for years. Devote more time and energy to the decisions with big outcomes.

Base your decisions on a life plan. The benefit of having long-term goals for our lives is that they provide a basis for many of our daily decisions. Being certain about what we want to accomplish this year and this month makes today's choices more clear.

Balance learning styles in decision making. To make decisions more effectively, use all four modes of learning explained in Chapter 9: First Steps. The key is to balance reflection with action, and thinking with experience. First, take the time to think creatively, and generate many options. Then think critically about the possible consequences of each option before choosing one. Remember, however, that thinking is no substitute for experience. Act on your chosen option, and notice what happens. If you're not getting the results that you want, then quickly return to creative thinking to invent new options.

Choose an overall strategy. Every time you make a decision, you choose a strategy—even when you're not aware of it. Effective decision makers can articulate and choose from among several strategies. For example:

- *Find all of the available options, and choose one deliberately.* Save this strategy for times when you have a relatively small number of options, each of which leads to noticeably different results.

- *Find all of the available options, and choose one randomly.* This strategy can be risky. Save it for times when your options are basically similar and fairness is the main issue.

- *Limit the options, and then choose.* When deciding which search engine to use on the World Wide Web, visit many sites and then narrow the list down to two or three that you choose.

Use time as an ally. Sometimes we face dilemmas—situations in which any course of action leads to undesirable consequences. In such cases, consider putting a decision on hold. Wait it out. Do nothing until the circumstances change, making one alternative clearly preferable to another.

Use intuition. Some decisions seem to make themselves. A solution pops into our mind, and we gain newfound clarity. Using intuition is not the same as forgetting about the decision or refusing to make it. Intuitive decisions usually arrive after we've gathered the relevant facts and faced a problem for some time.

Evaluate your decision. Hindsight is a source of insight. After you act on a decision, observe the consequences over time. Reflect on how well your decision worked and what you might have done differently.

Think choices. This final suggestion involves some creative thinking. Consider that the word *decide* derives from the same roots as *suicide* and *homicide*. In the spirit of those words, a decision forever "kills" all other options. That's kind of heavy. Instead, use the word *choice,* and see whether it frees up your thinking. When you *choose,* you express a preference for one option over others. However, those options remain live possibilities for the future. Choose for today, knowing that as you gain more wisdom and experience, you can choose again. ■

13

You're One Click Away...
from finding more strategies online for making decisions.

Four ways to
solve problems

Many people use the terms *decision making* and *problem solving* interchangeably, as if the two processes are the same. Of course, there are many overlaps. Both processes hinge on your ability to think critically and creatively. Yet when actually trying your hand at these processes, you'll discover that problem solving exists at an even higher level of complexity than decision making.

To understand this point, start by considering the nature of decision making. When faced with a decision, you're asked to make a judgment call. Often the decision boils down to a single question that can be answered yes or no, or a choice between two major options: Is the defendant guilty or not guilty? Do we hire this person or keep looking for another? Do I cast my vote for this candidate or someone else?

Problem solving, on the other hand, calls for making a *series* of decisions and answering questions that are more open ended: How can I raise enough money to fund my education? How can I manage my time so that I finish projects by the due date? How can I resolve conflicts with my partner?

Think of problem solving as a process with four P's: Define the *problem*, generate *possibilities*, create a *plan*, and *perform* your plan.

Define the **problem**	**What** is the problem?
Generate **possibilities**	**What if** there are several possible solutions?
Create a **plan**	**How** would this possible solution work?
Perform your plan	**Why** is one solution more workable than another?

1 Define the problem. To define a problem effectively, understand what a problem is—a mismatch between what you want and what you have. Problem solving is all about reducing the gap between these two factors.

Tell the truth about what's present in your life right now, without shame or blame. For example: "I often get sleepy while reading my physics assignments, and after closing the book I cannot remember what I just read."

Next, describe in detail what you want. Go for specifics: "I want to remain alert as I read about physics. I also want to accurately summarize each chapter I read."

Remember that when we define a problem in limiting ways, our solutions merely generate new problems. As Albert Einstein said,

"The world we have made is a result of the level of thinking we have done thus far. We cannot solve problems at the same level at which we created them."[6]

This idea has many applications for success in school. An example is the student who struggles with note taking. The problem, she thinks, is that her notes are too sketchy. The logical solution, she decides, is to take more notes, and her new goal is to write down almost everything her instructors say. No matter how fast and furiously she writes, she cannot capture all of the instructors' comments.

Consider what happens when this student defines the problem in a new way. After more thought, she decides that her dilemma is not the *quantity* of her notes but their *quality*. She adopts a new format for taking notes, dividing her notepaper into two columns. In the right-hand column, she writes down only the main points of each lecture. And in the left-hand column, she notes two or three supporting details for each point.

Over time, this student makes the joyous discovery that there are usually just three or four core ideas to remember from each lecture. She originally thought the solution was to take more notes. What really worked was taking notes in a new way.

For added clarity, see if you can state the problem as a single question. This focuses your thinking and makes it easier to isolate and analyze the underlying issues.

You might find it tempting to gloss over this first step in problem solving, especially if your learning style favors moving into action quickly. However, consider the advantages of delaying action until you've taken time to define a problem precisely. The definition phase paves the way for the remaining three. Once you define a problem, you're well on the way to no longer having a problem. A clear definition of the problem can immediately suggest appropriate ways to solve it.

Also remember that problems often come in pairs. First is the immediate problem that you want to solve. Next is the underlying issue—a breakdown in a system, policy, or procedure that *created* the immediate problem. To solve the underlying issue, ask: How can we prevent this problem from happening again?

2 Generate possibilities. Now put on your creative thinking hat. Open up. Brainstorm as many possible solutions to the problem as you can. At this stage, quantity counts. As you generate possibilities, gather relevant facts. For example, when you're faced with a dilemma about what courses to take next term, get information on class times, locations, and instructors. If you haven't decided which summer job offer to accept, gather information on salary, benefits, and working conditions.

Certain comments can put the brakes on new ideas and squelch creativity in record time. For example, when considering a new policy or procedure, people can speak from a mindset of inertia: "We've never done it that way before." They can also speak from a sense of resignation: "We'll never get this idea past the boss." Or they can use the weight of tradition to smother new ideas: "We've been using this procedure for years, and it's too late to change now." When you notice such voices and consciously choose to put them on hold, you start to unleash your imagination.

Alex Osborn, who first described brainstorming, compared the process of creating ideas to using the gas pedal on a car floorboard and evaluating ideas to using the brake pedal. If you drive with a foot on the brake pedal and the other foot on the gas pedal at the same time, you can damage your car. Likewise, trying to evaluate ideas at the same time that you create them compromises your ability to make innovative decisions.

3 Create a plan. After rereading your problem definition and list of possible solutions, choose the solution that seems most workable. Think about specific actions that will reduce the gap between what you have and what you want. Visualize the steps you will take to make this solution a reality, and arrange them in chronological order. To make your plan even more powerful, put it in writing.

If you're working in a group, ask participants to visualize what the solution will look like and how it will operate when it's fully implemented in the future. With that image in mind, ask participants to list the steps they'll take to make the solution a reality and arrange those steps in chronological order.

4 Perform your plan. This step gets you off your chair and out into the world. Now you actually *do* what you've planned. Ultimately, your skill in solving problems lies in how well you

> ## Visualize the steps you will take to make this solution a reality, and arrange them in chronological order. To make your plan even more powerful, put it writing.

perform your plan. Through the quality of your actions, you become the architect of your own success.

Be sure to evaluate the results of your actions. The messy complexity of life and the fact that people and circumstances are constantly changing means that solutions seldom "stay put." In fact, any solution has the potential to create new problems. If that happens, cycle through the four steps of problem solving again.

Bonus tip: Be grateful for problems. In the work world, problems create jobs. Problems create a reason for an employer, customer, or client to pay you. For example, medical assistants solve problems that prevent a physician's office or medical clinic from running smoothly. Paralegals solve problems with the accuracy and usefulness of legal research and records. People who develop "apps" solve problems for people who want their mobile devices to be as useful as their desktop computer.

Seen from this perspective, you can greet problems with gratitude, as explained in the "Power Process: Love your problems (and experience your barriers)." In fact, you can advance your career and boost your income by seeking out bigger problems at your job and gaining the skills to deal with them. There are plenty of jobs for people who know how to solve problems. ∎

You're One Click Away...
from finding more strategies online for problem solving.

13

✓ CRITICAL THINKING EXERCISE 20

Move from problems to solutions

p. 395-9398

Many students find it easy to complain about school and to dwell on problems. This exercise gives you an opportunity to change that habit and respond creatively to any problem you're currently experiencing—whether it be with memorizing or some other aspect of school or life.

The key is to dwell more on solutions than on problems. Do that by inventing as many solutions as possible for any given problem. See whether you can turn a problem into a *project* (a plan of action) or a *promise* to change some aspect of your life. Shifting the emphasis of your conversation from problems to solutions can raise your sense of possibility and unleash the master learner within you.

In the space below, describe at least three problems that could interfere with your success as a student. The problems can be related to transportation issues, lack of access to technology, teachers, relationships with coworkers, personal relationships, finances, or anything else that might get in the way of your success.

My problem is that . . .

> I tend to procrastinate and leave work for the last minute.

My problem is that . . .

> financial problems get in the way and I need to work more often.

My problem is that . . .

> I ~~have~~ tend to be timid and shy in asking questions sometimes.

Next, brainstorm at least five possible solutions to each of those problems. Ten solutions would be even better. (You can continue brainstorming on a separate piece of paper or on a computer.) You might find it hard to come up with that many ideas. That's okay. Stick with it. Stay in the inquiry, give yourself time, and ask other people for ideas.

I can solve my problem by . . .

> understanding the concepts on a topic in class, Analyzing better, and applying goals so my procrastination will stop and less effect me in the future.

I can solve my problem by . . .

> learning how to manage my money, and seperating the money for the needs.

I can solve my problem by . . .

> coming out of my shell and asking questions when they need to be ask. It will only help me in my career and help me succeed.

master**student**profile

Irshad Manji

(1969–) Controversial journalist, broadcaster, and author of *The Trouble with Islam*, who uses her "Muslim voice of reform, to concerned citizens worldwide" in an effort to explore faith and community, and the diversity of ideas.

It's to be expected that an author with a book on the verge of publication will lose her cool over a last-minute detail or two. Some might get nervous that their facts won't hold up and run a paranoid, final check. Others might worry about what to wear to their book party. When Irshad Manji's book was about to hit the stands, her concern was a bit different. She feared for her life.

Certain her incendiary book *The Trouble with Islam* would set off outrage in the Muslim community, she called the police, told them she was working on a book that was highly critical of Islam, and asked if they could advise her on safety precautions.

They came to visit her Toronto apartment building several times and suggested she install a state-of-the-art security system, bulletproof windows, and hire a counterterrorism expert to act as her personal bodyguard.

In her short, plucky book she comes down hard on modern-day Islam, charging that the religion's mainstream has come to be synonymous with literalism. Since the 13th century, she said, the faith hasn't encouraged—or tolerated—independent thinking (or as it's known in the faith, *ijtihad*).

The book, which is written like a letter, is both thoughtful and confrontational. In person, Ms. Manji embodied the same conflicting spirit. She was affable and wore a broad smile. Her upbeat, nervous energy rose to the task of filling in every potentially awkward pause. (One of her favorite factoids: "Prophet Mohammed was quite a feminist.")

Her journey scrutinizing Islam started when she was an 8-year-old and taking weekly religious classes at a *madrasa* (religious school) in suburban Vancouver. Her anti-Semitic teacher Mr. Khaki never took her questions seriously; he merely told her to accept everything because it was in the Koran. She wanted to know why she had to study it in Arabic, which she didn't understand, and was told the answers were "in the Koran."

Her questioning ended up getting her kicked out of school at 14, and she embarked on a 20-year-long private study of the religion. While she finds the treatment poured on women and foreigners in Islamic nations indefensible, she said that she continues to be a believer because the religion provides her with her values. "And I'm so glad I did because it was then I came to realize that there was this really progressive side of my religion and it was this tradition of critical thinking called *ijtihad*. This is what allows me to stay within the faith."

She calls herself a "Muslim refusenik" because she remains committed to the religion and yet she doesn't accept what's expected of Muslim women. As terrorist acts and suicide bombings refuse to subside, she said it's high time for serious reform within the Islamic faith.

She said many young Muslim supporters are still afraid to come out about their support of her. "Even before 9/11 it was the young Muslims who were emerging out of these audiences and gathering at the side of the stage. They'd walk over and say, 'Irshad, we need voices such as yours to help us open up this religion of ours because if it doesn't open up, we're leaving the mosques.'"

She wants Muslims to start thinking critically about their religion and to start asking more questions. "Most Muslims have never been introduced to the possibility, let alone the virtue, of asking questions about our holy book," she said. "We have never been taught the virtue of interpreting the Koran in different ways."

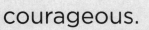

IRSHAD MANJI ... is courageous.

YOU ... can practice courage by questioning assumptions and creating bold, new ideas.

You're One Click Away...
from learning more about Irshad Manji online at the Master Student Profiles. You can also visit the Master Student Hall of Fame to learn about other master students.

FIVE Cs
FOR YOUR CAREER

CHARACTER • CRITICAL THINKING • CREATIVE THINKING • COLLABORATION • COMMUNICATION

Build character by making ethical decisions at work. Some workplace behaviors are clearly unethical. Examples are submitting false expense reports, operating machinery while intoxicated, stealing from a cash drawer, diverting corporate funds for personal uses, taking home office supplies, or using work time to download explicit sexual images from the Internet. Other behaviors fall into a "gray area" that calls for careful thinking about whether ethics are being violated.

You don't have to be a philosopher in order to make sound ethical decisions at work. Start with a working definition of *ethics* as using moral standards to guide your behavior. Next, turn your own moral standards into a checklist of pointed questions. For example, is this action legal? Is this action consistent with my organization's mission, goals, and policies? Will I be able to defend this action tomorrow, next month, and next year? Am I willing to make this decision public—to share it wholeheartedly with my boss, my family, and my friends? Has everyone who will be affected by this decision had the chance to voice their concerns?

Think creatively by looking for an unmet need. Sometimes needs are met as a result of serendipity—a happy and creative coincidence of ideas. Spence Silver, a research scientist at 3M, invented a new chemical by accident while looking for ways to improve tape adhesives. This chemical did not stick strongly when coated onto tape backings. Even so, Silver believed it had potential uses.

His invention languished for years until Art Fry, who worked in new product development at 3M, attended a seminar by Silver. Fry had long been frustrated with the scrap paper bookmarks he used to mark his place in his church hymnal during choir practice. One day it suddenly occurred to Fry that Silver's adhesive could be used to make a perfect bookmark—one that could be fastened temporarily to a page and then easily but securely refastened on another page. That "aha!" yielded the Post-it® in 1980, with billions sold since then.

Think critically to use your mind like an expert. In their book *The New Division of Labor: How Computers Are Creating the Next Job Market*, Frank Levy and Richard J. Murname argue that prospering in a global economy calls for expert thinking. This means "solving new problems for which there are no routine solutions."[7]

The chef who creates a new meal without increasing restaurant costs shows expert thinking. So does a car mechanic who solves a problem not covered in the owner's manual.

Jobs that do not involve expert thinking are more likely to be outsourced or automated. For example, travel agents and underwriters (people who determine eligibility for an insurance policy or loan) traditionally made decisions according to step-by-step formulas. Those kinds of decisions are now made by computers.

An expert has deep knowledge about a field along with an ability to identify new relationships between ideas. Develop expert thinking by taking advanced courses in your major or field and seizing opportunities to work on project teams.

Think collaboratively with the Decreasing Options Technique. The Decreasing Options Technique (DOT) offers an efficient way to sort and rank a large pool of ideas created by groups of people in meetings. With DOT, you can sort and prioritize dozens of ideas, reducing them to a manageable number for discussion. This technique is especially useful for large groups that are asked to arrive at a decision in a short time. DOT also allows for contribution from all participants—not just those who are most vocal. Here's how it works:

- *Conduct a brainstorm, summarizing each idea in a single, word, phrase, or sentence on a large sheet of paper.* Write letters that are big enough to be seen across the meeting room. Place only one idea on each sheet of paper.

- *Post the sheets where everyone can see them.* To save time, ask participants to submit ideas before the meeting takes place. That way you can summarize and post ideas ahead of time.

- *Ask participants whether they can eliminate some ideas as obviously unworkable.* Also group similar ideas together and eliminate duplications.

- *"Dot" ideas.* Give each participant a handful of sticker dots. Then ask participants to go around the room and place a dot next to the ideas that they consider most important. A variation on this process is to give each participant a limited number of dots. You can also assign different levels of priority to each color of sticker.

- *Stand back and review the ideas.* The group's favored ideas will stand out clearly as the sheets with the most dots. Now you can bring these high-priority ideas to the discussion table.

Communicate some ideas to individuals before groups. If you come up with an idea that has the potential to create big changes in your workplace, consider *not* sharing it first during a regular staff meeting. Instead, "pitch" the idea to key decision makers on an individual basis. Plan to do this over several weeks of months.

This strategy has several advantages. For one, these people can help you think critically about the idea. And if they like it, you can ask them for support when you decide to share it more publicly. At that time, you'll already have some "buy-in" for your big idea.

Now make a personal commitment to develop the five Cs. Take another look at the Discovery Wheel in Chapter 9—especially the sections labeled Character, Creative and Critical Thinking, Communicating, and Collaborating. Take a snapshot of your current skills in these areas after reading and doing this chapter.

DISCOVERY

My scores on the "Five C" sections of the Discovery Wheel were:	As of today, I would give myself the following scores in these areas:	At the end of this course, I would like my scores in these areas to be:
Character _____	Character _____	Character _____
Creative & Critical Thinking _____	Creative & Critical Thinking _____	Creative & Critical Thinking _____
Communicating _____	Communicating _____	Communicating _____
Collaborating _____	Collaborating _____	Collaborating _____

Next, skim this chapter and look for a creative or critical thinking technique that you want to explore in depth. Choose one that would enhance your self-rating in at least one of the five Cs.

I discovered that my preferred technique is . . .

_____

_____

_____

_____

In light of the five Cs, I can use this technique to become more . . .

_____

_____

_____

_____

INTENTION
To use this technique, I intend to . . .

_____

_____

_____

_____

NEXT ACTION
The specific action I will take is . . .

_____

_____

_____

_____

13

Name **Michelle Ramos**

Date _____

395

1. List the six levels of thinking described by Benjamin Bloom.

Level 1: Remembering   Level 4: Analyzing   Level 6: Creating
Level 2: Understanding   Level 5: Evaluating
Level 3: Applying

2. List the key question associated with each level of thinking of Bloom's taxonomy.

395-396
Level 1: Can I recall the key terms, factors or events?
Level 2: Can I explain this idea in my words?
Level 3: Can I use this idea to produce a desired result.
Level 4: Can I divide this idea into parts or steps
Level 5: Can I rate the truth, usefulness, quality of this idea — and give reasons for my rating?
Level 6: Can I invent something new based on this idea?

3. Briefly explain the difference between *creative thinking* and *critical thinking*.

p395. Creative thinking is the process of brainstorming, cultivating creative serendipity, and collecting + playing with ideas.
Critical thinking is being flexible and ask alot of questions

4. Discuss what is meant in this chapter by *aha!*

389
Central to creative thinking. It is the burst of creative energy heralded by the arrival of new, original idea

5. Briefly describe three strategies for creative thinking.

391.
Brainstorming by creating plans, finding solutions and discovering new ideas.
Focus and let go meaning intense focus taps the resources of your conscience mind.
Letting go gives subconscious mind time to work. Collect and play with ideas.

6. List three types of logical fallacies, and give an example of each type.

7. Name the logical fallacy involved in this statement: "Everyone who's ever visited this school agrees that it's the best in the state."

8. What cultivates an *aha!* moment, and what leads to following through from that moment?

389
Creative thinking, a burst of creative energy heralded by arrival of new, original idea.

9. List the three strategies for making a decision that were mentioned in the text.

Recognize decisions, establish priorities, Based your decisions on a life plan.

10. List three examples of questions you can ask to promote inquiry-based learning.

406
What am I willing to do to solve this problem?
Who can I ask for help?
What am I willing to do to get what I want?

Index